ORGANIZED CRIME IN AMERICA

Organized Crime
in America

DENNIS J. KENNEY

University of Nebraska at Omaha

JAMES O. FINCKENAUER

Rutgers University

Wadsworth Publishing Company
I(T)P™ An International Thomson Publishing Company

Belmont • Albany • Bonn • Boston • Cincinnati • Detroit • London • Madrid • Melbourne
Mexico City • New York • Paris • San Francisco • Singapore • Tokyo • Toronto • Washington

Editorial Assistant: *Jennifer Dunning*
Production Services Coordinator: *Debby Kramer*
Production: *Scratchgravel Publishing Services*
Designer: *Andrew H. Ogus*
Print Buyer: *Karen Hunt*
Permissions Editor: *Jeanne Bosschart*
Copy Editor: *Kay Mikel*
Illustrator: *Greg Draus, Scratchgravel Publishing Services*
Cover: *Marnie Deacon*
Compositor: *Scratchgravel Publishing Services*
Printer: *Arcata Graphics/Fairfield*

COPYRIGHT © 1995
By Wadsworth Publishing Company
A Division of International Thomson Publishing Inc.

I⟨T⟩P The ITP logo is a trademark under license.

Printed in the United States of America.

For more information, contact:

Wadsworth Publishing Company
10 Davis Drive
Belmont, California 94002, USA

International Thomson Publishing
Berkshire House 168-173
High Holborn
London, WC1V 7AA, England

Thomas Nelson Australia
102 Dodds Street
South Melbourne 3205
Victoria, Australia

Nelson Canada
1120 Birchmount Road
Scarborough, Ontario
Canada M1K 5G4

International Thomson Publishing GmbH
Königswinterer Strasse 418
53227 Bonn, Germany

International Thomson Publishing Asia
221 Henderson Road #05-10
Singapore 0315

International Thomson Publishing Japan
Hirakawacho Kyowa Building, 3F
2-2-1 Hirakawacho
Chiyoda-ku, Tokyo 102
Japan

4 5 6 7 8 9 10—01 00

Library of Congress Cataloging-in-Publication Data

Kenney, Dennis Jay.
   Organized crime in America / Dennis Jay Kenney, James O. Finckenauer.
      p. cm.
   Includes bibliographical references (p.   –   ) and index.
   ISBN 0-534-24702-4
   1. Organized crime—United States. 2. Organized crime—United States—History. I. Finckenauer, James O. II. Title.
HV6446.K46 1994
364.1'06'0973—dc20   94-18081

Contents

Preface

More than two decades have passed since the film *The Godfather* first arrived on the screen, dramatically portraying big-time crime in America to audiences around the world. In the ensuing years, drugs have shifted from the fringes of society into the mainstream where their effects and resulting profits have increased many times over. With the arrival of crack, mass marketing of cocaine became possible, leaving the newest gangsters to battle for market share and control as they had decades before during Prohibition. Despite state run lotteries and casinos on riverboats and on Indian reservations offering increased access to legal gambling, many localities have nevertheless seen an expansion of the more traditional numbers games sponsored by organized crime groups. Providing the most employment opportunities in some ghetto neighborhoods, drugs and gambling have increasingly become the only avenue out of the ghetto—a rung on the "queer ladder of social mobility." As we move toward the year 2000, the influence of organized crime on labor and business also continues to grow, and estimates of its effects on the country's overall economy are all but impossible to calculate.

As is often the case, the beginnings of this book arose some years ago from our need for materials in our own courses on organized crime. After reviewing (and in some cases using) the sources then available, we concluded that most were either general overviews or too narrowly focused on individual topics—in either case, insufficient for the approach we wished to take. As a result, we set out to develop a theory-based approach that would focus the lessons of yesterday on contemporary policy and explore the changing face of organized crime, including its internationalization and the emerging recognition of the myriad forms of the phenomenon. We hope we have succeeded on each count with a book that tells interesting stories about interesting people and places—but for a reason. With a more consistent view of the problem of organized crime, we believe that the success and failure of policy, both past and present, can more easily be examined and placed in context. In addition, it has been our intent to capture the vast complexity of the problem and its various solutions.

Originally begun at Brooks/Cole Publishing Company, this project had the early faith and support of Claire Verduin. Before and after the restructuring at Wadsworth, our editors Cindy Stormer and Brian Gore were not only helpful but a pleasure to work with as well. Their encouragement, their feedback, and, above all, their patience were invaluable to both the process and the product. Also inestimable were the advice and comments of the reviewers: Edward Tromanhauser, Chicago State University; N. Gary Holten, University of Central Florida; Joseph L. Albini, Wayne State University; and Clifford Karchmer, American University. Special recognition is due to Phyllis Schultze, the Information Specialist at the NCCD/Criminal Justice Collection at Rutgers. We are always amazed that no source, no matter how obscure, can escape her detection. And last but not least, without Rob Weidner's help at the Rutgers School of Criminal Justice the bibliography, indexes, and many of the tables we used would have been a lot longer in coming.

Dennis J. Kenney
James O. Finckenauer

ORGANIZED CRIME IN AMERICA

1

Problems of Definition:

What Is Organized Crime?

In its 1986 report, the President's Commission on Organized Crime indicated that the problem in defining organized crime came not from the word *crime*, but from the word *organized* (p. 19). Such behaviors as murder, robbery, and theft—behaviors said to be *mala in se*, or wrong in and of themselves—are well defined and accepted as crimes. Other behaviors, such as prostitution, drug dealing, bribery, and gambling—behaviors that are *mala prohibita*, or wrong because they are prohibited—are less clearly defined but are also generally accepted as crimes. All of these—and other crimes, such as hijacking, extortion, loan-sharking, bootlegging, and fixing sports events—have come to be associated with and a part of what is commonly known as organized crime. They do not, however, by themselves define organized crime; in part this is because they are also committed by other, what we can call for this purpose, "unorganized" criminals. Thus, one implication of the commission's statement is that the phenomenon known as organized crime cannot be defined by criminal acts alone but must also include in its definition what is meant by *organized*. In other words, we must take into account the attributes or characteristics of the actors as well as the acts involved in organized crime.

The definitional issue is very controversial, chiefly because how the problem of organized crime is defined goes a long way toward determining the solutions proposed and promulgated. Certain questions are part of the controversy surrounding the definition and understanding of organized crime. Is organized crime synonymous with the Mafia or La Cosa Nostra? Is there even such an entity as the Mafia or La Cosa Nostra? Can any other criminal groups or conspiracies be considered to be examples of organized crime? Or is this whole thing about organized crime, and particularly about the Mafia, only a myth exploited for political purposes and sustained by books, movies, and television? Does organized crime thrive, in whatever form, simply because of the weakness of the American public—a public that desires certain illegal goods and services? We will deal with all these questions and many others as well.

The relatively few academic criminologists who have written on this topic have differed dramatically in their conceptualizations. Legal definitions in criminal statutes have been either nonexistent, constitutionally vague or indefinite, or overbroad. Various government commissions and investigative bodies have likewise differed in their definitions and, in some cases, have failed to define the problem at all. The 1976 National Task Force on Organized Crime threw up its hands, stating: "Although organized crime has been considered a major problem for the American society for half a century, it remains one elusive in nature and difficult to define. . . . The Task Force concluded that until the scope of organized criminal activity has been researched thoroughly on a nationwide basis, a comprehensive definition of organized crime cannot be formulated" (p. 1).

We approach the question of what is organized crime from a number of directions. We will examine the attributes that characterize organized criminals and crime groups, the so-called actors in organized crime. Next, we will try to sort out the means by which organized crimes are committed, focusing on the attributes of the "acts" that make up organized crime. This will enable us to see how organized crime is different from other crime. We will describe a select group of major national commissions and investigative bodies that have offered definitions and examine them by means of content analysis, using our "actors" and "acts" dimensions. We will do the same with a sample of legal definitions found in criminal statutes or other legal documents. Together, these details comprise a pretty good picture of government efforts at defining organized crime.

Next we will turn to academic efforts at definition. Using our acts and actors schema, we will analyze a sample of definitions offered by the principal scholars who have written on organized crime in the United States over the last quarter-century. We will seek to identify a core criminological definition. Finally, we will draw the relevant conclusions and implications from all of this and frame our own definition of organized crime.

THE ACTORS: ORGANIZED CRIMINAL AND CRIME GROUPS

Focusing on the characteristics of organized criminal groups delineated in criminology texts, Hagan (1983) identified 11 dimensions of organized crime. A similar attempt by Maltz (1985) suggested 9 possible characteristics—some identical to Hagan's and some that partially overlapped. We have integrated and synthesized these two approaches and offer these dimensions and characteristics as one framework for an analysis of definitions of organized crime. Organized crime groups:

- are nonideological,
- have an organized hierarchy,
- have continuity over time,
- use force or the threat of force,
- restrict membership,
- obtain profit through illegal enterprises,
- provide illegal goods and services desired by the general populace,
- use corruption to neutralize public officials and politicians,
- seek a monopoly position to obtain exclusive control over specific goods and services,
- have job specialization within the group,
- have a code of secrecy, and
- plan extensively to achieve long-term goals.

While none of these attributes alone can adequately define organized criminals, when taken together they produce a clear picture of organized crime. Let's take a close look at what each of these attributes contributes to our definition of organized crime groups.

Organized crime groups are *nonideological* in the sense that they do not have political agendas of their own. They are not terrorists dedicated to political change. They do not espouse a particular radical, liberal, conservative, or other political ideology. Their interest in government is only in its nullification—through bribery, payoffs, and corruption. Despite the fact that they may engage in killings, bombings, or kidnappings and despite the fact that they may exist within political groups, such as is the case with certain elements of the Palestine Liberation Organization, for example, international terrorist organizations would not be a form of organized crime according to this criterion.

(2) There is widespread agreement that organized crime groups have a _well-structured hierarchy_ with leaders or bosses and with followers in some rank order of authority. The latter include various associates, hangers-on, and would-be members. The members of the group engage in conspiracies to commit crimes. Someone in the group is in a position to decide what will be done, by whom, how, and when. Outlaw motorcycle gangs (considered by many experts to be organized criminal groups) have chapters generally consisting of a president, vice president, secretary/treasurer, and even a sergeant at arms, who are elected by the membership (President's Commission, 1986).

(3) _Continuity_ means that the group is self-perpetuating; it continues beyond the life or participation of any particular individual. Leaders who die or go to jail are replaced by new leaders: Others may drop out for various reasons, but the organization—just like its counterparts in the noncriminal world—continues. Maltz (1985) suggests that the group's involvement in continuing enterprises (drug distribution, extortion, or gambling)—what he calls _continuity_—is one of the cohesive elements of a true organized crime group.

(4) Force or the threat of force is generally accepted as a dimension of organized crime. Organized criminal groups _use force_ or threaten its use to accomplish their ends. They engage in killings, beatings, burnings, and destruction. Use of predatory violence against sometimes innocent victims is an attribute of many of the groups we will look at later on. Drug gang shootings (sometimes of small children) in our cities is an example of this wanton violence. Violence is used both against other criminals and against victims who don't pay for their drugs or don't pay off their bets or don't pay back their loans.

(5) Organized crime groups _restrict membership_ and are characterized by some experts as limiting their membership to persons of certain ethnic backgrounds, kinship, race, or criminal record (Abadinsky, 1985). The Mafia, the Chinese Tongs, and the Japanese Yakuza are examples of groups that are formed based on ethnic considerations. Membership in the Aryan Brotherhood or the Black Guerilla Family depends on both racial and criminal considerations.

(7) It is widely agreed that organized crime exists for purposes of _economic gain._ Making a profit, through whatever means are considered necessary, is the primary goal of organized criminal groups. This is, in part, why they

are believed to be nonideological. This profit can come from *illegal* enterprises such as drugs, gambling, or loan-sharking, but it can also come from legal businesses. For example, investing in restaurants or bars gains respectable social status and is also a good way to launder illegal money. Money laundering is a method of accounting for money obtained through illegal means. For example, money gotten through extortion can be shown in financial records for tax purposes as having been obtained through a bar business. Maltz (1985) indicates that there are many good reasons for organized crime groups to diversify into *legitimate businesses*. Thus, organized crime groups almost always have legitimate enterprises in addition to their illegitimate enterprises.

Organized crime provides *public access* to goods and services that have been declared illegal but that are desired by a large enough segment of society to make their provision a profitable business. Americans want drugs, sex, and gambling. In addition, some of us want to dispose of toxic wastes cheaply and quickly. Others want to obtain guns that have been outlawed or to adopt babies without having to go through a lot of bureaucratic red tape. Still others want to collect prematurely on life insurance policies. The tug-of-war between our desires, our human weaknesses, on the one hand, and our morals, on the other, provides fat profits for organized crime. Francis Ianni and Elizabeth Ruess-Ianni (1976) focus on this dimension and describe organized crime as representing "a means of producing and distributing those goods and services which are officially declared illegal—thus, realistically, it represents an area of conflict between our desires and our morals" (p. xv).

Organized crime neutralizes or nullifies government by avoiding investigation, arrest, prosecution, and conviction through payoffs to the police, prosecutors, and judges. *Efforts to corrupt* public officials and the political process are characteristic of organized crime. Payoffs enable organized crime groups to operate with immunity. Bribes or kickbacks to purchasing agents, union officials, politicians, and others facilitate organized crime's infiltration of legitimate business. The huge profits and the temptations and inducements that can be offered to relatively low-paid public servants undermine the efforts of law enforcement to combat organized crime. Maltz (1985) suggests that only public sector corruption should be considered an element of organized crime.

Criminal groups seek partial or complete control over whatever endeavors they are engaged in. Schelling (1976) stresses this characteristic of *monopolization* as the unique definer of organized crime and writes: "The characteristic is exclusivity, or, to use a more focused term, monopoly. . . . Organized crime does not merely extend itself broadly, but brooks no competition. It seeks not merely influence, but exclusive influence. . . . We can apply to it some adjectives that are often associated with monopoly—ruthless, unscrupulous, greedy, exploitative, unprincipled" (p. 72). Organized crime is, says Schelling, usually monopolized crime and is most frequently found in those lines of business that lend themselves to monopoly.

 Some few scholars and government experts have described organized crime groups as being *specialized* and as having *a division of labor*. Abadinsky (1985), for example, says that these groups have certain functional positions, such as an enforcer, who uses violence and even murder to carry out assignments; a fixer, who handles corrupting criminal justice officials; and a money mover, who launders illegal money. Maltz (1985) suggests that some criminal organizations diversify their activities beyond a single criminal enterprise to *multiple enterprises*, whereas others concentrate on a single product, such as drugs.

 Membership, rituals of initiation, rules and regulations, activities, and the leadership of certain organized crime groups are *bound by rules of secrecy*. Violation of these rules—and of this code—can be punished by expulsion or death. This cultlike behavior and ritualism are said by some to distinguish organized crime groups from other criminal groups, which tend to be more informal. Maltz (1985) describes these rites as *bonding*, but he says this bonding is not necessarily an attribute of all organized crime groups.

The far-reaching and intricate activities and manipulations of certain organized crime groups require considerable *planning and coordination*. Methodical, systematic, highly disciplined, and secret actions do not just happen. They are not the actions of criminal groups or gangs noted for impulsiveness, simple thrill seeking, and hedonism. Maltz (1985) refers to this *sophistication* and suggests that organized crime groups do not conduct their illegal enterprises in a willy-nilly fashion.

We have now identified the attributes of the *actors* in this phenomenon called organized crime. To get a handle on that elusive term *organized*, we must look to the *acts* or the means by which organized crimes are committed.

THE ACTS: THE MEANS
OF ORGANIZED CRIME

Michael Maltz (1976) suggests a typology of organized crime consisting of six means by which organized crimes are executed. In some cases (for example, violence and corruption), this typology parallels the characteristics of organized crime groups. Violence and a willingness to use violence are both characteristic of the group and a means of executing the group's crimes. The same is true of corruption. They both fit whether we are describing the actors or the acts. Maltz (1976) identifies these six means by which organized crimes are executed:

- *Violence*—Gang wars over the control of drugs and drug territories; assassinations of gang or family leaders; and torching stores or bars that refuse to install certain cigarette vending machines.
- *Theft*—Burglary or stolen car rings; fencing stolen goods; the so-called ten percenter, in which a truck driver gives up a truckload of merchandise in exchange for erasing 10 percent of a gambling or loanshark debt; cargo theft; chop shops; and distribution of bootleg cigarettes and pirated records and tapes.
- *Corruption*—Gambling and narcotic payoffs to police, prosecutors, and judges; campaign contributions and other support for political candidates; backdoor influence of political leaders through powerful friends and through political and financial backers; and payoffs to influence public procurement and contracting.
- *Economic Coercion*—Refusing to lay off gambling bets, thereby bankrupting a bookmaker (bookmakers transfer some of their bets to other bookmakers to avoid having more winners than losers); price-fixing following infiltration of legitimate business; and illegal labor strikes.
- *Deception*—Fixing a sports event; creating a dummy corporation or business as a front for illegal enterprises; and being a silent partner in an otherwise legal enterprise such as a gambling casino.
- *Victim Participation*—The "johns" who use the services of prostitutes; the drug users who buy narcotics and drugs; the gamblers who bet on the numbers, on the horses (off-track), or on the Super Bowl; and the financially strapped individual who needs a fast loan without having to put up any collateral.

With this analytical framework in mind, we can now turn our attention to the definitions of organized crime prevalent in the literature.

MAJOR NATIONAL COMMISSIONS
AND INVESTIGATIVE BODIES

We have chosen five of the principal national bodies that have examined organized crime over the last 40 years as our first source of government efforts at defining organized crime.

Kefauver Committee

United States Senator Estes Kefauver chaired the Senate Special Committee to Investigate Organized Crime in Interstate Commerce in 1950 and 1951. The committee held public hearings in major cities across the country, and these hearings were televised in 1951, resulting in a great deal of public interest and attention to organized crime. The hearings helped sway both professional and popular opinion toward a belief that major aspects of organized crime were controlled and administered by a nationwide conspiracy called the Mafia (Moore, 1974). But historian William H. Moore (1974) and other scholars and experts as well suggest that the Kefauver committee exaggerated the degree of centralized planning in the underworld and misread its own evidence in finding the existence of a cohesive nationwide conspiracy. We will have much more to say about this issue in a later chapter. The Kefauver committee's definition of organized crime includes these four characteristics:

1. There is a Nation-wide crime syndicate known as the Mafia, whose tentacles are found in many large cities. It has international ramifications which appear most clearly in connection with the narcotics traffic.

2. Its leaders are usually found in control of the most lucrative rackets in their cities.

3. There are indications of a centralized direction and control of these rackets, but leadership appears to be in a group rather than in a single individual. . . .

4. The domination of the Mafia is based fundamentally on "muscle" and "murder." The Mafia is a secret conspiracy against law and order which will ruthlessly eliminate anyone who stands in the way of its success in any criminal enterprise in which it is interested. It will destroy anyone who betrays its secrets. It will use any means available—political influence, bribery, intimidation, etc., to defeat any attempt on the part of law-enforcement to touch its top figures or to interfere with its operations. (President's Commission, 1967:1)

Applying the attributes of actors and acts to this definition tells us that the emphasis here is on an organized hierarchy ("centralized direction and control," "leadership," "top figures") using violence ("muscle" and "murder," "ruthlessly eliminate," "destroy anyone") and corruption ("political influence, bribery, intimidation"). The Kefauver committee clearly defines the Mafia as a centrally organized, secret, criminal conspiracy that uses violence and corruption to accomplish its ends. And since one of its ends is trafficking in narcotics, victim participation is also a necessary component of this definition of organized crime.

Oyster Bay Conferences

The next major national event was a series of conferences on organized crime held during 1965-1966 at Oyster Bay, Long Island. These conferences are important because they were conducted outside the television limelight. They did not have a particular political purpose, and they brought together experts from across the country to share their views, experiences, and expertise. As such, the Oyster Bay conferences were the first meetings of their kind devoted to the problem of organized crime.

The participants represented a cross section of government officials, academics, law enforcement officials, lawyers, information specialists, and others. Their charge was to "determine if it would be possible or useful to create a new doctrine defining the nature of organized crime and developing the most effective means of controlling it" (Smith, 1975:244). The emphasis in the conferences was on the economic function of organized crime as opposed to any political role it might have. "The notion of an 'invisible government of crime' was rejected in favor of 'criminal enterprises.' There was seen to be a conceptual link between conventional organized crime and other criminal groups like youth gangs and confidence rings; the distinguishing factor [being] 'sophistication'" (Smith, 1975:244).

A final report of the conferences stressed the need for development of a systematic and accurate definition of organized crime. Such a definition would, it was supposed, make enforcement activities more effective. The report, called *Combating Organized Crime,* said: "In the absence of a definition derived from the experience of informed persons, public understanding of organized crime would continue to be influenced by folklore and rumor." Let's see how organized crime was defined in this report:

> Organized crime is the product of a self-perpetuating criminal conspiracy to wring exorbitant profits from our society by any means—fair and foul, legal and illegal. Despite personnel changes, the conspiratorial entity continues. It is a malignant parasite which fattens on human weakness. It survives on fear and corruption. By one or another means, it obtains a high degree of immunity from the law. It is totalitarian in its organization. A way of life, it imposes rigid discipline on underlings who do the dirty work while the top

men of organized crime are generally insulated from the criminal act and the consequent danger of prosecution. (1966:19)

This rather dramatic definition again focuses on organized crime as being a rigidly organized and continuing hierarchy—"self-perpetuating" and "totalitarian in its organization." This hierarchy employs violence and corruption to gain great profits, in part by meeting public demands for illegal goods and services ("fattens on human weakness") again requiring victim participation.

Task Force on Organized Crime (1967)

Just a few years later, a Task Force on Organized Crime was created as part of the President's Commission on Law Enforcement and Administration of Justice, established by President Lyndon Johnson in 1965. It looked into the types of activities organized crime engaged in, the locations of these activities, and how the so-called criminal cartels were organized and who their members were. The task force reviewed the country's existing efforts to control organized crime and set out what it called a national strategy against organized crime.

The task force was greatly influenced by the work of the Kefauver committee. But even more, it was influenced by the hearings of the U.S. Senate Committee on Government Operations Permanent Subcommittee on Investigations (also known as the McClellan committee, after its chairman, Senator John McClellan). It was at these hearings in 1963 that a small-time hoodlum of Italian descent named Joseph Valachi testified about the existence of a nationwide, organized criminal conspiracy he called La Cosa Nostra. In sensational and shocking fashion, Valachi described highly structured organized crime families. The task force concluded that there were 24 such families in all—each with a boss, a consigliere or counselor, an underboss, a number of *caporegimas* or lieutenants, and soldiers or members. Valachi also described gang wars, killings, and secret initiation rituals required to gain membership in an organization that sounded like an alien conspiracy. (We will be saying much more about Valachi's testimony in Chapter 9 on the Mafia.)

Perhaps not surprisingly given its orientation, the task force concluded that organized crime was "the most sinister kind of crime in America." To dramatize this conclusion, the task force stressed that organized crime was, in a very real sense, "dedicated to subverting not only American institutions, but the very decency and integrity that are the most cherished attributes of a free society" (President's Commission, 1967:24). It painted a picture of organized crime as a large, sinister, alien force sapping the lifeblood of

American society. Let's analyze the definition of organized crime set out on the first page of its report:

> ORGANIZED CRIME is a society that seeks to operate outside the control of the American people and their governments. It involves thousands of criminals, working within structures as complex as those of any large corporation, subject to laws more rigidly enforced than those of legitimate governments. Its actions are not impulsive but rather the result of intricate conspiracies, carried on over many years and aimed at gaining control over whole fields of activity in order to amass huge profits.
>
> The core of organized crime activity is the supplying of illegal goods and services—gambling, loan sharking, narcotics, and other forms of vice—to countless numbers of citizen customers. But organized crime is also extensively and deeply involved in legitimate business and in labor unions. Here it employs illegitimate methods—monopolization, terrorism, extortion, tax evasion—to drive out or control lawful ownership and leadership and to exact illegal profits from the public. And to carry on its many activities secure from governmental interference, organized crime corrupts public officials. . . .
>
> What organized crime wants is money and power. . . . The ethical and moral standards the criminals adhere to, the laws and regulations they obey, the procedures they use are private and secret ones that they devise themselves, change when they see fit, and administer summarily and invisibly. (President's Commission, 1967:1)

Table 1.1 lists the prominent features of the task force's definition of organized crime. As can be seen, this definition addresses a large array of the attributes of the actors and the acts that make up organized crime. It was the most comprehensive definition of its time. In particular, the task force introduced the concepts of extensive planning and monopolization as characterizing organized crime activities.

Task Force on Organized Crime (1976)

Ten years after the President's first crime commission, another national task force undertook an examination of organized crime. Part of the National Advisory Committee on Criminal Justice Standards and Goals, this task force was to offer, in the form of standards, a number of tools for dealing with organized crime. The 1976 National Task Force on Organized Crime

Table 1.1 Elements of Organized Crime

ATTRIBUTE	ELEMENTS OF DEFINITION
Organized hierarchy, continuing	thousands of criminals working within complex structures; carried on over many years
Extensive planning	intricate conspiracies; actions not impulsive
Rational profit through illegal activities	amass huge profits; exact illegal profits
Monopoly	control whole fields of activity; monopolization
Public demand	illegal goods and services
Victim participation	countless numbers of citizen customers
Violence	terrorism ; extortion
Deception	tax evasion
Corruption	corrupts public officials
Code of secrecy	private and secret procedures, laws and regulations, and standards

pointed out that this is one of the least understood and most neglected areas of criminal activity in America. The chairman referred to organized crime as "a secret, conspiratorial activity" that operates in an extralegal world insulated from both prosecution and regulation. He said it results in losses of tax revenues, takeovers of legitimate businesses, intimidation of witnesses, concealment of wrongdoing, and corruption of public officials (National Task Force on Organized Crime, 1976, preface). Despite the lack of understanding of the phenomenon, or perhaps because of it, this group decided it could not formulate a comprehensive definition of organized crime. Instead, it proposed what it called a working description based on the general characteristics of organized criminal activity. Those characteristics were outlined as follows:

1. Organized crime is a type of conspiratorial crime, sometimes involving the hierarchical coordination of a number of persons in the planning and execution of illegal acts, or in the pursuit of a legitimate objective by unlawful means. Organized crime involves continuous commitment by key members, although some individuals with specialized skills may participate only briefly in the ongoing conspiracies. . . .

2. Organized crime has economic gain as its primary goal, though some of the participants in the conspiracy may have achievement of power or status as their objective.

3. Organized crime is not limited to patently illegal enterprises or unlawful services such as gambling, prostitution, drugs, loan-sharking, or racketeering. It also includes such sophisticated activities as laundering of illegal money through a legitimate business, land fraud, and computer manipulation. . . .

4. Organized crime employs predatory tactics such as intimidation, violence, and corruption, and it appeals to greed to accomplish its objectives and preserve its gains. . . .

5. By experience, custom, and practice, organized crime's conspiratorial groups are usually very quick and effective in controlling and disciplining their members, associates, and victims. Therefore, organized crime participants are unlikely to disassociate themselves from the conspiracies and are in the main incorrigible. . . .

6. Organized crime is not synonymous with the Mafia or La Cosa Nostra, the most experienced, diversified, and possibly best disciplined of the conspiratorial groups.

7. Organized crime does not include terrorists dedicated to political change, although organized criminals and terrorists have some characteristics in common, including types of crimes committed and strict organizational structures. (National Task Force on Organized Crime, 1976:7–8)

In addition to stressing some of the same attributes as the earlier investigative bodies—organized hierarchy, public demand, violence, profit through illegal activities, and corruption—this definition also points to the sophistication of some organized crime activities. Deception of a sophisticated kind is certainly required in order to engage in land fraud and computer manipulation. This is also the first definition to specifically exclude political terrorists, thus defining organized crime as nonideological. But perhaps of most importance, the 1976 task force explicitly stated that organized crime "is not synonymous with the Mafia or La Cosa Nostra." While acknowledging the existence of such an entity, the task force widens the scope of the definition of organized crime to include a host of other criminal groups as well. This broader scope becomes even more evident when we turn to our final definition of organized crime by a national commission.

President's Commission on Organized Crime (1986)

Created by executive order of President Reagan on July 28, 1983, this national commission was chaired by retired federal judge Irving R. Kaufman. The executive order directed the commission to, among other things, "Make a full and complete national region-by-region analysis of organized crime; define the nature of traditional organized crime as well as emerging organized crime groups ... [and] develop in-depth information on the participants in organized crime networks" (President's Commission, 1986:9). The commission engaged in a wide variety of activities to fulfill its mandate, including public hearings, litigation, research studies and surveys, and investigations. The seven public hearings focused on:

- federal law enforcement strategies,
- money laundering,
- the activities of organized crime groups of Asian origin (Chinese, Japanese, and Vietnamese groups),
- narcotics trafficking (specifically cocaine and heroin importation and distribution),
- labor and management racketeering, and
- legal and illegal gambling activities.

According to the commission's final report, one of its principal aims was "to expose the existence of other organized crime groups, whose importance was only recently recognized." "These groups," said the commission, "operate independently and occasionally in collaboration with other groups" (p. 11). All the groups were said to share a common greed and ambition, a disrespect for the law, and a willingness to rely on violence, criminality, and corruption to achieve their ends. The commission said that the failure of authorities to recognize organized crime in any group but La Cosa Nostra had been a barrier to law enforcement. The commission went on to describe a host of other organized crime entities:

- outlaw motorcycle gangs (Outlaws, Hells Angels, Bandidos, and Pagans),
- prison gangs (Mexican Mafia, La Nuestra Familia, Aryan Brotherhood, Black Guerilla Family, and Texas Syndicate),

- Cuban Marielito crime gangs,
- Colombian cocaine rings, and
- Russian organized crime groups or gangs allegedly operating in a number of cities across the country.

The commission concluded that the Japanese Yakuza is the largest organized criminal group in the world, with 110,000 members in 2,500 gangs. Many of these organized crime actors will be dealt with in some detail in later chapters.

The commission concluded that drug trafficking was the "single most serious organized crime problem in the United States and the largest source of income for organized crime" (p. 11). This was a significant change from the report of the 1967 President's Commission of a generation earlier, which concluded that gambling was the largest source of revenue to organized crime. In 20 years, organized crime appeared to have moved from domination by Italian–Sicilian groups principally engaged in gambling enterprises to a plethora of groups (perhaps better labeled gangs) involved heavily in drug-related activities.

The work of the President's Commission was surrounded by controversy. For example, a separate statement by a majority of the commissioners, attached to the final report, concluded that "[t]he true history of the President's Commission on Organized Crime is a saga of missed opportunity" (President's Commission, 1986:173). These commissioners accused the commission of leaving important issues unexamined, particularly questions about the effectiveness of federal and state anti-organized crime efforts. This same group, however, concluded that the commission had done a useful job in redefining the nature of organized crime.

> Histories of American organized crime have been ordinarily drawn too narrowly in that they have focused nearly exclusively on the Mafia or La Cosa Nostra. Drawing in part upon sources frequently ignored or overlooked, we have concluded that a broadened historical view on organized crime is essential. To adhere inadvertently to a misperception of organized crime in America as essentially the activities of members of the organization called La Cosa Nostra is to imply that organized crime and La Cosa Nostra are synonymous.
>
> This would perpetuate an unfortunate myth and divert potential attention from the broad range of persons and groups which are in fact responsible for much of the organized criminal activity in America today. (President's Commission, 1986:176)

The commission outlined three significant developments regarding U.S. organized crime in the prior two decades: (1) an increasing awareness that other organized crime groups exist; (2) the success of law enforcement against La Cosa Nostra, which it called "the largest, most extensive, and most influential crime group in this country"; and (3) the increased involvement of organized crime in drug trafficking operations.

With this background, let's turn now to the commission's definition of organized crime.

> Organized crime is the collective result of the commitment, knowledge and actions of three components: the criminal groups, each of which has at its core persons tied by racial, linguistic, ethnic or other bonds; the protectors, persons who protect the group's interests; and specialist support, persons who knowingly render services on an *ad hoc* basis to enhance the group's interests.
>
> *The criminal group* is a continuing, structured collectivity of persons who utilize criminality, violence, and a willingness to corrupt in order to gain and maintain power and profit. The characteristics of the criminal group, which must be evidenced concurrently, are: continuity, structure, criminality, violence, membership based on a common denominator, a willingness to corrupt and a power/profit goal. . . .
>
> *The protectors* are a complement of corrupt public officials, attorneys and businessmen, who individually or collectively protect the criminal group through abuses of status and/or privilege and violation of the law. . . . As a result of the protectors' efforts, the criminal group is insulated from both civil and criminal government actions. . . .
>
> Corruption is the central tool of the criminal protectors. . . .
>
> *Specialist support* includes individuals and groups who provide specialized contract services which facilitate organized crime activity. . . . *User support* includes those individuals who purchase organized crime's illegal goods and services, such as drug users and patrons of bookmakers.
>
> *Social support* includes individuals and organizations that grant power and an air of legitimacy to organized crime generally and to certain criminal groups and their members specifically. (President's Commission, 1986:25–32)

This definition contains the actor attributes of groups being defined by restricted membership (bonding), by a continuing, organized hierarchy, by use of violence and corruption, by seeking profit through illegal activities, and by meeting a public demand. In addition, it includes such attributes of organized crime acts as violence and corruption and victim participation.

THE LEGAL DEFINITION: LAWS PRESCRIBING INVESTIGATION, PROSECUTION, AND PUNISHMENT

Unlike the definitions of organized crime set forth by the various commissions and investigative bodies just described, which had no particular restrictions, legal definitions—that is, the definitions contained in criminal or civil statutes—must target specific acts as being legally proscribed. They must sharply and narrowly define what behavior is to be subject to criminal or civil remedy. Criminals, whether organized or otherwise, cannot be prosecuted and punished simply because they have certain characteristics or belong to certain groups. They can only be prosecuted and punished because they have committed certain acts that are illegal. While it may be that the old adage, "If it looks like a duck, walks like a duck, and hangs around with ducks, then it is a duck," fits members of organized crime, no one can be prosecuted for looking like, walking like, or hanging around with members of organized crime groups.

G. Robert Blakey, the father of the Racketeer Influenced and Corrupt Organizations (RICO) concept, addresses this issue in an appendix to the final report of the 1986 President's Commission on Organized Crime. Blakey says that there is "no generally applicable legal definition of concepts of 'organized crime,' 'corruption' or 'racket' or 'racketeering'" (President's Commission, 1986:511). The legal definitions, according to Blakey, are often constitutionally vague or indefinite. They may violate constitutional rights to association and assembly. They may violate concepts of due process or equal protection. Or they may raise other civil liberties issues and problems. In any or all of these instances, criminal charges against suspected organized crime defendants can be dismissed or convictions overturned upon appeal.

The only definition of organized crime contained in a federal statute is that in Public Law 90–351, the Omnibus Crime Control and Safe Streets Act of 1968:

> Organized crime means the unlawful activities of the members of a highly organized, disciplined association engaged in supplying illegal goods and services, including but not limited to gambling, prostitution, loan sharking, narcotics, labor racketeering, and other unlawful activities of members of organizations.

This statement defines organized crime both in terms of its actors (organized hierarchy and public demand) and in terms of its acts (victim participation offenses).

The difficulty arises when this definition is used as the basis for bringing criminal charges against a defendant or defendants. What, for example, constitutes a "highly organized, disciplined association" as opposed to a less highly organized, less disciplined association? This distinction is critical to separating the organized crime defendant from defendants who, as individuals, gamble, prostitute themselves, make loans for exorbitant interest rates, or sell drugs. Law enforcement can readily proceed against individuals charged with unlawful activities, but it is much less clear that it can proceed against individuals for being members of organizations, even when those organizations are suspected of being involved in unlawful activities. And it is still less clear that it can proceed against criminally suspect organizations themselves. Organized criminal groups may be highly structured, but that does not mean they look like General Motors or the Teamsters Union. Responsibility, accountability, and legal liability are much more complex and difficult to sort out.

Interestingly, but perhaps not surprising given the difficulties in so doing, the federal Organized Crime Control Act of 1970 (PL 91–452) did not define organized crime. Particular provisions of this act, especially the RICO statute, have been subjected to legal tests and appellate reviews to determine the constitutionality of their legal definitions. The RICO provision enables prosecutors to charge groups affiliated with a criminal enterprise, to obtain a pretrial freeze and posttrial forfeiture of assets either used in or derived from a pattern of racketeering activity, and to seek stiffer penalties upon conviction. A "pattern of racketeering" has generally been defined as participation in any two incidents of whatever crimes are specified, for example, murder or theft, within a ten-year period.

Legal definitions or, more properly, attempts at legal definitions can be found in a number of sources. In his 1983 testimony before a Congressional Appropriations Committee, then FBI Director William Webster defined an organized crime investigation as an investigation

> targeted against any member or members of an organized crime group involved in violation of Federal statute(s) specifically aimed at racketeering activities. . . . [A]n organized crime group is defined as any group having some manner of formalized structure whose primary objective is to obtain money through illegal activities and maintains its position through the use of violence or threat of violence, corrupt public officials, graft and extortion, and has a significant adverse effect on the people in its locale or region, or the country as a whole. (cited by Blakey, in President's Commission, 1986:540–541)

This definition includes a number of attributes: organized hierarchy ("formalized structure"), rational profit through illegal activities ("obtain money through illegal activities"), violence ("use of violence or threat of violence"), and corruption ("corrupt public officials"). But again, the phrase "having some manner of formalized structure" is not exactly crystal clear for prosecution purposes. Nor perhaps is the phrase "primary objective is to obtain money through illegal activities." Suppose this group has a thriving restaurant or bar business or a motorcycle shop? Who is to say, or prove, that these are not the primary sources of income? And just what is a "significant adverse effect on the people"?

Legal definitions of organized crime have become part of international agreements between the United States and other countries. For example, the 1973 Treaty on Mutual Assistance in Criminal Matters between the United States and Switzerland defined (in the somewhat convoluted language of international diplomacy) an organized group as:

> an association or group of persons combined together for a substantial or indefinite period for the purposes of obtaining monetary or commercial gains or profits for itself or for others, wholly or in part by illegal means, and of protecting its illegal activities against criminal prosecution and which, in carrying out its purposes, in a methodical and systematic manner:
>
> > a.) at least in part of its activities, commits or threatens to commit acts of violence or other acts which are likely to intimidate and are punishable. . . . (27 U.S.T. 2019, T.I.A.S. No. 8302)

Most states have attempted to define organized crime in their criminal statutes. These definitions range from Delaware's "[a] group of individuals working outside the law for economic gain" to Mississippi's "[t]wo or more persons conspiring together to commit crimes for profit on a continuing basis" to Pennsylvania's "[t]he unlawful activity of an association trafficking in illegal goods and services, including but not limited to gambling, prostitution, loan sharking, controlled substances, labor racketeering, or other unlawful activities; any continuing criminal conspiracy or other unlawful practice which has as its objective (1) large economic gain through fraudulent or coercive practices; or (2) improper governmental influence."

Delaware and Mississippi throw their nets so wide as to capture almost anything and everything as organized crime; such legal definitions are meaningless for prescribing effective law enforcement against organized crime.

Finally, the U.S. Bureau of Prisons uses an inmate classification system that designates certain inmates as having been involved in "sophisticated criminal activity." Three factors constitute the criteria for this classification:

(1) the offense was planned and organized and involved criminal activity that geographically operated on a municipal, county, state, national, or international scale;

(2) the offender occupied a position of organizer, a supervisory position, or any other position of management in the criminal organization or activity from which substantial income or resources could be obtained; and

(3) the monetary value of the offense totaled $500,000 or more for drug offenses and $250,000 or more for property offenses or white collar offenses. (cited by Blakey, in President's Commission 1986:536–537)

This definition emphasizes extensive planning, organized hierarchy, and rational profit through illegal activities—attributes of the actors involved in organized criminal activity. This definition, along with the many others we have cited, attempts to define that elusive term *organized* in the phenomenon known as organized crime.

Now let's look at the work of the scholars of organized crime—those who have researched, studied, and written about the subject—to see how they define it.

ORGANIZED CRIME FROM THE IVORY TOWER

We have already referred to the work of a number of academics in this field—Hagan (1983), Maltz (1976, 1985), Schelling (1976), and Blakey (President's Commission, 1986)—in some cases drawing extensively upon them. Here we will limit ourselves to a relatively few additional scholars who have made major contributions to our knowledge and understanding of organized crime over the last two decades.

Sociologist Donald R. Cressey served as a consultant to the 1967 President's Commission Task Force on Organized Crime. He also authored a subsequent influential book called *Theft of the Nation* (1969). Cressey outlined a theory of organized crime that was heavily influenced by the Joseph Valachi testimony before the McClellan committee. As a result, Cressey's definition of organized crime equated it largely with the Mafia/La Cosa Nostra.

In his report to the President's Commission, Cressey criticized prior efforts of social scientists to define organized crime for not being concerned with formal and informal structure and for not attending to the antilegal attitudes that permit engagement in a "continuous" or "self-perpetuating" conspiracy. Organized criminals, said Cressey, exhibit certain attitudes about the rules, agreements, and understandings that form the foundation of the criminal social structure. It is this social structure and these attitudes that differentiate organized crime and the organized criminal from other crimes and criminals. In Cressey's own words:

> Organized crime is any crime committed by a person occupying a position in an established division of labor designed for the commission of crime. This means that the organized criminal's activities are coordinated with the activities of others by means of rules. . . .
>
> If the positions of Corrupter, Corruptee, and Enforcer are in fact essential to the operation of the business of gambling, prostitution, usury, distribution of narcotics and untaxed liquor, and extortion, then identification of a defendant as an "organized criminal" becomes clearly a matter of identifying the structure of the illicit business in connection with which he has committed his crime. An organized crime becomes any crime committed by a person occupying, in an established division of labor, a position designed for the commission of crime, providing that such division of labor also includes at least one position for a Corrupter, one position for a Corruptee, and one position for an Enforcer. . . .
>
> Our view is that an "organized criminal" is one who has committed a crime while occupying an organizational position for committing that crime. (President's Commission, 1967:58–59)

Cressey's definition focuses on the attributes of organized hierarchy and corruption. It also alludes to, but without stressing, violence and public demand/victim participation. Cressey was later accused of being one of the principal promulgators of the myth of the Mafia. Dwight Smith (1975) says that Cressey had bought a perspective of organized crime that assumed it and the Mafia were synonymous labels for a real world phenomenon. "It gave him," says Smith, "a way of viewing a set of circumstances associated with organized crime, of seeing certain characteristics in them and ignoring (or dismissing) others, of interpreting what it allowed him to see, and of categorizing the results into a logical description of organized crime. The perspective was based on assumptions about how the real world 'ought' to look" (1975:311). Given this criticism, perhaps we should look at how Smith defines organized crime.

In a series of articles and in a well-regarded book, *The Mafia Mystique* (1975), Smith argues for a theory of illicit enterprise to explain organized crime. This approach is a socioeconomic one, putting more emphasis on the activities (the enterprise) than on the group or groups undertaking the enterprise. Organized crime is different from legitimate organized business only because its activities fall at a different place on a spectrum of economic enterprise. Organized crime is essentially an ongoing economic operation whose business is to provide illegal goods and services.

Smith describes marketplace dynamics where market demand is neither licit nor illicit. The need (demand) for a loan is an example. Financial institutions such as banks, credit unions, and finance companies are legal sources of loans. These institutions are governed by certain rules about the conditions under which a loan can be extended, collateral accepted, and an amount of interest set. As long as these conditions are met, a loan is legal. But some people in need of a loan cannot meet these conditions, perhaps because they cannot meet collateral requirements or their borrowing purposes are not acceptable. Their need (demand), however, does not go away, and an entrepreneur fills the gap by taking the risk of extending the loan and meeting the demand. This entrepreneur—if it's not your grandmother or your uncle—is called a loan shark. Bankers and loan sharks are really in the same business, but they operate under slightly different conditions. This, in a nutshell, is Smith's spectrum-based theory of enterprise. He links it to other explanations of organized crime in this way:

> It is clear that each [of conspiracy, ethnicity, and enterprise as ex-
> planations for organized crime] contains some truth, and that a
> complete explanation for organized crime must call on each theory
> in some integrated way. . . .
>
> It is my contention that enterprise is the principal but not exclu-
> sive explanation for the events we identify as organized crime. Mar-
> ket dynamics operating past the point of legitimacy establish the
> primary context for the illicit entrepreneur, regardless of his organi-
> zational style or ethnic roots. . . . The device of conspiracy may be
> the best way to further outlawed economic activity. . . . Ethnic ties
> provide the strongest possibility of ensuring trust among persons
> who cannot rely on the law to protect their rights and obligations
> within cooperative but outlawed economic activity. (Smith,
> 1980:375)

If we assume public demand to be the stimulus for the illicit entrepreneur, rational profit through illegal activities to be the economic objective of the illegal enterprise, and ethnic ties to result in restricted membership, we have identified three of our attributes of organized crime in this definition. This definition says nothing about the other characteristics of organized criminal groups, nor does it say anything about the use of violence or corruption.

Another sociologist, Joseph L. Albini, defined organized crime as syndicated crime. This, he said, is "a system of loosely structured patron–client relationships in which the roles, role expectations, and benefits of participants are based upon agreement or obligation" (cited in Ianni & Reuss-Ianni, 1976:24). Further, these patron–client relationships are structured as a continuous system, are secretive, and may involve violence or the threat of it. Albini indicated that syndicate criminals take advantage of needs in meeting public demand rather than creating needs or demands. He stressed this latter point, saying that syndicated crime functions because it fulfills a demand for illicit goods and services in a society that is basically puritanical and suppressive. "Traditionally," he said, "Americans have spoken out openly against vice but in practice have always allowed a controlled mechanism to make such vices available to the public" (Albini & Bajon, 1978:288).

This idea is similar to Smith's contention about the illicit entrepreneur. Again we have a focus on making profits through illegal activities that are a response to public demands for illegal goods and services. We also have the description of an organization that uses force or the threat of force and that assures immunity of its operations through corruption.

Anthropologists Francis Ianni and Elizabeth Ruess-Ianni have made significant contributions to our understanding of organized crime through their studies of organized criminal groups. Their work on ethnic succession in such groups as the so-called black Mafia, for example, helped shift attention away from the traditional Mafia/La Cosa Nostra toward other ethnic groups engaged in organized crime. Recognition of the existence of these emerging groups has been one of the major developments in the research on organized crime in the last 20 years. Emergence of groups such as the Dixie Mafia, the Mexican Connection, or other Cuban, Puerto Rican, and black criminal organizations does not, however, appear to give much support to the Iannis' theory of ethnic succession. Instead, it appears that as a result of advantages of language and geography, these groups establish temporary or even more than temporary monopolies over certain criminal enterprises but do not achieve syndication or consolidation of these activities across broad geographical areas. Thus, La Cosa Nostra is not being succeeded by Chinese, Japanese, Mexican, or any other ethnic-based organized crime group.

In addition to their work on ethnic succession, the Iannis have also set forth a definition of organized crime that shifts the focus away from organized criminals themselves.

We have preferred to take what we consider both a more systematic and a more empirical view of organized crime as a social institution which is symbiotic rather than parasitic in American society. Thus we have not focused on the specific aggregation of individuals who join together to perform specific criminal acts or even on particular types of crime. Rather, we have defined organized crime as an integral part of the American social system that brings together (1) a public that demands certain goods and services that are defined as illegal, (2) an organization of individuals who produce or supply those goods and services, and (3) corrupt public officials who protect such individuals for their own profit or gain. (Ianni & Ruess-Ianni, 1976:xvi)

Despite the disclaimer of focusing upon neither organized crime actors nor acts, this definition cites certain attributes we have associated with these two categories: public demand, organized hierarchy, and corruption. The notion of organized crime being symbiotic is important. The schizoid or hypocritical nature of American society with regard to desires and morals is, according to these researchers, at the root of American organized crime.

Finally, we turn to the more contemporary work of Howard Abadinsky. He has written several books on organized crime, the most recent published in 1990. Abadinsky was also a consultant to President Reagan's Commission on Organized Crime. Abadinsky (1985) suggests that organized crime encompasses only those groups that engage in ongoing criminal activity and that share these attributes:

- nonideological,
- hierarchical,
- limited or exclusive in membership,
- perpetuitous,
- organized through specialization or division of labor,
- monopolistic,
- and governed by rules and regulations.

Many of these attributes are identical to or overlap those in the analytical framework we have been using because they have been drawn from common sources. Abadinsky's definition incorporates all these attributes and should prove fertile soil for our own content analysis using actors and acts attributes.

Organized crime is a nonideological enterprise that involves a number of persons in close social interaction, organized on a hierarchical basis for the purpose of securing profit and power by engaging in illegal and legal activities. Positions in the hierarchy and positions involving functional specialization may be assigned on the basis of kinship or friendship, or rationally assigned according to skill. The positions are not dependent on the individuals occupying them at any particular time. Permanency is assumed by the members who strive to keep the enterprise integral and active in pursuit of its goals. It eschews competition and strives for monopoly over particular activities on an industry or territorial basis. There is a willingness to use violence and/or bribery to achieve ends or to maintain discipline. Membership is restricted, although nonmembers may be involved on a contingency basis. (Abadinsky, 1985:7)

As expected, we find many of our attributes in this definition: non-ideological, organized hierarchy, violence, restricted membership, rational profit through illegal activities, corruption, monopoly, and specialization. These are all characteristics of organized crime groups—of the actors in organized crime—and they include a willingness to use violence and bribery. There is no reference to the acts, to the means (other than violence and corruption) by which organized crimes are carried out—for example, by economic coercion or deception or victim participation.

Abadinsky's definition is much more comprehensive than the others we have examined because it is not derived from a particular theoretical perspective as were the definitions of Cressey, Smith, Albini, and the Iannis. It is eclectic in nature. This is neither necessarily bad nor good. It simply means that it is limited to describing the phenomenon of organized crime rather than attempting to explain it. Organized crime is sufficiently varied and complex that perhaps one explanation or one theory cannot cover all the bases. We will be dealing with the theories of organized crime in the next chapter.

We have summarized the perspectives of the national commissions and investigative bodies, the legal definitions, and the academics on the attributes of both organized crime actors and organized crime acts in Table 1.2 and Table 1.3. With this information at hand, we can propose our own working definition of organized crime.

CONCLUSION

So what is organized crime? The difficulty lies in defining the word *organized*. The attributes of the actors and the acts that make organized crime in fact *organized* include a self-perpetuating, organized hierarchy, a criminal conspiracy, which exists to profit from providing illicit goods and services in public demand or providing legal goods and services in an illicit manner.

Table 1.2 Attributes of Organized Crime Actors: National Commissions, Scholars, and Legal Definitions

ATTRIBUTES	Kefauver Committee (1951)	Oyster Bay Conferences (1966)	TFR (1967)	NAC Task Force (1976)	President's Commission (1986)	Cressey	Smith	Albini	Ianni	Abadinsky	1968 Law	FBI	PA Law	CIM	U.S.-Swiss Treaty
Nonideological				X											
Organized hierarchy, continuing	X	X	X	X	X				X	X					
Violence	X	X	X	X	X		X	X		X		X			
Restricted membership			X			X	X	X							
Rational profit through illegal activities	X	X	X	X	X	X	X	X	X	X		X	X	X	X
Public demand	X	X	X	X	X	X	X	X	X		X			X	
Corruption (immunity)	X	X	X	X	X	X	X	X	X	X		X	X		
Monopoly		X								X					
Specialization										X					
Code of secrecy	X		X												
Extensive planning	X	X													X

Table 1.3 Attributes of Organized Crime Acts: National Commissions, Scholars, and Legal Definitions

ATTRIBUTES	Kefauver Committee (1951)	Oyster Bay Conferences (1966)	TFR (1967)	NAC Task Force (1976)	President's Commission (1986)	Cressey	Smith	Albini	Ianni	Abadinsky	1968 Law	FBI	PA Law	CIM	U.S.–Swiss Treaty
Violence	X	X	X	X	X			X		X		X			X
Theft		X		X						X		X			
Corruption	X	X	X	X	X			X		X		X	X		
Economic coercion													X		
Deception		X	X										X		
Victim participation		X	X	X							X				

27

The co-conspirators may comprise a crime family, a gang, a cartel, or a criminal network, but these characteristics are not important to the definition. These same co-conspirators may also share certain ethnic identities; but that too is not essential to their being defined as organized crime groups.

Essential to the definition of organized crime is the use of violence or the threat of violence to facilitate criminal activities and to maintain monopoly control of markets. Also essential is that organized crime employs corruption of public officials to assure immunity for its operations. These factors define organized crime and it is that phenomenon we will focus on in the remainder of our book.

2

The Theories of
Organized Crime :

Explaining the Past, the
Present, and the Future

I n the 15 years following the 1967 President's Commission, the most important change in outlook was the new focus on organized crime as
a form of illicit enterprise (Walsh, 1983). This focus is exemplified in the
Racketeer Influenced and Corrupt Organizations (RICO) legislation of the
1970 Organized Crime Control Act. One result of the change in focus has
been a growing awareness of and attention to organized crime groups other
than the traditional Mafia or La Cosa Nostra. One example of this expanded perspective is the 1986 President's Commission description of outlaw motorcycle gangs, prison gangs, and a host of ethnically based organized
criminal groups—Chinese, Cuban, Colombian, Japanese, Vietnamese, and
Russian (President's Commission, 1986).

Despite a number of positive developments since 1967, Walsh (1983)
concluded that no "coherent" theoretical base nor organized crime control
policy had yet been developed and relatively little empirical research on organized crime had been done. In a later paper, Reuter (1987) reached a
similar conclusion: "What is notably lacking, and is critical in the development of a research tradition, is any theoretical framework for the formation
and testing of hypotheses. There is [only] a very slight theoretical literature

dealing with organized crime" (p. 170). Unfortunately, these same circumstances remain true today.

But is a theory of organized crime necessary? To answer that question, we must first explore these questions:

- Why is theory needed?
- Just what is a theory?
- Of what value is it?
- What should a theory do?
- What is a criminological theory, and what should it do?
- Why should organized crime theory be different from any general theory or theories about crime?
- Are there any "good" theories of organized crime?

In the next section, we will begin to answer these questions.

WHY THEORY?

A theory is an effort to explain some real world phenomenon. It organizes what we know, or think we know, at a particular time about some question or issue; for example, what causes organized crime? A theory answers questions, both deductively and inductively, about why something should be the way it appears. Theory has a descriptive function; it describes the real world by taking into account what is known. And theory has an explanatory function; it helps explain and interpret the apparent relationships among observed phenomena. For example, we observe that when X is present, Y is also always present. (What X and Y are makes no difference for purposes of this example.) The simultaneous presence of X and Y could mean that one causes the other or that both are caused by some third factor, Z. But in any event they are related—or at least appear to be related—in some way.

Theory also has a predictive function—it makes predictions about future relations among events possible. In the case of our simple example, if X is present, then we can predict that Y will also be present. If a theory's explanation of what has been observed in the past is correct, then similar observations should occur in the future, making prediction possible.

Finally, theory has a control or influencing function—it suggests steps or directions for controlling or altering the relations among events. We can use theory as a basis for trying to alter the predicted happenings. If Y is something that is undesirable, for example, lung cancer, then perhaps we can reduce or even eliminate it by altering X, the desire to smoke.

By helping to organize what we know, theory makes the important contribution of serving as a heuristic device; that is, it stimulates and guides further investigation and discovery. One sociologist has defined theory this way:

> A theory is a set of propositions complying, ideally, with the following conditions: one, the propositions must be couched in terms of exactly defined concepts; two, they must be consistent with one another; three, they must be such that from them the existing generalizations could be deductively derived; four, they must be fruitful—show the way to further observations and generalizations increasing the scope of knowledge. (Timasheff, 1957:9–10)

In sum, a theory must have well-defined and specific elements that are measurable; these elements must fit together logically; the elements must give forth certain derivable assumptions and hypotheses; and they must be heuristic. If criminology is to be scientific, then theories that purport to explain crime and delinquency should have the same characteristics as scientific explanations in other fields. Such theories should stimulate, simplify, and give direction to criminological research; provide a framework for understanding the significance of our knowledge about crime and criminal behavior; and be useful in the control of crime (Sutherland & Cressey, 1960).

It is important to make a distinction between crime and criminal behavior because the factors associated with each of them are different. The factors or circumstances associated with crime include poor socioeconomic circumstances, criminal opportunities, and unpopular laws. These are quite different from the factors associated with individual criminal behavior, which include impulsivity, low self-control, low self-esteem, and greed. Given the same set of factors, not everyone will engage in criminal behavior. All poor people do not become criminals, just as all bank employees do not become embezzlers. A comprehensive theory of crime must address both sets of circumstances—crime and criminal behavior. It must account for both the social factors and the individual factors.

Theories of organized crime should also have these attributes. They should distinguish between and reconcile explanations of crime as distinct from criminal behavior (descriptive and explanatory functions). They should stimulate and give direction to research (heuristic functions). They should provide a framework for understanding all that is known about organized crime (explanatory and predictive functions). And they should have application value in the control and prevention of organized crime (control function). These are admittedly tough criteria; nevertheless, they provide a useful framework for us to examine and analyze a number of the most popular theories of organized crime. We will also explore several new theoretical perspectives that, for various reasons, have not been examined in this way before. We begin with the old "alien conspiracy" theory of organized crime.

ALIEN AND OTHER CONSPIRACIES

The idea that organized crime is caused by a particular group of alien foreigners (most commonly, Italians and Sicilians) invading and infiltrating an otherwise law-abiding America and forming a highly structured, secret, nationwide criminal organization is a popular myth but a very tenuous "theory" of organized crime. Serious questions abound about whether it was ever a full-fledged theory or, for that matter, even a partial explanation of the phenomenon of organized crime. Today it is, for the most part, discredited. Although a Mafia myth persists, most experts now agree that the Mafia or La Cosa Nostra and organized crime are not synonymous. This is not to deny the existence of such groups but rather to deny their exclusivity and monopoly. In the context of alien conspiracies, it is interesting to note that this characterization is now being applied to the so-called Chinese Mafia (Posner, 1988) and the Japanese Yakuza (Kaplan & Dubro, 1986). Apparently, the desire for simple answers to complex problems—and for scapegoats—dies hard.

The alien conspiracy idea suggested that the crimes and the criminal behaviors of organized crime in the United States originated elsewhere: Thus, it was an international conspiracy. Members of the Sicilian Mafia brought their crimes and their criminal traditions to the United States in the early 1900s. They were simply transplanted here, bag and baggage. Once here, these Sicilians (and southern Italians) organized themselves in a highly rational and orderly manner, creating a national Mafia Commission that dictated local policies to all crime "families" around the country and controlled all organized crime in the United States. The structure was a highly organized hierarchy with clearly delineated roles and functions.

The explanatory power of the alien conspiracy theory is poor. For instance, if organized crime originated with this Sicilian/Italian immigration, there should have been no such crime in the United States prior to this immigration. According to the historical record, however, that is clearly not the case. As numerous studies have demonstrated, plenty of organized crime existed among WASPs, Irish, Jews, and others (Lupsha, 1986; Fox, 1989) well before the arrival on our shores of the Mafia. Second, if this is purely and exclusively a Sicilian/Italian phenomenon, no other ethnic groups should be involved. This is clearly not the case. Ethnic diversity and the number of independent entrepreneurs refute the notion of the Mafia having some kind of total national control of all organized crime. Third, if organized crime is simply a transplant, Mafia operations in Sicily and the United States ought to be similar. Is that the case? Once again, the answer is no. Mafiosi in Sicily and southern Italy were, and to some extent still are, integral parts of the social system there. They play significant economic and political roles that are only partly based on social control, fear, and power. This has never been the case in the United States, where their role has been exclusively a criminal one, based on the fear produced by their use or threatened use of violence.

Finally, we ask whether the alien conspiracy theory has heuristic value? Again, no. On the contrary, acceptance and adoption of this theory and its attendant myth of the Mafia actually served to discourage research and investigation rather than to encourage it. It became more of an ideology than a theory. Myth and ideology tend to be closed-minded rather than open-minded influences, accepting confirming evidence only. Naysayers were generally not welcome to examine the tenets of the alien conspiracy explanation. Therefore, research designed to test the theory was impossible because such research was seen as neither desirable nor necessary.

Does the notion of conspiracy (as opposed to "alien" conspiracy) play any part in helping to describe and explain and possibly predict and control organized crime? Yes, we believe it does. As Albanese (1989) points out, provision of illicit goods and services involves the crime of conspiracy when carried out in an organized manner by two or more persons. By definition, people who organize to violate the law, that is, to engage in organized crime, are engaging in a criminal conspiracy. Albanese (1989) says that "the crime of conspiracy lies at the heart of organized crime, due to [the] goal of punishment for those who organize to commit a crime" (p. 9). We do not believe, however, that that is the only reason conspiracy is important. The fact that conspiracy is itself a crime goes to the crime part of the explanation, but who conspires with whom, and under what circumstances, goes to the criminal behavior part of the explanation.

If there has to be a criminal conspiracy for there to be organized crime, then conspiracy must be taken into account, but it is not a theory. Conspiracy does have instrumental value in stimulating the question of who the conspirators are and on what basis they decide to conspire. We will come back to this question later in the chapter and explain how conspiracy may fit into an integrated theory of organized crime.

CULTURAL TRANSMISSION, CULTURE CONFLICT, AND STRAIN THEORIES

Cultural Transmission Theories

As with so many criminological theories, the examples we have grouped under the rubic of *cultural transmission* were originally conceived as descriptions and explanations of juvenile delinquency. Sociologists such as Shaw and McKay (1942) and Miller (1958) suggested that offenders (in this case lower-class slum youth) violate the law because they adhere to a unique, independent value system that exists in and is the product of the lower socioeconomic slum areas of major cities. This value system is different from the middle-class value system and is in conflict with it. Further, the lower-class, criminally oriented value system and its traditions are passed down from generation to generation in a process of cultural transmission. No strong ethnic or racial correlation with criminal behavior is posited, except as people living in lower-class urban environments also happen to have particular ethnic or racial backgrounds.

Referring to the difference between lower-class and middle-class values and to the importance of that difference, Schrag (1971) said many lower-class persons have little interest in middle-class definitions of economic, social, and political success.

> Lower class ambitions are often aimed in another direction, involving such personal goals as excitement, enjoyment, freedom, and leisure. Reconciled to a world of dull, intermittent, and unrewarding employment, these people may seek their pleasures in expressive activities and in the consumption of goods and services. It therefore should not be surprising if the earnings from illicit activities (gambling, drug traffic, numbers and other rackets, graft, prostitution, loan sharking, and the like) [become] chief sources of financial support in some of the slums of our large cities. (Schrag, 1971:7)

To test these ideas as a valid theory of organized crime, it would be necessary to operationalize and measure lower-class as opposed to middle-class values and criminal versus noncriminal values. There is some precedent for doing that, but to show that these lower-class and criminal values are unique to certain areas and certain people, that these are the only areas where organized crime is located, and that these people are the only ones involved in organized crime would be a pretty tall order.

Questions that would have to be addressed in considering the idea of cultural transmission as a complete theory of organized crime are:

- Is it reasonable to believe that organized criminals are not interested in economic, social, and political success—even though these may be defined in middle-class terms?
- Is it possible that middle-class people (and noncriminals) as well as lower-class people are interested in excitement, enjoyment, freedom, and leisure?
- Is it possible that they may obtain these things by gambling, drugs, or prostitution as well?

We know that members of organized crime seem to be very interested in legitimate upward social mobility. Children of alleged mobsters have been encouraged by their families to become doctors, lawyers, teachers, and government officials. We also know that the last two hypothetical questions about the middle class are not only possibly true but are highly probable. In fact, much of the victim participation in organized crime is by the middle class.

Another form of cultural transmission, proposed in Edwin Sutherland's differential association theory (Sutherland & Cressey, 1960), suggests that criminal behavior is learned in a process of interaction with other persons in intimate personal groups. People are said to become criminals because they take on an excess of definitions favorable to violation of the law. The definitions, skills, and rationalizations for crime that are learned are not restricted to city slums or to the lower classes. The kind of intense interaction with significant others in which criminal ways of thinking and acting are passed on and adopted can occur anywhere. People (particularly young people) living in certain areas—(a) where there are considerable amounts of gambling, prostitution, drug trafficking, loan-sharking, numbers, and extortion; (b) where there are criminally successful role models pursuing these activities; (c) where there is intimate personal contact between young people and successful criminals; and (d) where there is a prevailing atmosphere of contempt for and disregard of the law—are especially vulnerable to learning organized crime orientations.

The practice of organized crime groups attracting and recruiting youngsters from urban street gangs would seem to support the validity of this explanation. Although much work has been done testing differential association as a general theory of crime and delinquency, very little work has actually been done applying it to organized crime per se. On the other hand, it could be argued that the form of the crime and the criminal behavior being explained by differential association theory—that is, whether it is organized or unorganized—really makes no difference. In either case, the behavior is learned in the manner described and the specific forms of crime are determined by the particular criminal opportunities available. Learning (with all that is entailed in that learning) such skills as how to steal cars, how to snatch pocketbooks, and how to break into houses is pretty much the same as learning to organize to deal drugs, run numbers, or run a protection racket.

Culture Conflict Theory

Criminologist Thorsten Sellin (1938) first put forward the theory of culture conflict and crime. He said that crime should be understood in terms of normative conflict. Different cultures have different conduct norms as well as different beliefs and values. As these different cultures come into contact in a more complex pluralistic society, the stage is set for intercultural and intergroup conflict. People may be expected to conform not only to the norms of the larger society in which they find themselves but also to the norms of their individual cultural group. Where these are different—are in conflict—the person is torn as to which norms to follow.

It is out of this conflict, said Sellin, that crime and delinquency arise. When one set of norms, usually those of the larger society, are given the force of law, failure to abide by them amounts to lawbreaking. Culture conflict is common following immigration from one country to another. The norms of the old country may have sanctioned certain kinds of behavior, whereas the laws of the new country may outlaw that same behavior. Because the United States is especially a country of immigrants, the potential for culture conflict, and its ensuing crime, is especially high here.

Sykes and Matza (1957) argued that American culture is a complex and pluralistic culture that has certain *subterranean* or deviant traditions that are in conflict with prosocial traditions. (This may be true for other pluralistic societies as well.) Our society's two sets of traditions—conventional and deviant—are held simultaneously by almost everyone. While certain individuals and groups may be influenced more by one than the other, both traditions act to determine behavior. In fact, cheating or otherwise using unethical or unlawful means has, unfortunately, been a major means by which a variety of people have attempted to achieve the American dream of financial and social success.

The Sellin form of culture conflict could be a basis for explaining the involvement of certain immigrant groups in organized crime. Have certain cultural norms, traditions, or behaviors been brought to the United States that conflict with the norms, traditions, and behaviors here? For example, goods and services legally available in the country of origin may not be legally available here. If, however, a demand for these goods and services exists here, then there is obviously money to be made from providing them. The Sykes and Matza version has been used to explain organized crime by Bell (1953) and others. We will consider both these approaches in our discussion of ethnicity.

Strain Theory

The strain theorists view crime and delinquency as resulting from the frustration and anger people feel over their inability to achieve legitimate social and financial success. Unlike the cultural transmission view, in this view people are believed to share similar values and goals. But the chances of reaching their goals are believed to be enhanced or limited by their particular socioeconomic class. In lower-class slum areas, legitimate avenues to success are closed or severely limited. When acceptable means for obtaining success do not exist, people may either use deviant means or reject societal goals and substitute others for them. Merton (1957) described American society as stressing the goals of acquiring wealth, success, and power. The socially permissible means for achieving these goals are hard work, education, and thrift. However, opportunity is very much shaped by social class and status. Those with little formal education and few economic resources find that they are denied the opportunity to acquire money and other success symbols legally. This is where the strain comes in. One response to this strain may be development of criminal solutions to the problem of attaining goals. "A cardinal American virtue, ambition," said Merton, "promotes a cardinal American vice, deviant behavior" (1957:146).

Cloward and Ohlin (1960) took this idea one step further. They agreed with Merton that socioeconomic class membership controls access to legitimate means of achieving social goals. However, they went beyond this to state that illegitimate means for goal attainment were also unevenly distributed and thus unevenly available. Some lower-class neighborhoods provide more opportunity for illegal gain than do others in the form of access to rackets and other organized crimes. Thus, we have a possible connection to organized crime.

Cloward and Ohlin said that illegitimate opportunities for success were present in areas where "stable patterns of accommodation" existed between the criminal world and the conventional world. In these areas, adult criminals have worked out relationships with businesses and with the police and other criminal justice officials through bribery and corruption, so they are immune from arrest and prosecution. Their criminal activity—drugs, gambling, loan-sharking, prostitution—provides a relatively stable and perhaps substantial income and, most important, an alternative means to the success goals of money, power, and status. Under the tutelage of adult criminals, youth in these areas can be recruited into a criminal subculture. In this model, lower-class urban youth would join gangs specializing in theft, extortion, and so on. Later, they would become part of the adult criminal organizations. Just as middle-class boys learn to become bankers, lawyers, or businessmen, lower-class boys learn to become professional burglars, numbers runners, bookies, or fences (similar to differential association). Further, they learn how to build strong political ties and the importance of hiring the best lawyers to avoid prosecution and conviction. Crime in general, and organized crime in particular, is simply an alternate route to the American Dream.

Donald Cressey (1970) likewise pointed out how organized crime can be an attractive field of endeavor for poor youths growing up in urban ghettos. Organized criminals, said Cressey, demonstrate to young people that crime does pay. Organized crime is seen as attractive, natural, and relatively painless. Its presence demonstrates the corruption of the law enforcement and political apparatuses. Respect for, commitment to, and belief in the moral validity of the law are all diminished by this demonstration. All of this makes it very difficult for parents to teach their children that the way to get ahead is through hard, honest labor. Finally, the damaging economic effects of numbers rackets, drugs, and so on reduces even further the economic viability of the neighborhood. Already sparse legitimate opportunities become even more limited and less available, and there is even less to lose if convicted of a crime.

Each of these theories comes at organized crime in a slightly different way, but they share many similarities. One of the major ones is the proposition that poor urban neighborhoods provide a fertile environment for the cultivation and growth of organized crime. Another is that choosing to become involved in this kind of criminal behavior is a rational choice from among a set of less desirable alternatives, although it is to some degree a forced choice because attractive alternatives are simply not available. One other characteristic the neighborhoods referred to here share is that they are frequently populated by various ethnic groups and newly arrived immigrants. Let us turn to the role of ethnicity in organized crime.

ETHNICITY AND ETHNIC SUCCESSION

Beginning with the work of Daniel Bell (1953) and later that of Francis Ianni (1972, 1974), organized crime has been described as being "caused" by the efforts of successive immigrant groups to make it in America. Cut off from legitimate opportunities for achieving socioeconomic and political success, immigrants have been forced by circumstances to climb what Bell called the "queer ladder" of upward social mobility, namely, crime, and especially organized crime. Ianni advanced the role of ethnicity in explaining organized crime by arguing for the notion of ethnic succession. This is said to come about as one ethnic group replaces another on the queer ladder of mobility, and the preceding groups move on to social respectability. This presumably means that they move out of organized crime. Thus, the Irish are replaced by the Jews, who are in turn replaced by the Italians, who in turn are replaced by African Americans, and so on.

More recently, Kelly (1986) reflected on the important role attributed to ethnicity in describing a study of Georgian Jews in Israel. The study, he said, "shows the relationships between ethnicity and organized crime; it reveals the dilemma ethnic groups not fully acculturated into their host society face: how does one gain acceptance and approval when the traditional routes to these desired goals are either closed off or sharply circumscribed by cultural values within the ethnic group?" (p. 23).

There are several major problems with ethnicity as a general explanation of organized crime. One is that the ethnicity variable by itself does not appear to be the proximate cause of organized criminal behavior. Instead, it is the difficult socioeconomic circumstances ethnic immigrants, but certainly nonimmigrant ethnic minorities as well, find themselves in that explains their potential risk for this kind of criminality. If that is so, then any socioeconomically disadvantaged individuals and groups should be prime candidates for recruitment into organized crime. Ethnicity would then be a secondary attribute characterizing some of these individuals and groups, meaning we should find nonethnic as well as ethnic organized criminal groups. And, in fact, that is the case. The ethnicity theory cannot account for the emergence of such nonethnic groups in organized crime as outlaw motorcycle gangs and at least some prison gangs. Although some of these crime groups have ethnic identifications, many of them do not. They may, however, share certain other characteristics historically associated with ethnic immigrants—alienation, distrust, fear, and discrimination.

The limitation of this explanation is that not all members of all ethnic groups, nor all immigrants, become organized criminals or criminals of any kind. Therefore, ethnicity cannot be the cause of organized crime.

Further, contrary to the notion of ethnic succession, emergence of other organized crime groups has not necessarily resulted in the displacement of earlier groups. This has been particularly true of the Italians and Sicilians. The President's Commission (1986) concluded that despite tremendous pressure from law enforcement in recent years, La Cosa Nostra remains the most formally organized, broadly established, and effective crime group in the United States. Many young Italian Americans have become doctors, lawyers, teachers, plumbers, and carpenters, but many others are still apparently eager and willing to join criminal organizations.

If ethnicity is not the cause of organized crime, then a theory of ethnicity cannot be a comprehensive theory of organized crime. We agree with Albini (1988) that "ethnicity must be viewed as a variable that becomes significant only when it is found in combination with a host of other variables that seek to explain the complex puzzle of organized criminal involvement" (pp. 347–348).

Many of the causal factors identified by cultural transmission theorists, strain theorists, and culture conflict theorists are also found in the work of ethnicity theorists as these factors frequently exist in conjunction with ethnic identification. Thus, in addition to sharing a common ethnicity, potential criminals with particular ethnic backgrounds often share other characteristics that are especially (but not exclusively) associated with new immigrants. Living in socially disorganized neighborhoods, being poor, suffering language problems, being unskilled or uneducated—all of these limit their access to and their ability to take advantage of legitimate opportunities. And all of these characteristics have been said to be linked to the cause of crime. Ethnicity is confounded by a number of other variables, and it is difficult, if not impossible, to sort out its individual and special effects.

Lupsha (1981) and Fox (1989) claim that there is little causal relationship between ethnicity and organized crime in any event. To quote Fox: "to stress ethnicity may obscure the individual gangsters and the options available to them. . . . [Organized crime] derived less from social conditions or difficult childhoods or there-but-for-fortune bad luck than from a durable human condition: the dark, strong pull of selfish, greedy, impatient, unscrupulous ambition" (p. 76).

Ethnicity does have a role in explaining organized crime, but it neither works alone nor does it necessarily work in the fashion some theorists have proposed. But before we get to that, we have another theoretical perspective to present.

ENTERPRISE THEORY

The theory of enterprise explains the existence of illicit entrepreneurs as due to the fact that the legitimate marketplace leaves potential customers for goods and services unserved or unsatisfied (Smith, 1980). It postulates that economic activities (enterprises) take place across a spectrum that includes both legitimate businesses and certain kinds of crime. There is a range of behavior along which any business can be conducted, and legality is an arbitrary point on that range. This point can be shifted by passing new laws or promulgating regulations. These do not, however, necessarily change behavior. They may only make behavior that was formerly legal, illegal—or vice versa.

Prohibition is a prime example of the spectrum of enterprises idea. When the Volstead Act of 1920 set conditions on the distribution and consumption of alcohol, it did not really affect the demand nor change the technology for producing alcohol. It did, however, create illegal markets and produce the conditions for the formation of large criminal enterprises. How much did Prohibition contribute to organized crime? According to Fox:

> Organized crime in America was permanently transformed by thirteen years of Prohibition. The old, clear line between underworld and upperworld became vague and easily crossed. With so many Americans casually defying the law, gangsters took on an oblique legitimacy. . . . Crime was nationalized by Prohibition, as most of the men who would dominate organized crime for the next three or four decades got their start as bootleggers. (1989:51)

It is, according to Smith (1980), "market dynamics operating past the point of legitimacy [which] establish the primary context for the illicit entrepreneur"(p. 375). A high level of demand for a particular form of goods (such as drugs) or services (such as gambling) that are illegal, when combined with a relatively low level of risk of arrest and very high profits, provide "ideal conditions for illicit business groups to enter the market to seek profits by organizing the supply" (Lodhi & Vaz, 1980:145).

Just as there is a spectrum of entrepreneurship, there is a spectrum of customers, including customers whose legitimate needs are met on the legal side of the spectrum. On the illegal side are customers whose legitimate needs are not met for some reason; customers with illicit needs or demands; and extortionists who exploit the domains of other entrepreneurs. The latter, according to Schelling (1971), are the ones engaging in the "true" business of organized crime, namely, extortionate monopoly.

Whether the product is legal goods or services being illegally produced and distributed or illegal goods and services, a market must be available. A certain rate of consumption must be maintained to justify the risk and to produce a profit. Just as in legitimate businesses, the usual practice is to expand the market to expand profits. Competition must be discouraged and eliminated. Recognizing that certain unsavory and illegal practices such as violence, corruption, and extortion are used to develop, maintain, control, and expand these markets, the organized criminal is nevertheless said to be principally a businessperson, albeit an illegal one.

Enterprise theory employs propositions taken from the economic laws of supply and demand. Its ability to describe, explain, and predict organized crime can be tested using these propositions. Drugs, for example, are an illegal substance—except in certain forms and in certain circumstances. There is a substantial demand for illegal drugs, creating a market for organized crime in which huge profits can be made by meeting this demand.

What if we shift the demarcation point on the spectrum that divides what is legal from what is illegal about drugs? Suppose, for instance, we were to legalize drugs—as some people are in fact advocating? Assuming this was done with necessary controls and conditions in place, what would be the effect on the supply side of the equation? If people wanting drugs could go into a clinic or drugstore or other such place and purchase them for less than they had been costing on the illegal market, what would happen to the illegal suppliers? Or suppose a tremendously effective form of public education and drug prevention drastically reduced demand? What would be the effect? In both instances we would be altering the market conditions under which the lucrative drug market is being exploited by organized crime. Recognizing that we have oversimplified this example, it nevertheless illustrates the potential applications of enterprise theory for public policy.

AN INTEGRATED THEORY

In an article on enterprise theory, Dwight Smith (1980) explored, in a very preliminary way, the possible integration of ethnicity, conspiracy, and enterprise. "It is clear," Smith wrote, "that each contains some truth, and that a complete explanation for organized crime must call on each theory in some integrated way"(p. 375). To our knowledge, no further theoretical or empirical work has been done on such an integrated theory.

"Conspiracy may be the best way to further outlawed economic activity" (Smith, 1980:375). Smith pointed out that conspiracies exist not only in organized crime but also in white-collar crime, and perhaps in legitimate business operations as well. Putting the latter aside, we go beyond the modest notion that conspiracy may be the best way to proceed. Criminal conspiracy is the only way to engage in organized crime. It is the agreement, usually oral or tacit, between two or more persons to commit a criminal act or to commit by illegal means an act not in itself criminal, which is one of the critical elements distinguishing organized crime from all other crime. Conspiracy addresses the issue of *how* a particular criminal activity is planned. It is, as Smith pointed out, the operating strategy.

Who the conspirators are is where ethnicity comes in. Because engaging in a criminal conspiracy puts the individual at risk, keeping in mind that conspiracy itself is a crime, there must be an element of trust among the co-conspirators. Smith argued that ethnic ties provided the strongest possibility for ensuring trust among people who had nothing else to rely on. Lupsha (1986) made a similar argument:

> What one can note about ethnicity is that like family or blood tie, it is a useful trust variable. If a group all speaks the same language, has the same village roots, possesses the same myth and culture norms, then it can function as a unit with greater trust and understanding. . . . It is the organizational need for trust, loyalty, intimate knowledge of character, security, sense of courage, prowess, honesty, ease of understanding, communication and control, that makes ethnicity, kinship, blood-tie, language, and race important variables for group bonding, organization and identification. (p. 34)

Similarly, Reuter argues that loyal performance by employees in illegal markets may be sought by recruiting relatives or by incorporating these employees into the extended family (Reuter, 1985). These actions seem to assume a common ethnic background.

In addition to the ethnic factors of trust and kinship, a number of other issues are related to ethnicity and, in at least one case, to conspiracy as well. The latter raises the question of indigenous criminality versus imported criminality. Do newly arrived, formerly law-abiding emigres become criminals because of the force of limited circumstances? Or, were they possibly already criminals in their country of origin? If the latter, were they conspirators there as well? The answers to these questions have implications for both the ethnicity and the conspiracy explanations of organized crime. Other ethnic issues pertain to (1) the phenomenon of within group victimization—ethnic groups, for example, the Chinese, seem particularly to victimize their fellow ethnics; (2) the issue of limited socioeconomic mobility for newly arrived ethnic groups precipitating their involvement in organized crime; and (3) the role of any feelings of distrust, fear, and lack of respect and general ignorance of American customs and the American system that may be particularly prevalent in specific ethnic groups.

Having decided to engage in criminality and on who the co-conspirators are to be, the only remaining question is *what* is going to be done. This is not the only order in which these events can occur, but it is important that a *how* (conspiracy), a *who* (ethnicity), and a *what* (illicit enterprise) come together at some point to produce organized crime. The ethnic conspirators must decide what it is they are going to market. What products or services? To whom? Is there an existing demand for this product or service that is not being met, either in whole or in part? Can a demand be created or expanded? What is the competition? What is the territory? What are the risks, and how can they be controlled? Where will the capital investment come from? What about raw materials, supply, and distribution? And what of supervision and management of employees? How will the profits be handled? Should they be laundered? Reinvested? Or invested in legitimate businesses? These are all decisions that must be made to carry out a successful criminal enterprise. Some are one-time decisions, others are decisions that must be made over and over.

Whether a particular market is driven mainly by demand (reactive) or mainly by supply (proactive) has implications for entrepreneurial emphasis, but it also has implications for control strategies. The current drug market in the United States is an obvious example of this. Implications for control and prevention (the control function of the theory) can also be derived from these enterprise issues:

- If the product/service being provided is illegal, might it be legalized? This would remove it from the realm of illicit enterprise; and, if the theory is correct, it would eliminate it as one form of organized crime.

- If the product/service provided is legal, but in short supply, can the legal supply be expanded? This would take away the profit of illegal supply and again eliminate one form of organized crime.

- If the product/service is restricted, for example, licenses or other documentation, can that be revised or better enforced?

- Can demand be reduced through public education? "Just say no to drugs" is an example of this approach. If some product or service is no longer in demand, then there will be no money to be made in providing it, therefore another form of organized crime should be eliminated.

- Can supply be reduced through control or elimination of necessary raw materials and distribution systems?
- Can risk be increased by attacking corruption?

Each of these factors could make it more costly to do business. Reducing or minimizing the profit margin on any product or service reduces its attractiveness as a marketable commodity.

CRIMINALITY AS CHOICE OR AS LOW SELF-CONTROL

These two theoretical perspectives may shed some new light on organized crime. They are both relatively recent and relatively unexplored theories.

Choice and Consequences

James Q. Wilson and Richard Herrnstein (1985) offer a theory of criminal behavior based on behavioral psychology that purports to explain why individuals choose to engage in crime:

> At any given moment, a person can choose between committing a crime and not committing it. The consequences of committing the crime consist of rewards and punishments; the consequences of not committing the crime also entail gains and losses. The larger the ratio of the net rewards of crime to the net rewards of noncrime, the greater tendency to commit the crime. The net rewards of crime include, obviously, the likely material gains from the crime, but they also include intangible benefits, such as obtaining emotional or sexual gratification, receiving the approval of peers, satisfying an old score against an enemy, or enhancing one's sense of justice. One must deduct from these rewards of crime any losses that accrue immediately—that are, so to speak, contemporaneous with the crime. They include the pangs of conscience, the disapproval of onlookers, and the retaliation of the victim. (p. 44)

Most of the rewards of noncrime (of not engaging in criminality) lie in the future. They include avoiding the risk of being caught and punished as well as avoiding other negative side effects, such as loss of reputation, a sense of shame, and such practical losses as being unable to get a job or losing the job you have.

The value of any rewards and punishments associated with crime and noncrime are uncertain. The stolen pocketbook may or may not have any money in it; you may or may not get caught; your friends may or may not be impressed with your exploits.

Time is an important compounding factor in these uncertainties. Because the rewards of noncrime, of being honest and hardworking, are almost always in the relatively distant future, the choice between immediate or delayed gratification is a critical element in choosing crime or noncrime.

Wilson and Herrnstein (1985) focus on so-called serious high-rate offenders—predatory street crime. While Wilson and Herrnstein would have wished to draw upon a wider variety of crimes, such as embezzlement, bribery, extortion, and fraud, there has been very little research on these types of crimes. This focus obviously constrains the application of their theory to organized crime. Violence, for example, is certainly one of the means and methods of organized crime, but it is usually not the central purpose. Violence, in the form of threats, assaults, and even murders, is one of the ways of "doing" organized crime. But violence is not an end in itself. It is a means to the main end—running illegal markets to make money.

In their description of time, and discounting time as a factor in choosing between crime and noncrime, Wilson and Herrnstein distinguish between "professional" criminals and "impulsive" or "opportunistic" offenders. Professional criminals, who *might* be more characteristic of organized criminals, attach little value to the benefits of noncrime, are willing to work to obtain a large payoff, and attach value to future, as opposed to immediate, rewards from crime. Opportunistic offenders, on the other hand, seek even the smallest gain if it is immediate and are generally uninterested in distant events. These two factors can be used to separate organized criminals (assuming we are correctly classifying them as being of the professional criminal type) from other criminals and from noncriminals as well. For example, successful law-abiding individuals also are willing to work over an extended period for some worthy future reward, for example, a college degree, a promotion to partner or to supervisor, or the recognition and esteem of their peers. They do, however, apparently attach greater value to the benefits of noncrime, which at least in part differentiates them from the professional criminal. At the same time, there are some law-abiding individuals who are impulsive and opportunistic. They live for today and let tomorrow take care of itself. But, they choose not to act out their impulsivity in the form of criminal behavior.

The other possible explanation of organized crime that can be drawn from reading Wilson and Herrnstein comes not from their theory as such but from their description of the research on organized inner-city gangs. These gangs, they say, "may well have a much stronger effect on individual crime rates."

> Under some circumstances . . . the gang becomes an enduring, highly organized, territorially based social unit that shapes the behavior of its members over a long period of time and provides the organizational structure necessary to commit certain kinds of crime, such as drug dealing (among Chicanos) or gambling and loan-sharking (among Italians). (Wilson & Herrnstein, 1985:299)

The gang, or organized criminal group, is said to be a source of peer approval and disapproval. It materially rewards "good work"; and it creates opportunities for and provides the structure necessary for committing certain kinds of crimes—particularly those that are difficult or impossible to commit alone or in an unorganized group. The gang furnishes the social environment and opportunity structure that shapes the choices of criminality made by its members. This is one of the critical elements that marks the difference between organized and unorganized crime.

Low Self-Control

Michael Gottfredson and Travis Hirschi (1990) have even more recently set forth a general theory of crime they ambitiously claim is intended to apply to all cases: female as well as male crime, crime in different cultures, occupational as well as street crime, crime by children as well as by adults, and so forth. "Our theory," they say, "is meant to explain all crime, at all times" (p. 117). If this is the case, it certainly ought to apply to organized crime. And, in fact, one chapter in their book discusses organized crime. But before dealing with that, we need to understand what their theory is about.

Self-control is the central feature of this general theory. Defined as the differential tendency of people to avoid criminal acts whatever the circumstances in which they find themselves, an absence of self-control is said to characterize those who engage in crime. Low self-control types are described as being impulsive and insensitive, and as being physical risk-takers who are shortsighted and nonverbal. They have minimal tolerance for frustration and little ability to respond to conflict through verbal rather than physical means. People who lack self-control also lack diligence, tenacity, and persistence. They thirst for the adventure and physical pleasures that might be derived from a whole range of deviant activities, both criminal and noncriminal. Such individuals sound very much like Wilson and Herrnstein's impulsive criminals.

Criminal behavior is only one of the many manifestations of low self-control. Others include employment instability, alcohol and drug abuse, child and spouse abuse, and motor vehicle accidents. Gottfredson and Hirschi suggest that low self-control types are very versatile, usually engaging in a range of criminal as well as noncriminal (but deviant) behaviors. Crime is said to be particularly attractive to them because it can provide easy, immediate gratification and because it is exciting, risky, and even thrilling.

Where does self-control come from? According to Gottfredson and Hirschi, it comes principally from families that care about and monitor their children's behavior, recognize deviant behavior, sanction their children's deviant behavior, and instill a concern in them for the long-term negative consequences of deviant behavior. To a lesser degree, the school plays a role in development of self-control, acting in concert with and complementing the family.

So what does all this have to do with organized crime? Gottfredson and Hirschi hypothesize that the very existence of something called organized crime might be taken as evidence that contradicts their theory:

> The idea of organized crime argues against our view in at least four ways: (1) it challenges the notion that self-control is a general characteristic with multiple manifestations . . . ; (2) it challenges the notion that characteristics reliably accompanying the low self-control of offenders make their long-term participation in cooperative activities unlikely or problematic; (3) it challenges the notion that crime involves easy pursuit of immediate pleasure without concern for long-term values; and (4) it suggests that a complete theory of [crime] . . . must take into account the causal influence of the group or organization. (Gottfredson & Hirschi, 1990: 202)

They conclude that none of these objections is valid and that the above hypothesis should therefore be rejected. We respectfully disagree!

Although Gottfredson and Hirschi assert that American criminology has devoted considerable attention to organized crime over the years (an assertion itself contrary to the reality), they pick just a few select targets to attack to support their arguments. Further, although they refer to the problem of "other highly organized criminal activities of adults," their main point of attack is the old standby—the alien conspiracy theory—associated with Donald Cressey, which, as we pointed out, has already been largely discredited as a comprehensive theory of organized crime. Gottfredson and Hirschi indicate that they agree with Hawkins's conceptualization of the Mafia myth in regard to this explanation. Gordon

Hawkins (1969) drew an analogy between assertions about the existence of the Mafia and the existence of God. He was criticizing Cressey's failure to demonstrate the existence of a nationwide criminal confederation called La Cosa Nostra; however, Hawkins did not deny the existence of organized crime. Nor have many others who have criticized the Mafia myth—for example, Bell (1963) and Smith (1975). Yet Gottfredson and Hirschi reach the sweeping conclusion that "whereas Hawkins was (rightly) impressed by the flimsiness of the evidence favoring the existence of organized crime (comparing it to the evidence for the existence of God), we are impressed by the incompatibility of the idea of organized crime and the ideas of crime and self-control" (1990:213).

It was not the existence of organized crime that Hawkins was comparing to the existence of God, but rather the existence of the Mafia. In fact, Hawkins said quite clearly that there is "little dispute" that in supplying illegal goods and services, "large-scale continuing firms with the internal organization of a large enterprise, and with a conscious effort to control the market" have arisen (1969:34).

We too, along with a number of others, are skeptical of the conspiracy theory, and we too recognize the existence of a Mafia myth. Both the conspiracy theory and the Mafia myth have equated organized crime with the Mafia and La Cosa Nostra. But what if the Mafia and organized crime are not synonymous? What if the Mafia is not the only game in town? What about the other forms of organized crime—the outlaw motorcycle gangs, the Chinese Tongs, the Japanese Yakuza, the international drug cartels? How are these criminal organizations to be explained? Gottfredson and Hirschi seem to be making the claim that such criminal organizations are comparatively "ephemeral" (their term), are composed of individuals who only occasionally work together off and on over a period of time, and have only the illusion of organization and continuity. This seems to us to fly in the face of a considerable amount of evidence that a number of the criminal organizations we will describe do in fact have organized, continuing, hierarchical structures; that they do have sophisticated operations; that they do engage in multiple criminal enterprises; and that they do systematically employ corruption and violence. These characteristics do not suggest a casual, ephemeral type of organization to us. Nor do the crimes in which they are involved suggest that little skill or planning is required, nor that the criminals themselves are reaping few and meager long-term benefits. On the contrary, there is considerable planning and organizational management going on, and the benefits in some cases run into the multi-millions of dollars.

Gottfredson and Hirschi assert further that the careers of organized crime figures, as described by the figures themselves, are consistent with their general theory of crime. But who are these figures? The only one they specifically name, Vincent Teresa, was alleged to be a member of the self-same Mafia. We should assume, therefore, that he could only be writing about that particular form of organized crime. There are considerable problems with self-reports. Informants of the "kiss and tell" genre have their own specific and limited descriptions, understandings, and interpretations. Sometimes, as in the case of Joseph Valachi, they are only lowly members of the organization and their observation point is limited. And often, they are reporting hearsay and depending upon fuzzy recollections of people and events that are far in the past. But not withstanding these general limitations, from such testimony Gottfredson and Hirschi conclude that "organized crime is incapable of perpetuating itself." If that were true, how do they explain the continued existence of some of the above mentioned criminal organizations over many years?

Gottfredson and Hirschi appear to have put forth a straw man argument to bolster their theory. They pick on a 25-year-old theoretical perspective, and attack it as if no other theoretical work had occurred in the interim and as if no one else had recognized its limitations. They totally ignore other perspectives of the kind we presented earlier in this chapter. They also ignore any other work done on organized crime in the last 25 years. Ironically, therefore, they appear to have succumbed, in a reverse kind of way, to the Mafia myth they criticize.

Gottfredson and Hirschi conclude, finally, that "there is no need for theories designed specifically to account for . . . organized crime. . . . The theory of crime and self-control is capable of accounting for the facts about 'organized' crime once they have been stripped of the social-organization myth" (1990:214). In other words, there is no such thing as "organized" crime as something distinct and different from "nonorganized" crime. We emphatically do not believe that is the case; but even if it were, we do not believe Gottfredson and Hirschi have made the case that would support their conclusion.

AN OUTLINE OF A THEORY

We want to end this discussion of organized crime theory by describing the conjectures of Peter Reuter (1987) about another possible theoretical perspective. This outline was contained in a paper done for a National Institute of Justice symposium on organized crime, and was published in the proceedings of that symposium.

Reuter was attempting "to explain under what circumstances some gangs acquire the defining characteristic of organized crime, namely broad and durable reputation, and to determine the consequences of the existence of such gangs" (1987:179). Reuter believes that adult gangs are mainly instrumental, that is, they exist for economic purposes—to make money. Although there are many such gangs in large American cities, only some acquire the distinctive capabilities of organized crime. This, he says, is determined by supply and demand conditions. There has to be a demand for the services that only organized crime can provide, and there have to be certain supply conditions that require distinctive capabilities. Each of these in turn is determined by the defining characteristics of durability and reputation.

The factors that affect the extent of organized crime in a given city, according to Reuter, are: (1) illegal market opportunities, such as gambling, drugs, and loan-sharking, which require enterprises that coordinate ongoing groups of people involved in frequent interaction; (2) the extent of recent migration of important ethnic groups into the community, which provides a recruiting base for organized crime (and a base of clients for goods and services as well); and (3) the strength and corruptness of local political authority.

Organized criminal networks have a unique capacity for extortion and intimidation. This threat of violence and their willingness to use violence or other means of coercion enables them to organize cartels involving large numbers of firms. It also enables them to extort other entrepreneurs (both legal and illegal) who are providing goods and services. Bookmakers or drug dealers, for example, may be required to pay kickbacks for the privilege of operating in particular territories. Operators of bars, restaurants, or small stores may be forced to pay protection money. This works only when, and if, the exploiting organization has a durable reputation.

Reuter's stated purpose in sketching out this minitheory is to provide a heuristic foundation for conceptual and empirical research. "It will be successful," Reuter says, "not to the extent that any of the hypotheses or suggested measurements turn out to be correct, but inasmuch as it persuades readers of the need (and possibility) to move beyond descriptive studies of actual organizations and imbed empirical research in a broader theoretical framework" (1987:183).

This then brings us full circle back to where we started on the need for and purposes of a theory of organized crime. Time will tell whether Reuter's ideas (or the ideas of others mentioned here) serve this purpose. Describing and explaining organized crime requires a comprehensive theory, as does making valid predictions about the growth and development of organized crime. Finally, and very practically, effective intervention efforts to prevent and control organized crime also demand sound theory. This should be taken as a challenge by all students of organized crime.

3

In the Beginning:

Blackbeard and the Others

> No sooner had crime become profitable in America than it became organized. And no sooner did it become organized than it became a regular part of the American way of life, thanks to the cooperation and collusion of government officials. Organized crime did not begin with twentieth century Prohibition. It began with the colonial pirates. (Browning & Gerassi, 1980:53)

Despite the efforts of numerous investigative commissions and theoreticians, it is difficult to achieve a consensus about what actually constitutes organized crime. In his popular text, Abadinsky (1981) writes that "what is needed is a definition that includes Al Capone while excluding Jesse James" (p. 6). In a later edition, Abadinsky (1990) clarifies his reasons for this distinction but raises the issue again by offering robber barons and machine politicians as "historical antecedents" of organized crime. While recognizing the significance of the crimes of both, he declares that the roots of organized crime belong in the Prohibition era from 1920 to 1933. Inevitably, students following these arguments become confused as they attempt to separate organized crime from crimes by organizations and from crimes committed by individuals in concert with others. Further, they wonder, if organized crime is itself little more than 60 years old, can our experiences be broad enough to guide meaningful policy considerations? Is it possible that there is little that can be accomplished against so elusive a concept?

In fact, we agree with Browning and Gerassi (1980) and take a more long-term approach to organized crime. As Michael Woodiwiss (1987) observed, the crimes of Al Capone were not new, only the labels we attached to them were new. If so, then only the terminology of modern organized crime has its roots in "the 1920s and the Prohibition era when academics and newspaper editors found it to be a convenient new label for an old phenomenon" (Woodiwiss, 1987:8). Examined from this perspective, our experience with organized crime is quite lengthy and our successes substantial.

PRIVATEERS, BUCCANEERS, AND PIRATES

Piracy, an original and early form of organized crime, can be attributed to 17th century efforts of the English throne to harass and disrupt Spain and her settlers and traders. Both the British and the Spanish laid early claim to the newly settled North American continent and its rich supply of natural resources. The British claimed colonies to the north, and the Spanish primarily claimed settlements in the south. Being far from the European mainland, each nation soon realized that the expansions they had envisioned would require costly naval expeditions capable of surviving an Atlantic voyage and defending their respective settlers from attack. Faced with a weak economy at home and a restless populous with limited employment options, the English kings and queens responded by offering commissions to an assortment of private freebooters and buccaneers and sending them out to "attack, burn, loot, and otherwise decimate Spain's military and commercial ships" (Browning & Gerassi, 1980:54). By the late 1600s, the pirates and privateers were the only reliable defenders of the precarious colonies.

As one war spilled into the next, entire fleets of privateers were commissioned to roam throughout the Caribbean and as far north on the eastern coast as Rhode Island. Technically innocent of piracy, a privateer was authorized only to seize the ships of the enemy. However, since their pay came from their plunder, their campaigns often depended largely upon opportunity and need, which made the line between privateering and piracy exceptionally fine and variable. Captain Kidd, among the most notorious of all pirates, perhaps best illustrates just how variable this fine line could be.

Transition from Privateer to Pirate

Acting on orders from King William in 1695, Richard Coote, the Earl of Bellomont and newly appointed Governor of New York, devised a plan to suppress the now growing problem of piracy. With backing from a syndicate of British investors that included merchants, political figures, and the wealthy East India Company, Bellomont's plan called for construction of a swift and powerful "pirate killer" ship to be manned by a crew of trusted privateers and supported in action by profits earned from its seizures of both French (with whom the English were now at war) and pirate vessels. In one stroke, Bellomont reasoned, he could please his King, launch his career as governor, and profit handsomely from the prizes taken from the captured ships of enemies. To complete his plan, Bellomont persuaded Captain William Kidd, one of New York's most successful merchant captains, to head his expedition.

Apparently believing that success would earn him a Royal Navy command, Kidd and an initial crew of 70 sailors set sail for New York aboard the *Adventure Galley* in February 1696. Once there, he intended to visit with his family, settle remaining personal affairs, and recruit an additional 80 sailors before setting out on his assignment. As an experienced seaman and veteran privateer, however, the terms of the project must have left him uneasy.

First, since the final agreement called for Lord Bellomont and his investors to put up 80 percent of the startup costs, the agreement carefully spelled out how the prizes seized were to be shared: 10 percent to the Crown; 55 percent for Bellomont and his partners; 22.5 percent to the crew (an unusually small share); and 12.5 percent to Kidd and an American merchant backing his share of the venture. Worse, however, was the stipulation that should their seizures fail to cover the initial costs, Kidd was to personally reimburse the other investors and retain only the ship as his own compensation. And finally, the cruise was to be completed in only 14 months—an unrealistic requirement (Sherry, 1986). In other words, Kidd had to find booty by March 1697. Should anything go wrong, Kidd alone would be responsible.

Predictably, things did go wrong. Recruiting the remaining crew under such unfavorable terms of pay was more difficult and time consuming than was originally imagined. What crewmen Kidd did find were more often drifters or deserters than loyal and experienced sailors. Eventually, a full complement of 150 men were selected, but only after Kidd unilaterally revised the ship's articles to boost the crew's share of profits to 60 percent. When the *Adventure Galley* was, at last, ready to sail, seven months had passed and a successful mission was no longer a possibility. Still, as the King's privateer on an important assignment, Kidd remained unconcerned, believing that each problem could be explained away at the appropriate time. What he didn't know, of course, was that he would spend the next 14 months searching in vain for prey that his commission entitled him to take. In the interim, at least 60 of his crewmen would die from disease and other causes, while the patience of those who remained grew increasingly short.

Although they frequently encountered neutral shipping, it was not until late November 1697—nearly two years after the *Adventure Galley* initially set sail for New York—that Kidd and his crew finally sighted the sails of a potential prey. As they closed on the unknown ship, Kidd followed the standard tactic of showing the French flag as a subterfuge to encourage the other ship to reveal its true colors. After overtaking and boarding her, however, Kidd learned that the ship's captain and officers were in fact Dutch and that most of the crew were Moors—all neutrals in the war with France. The ship itself, the *Rouparelle*, was owned by Moors and was transporting a cargo of cotton, quilts, sugar, and two horses. Unfortunately for the *Rouparelle*, her captain, still unaware of Kidd's true identity, produced a French pass requesting safe passage. Although issuance of such passes to commercial vessels was common and the captain carried several issued by different countries, Kidd nevertheless declared the ship French and a legitimate prize for plunder. After turning out her crew on lifeboats, the *Rouparelle* cargo was transported ashore and sold to traders. To satisfy his now unruly crewmen, Kidd divided the proceeds evenly among his sailors (Sherry, 1986:175). Having clearly committed an act of piracy, Kidd seemed now to lose his inhibitions and began to hunt for larger game regardless of its origination.

The Organization of Crimes at Sea

The most permanent and successful of the pirate groups to emerge were neither undisciplined bands of vicious predators nor swashbuckling soldiers of fortune. Far from either, most pirates were simple seafaring men who had first gone to sea years earlier as boys. Wronged noblemen, escaped convicts, and bored landlubbers were seldom welcome. No matter how lax the discipline aboard a pirate vessel may have been, knowledgeable sailors were still essential to its workings. With the exception of doctors, surgeons, and musicians, the outlaws of piracy were largely all ordinary, uneducated seamen who had scorned the institutions of society in favor of opportunities for considerable wealth and camaraderie. Even the most feared of pirate captains began their careers as ordinary sailors; discovering their abilities at command only after turning pirate, where merit, rather than birth, brought leadership (Sherry, 1986). Ironically, their complete rejection of autocratic authority leaves the pirates of the early 18th century as perhaps the most remarkable examples of democratic planning in the workplace.

Unlike their counterparts in "honest service" on commercial and naval vessels, pirates generally came to regard themselves more as collective owners than as hired hands. Since they had acquired their ships by common effort and participated equally in the work, sacrifices, and risks of building their bounties, they came to accept that the responsibilities for decision making about most matters regarding life aboard their ships should be shared. Issues such as where and when to anchor, what sailing courses to follow, which targets to seek and seize, and even whether to fight became subject to vote with each man entitled to an equal say in the decision. Sherry (1986) reports that only in battle did the pirates abandon this system of decision by referendum.

Certainly, most pirates were angry men whose primary motives were gratification of personal desire and pursuit of individual wealth. Still, to operate effectively, all sailing crews had to subscribe to specific rules, or "ship's articles," which spelled out the rights and duties of all crew members. While these articles differed from ship to ship, all were intended to regulate the difficulties of life that could be expected when several hundred men were crammed into ships usually no larger than 130 by 40 feet. Even Bartholomew Roberts, perhaps the most successful of all pirates, required each of his crew to take an oath. Among the things Roberts's crewmen agreed to were these articles:

I. Every man has a vote in affairs of moment; has equal title to the fresh provisions, or strong liquors, at any time seized, and may use them at pleasure, unless a scarcity make it necessary, for the good of all, to vote a retrenchment.

II. Every man to be called fairly in turn, by list, on board of prizes, because (over and above their proper share) they were on occasions allowed a shift of cloaths: but if they defrauded the Company to the value of a dollar, in plate, jewels, or money, marooning was their punishment. If the robbery was only betwixt one another, they contented themselves with slitting the ears and nose of him that was guilty, and set him on shore, not in an uninhabited place, but somewhere, where he was sure to encounter hardships.

III. No person to game at dice or cards for money.

IV. The lights and candles to be put out at eight a-clock at night: if any of the crew, after that hour, still remained enclined for drinking, they were to do it on the open deck.

V. To keep their piece, pistols, and cutlash clean, and fit for service.

VI. No boy or woman to be allowed amongst them. If any man were found seducing any of the latter sex, and carry'd her to sea, disguised, he was to suffer death.

VII. To desert the ship, or their quarters in battle, was punished with death, or marooning.

VIII. No striking one another on board, but every man's quarrels to be ended on shore, at sword and pistol.

IX. No man to talk of breaking up their way of living, till each had shared a 1000 *l*. If in order to this, any man should lose a limb, or become a cripple in their service, he was to have 800 dollars, out of the public stock, and for lesser hurts, proportionately.

X. The captain and quarter-master to receive two shares of a prize; the master, boatswain, and gunner, one share and a half, and other officers, one and a quarter.

XI. The musicians to have rest on the Sabbath Day, but the other six days and nights, none without special favour. (Defoe, 1972:211–212)

Nor does it appear that Roberts's company or the rules aboard his ship the *Rover* were especially unique. From the diary of Alexander Esquemeling, a young French surgeon who served as surgeon-barber to the pirate Sir Henry Morgan, we learn that the articles established by the crews of his knowledge stipulated:

what recompense or reward each one ought to have, this is either wounded or maimed in his body, suffering the loss of any limb, by that voyage. Thus they order for the loss of a right arm 600 pieces of eight or six slaves; for the loss of a left arm 500 pieces of eight, or five slaves; for an eye 100 pieces of eight, or one slave; for a finger of the hand the same reward as for an eye. (1951:59)

Despite these noble sounding accounts, it is highly unlikely that the pirates were entirely egalitarian. While captains and other officers served at the pleasure of their crews and could be removed or replaced by majority will, accounts of captains with unquestioned power acting capriciously are not uncommon. For example, after shooting a crewman in the knee during a card game, Blackbeard reportedly explained that such demonstrations of who was in charge were occasionally necessary (Browning & Gerassi, 1980). When confronted by an insolent gunner angry because he had refused to attack an English merchant vessel, Captain Kidd flew into a rage and beat his crewman to death with a wooden bucket (Sherry, 1986). And Edward Low, among the most violent and sadistic of all pirates, was known to welcome blacks aboard his ships, allowing them to voluntarily sign ship's articles to become full members of the crew. At a convenient time, however, he would throw them into irons and sell these "crewmen" into slavery (Sherry, 1986).

The important point is not how well the pirates lived up to their own principles but rather that they were highly organized with a fixed hierarchy including a captain, a quartermaster (who enforced ship's rules and served as a second in command), a master (navigator), a boatswain (who maintained the vessel), and a gunner (who maintained the weapons). Others in the hierarchy usually included a carpenter, a sailmaker, and a surgeon. In virtually every instance, the selection of these hierarchies was such that any individual band of pirates was both self-supporting and self-perpetuating—that is, they continued on beyond the life or participation of any single leader. For example, Bartholomew Roberts, more commonly known as Black Bart, originally entered into piracy after his capture from the slave trader *Princess*. Within six weeks, however, he had impressed his captors sufficiently that he was chosen to lead the group after Howell Davis, their previous captain, was ambushed and killed by the Portuguese (Karraker, 1953). As we can see, pirates were highly organized, continuing, willing to use violence and, in time, absent an ideology beyond self-gratification and wealth.

THE ROLE OF THE COLONISTS

Certainly, the victims of the pirates attempted to fight back. While there was little stigma attached to privateering, outright piracy was officially condemned throughout the colonies and among each of the European trading partners. Strict laws were passed, and naval escorts were employed whenever possible. Military campaigns and law enforcement crackdowns were routinely launched against both pirates and their supporters. Finally, as these efforts failed, special "pirate killer" commissions with royal support and private backing were undertaken.

Although each of these steps produced individual successes, some quite spectacular, most military and law enforcement efforts had little impact on piracy as a whole. Captain Kidd initially set out to attack piracy by raiding pirate ships and returning with the prizes he had seized. Instead, he became an outlaw himself. After his arrest in New York, Kidd was returned to London where he was convicted and hanged for his crimes. Following his execution, his body was tarred for preservation and publicly displayed for years along the banks of the Thames River as a deterrent to others so inclined (Ritchie, 1986).

Bartholomew Roberts, who roamed the east coast from Newfoundland to Brazil taking more than 400 ships in his three-year career as a pirate (1719–1722), met his end from the guns of the English warship *Swallow*. After a painstaking search of nearly eight months, the *Swallow* and her companion ship HMS *Weymouth* caught up with Roberts and his company as they attempted to hide themselves among the swamps and lagoons near Annobon, a tiny island northwest of Africa. Sighting the *Swallow's* sails from a distance and mistaking her for a large merchant vessel, Roberts sent the *Great Ranger*, one of his three ships, out to take her. After luring the pirates far out to sea—out of sight and sound of their companions—the *Swallow* quickly turned and destroyed the pirate ship with broadsides from her 60 guns. The next day, the Royal Navy man-of-war returned to the coastal swamp where she engaged and captured Roberts's remaining ships, the *Royal Fortune* and *Little Ranger*. Roberts himself was killed during the battle by a gunshot to his throat. Of the 254 pirates captured, most were either imprisoned at length or hanged after convictions in England. As with Kidd almost 20 years earlier, 18 of the prisoners were tarred and hung for display following their execution (Sherry, 1986).

Finally, Blackbeard, who terrified east coast shipping for almost two years (1716–1718), died as a result of a special expedition planned and personally financed by Governor Spotswood of Virginia. Born Edward Thach in Bristol, England, Blackbeard possessed all of the romantic qualifications required for pirate fame. With his black beard grown "as high up as his eyes," his "animal-like features" were such that "imagination cannot form an idea of a fury from Hell to look more frightful" (Karraker, 1953:144). Once trapped by the governor's forces in the Okracoke Inlet of North Carolina, Blackbeard and his men resisted fiercely. During the battle, one of the attacking ships was forced to withdraw due to damage and injuries; the second was then boarded by the pirates. Befitting his image and reputation, Blackbeard fought with abandon. Nonetheless, after receiving 25 wounds—five from gunshots, several fired point blank—Blackbeard was dead. To celebrate the victory, his head was cut off and hung from the bowsprit of the governor's ship (Defoe, 1972:78-83).

Despite these bold successes, however, piracy continued to flourish. By 1718, the year Blackbeard died, an estimated 1,500 to 2,000 pirates roamed the waters off the eastern seaboard, at times sailing openly into Long Island Sound and the ports of Rhode Island, New York, and the Carolinas. The pirates had become so bold, in fact, that many shipping lanes used by the colonies had fallen completely under pirate control. As one Carolina historian noted, for several years few months passed without some pirate company sailing into a Carolina port laden with the spoils of a recent expedition.

> Not infrequently they would meet with rich prizes, ships of trea-
> sure and plate, and on coming into the colony would scatter their
> gold and silver about with so generous a hand that their appearance
> would soon come to be welcomed by the trading classes; and by
> means of their money they ingratiated themselves not only with the
> people, but with the highest officials of the government. (Browning
> & Gerassi, 1980:56)

In short, despite strict laws against piracy and in spite of the regular stream
of governors sent by the king to eliminate them, the pirates were viewed by
many in the colonies as little more than "gentlemanly outlaws" providing
goods of considerable value. It was the pirates who enabled the colonists to
circumvent the restrictive English Trade and Navigation Laws enacted to
prevent those in the colonies from buying goods not shipped through England on English ships. Because of the sizable black market resulting from
the resale of property plundered from the ships of others, many consumers
could buy goods, especially luxury items, at prices far lower than those offered by legal markets. The pirates and a large portion of many American
colonial communities had quietly become partners in a vast system of
wholesale theft and fencing. Simply put, piracy flourished because the colonists wanted it to.

Corruption in the Northern Colonies

While the adventure and camaraderie of piracy appealed to the working
classes, pirate goods and gold were equally alluring to colonial merchants
and officials. By the close of the 1600s, pirate companies had become regu-
lars in the ports and taverns of Boston, New York, Philadelphia, and Newport where they traded openly with merchants and enlisted recruits for new
expeditions. For merchants, the benefits of trade could be considerable. Not
only could merchants obtain goods at prices not otherwise available but
they also profited handsomely as the pirates resupplied their ships with food,
rum, and ammunition and relaxed on shore leave. In describing this growing trade relationship to the Lords of Trade in London, Governor Cranfield
of New Hampshire complained of a visit by one pirate company to Boston
in 1684. To ensure the safe arrival of the pirates, local merchants provided a
pilot for navigation into the harbor. In turn, once in port, the pirates
bought "most of the choice goods" in the city (Karraker, 1953:66). While
colonists loudly condemned piracy itself, it appears that it made little difference to many colonists whether the ships in port had bought their cargos or
had stolen them.

Even with such support, it is difficult to imagine the pirates surviving, much less operating so openly and boldly, if they had not had protection from the laws of the day. As we saw with captains Kidd, Roberts, and Blackbeard, the laws against piracy were clear, and the forces against them both patient and formidable. Still, by the spring of 1700, American waters had become so infested with pirates bringing in their plunder that one official described the entire coastline as being virtually in a state of war.

Official corruption in support of the pirates reached its peak with the administration of Governor Benjamin Fletcher of New York. Upon taking office in 1682, Fletcher immediately surrounded himself with the region's most successful merchants and traders. Men such as Frederick Philipse were well established and could offer Fletcher both support and introduction into the community's social networks. In return, members of this group soon became the governor's closest council, were appointed to a majority of judgeships of the superior courts, and received or controlled assignments to most bureaucratic and military posts throughout the area. To his closest supporters, Fletcher also granted large tracts of choice land along the Hudson River.

In the 12 years that followed, Fletcher and his colleagues found the profits from illegal trade irresistible. Known widely as a man who understood the needs of privateers, the new governor soon was investing covertly in privateering ventures of his own. As the years passed, he developed many friendships among known pirate captains and allowed them to officially conceal their acts of piracy by declaring them to be sanctioned privateers. In doing so, Fletcher profited both by selling privateering commissions and later by accepting bribes to allow the resulting plunder to be brought ashore for sale. So long as he was the King's governor, and the pirates continued to offer appropriate "gifts," Fletcher made it clear that his newly met friends could continue to operate with impunity. And besides, as their collusion grew, the governor discovered that he actually liked the company of these tough seamen with their gruff, straightforward ways (Sherry, 1986).

Although perhaps the most flagrant, Governor Fletcher of New York was certainly not the only corrupt official profiting from trade with the pirates. Enterprising Bostonians established a special mint so that smuggled gold and silver could be pressed into coins and quickly circulated. In an effort to protect their illegal suppliers, Rhode Island officials not only refused to enforce navigation laws but refused permission to an Admiralty Court to even sit within their colony's boundaries (Sherry, 1986). Governor Bass of New Jersey complained to the Board of Trade in London that his efforts were being severely hampered by farmers and shopkeepers who resupplied the trading pirates, informed them of his men's whereabouts, hid them in their homes and, when pirates were caught and imprisoned, broke them out of his jails. When he insisted on strict confinement in an effort to prevent escape, he often found that the sheriff and other officials would either come to the pirates' aid or refuse to provide sufficient money to pay for guards.

Governor Markham of Pennsylvania, whose daughter was married to a notorious pirate, both declined to prosecute those outlaws found in his jurisdiction and refused to provide the resources requested by his officers so that they might do so (Karraker, 1953). As bad as these abuses may have been, however, no colony's corruption matched that found in New York.

By the time Governor Bellomont arrived in New York to replace the corrupt Fletcher, the complicity between Fletcher's men and the east coast pirates was well established. While Fletcher profited by protecting his pirate friends, Frederick Philipse, a member of the Governor's Council, became the primary trading partner for pirate companies from as far away as Madagascar and the Red Sea. As New York became the center for pirate trade, Philipse, who was by then a leading merchant, ship builder, slave trader, and landowner, was ideally positioned to profit by resupplying and repairing the pirate ships. Eventually, Philipse dealt even more directly with the pirates, undertaking salvage efforts in search of lost treasures and later directly underwriting expeditions themselves. Philipse employed five ships and at least as many pirate captains in his extensive robbery, fencing, and supply operations (Karraker, 1953). By the end of the 1600s, Fletcher, Philipse, and their colleagues had succeeded making themselves the richest men in the region and making New York the headquarters for most of the world's pirate trade.

Corruption in the Middle and Southern Colonies

The two areas along the North American coastline most preferred by pirates were the waters and inlets off Charleston, South Carolina, and Virginia's Chesapeake Bay. For her part, Charleston was perhaps the wealthiest and most important port community in the southern colonies. Her status and size ensured that shipping to her ports, trade with her merchants, and the recreation in her taverns would be plentiful, at least relative to other ports in the region. Additionally, a massive bar blocking the mouth of Charleston's harbor allowed heavily laden ships to navigate only at high tide. This made them easy prey for the more agile pirate vessels.

Virginia was appealing for altogether different reasons. While the rest of the colonies were profiting from pirate trade and the dumping of stolen goods, Virginia was largely excluded from the prosperity. There were no concentrations of people to serve as a market for plundered goods, and without major cities or towns, few pleasures were available for the pirates to enjoy with their proceeds. Virginia's primary value to the pirates was as plunder rather than as an outlet for trade or rest and relaxation.

Shipping for Virginia and neighboring Maryland was funneled through the narrow mouth of the Chesapeake Bay, and most of the protecting forts had been neglected to ruin. The remaining forts offered little defense from pirates operating outside the range of land-based guns during the day and closer in under the cover of dark at night. In short, the rural character of the region practically begged the pirates to lie in wait for merchant shipping and then later come ashore to raid the plantations and small communities along the coast. In either case, it was a simple matter to slip back to sea before a defense could be attempted (Rankin, 1969). Virginia was literally a pirate's delight—substantial rewards to be seized at little risk to themselves.

The differences in these two important coastal areas led to very different results.

Piracy in the Carolinas For at least a generation, pirates had visited the coastal towns of the Carolinas. The numerous inlets, islands, and rivers in the region kept them close to the wealthy northern cities with which they traded while offering sanctuary from the naval vessels and others in their pursuit. Each time they arrived in a port community, the pirates were generous with their profits, ingratiating themselves among officials and merchants alike. So popular was the area that by 1718 the volume of pirate traffic in the region had grown to near epic proportions. Officials from as far away as Jamaica were declaring the Carolinas to be among the worst for harboring and encouraging piracy.

In late January 1718, Blackbeard and Major Stede Bonnet, a largely inept pirate captain who had been befriended by Blackbeard, sailed into Bath, North Carolina. They asked for and were given full pardons for all previous crimes by Governor Charles Eden, Blackbeard's friend and ally. With their pardons in hand, the pirates proceeded to dispose of the prizes from their previous expedition (of course, sharing generously with Governor Eden and Tobias Knight, the secretary of the colony and customs collector). Using Bath as their base of operations, they refit for their next expedition. And after a few weeks rest, they set sail, heading southward for the Caribbean. Over the next two months, Blackbeard made a series of captures, pausing in Havana and Nassau, and then once again started north along the American coast. Aware that a dozen or more ships were anchored and preparing to get under way in Charleston, Blackbeard and his men decided to blockade beyond the mouth of the harbor and seize prey on their way home. They were about to perform one of the most audacious acts of piracy ever.

Within a few days, several unsuspecting merchantmen, each richly loaded, had fallen into the trap. Blackbeard discovered four important passengers aboard one of the ships, including a member of the South Carolina Governor's Council and his four-year-old son. All four were taken hostage, and a plan was devised to ransom them back to the town in exchange for medicine to treat an outbreak of syphilis plaguing his crew. A delegation of Blackbeard's men, accompanied by one prisoner, was sent to meet with the governor to deliver the pirates' demands. With the ransom message, Blackbeard sent a warning that should the pirates not be paid within two days, the hostages, including the boy, would be killed and their heads delivered to the town. He added that he and his men would then destroy the town and burn the remaining ships in the harbor (Sherry, 1986).

Since there were no warships in the area, the governor had little choice but to comply. Although bad weather kept Blackbeard's men from returning until after the deadline, he had not carried out his threat to behead his prisoners. Upon receiving £300 worth of medical supplies and stripping his prisoners of all their belongings—including their clothing—Blackbeard lifted his blockade and sailed on to North Carolina. Once there he again "surrendered" to his friend Governor Eden and received still another pardon for all his previous illegal activities (Sherry, 1986). Behind him, however, Blackbeard left a frightening reputation and a citizenry that now recognized that he and his fellow pirates represented a real danger to the future of their colonies. Knowing that their own governments were too corrupt to act, they secretly appealed to Governor Spotswood of Virginia for help.

Piracy in Virginia Piracy came early to Virginia. From the first recorded incident in 1610 until 1660 when William Berkeley, then governor, complained that the "Seas were soe full of Pyrates that it is almost impossible for any Ships to goe home in safety," the pirates discovered the Virginia coastline to be ripe for plunder. Efforts at defense were attempted, though the small vessels sent out to clear the shipping lanes were usually outgunned and unable to either capture pirates or prevent their more powerful ships from entering the Chesapeake. By 1682, the Council of Virginia had become so alarmed that appropriations were authorized to maintain a garrison of 60 soldiers and to build and send an armed ketch with a crew of 8 out into the bay. Unfortunately, this too proved inadequate as the captain, likely aware of the futility of his assignment, began to profit from "his advising, trading with and sheltering severall Pyrates and unlawfull Traders, instead of doeing his duty and Seizing them" (Rankin, 1969:45).

With the arrival of each successive governor, the hopes of Virginians that matters would improve were repeatedly raised only to be dashed again. Almost immediately upon his arrival in 1684, Governor Francis Howard issued a proclamation warning that all who might be tempted to "Entertaine, harbour, Conceale, Trade, or hold any Correspondency, in any kind, with any Privateers or Pyrates, upon any pretence whatsoever . . ." would be "prosecuted as Notorious Offenders, and shall be lyable unto such paines, punishments, and poenalties, as by Law shall be Judged against them." Unfortunately, such proclamations had little effect on the pirates plaguing them. With the arrival of Francis Nicholson as governor in 1698, Virginia received still another vigorous opponent of piracy. Nicholson had earlier declared: "I confess that I have always abhorred such sort of profligate men and their barbarous actions; for sure they are the disgrace of mankind in general, and of the noble, valiant, generous English in particular" (Rankin, 1969:53). While Governor of Maryland, Nicholson had publicly berated Pennsylvania Governor Markham, dispatching an armed force into Pennsylvania in pursuit of the pirate John Day (Rankin, 1969). The resulting jurisdictional dispute was not easily settled. Still, even with Nicholson's resolve, the attacks on Virginia continued. Despite the addition of two local sloops and the arrival at differing times of at least six royal warships for protection, homes and communities along the shore were still being plundered, with the pirates quickly fleeing into the shallow sounds and rivers of North Carolina. As we have seen, Virginia's southern neighbor was by now a pirate haven where official letters of protest received little notice and even less action.

With the Chesapeake Bay to the north and Charleston to the south, North Carolina was the primary pirate sanctuary in the middle and southern colonies. Governor Seth Sothel, once captured and held for ransom himself, openly traded with pirates and willingly offered commissions and pardons for only 20 guineas each. It was also charged that he would seize the property of respectable merchants, charging them as pirates and forfeiting whatever possible to himself. During John Archdale's administration in 1693, pirates regularly came ashore with a "vaste quantity of gold" and once in port, "they were entertained, and had liberty to goe to any other place" (Rankin, 1969:58). And, of course, in the early 1700s, Charles Eden and Tobias Knight befriended Blackbeard and profited personally by providing him with a home port in Bath.

With each administration, an occasional pirate was charged and executed to satisfy critics. It was observed, however, that even then only the least successful were chosen. "There were abt half a dousin Pyrats lately hang'd in Carolina, but it was they were poor. . . . These rich ones appear'd publickly and were not molested in the least" (Rankin, 1969:58). Following Blackbeard's raid on Charleston and the increased incidence of pirates taking ships carrying exports from South Carolina, the problem of piracy was soon to change.

THE DEATH OF AN ERA

Piracy peaked in 1720 but quickly diminished thereafter, and over the next decade the pirates would disappear almost entirely. Certainly the expeditions that resulted in the death or capture of captains Kidd, Blackbeard, Bartholomew Roberts, and others such as Anne Bonney, Mary Read, and Jack Rackham played an important part in the decline. As English determination to stop the pirates increased, the price for piracy clearly became quite high. But legal and naval efforts alone were insufficient; indeed, piracy reached its highest level nearly two years after the last of these major enforcement efforts.

Nor did the rehabilitation efforts pushed by London humanitarians have much measurable impact. A decade or so of failed efforts to force an end to piracy had led the English Admiralty to conclude that a strategy alternating between pardons and outright attacks might be necessary. Perhaps the pirates could be killed with kindness.

Early on, the value of pardons to pirates was debated hotly. Many who knew the pirates well through direct contact opposed the idea arguing that a blanket issuance of pardons, regardless of merit, would encourage further piracy rather than undermine it. On the other hand, the Board of Trade, whose involvement with pirates was primarily second hand, favored a merit-based strategy that required some signal act of loyalty to the King. They went further and advocated pardons issued to entire companies of pirates willing to give unanimous pledges to discontinue their criminal ways. After much debate and many conferences, ships filled with bundles of pardons were eventually dispatched to search for pirate havens with hopes of returning with volunteers and their illegally seized and now much desired plunder.

Initially, these offers of forgiveness were viewed by the pirates with much skepticism. However, individuals and later masses of pirates came forward to accept absolution, seldom offering more than a confession of sin and a show of penitence in return. Shortly thereafter, most of these pirates were observed returning to their old ways in violation of their pledges. Perhaps these failures resulted from bad faith on the part of the pirates. Equally likely, the absence of any programs of employment rehabilitation and the knowledge that many pirates had been severely punished by officials who chose to disregard the pardons may have contributed greatly. In either case, none of the problems of piracy were solved.

While the twin strategies of enforcement and forgiveness can't account for the collapse of piracy, fundamental changes in the politics and economics of the colonies can. These changes were set into motion as early as 1695 when King William, determined to attack corruption in the colonies, decided to replace the notorious Governor Fletcher of New York.

Where Fletcher had overlooked the pirates, the King was determined that his replacement would not. What was needed was an administrator who could be counted on to enforce the laws, especially the Navigation Acts. The King determined that his new appointee would have authority as governor over New York, Massachusetts, and New Hampshire and as captain-general of all military and naval forces in Connecticut, Rhode Island, and New Jersey. King William chose the Earl of Bellomont for the post. Bellomont was enticed to accept the post with appeals to duty and a salary sufficient to eliminate the need for bribes.

In his instructions to Bellomont, King William authorized his new governor to take whatever action was necessary to enforce the Navigation Acts and suppress the pirates. The East India Company, perhaps the biggest victim of piracy, hailed the appointment while noting that Bellomont alone would not be enough. For his part, Bellomont quickly let it be known that, unlike his predecessors, he could not be bribed. On his arrival in New York, he immediately initiated a campaign to remove corrupt officials, beginning with Fletcher whom he returned to England under arrest. Others he suspected of dealing with pirates were soon removed from their posts as well.

To enforce his assignment, the governor next deployed his limited naval forces in the waters off New York and New England where they boarded suspect vessels and seized illegal cargos. Although the embargo was far from complete, in a short time many of New York's premier pirate traders, including Frederick Philipse, had been forced from business. So effective was the campaign that by the early 1700s, New York's merchants were petitioning London to recall their governor and reinstate the Fletcher administration (Sherry, 1986).

What Bellomont began, the appointments of Alexander Spotswood in Virginia and Woodes Rogers in the Bahamas continued. Unlike Lord Bellomont, Colonel Spotswood had the good fortune to assume an administration largely free of corruption and already engaging the pirates. Originally underestimating the extent and problems of piracy in the lower colonies, Spotswood became perhaps the most energetic of all colonial governors in the prosecution of pirates. By the time the outraged citizens of the Carolinas requested his protection from Blackbeard, Virginia's governor had already begun to act. After offering rewards for the capture of Blackbeard and his men, Spotswood wrote to Governor Eden of North Carolina warning him of the dangers of maintaining so special a relationship with the pirate. Following one final appeal for Eden's assistance, the expedition against Blackbeard was launched.

The evidence seized following Blackbeard's death so implicated the North Carolina administration that numerous indictments (although few convictions) resulted. Pressured from office, Governor Eden soon fell ill and died within a few months. By the end of his term in 1722, Spotswood had largely succeeded in his efforts to improve government in the middle and southern colonies while driving the pirates' allies from office. But two years later he still feared returning to England because of "the Vigorous part I've acted to Suppress Pirates: and if those barbarous Wretches can be moved to cut off the Nose and Ears of a Master for but correcting his own Sailors, what inhuman Treatment must I expect, should I fall within their power" (Rankin, 1969:138).

As corruption in the colonies diminished, rumors of the migration of large companies of pirates into the Bahamas were common. Claiming admiralty jurisdiction over the entire region, Governor Spotswood sent ships to investigate the strength of these newcomers and to learn of their plans. Those that returned came with ominous news; quick action was necessary or the pirates would soon seize the Bahamas. Warning that all trade in the region was at risk, Spotswood immediately appealed for naval support. Instead, Woodes Rogers, among the most illustrious sea captains of the day, was sent to be Governor of the Bahamas. His instructions were to do for that jurisdiction as Bellomont and Spotswood had done for theirs. Rogers, who had previously won fame as the commander of English privateering expeditions, needed several years and an outside threat of attack from the Spanish before order was imposed and enforcement of laws begun in the Bahamas (Karraker, 1953). Unlike his fellow governors, Rogers found the issue to be more a total absence of government than a problem of corruption.

Although the cessation of large-scale corruption and the considerable improvements in government administration deprived the pirates of their official consorts, it was not until the colonists themselves began to withhold their support that the era of piracy began to draw to a close. By the beginning of the 18th century, colonial America was becoming commercial America. Much of the colonial industry, especially shipbuilding, now rivaled that found in England. Crewmen on American commercial ships were better paid than those on English vessels, while the demand, both domestic and international, for raw materials from the south and finished goods from the north was increasing rapidly. As the economy of the colonies became increasingly dependent upon export products, frictions between the pirates and the businessmen they had previously been in league with became inevitable. Piracy was no longer simply a blight on the Crown; it had become an inconvenience and an embarrassment for the colonists. No longer could the pirates buy protection from corrupt officials. As the Piracy Act was extended to include accessories, earlier markets for plunder were closed and problems of resupply and repair became insurmountable. Where the pirates as hunters had previously been openly welcomed in port towns, as the hunted they were welcome no longer. Once the atmosphere that had supported the pirates and their flamboyant ways turned against them, piracy collapsed under its own weight.

> If there has to be a specific date for the end of the era known as the Golden Age of Piracy, it would be 1728. Official correspondency up to that date is filled with details of, and concerns about, piracy, but the word is seldom mentioned after 1728. From that year on there would be frequent alarms, an occasional ship would be taken, but in general the seas became relatively clear of the depredations of the freebooters. (Rankin, 1969:156)

LESSONS FROM THE PAST

Were the pirates an early American form of organized crime? We certainly believe so. Clearly they were *organized* into a well-structured hierarchy with leaders and followers in a rank order of authority. Further, given the democratic nature of most pirate companies, unless defeated as a group in battle they were virtually assured of *perpetuation*—the departure of any single individual led to replacement with the company itself continuing on as before. Additionally, as we saw during Captain Kidd's expedition, the pirates either were or became *nonideological* in order to survive. Originally begun as privateers commissioned by the English to harass first the Spanish and later the French, the crews of most companies included sailors of varied ethnic and national backgrounds willing to take ships under any flag. For them to do so, *violence*, or at least the threat of it, was almost always a necessity. In fact, the most successful pirate companies developed fearsome reputations that were often sufficient to induce commercial vessels to surrender to avoid the consequences of flight or a struggle. The crews themselves typically *restricted membership* to experienced sailors seeking freedom from social norms and willing to take bold risks in pursuit of great *profits from illegal activities*. Included were theft, robbery, extortion, kidnapping, smuggling, and a host of crimes of commerce and trade against the Crown. Perhaps of greatest interest to our studies, however, was the use of *corruption* by the pirates and the *public's demand* for their goods and trade.

As we noted earlier, colonial piracy flourished only because the colonists wanted it to. True, piracy came into being as a criminal conspiracy fed by a series of wars that dislocated and impoverished large segments of society, by the mistreatment of seamen (both commercial and military), and by a general absence of competing employment options. Still, the promotion and assistance given the pirates by merchants and the ability to buy immunity and legitimacy from officials transformed these "free-roaming brethren of the coast" into an integrated system of international trade. Reform became possible only after the governors Bellomont, Spotswood, and Rogers, along with William Penn in Philadelphia removed the protective cover and turned the spotlight of publicity on those secretly doing business with the pirates. Even then, the pirates would not be defeated and piracy itself would not disappear until the merchants and coastal communities became aware of the danger and losses they were receiving from the pirate trade. At that point, the markets for pirate goods dried up, and the public demand for their services and support for their existence disappeared. As Karraker (1953) describes it:

> Then and only then did piracy become to this class "an outrageous crime against mankind," the expression of which certain of its members had so piously mouthed while they continued to do business with the pirates.
>
> Piracy as a business has been dead in the western world for more than a hundred years, but its spirit and its methods persist in present day racketeering. The pattern was set in Colonial America in 1699. (p. 229)

In the chapters that follow, this pattern will be repeated many times.

4

Organized Crime as an Evolving Enterprise:

Crime in New York

With the close of the age of piracy, crime in America was largely disorganized. With an economy expanding rapidly but roughly, conflict and disparities were inevitable. Farmers fought with port merchants; town councils argued with the King's governors. Tax laws were both arbitrary and punitive. And governors, merchants, and local officials freely rewarded themselves and their friends with favors and concessions consuming vast sums of public money. Disproportionate wealth was soon obvious in a land where most farmers and many workers were barely eking out subsistence livings.

No one, it seemed, felt any real sympathy for the poor, growing in both number and their willingness to use crime as a means of support and gain. In fact, by the mid-1740s, crime had become the most serious public issue in cities such as Boston, Newport, Charleston, and Philadelphia. William Penn had already declared his the most "wicked city he knew, a place where deeds 'so very Scandalous [are] openly committed in defiance of Law and Virtue: facts so foul, I am forbit by common modesty to relate them'" (Browning & Gerassi, 1980:75).

As before, the more enterprising thieves, smugglers, and outlaws soon realized the benefits of organizing, giving rise to a new generation of organized crime in America. Nowhere was this evolution more dramatic than in New York.

THE CLIMATE FOR ORGANIZED CRIME

By the turn of the 19th century, New York City had become a truly tough place to live. The entrepreneurial center of the nation, New York was the gateway for immigrants pouring into the country in search of various freedoms, opportunities, and fortunes. As the launching point for commerce, the city also became the center for conspiracies and a magnet for con-men, crooks, and criminals.

Of the nearly 1 million people packed in the city's two-square-mile center, no less than 44 percent were recent immigrants. Sadly, most of these New Yorkers were indeed poor. Some 300,000 people were jammed into one East Side district of tenements without toilet facilities, heating, dry roofs, or fire protection. The streets were full of trash and sludge, and the death and unemployment rates were high and increasing steadily. Lacking the job skills now required (first for manufacturing and later for an increasingly financial city), large numbers of the unemployed had little choice but to roam the streets begging and stealing for survival. As they began to band together into gangs, New York became America's most terrifying city (Browning & Gerassi, 1980).

Recreation was frequently violent and almost always took place in the many saloons and taverns throughout midtown. Admission to a then illegal prizefight cost patrons around 50 cents, dogfights and cockfights were $2.00, and the more popular fights pitting a dog against rats ranged from $1.50 to $5.00, depending on the number of rats challenged. The dogs of choice were always fox terriers. Good dogs received as much as six months of training before they began fighting at about two years of age. A good rat dog could kill 100 rats in less than two hours. No fewer than 100 spectators would attend a match where purses typically started at $125—a considerable sum at the time (Sante, 1991).

As for the saloons, most were dirty, brawling places run by well-known crooks. The "Hole-in-the-Wall," for example, was the headquarters for a local gang run by One-Armed Charley Monell. Kate Flannery and Gallus Mag—both women adjutants to Monell—actually managed the bar, using it to organize gang activities. Able to handle most any contingency, both women were physically imposing and always armed with a pistol, a bludgeon, or both. An unruly customer who protested rough treatment in the bar was knocked to the floor where Gallus Mag would bite him on the ear and drag him into the street by her teeth. Further resistance would lead to the ear being ripped off and deposited in a jar of alcohol kept behind the bar for trophies. So fierce was her reputation that the police came to refer her as the most savage female they had ever encountered (Asbury, 1927).

Nearby on Cherry Street, "crimps" specialized in drugging and robbing sailors who they would shanghai aboard tramp boats for commissions. The Fourth Ward Hotel went so far as to install trap doors so that victims too badly injured or not otherwise suitable for sailing could be dumped directly into the East River where they would presumably drown (Sante, 1991).

By the mid–1800s, conditions throughout the Fourth Ward were such that in many areas practically every house held one or more dives with most offering either a saloon, a dance hall, or a house of prostitution on every floor. So crime ridden were the streets that virtually no one was safe and certainly no well-dressed man could expect to travel far without being robbed, murdered, or both. If he could not be lured into a saloon, an intended victim would be followed until he passed beneath a designated window. An accomplice, usually a woman, would dump a bucket of ash on the victim's head, leaving him choking and gasping for air. Thugs could then easily pull him into a nearby cellar where the passerby would be killed, robbed, and stripped of his clothes. The naked body was dumped on the sidewalk as a final indignity. For their part, the police refused to respond to the crimes in these Fourth Ward passageways in groups smaller than half a dozen or so. Even then, when a suspect managed to flee into one of the more notorious saloons, officers would lay siege to the building—often for as long as a week—until the wanted man grew tired or hungry and emerged (Asbury, 1927).

The growth of vice activities should be expected in such environments as well. While a young man born into a poor family might, through hard work, careful investments, and cunning, still manage wealth and status, a poor young woman with similar ambition generally had but one route available—prostitution. Along with the theater, prostitution was one of the few means available for lower-class women to meet men of a higher economic station. By the late 1800s, no family below the middle class could afford to support a child past the age of 12 (and many not past infancy). As a result, girls went to work as early as boys, usually as pieceworkers in manufacturing or as shop assistants. Such jobs seldom paid more than a dollar or two a week, which was barely enough for life in a flophouse. For those not forced into prostitution by their families or a lover, the life often was appealing as a means of avoiding sweatshop labor while giving at least an illusion of leisure, pleasure, independence, and a better way of life including fancy clothes and jewelry (Sante, 1991). And the opportunities were abundant.

Prior to the Civil War, many women freelanced by approaching men on the streets or in saloons or other places of amusement. A smaller but more regular income could be assured by entering a brothel. Although far more restrictive, the hazards were greatly reduced. As the war closed, opportunities expanded as prostitution spread from the slums of the waterfront, the Bowery, and the Five Points (a slum district so named because it sat at the intersection of Little Water, Cross, Anthony, Orange, and Mulberry Streets) into midtown and soon the Tenderloin, Fifth Avenue, and Seventh Avenue. In the Broadway district, the price, quality, and safety of service progressed upward as you moved uptown from the houses near Canal Street catering to sailors to the luxurious parlor houses on Clinton Street (now 8th Street).

In the Tenderloin, however, the sex trade was hardly so organized. Often called Satan's Circus, it is estimated that by 1885 at least half the buildings in this district housed some kind of immorality with the whorehouses being clustered around 24th, 25th, 31st, 32nd, and 35th Streets (Sante, 1991). With their red door lights in place, the brothels here ranged in tone from the Seven Sisters Row where customers were solicited with engraved invitations to the dirty, unnamed houses where the robbery of customers was the foremost concern. Perhaps the worst of these was John McGurk's Suicide Hall, a well-known dive in the Bowery. The lowest rung for prostitutes, McGurk's was given its name (and its attraction as a tourist spot) in response to the regularity with which suicides occurred. During 1899 alone, there were at least six successful and seven attempted suicides. Following Tina Gordon's self-inflicted death, McGurk stood over the body and declared:

> Most of the women who come to my place have been on the
> down grade too long to think of reforming. I just want to say that I
> never pushed a girl downhill any more than I ever refused a helping
> hand to one who wanted to climb. (Sante, 1991:29)

ORGANIZING THE GANGS

To the entrepreneurs and upper classes of the city, the poor and the slums in which they lived were both an embarrassment and a source of fear. Denounced as "a co-mingled mass of venomous filth and seething sin, of lust and drunkenness, of pauperism and crime of every sort" (Bremner, 1956:5–6), easily frightened property owners periodically brought pressure on city leaders to keep these "dangerous classes" in their place. During one such purge, in advance of Lafayette's 1824 tour of the United States, 20 thieves and robbers were rounded up and publicly hanged in Washington Park as examples. Against such odds, the more enterprising criminals soon realized that they had little choice but to organize.

The earliest gangs were spontaneous occurrences without a fixed structure or leadership. Gradually, however, well-organized groups began to appear, usually headquartered in the small, greengroceries that sprung up throughout the neighborhoods near Five Points. Ostensibly food stores, these greengroceries would display racks of vegetables outside while serving cut-rate drinks in backroom speakeasies. The Forty Thieves, apparently the first gang with a definite, acknowledged leadership, appeared in the first of these grocery-speakeasies shortly after it was opened.

While the Forty Thieves may have been first, other gangs turned up in many of the taverns and other greengroceries in the area. The Chickesters, Roach Guards, Plug Uglies, Shirt Tails, and Dead Rabbits appeared, each possessing its own distinctive mystique. The Roach Guards, for example, took their name from a Five Points liquor dealer. During one angry meeting, as internal dissension was mounting a dead rabbit was hurled to the center of the room. One of the squabbling factions took this as an omen and its members withdrew, forming a splinter gang and naming themselves appropriately. While the battle uniform of the Roach Guards included a blue stripe, the Dead Rabbits adopted a red stripe with their leader carrying the body of a dead rabbit impaled on a pike into battle. These two factions fought constantly, achieving great renown both as thieves and thugs (Asbury, 1927).

Equally colorful, the Shirt Tail gang was so named because they habitually wore their shirttails outside their trousers. Similarly, the Plug Uglies got their name from the oversized plug hats they stuffed with wool and leather. These hats could then be pulled down over the ears to serve as helmets during battles (Peterson, 1983). Mostly gigantic Irishmen, the Plug Uglies were known to be among the toughest of the Five Pointers. Always armed with a bludgeon, a brickbat, and a pistol, these gangsters wore heavy boots studded with nails to be used for stomping victims knocked helplessly to the ground (Asbury, 1927). In all, the Five Points was perhaps the toughest district in the nation. It was also a training ground for many of the most powerful organized crime leaders in America.

Although tough, the mean streets of the Five Points had no monopoly on crime and violence. Nearby in the Bowery, rough and tumble gangs such as the Bowery Boys, the True Blue Americans, the American Guards, the O'Connell Guards, and the Atlantic Guards sprang up in the beer and pool halls that proliferated as the area grew into a center for theater and amusement. Principally Irish, the Bowery gangs appear not to have been as criminal or as violent as their Five Point counterparts. Still, many were known as gifted brawlers. For many years, the Bowery Boys and the Dead Rabbits waged a bitter feud with frequent battles either along the Bowery, in Five Points, or in the ancient battlefield of Bunker Hill. Far more acceptable than the gangs of the Five Points, some historians have even attached a certain glamour to the Bowery Boys, characterizing them as "ready for a lark, eager for a spree, reckless of the consequences, and unreckoning of the future" (Peterson, 1983:14). Undoubtedly, however, such appraisals overlook the brutality of the gang and its members.

South of the Bowery to the waterfront lay the city's Fourth Ward. It was here that gangs, including the Daybreak Boys, the Swamp Angels, and the Slaughter Housers, systematically robbed passersby from saloons such as One-Armed Charley Monell's Hole-in-the-Wall. The Daybreak Boys, who did most of their work in the hours suggested by their name, were known to be especially vicious; the police claimed each member to be a cold, professional killer. From 1850 to 1852 this gang was credited with 20 known murders and the theft of at least $100,000 in property. By the middle of 1853, the gang's two leaders were both convicted of murder and hanged, causing the eventual collapse of the gang. According to an 1850s police report, however, the end of the Daybreak Boys left at least 50 gangs roaming the Fourth Ward. "Nothing comes amiss to them," wrote Police Chief George Matsell. "They prowl around the wharves and vessels in a stream, and dexterously snatch up every piece of loose property left for a moment unguarded" (Browning & Gerassi, 1980:139). By the time the chief's report was issued, the gangs had become a normal part of New York life. South from what is now Houston Street, no portion of the city was free of them.

AN ALLIANCE OF POLITICIANS, GAMBLERS, AND GANGSTERS

The first real test of gang power and influence occurred in 1834. At least a decade earlier, the politicians of Tammany Hall had begun to recognize the importance of the growing foreign population to their election efforts. Making a complete turnabout, the politicians reasoned that instead of excluding immigrants from the political process it was far more expedient to use them to win elections. As such, by the November 1827 federal election, immigrant influence began to be felt.

As the political net was widened, however, so too was the willingness to use fraud and violence as electoral tools. During the 1827 election, groups of men—many of them foreigners not yet eligible to vote—were used as "repeaters" to vote in several different wards. In one of the few documented instances, a cartload of six men was hauled to six different polling places, and the men voted in each. Meanwhile, in one predominately foreign ward, a registered native American was repeatedly turned away at the polls. When he persisted, he was arrested with a substitute ballot being entered for him. All of this was shocking to both political parties, which insisted that the improprieties were proof that only natives of the country (meaning English descendants) should possess political privileges (Peterson, 1983). Nonetheless, by the end of the decade, Tammany Hall men had gained control of virtually all the most influential federal positions in New York City.

By 1830, the population of the city had climbed to over 200,000 and the problems of crime, health, and public services were climbing as well. Additionally, the city was now struggling with a series of spontaneous riots, many started in the theaters of the Bowery. By 1831, city officials were also under reform pressure to permit direct election of the mayor by the people.

Originally opposed to direct elections, claiming that the people could not be trusted with selection of so important a figure as mayor, the Tammany Hall aldermen were perhaps the first to recognize the inevitable and to move to make it an advantage. If the people wanted to control their local government, then a way to reliably and systematically manipulate their votes would be necessary. To do so, a political–gang alliance was ideal. For their part, the gangs too were coming to realize that in a city with competing ethnic and economic interests, they could no longer stand aside from politics. In short, the physical strength of their leaders was no longer sufficient to gain and hold real power.

To initiate a connection, ward and district leaders moved into the waterfront, Bowery, and Five Points districts. Almost as soon as a gang became well organized, the greengrocery, saloon, or dance hall that was their headquarters would be acquired. Political leaders could then protect the gang from police and reformers, ensuring their survival and even growth at the expense of their unprotected or less well-protected competitors. In turn, the gangs could be commanded as "goon squads" on election day, working to ensure their sponsor's reelection. The 1834 mayoralty contest offered the first real test of this newly formed, mutually beneficial alliance.

As election day neared, the Tammany Hall ward leaders worked hard to build an effective machine to employ gang skills at the polling places. The election itself began on April 8 and lasted for three turbulent days. Pitting the Tammany Democrats and their Irish gangs against the incumbent Whigs and the supporters of a "native American" movement, the contest quickly degenerated into widespread fighting and rioting led by toughs from each side. Throughout the Sixth Ward, conditions grew so violent that when the mayor and a large body of his watchmen began visiting the polls in an attempt to restore order, they too were attacked and driven away. Several of the watchmen were wounded severely in the attack with at least eight requiring hospitalization for their injuries. In desperation, the National Guard was called out to suppress the riots. By then, however, the Tammany candidate, Cornelius W. Lawrence, had claimed victory.

For the next decade, the city was plagued by random rioting, widespread looting, corruption, and an almost complete breakdown in the delivery of city services. Showing little interest in reform, the corrupt and incompetent political leaders appeared concerned only with winning elections and satisfying their own greed. Weak and disorganized, the police demonstrated little ability to restore order. Instead, they seemed content to find ways of peaceful coexistence with protected gangs while cracking down on those like the Daybreak Boys who had failed to learn the lesson that crime without political organization did not pay. The gangs, meanwhile, continued to grow stronger, almost without interruption. Figure 4.1 outlines this growth and the men who led it and shaped organized crime in New York City.

The Rise of the Bosses

During the middle 1800s, the gangs became solidly entrenched in the political life of the city. Using force to compel votes while acting as repeaters to stuff ballot boxes, several gangs were a significant and perhaps deciding factor in the election of Robert H. Morris to Mayor in 1841 and 1842. As the elections neared, Sixth Ward violence grew to fearful proportions. As evidence of their importance, several of the Five Points gang members were reportedly on such familiar terms with Mayor Morris that they felt free to openly pat him on the shoulder and publicly refer to him as Bob. Other gangsters, such as Mike Walsh of the Plug Uglies, became so bold as to feel secure demanding nomination to office under threat of gang retaliation. Although Walsh—apparently the first to use extortion as a campaign strategy—was subsequently defeated in the election, he nonetheless demonstrated to others the power that was possible with sufficient gangster backing (Peterson, 1983). It was to this political environment that Captain Isaiah Rynders arrived in New York and began his rise to power.

Rynders rode a turbulent career as a Mississippi River gambler into the city. After a brief stop in Washington, D.C., where he was arrested in the

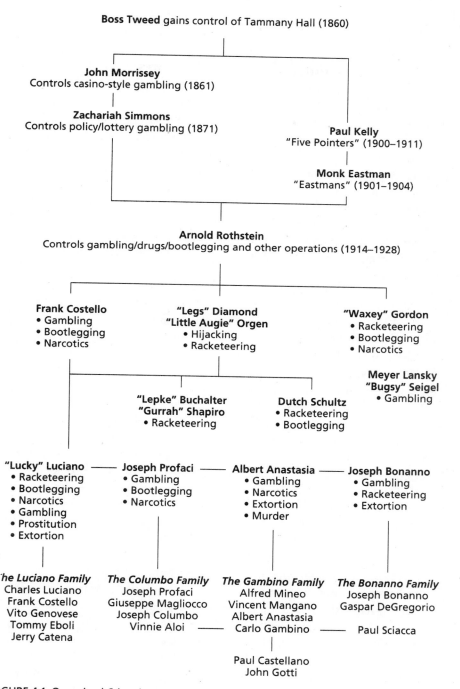

IGURE 4.1 Organized Crime in New York

theft of U.S. Treasury notes, Rynders moved on to New York City, which he discovered was ideal for his special talents. Successful as a gambler and saloon-keeper, he quickly recognized the role of the gangs and branched out, buying half a dozen greengroceries and numerous popular saloons such as Sweeney's House of Refreshment and the Arena, which he later renamed the Empire Club. From there he gained absolute control over the Five Points gangs, using them to tightly govern the politics of the Sixth Ward.

Also rising rapidly during this period was John Morrissey, a professional boxer and gambler. Born in Ireland, Morrissey spent his formative years among the bars and taverns of both Troy, New York, and the Hudson River boats. Learning well from the gamblers and thieves who frequented these dives, Morrissey soon polished his skills so well that by 1849, still only a teenager, he had been indicted twice for burglary, once for assault with the intent to kill, and again for assault and battery. After serving a short term in jail, Morrissey resettled in the city where he began work as an enforcer for Captain Rynders. Reportedly, he had come to Rynders's attention one evening when he boldly challenged everyone in Rynders's Arena saloon to fight. They accepted the challenge and, although beaten, Morrissey fought so fiercely that he won Rynders's admiration and an offer to settle permanently in New York City. Rynders placed Morrissey in charge of the Dead Rabbits, where he won the support of important Tammany leaders (Asbury, 1927). Eventually, that support would lead him to the state legislature, Congress, and a turn as a coleader of Tammany Hall.

Meanwhile, a city-wide struggle for the heart of Tammany Society was also being waged. While a successful and continuing pattern of corruption had been established during the first 60 years of its existence, no single individual had managed to rise from Tammany Hall to exercise consistent boss control over the city. Fernando Wood changed that when he took control of the mayor's office in January 1855. Unfortunately for the city, Wood's election and subsequent reelection in 1857—both marred by unprecedented violence and voter fraud—also resulted in a power struggle that brought about the collapse of what little formal authority to resist the gangs remained in New York City.

Previously, all police appointments were controlled by the aldermen and leaders of each of the city's wards. As ward elections were won by either the Democrats or the Whigs, officers from the winning party were soon appointed. For example, following the 1848 Whig victory in the First Ward, only 2 of 28 Democratic officers were reappointed. In the Second Ward, where the Democrats won reelection, 28 of 30 officers retained their appointments (Browning & Gerassi, 1980). With such control, it was an easy matter to coordinate police and gang activities. Arrests of gang members and the success of a gang itself were directly dependent on a connection to an important political leader.

By the end of Mayor Wood's first term, corruption permeated virtually every aspect of city government. City jobs and contracts were for sale. Cash was necessary for appointment, and kickbacks were required for the length of the term for continued employment. Brothels and gambling dens were also sources of income for the mayor who would limit police enforcement and guarantee issuance of licenses in exchange for regular payments. Uptown, many bankers, merchants, and property owners found that for appropriate campaign donations, the mayor's assistance in expediting business dealings could be invaluable. And in the slums of the waterfront and Five Points, Isaiah Rynders, John Morrissey, and several of the largest and most powerful gangs were solidly on the mayor's side. So badly was the city being misgoverned that within only a few days of Wood's re-election, Governor John King was calling for major reforms. In particular, he said, a "new police system for the city of New York is . . . required" (Peterson, 1983:39). That system, he added, should not be left to the management of the mayor.

Within three months, the New York State Legislature responded to the governor's call by enacting a bill to create the Metropolitan Police District— a special agency with jurisdiction over New York, Westchester, Kings, and Richmond counties. Governed by a five-member Board of Commissioners chosen by the governor, this new agency was to assimilate the existing police forces in both New York City and Brooklyn (then a separate municipality). All local police authority was to be divested.

But Mayor Wood had no intention of losing control over the municipal department. Supported by his Board of Aldermen, he decided instead to ignore the legislative act and refuse to surrender police property or power. As a result, New York City soon found itself with two police departments—one local and one under state control. Predictably, law enforcement in the city quickly turned even more chaotic as clashes between the forces became inevitable. Peterson (1983) describes the confusion as a "tragicomedy" producing a "boon to the criminal classes and a disaster for the decent citizens" (p. 41).

> Almost invariably when a burglar or robber was arrested by an officer of the Metropolitan department, a municipal policeman would appear on the scene and challenge his rival's jurisdiction. While the two officers were flailing away at each other with their clubs, the criminal would walk away unmolested. This situation prevailed much of the summer while the validity of the act creating

the Metropolitan Police District was being challenged in the courts. (Peterson, 1983:41)

Eventually, the New York Court of Appeals upheld the act, and the municipal police were reluctantly disbanded. By then, however, the damage had been done.

By the start of the Civil War, the city's collapsing economy, constant and widespread rioting and violence, and unrestricted corruption had grown to such proportions that observers were pessimistically noting a plunge into barbarism. "Our civilization is decaying," wrote George Strong, one of the city's few remaining distinguished citizens (1952:425). With war inevitable and the city's collapse near complete, even Mayor Fernando Wood apparently recognized that the time for change was near. As such, in exchange for seats in Congress for himself and his brother Benjamin, Wood agreed to relinquish control of the city. The ascension of Boss Tweed could now begin.

The Era of William M. Tweed

Born in the city to a Scottish chair maker, William M. Tweed rode a combination of savvy, cunning, and untiring labor to a position of political power unmatched in New York City. Leaving school at age 11, he was first sent to learn a trade. By 15, he was a bookkeeper, working first in an office and later for a brush factory his father had bought. At 21, he married the daughter of the factory's largest stockholder, a marriage that would eventually produce eight children (Browning & Gerassi, 1980). Always active in the politically connected fire companies, by 27, Tweed had organized his own engine company (the Americus Engine Company No. 6, or the "Big Six" as it was later known), naming himself the foreman and "Honored Leader." It was from there that he launched his political career. Using his contacts with firemen, cops, and street hustlers, Tweed became known for his ability to deliver votes when they were most needed—a skill that moved him quickly up the ladder of the Democratic party machine. By 1851, Tweed was elected alderman of the Seventh Ward. Only one year later, while continuing as an alderman, he was elected to Congress.

As an alderman, Tweed was not shy about wielding his considerable power. All police appointments in his ward required his approval, from the lowest patrolman to the precinct commander. Licenses to saloons and franchises to ferry, bus, and streetcar operators were issued by Tweed and his associates. In addition, he sat as a justice in the Mayor's Court and as a judge in Criminal Court. As alderman, Tweed also selected the pool from which grand jurors were drawn.

In 1857, Tweed moved on to the city's Board of Supervisors, rising to president of the board in 1863. By then he had also been selected as chairman of the Tammany General Committee and "Grand Sachem" of the Tammany Society. With approval from his friend Judge George Barnard, Tweed was then admitted to the practice of law, an act granting him the right to try cases in both the State Supreme Court and the New York Court of Appeals. This, in turn, enabled him to collect large sums for unspecified legal services from the Erie Railroad and others doing business with the city while also accepting appointment to the board of the Tenth National Bank where city funds were invested (Peterson, 1983). After ousting Mayor Wood, Tweed used his unchallenged control over Tammany Hall to add school commissioner, assistant street commissioner, New York County Democratic chairman, and state senator to his list of positions held. By engineering the election of his allies Abraham Hall, John Hoffman, and "Slippery" Dick Connolly to the offices of mayor, governor, and city comptroller, Boss Tweed's hold on the city of New York was complete.

Whether out of self-interest or from concern for the working classes, among Tweed's primary obligations was patronage for his supporters. Browning and Gerassi (1980) report that over 12,000 new city jobs were created for Tammany stalwarts who came to be known as the Shiny Hat Brigade. In no time, virtually every branch of city government was overwhelmed by patronage. Under threat of contract cancellations, still other jobs were created by the thousands for Tweed loyalists by companies doing business with the city. Additionally, Tweed also arranged for hundreds of thousands of immigrants to be naturalized. Of course, these new citizens could be counted on to express their appreciation in the voting booth. When added to the votes of gang members (who often voted dozens of times each per election), corrupt officials, and ward healers, the immigrants and new job holders were sufficient to guarantee Tammany Hall power through reelections.

Financially, the Tweed machine prospered as well. Companies doing business with the city had to offer kickbacks. Tammany friends were encouraged to file suits against the city which, thanks to Tweed's ally Judge Barnard, were inevitably decided in favor of the plaintiffs. Fat "commissions" and fees for "legal services" were then paid from the judgments to Tweed and his associates. But the biggest boondoggle of the era was easily New York's new county courthouse.

> Begun in 1858 on a budget of $250,000, it had cost almost $13 million by 1871 and was still not finished. Among the itemized expenses were: $1,575,782 for furniture, including so many chairs at $5.00 apiece that were they to be put side by side, they would

have extended seventeen miles; almost $3 million for plastering; $41,190 for "brooms, etc."; $7,500 for thermometers; $75,716 for "not defined" repairs; $5,691,144 for carpets and carpet repairs. The companies cashing in on these "expenses," all Tammany faithfuls, paid some of the money to the Tweed Ring, some to the hundreds of new employees, and pocketed huge profits. Just to maintain the heating apparatus, for example, the maintenance subcontractors had to hire thirty-two engineers, firemen, secretaries, clerks, messengers, and inspectors for a total wage package of $42,000 a year. In addition to the bills on the new courthouse the city government paid out another $15,750,000 in fraudulent bills by 1871. (Browning & Gerassi, 1980:294)

Until massive investigations by *Harper's Weekly* and the *New York Times* began to cause cracks in the Tweed machine, his popularity was enormous and his power, influence, and wealth virtually unquestioned. With his help, organized crime also flourished.

Generating the Organizations of Crime

During his rise to power, Tweed's organization and the city's gangs and criminals were intricately interwoven. The gangs provided toughs and bullies to intimidate voters and attack political opponents. Prostitutes and confidence artists assisted as repeaters at the polls, but more importantly they represented revenue to their political patrons. Even after local control of the police was returned in 1870, the criminal justice system remained largely impotent in the face of the increasingly organized and protected criminals. "Law protects life no longer," lamented George Strong. "Any scoundrel who is backed by a little political influence in the corner groceries of his ward can commit murder with almost absolute impunity. . . . Municipal law is a failure in New York" (Strong, 1952:425). While it seemed that almost everyone was involved in some manner of crime in the city, by the close of the Civil War the gamblers were emerging as the principal beneficiaries and dominate influence over the mayhem. The man who controlled the city's now thriving gambling industry was Tammany Hall politician John Morrissey.

Beginning with a simple gambling house on Broadway, Morrissey expanded rapidly with his considerable profits. Before long, he owned additional establishments—all elegant and widely celebrated—on Ann Street, Barclay Street, West 24th Street, and Broadway Avenue. Not content to be the city's most powerful gambler, Morrissey expanded upstate to Saratoga Springs, adding a gambling house on Matilda Street and a horse-racing track known as Horse Haven. From there he began building the Club House, soon the most famous gambling establishment in the country. Elegantly furnished, the Club House featured faro and roulette on the first floor and high-stakes poker upstairs. Among the Club House patrons were U.S. generals, senators, and well-known business and political leaders such as Cornelius Vanderbilt, Samuel J. Tilden, and former mayor Fernando Wood's brother, Benjamin. Peterson (1983:73) writes that in one game Benjamin dropped $120,000 to Morrissey; in another his winnings topped $124,000.

Morrissey's political future shone brightly as well. With Boss Tweed's support, he was elected to Congress in 1866, representing New York's Fifth District. Not overlooking his principal business while in the capital, however, Morrissey soon opened the Congressional Faro Bank on Pennsylvania Avenue near 14th Street—roughly the heart of most government activity. Meanwhile, Morrissey's political connections in New York allowed him to gain such dominance of that city's gambling industry that he could demand and collect operating fees from his fellow gamesters. In effect, to conduct gambling in New York City, now the center of gambling in the United States, you first needed a franchise from John Morrissey. Such unquestioned power could only occur with the backing of the Tammany organization and William M. Tweed who had by then known Morrissey for more than 24 years. According to Tweed, as an organizer of elections, Morrissey had no peers. Tweed added in a lengthy statement to the Board of Aldermen that Morrissey was "a professional prizefighter and public gambler—a proprietor and owner of the worst places in the city of New York, the resort of thieves and persons of the lowest character. Perhaps the worst faults which can fairly be attributed to me, is having been the means of keeping his gambling houses protected from the police" (Peterson, 1983:74). Of course, the aldermen refused to make Tweed's admission a part of the public record.

While Morrissey ran casino-type operations almost exclusively, John Frink and Reubin Parsons were successfully reestablishing the city's policy and lottery businesses. By the end of the Civil War, these "poor people's casinos" had proliferated such that an estimated one-fourth of the city's population were regular players and patrons of the 600 to 700 known policy shops. Frink and Parsons apparently were unprepared for such success, so Zachariah Simmons stepped in to seize control and force organization here too. His first step was to form an alliance with Tweed to gain the protection of Tammany Hall. Once done, those policy dealers reluctant to join him soon found themselves the repeated targets of police raids until little choice remained but to capitulate and join forces with Simmons. Dubbed the Central Organization, the resulting policy combination divided the city into districts, assigned policy writing privileges, and took most of each member's profits for itself. Within a year, Simmons and his brother were firmly in control of at least three-fourths of the city's known policy operations. Eventually extending his reach to 20 other cities, the "Policy King of New York" would later gain managing control of the Kentucky State Lottery and the Frankfort Lottery of Kentucky as well. True to form, both would become entangled with fraudulent drawings (Asbury, 1932).

By the late 1800s, even the prostitutes were becoming organized as a rich source of revenue for Tammany Hall supporters. Although less organized than the gamblers, by the end of the Civil War many of the more notorious madams began to move their houses from the Five Points, the Bowery, and along the East River waterfront into almost every other area of the city. And, of course, they too received protection allowing them to operate without fear of interference so long as regular payments to the police, prosecutors, and politicians were made. Some felt so safe as to boldly advertise their services in newspapers and with handbills on street corners. Callow (1966) reports that more than a few houses had direct telegraph connections with police so that officers could be called when disturbances broke out. By 1866, Bishop Simpson of the Methodist Episcopal Church declared that the business of sex had grown to such proportions that prostitutes were by then as numerous in New York as were Methodists. Offering considerable proof to support his claim, Simpson fixed their number as high as 20,000, roughly one-fortieth of the city's population (Asbury, 1927). Like gambling, prostitution was now big business.

Gamblers and Gangs: A Need for Consolidation

As the city began to mature and the influence and wealth from vice coalesced, so too did the power of the gangsters. By the early 1900s, two principal federations of gangs had evolved to divide Manhattan into fiefdoms. On one side were the Five Pointers who had evolved from the Dead Rabbits, the Plug Uglies, and the Whyos, perhaps the most feared of the earlier gangs. Led by Paolo Antonini Vaccarelli, more commonly known as Paul Kelly, the Five Pointers ruled an area between Broadway and the Bowery. The several hundred members would congregate at the New Brighton Dance Hall, which was owned by Kelly, where they would socialize and plan their various activities.

Nearby, the rival Eastmans dominated the stretch of New York from the Bowery to the East River. Named after Monk Eastman, the gang federation's leader, these gang members headquartered in an unsavory bar near the Bowery.

Although both leaders maintained close ties with Tammany Hall politicians, and members of both were similarly involved in vice and violence, their styles could hardly have been more different. Eastman (whose real name was Edward Osterman) was the son of a Jewish restauranteur from Brooklyn. A typical looking gangster, his short neck, broken nose, and numerous knife scars gave him a ferocious appearance that helped him command by the force of his personality.

Kelly, on the other hand, was a small, soft-spoken man who was usually neatly dressed. Although previously a professional prizefighter (bantamweight), Kelly seldom engaged in brawling. Instead, he was an efficient organizer who was self-educated and possessed varied cultural tastes. Among the gang leaders to follow and emulate Kelly was Johnny Torrio, who would later dominate Chicago crime and establish Al Capone in business. Capone himself was a Five Pointer.

While each gang federation had its own area of dominance, the battles between the two were fierce and continuous. Peterson describes one encounter:

> Around eleven o'clock on a hot night in mid–August 1903, several Five Pointers were about to raid an Eastman stuss game on Rivington Street under the Allen Street arch of the Second Avenue elevated railroad. Six Eastmans appeared on the scene and opened fire, killing a Five Pointer. The Five Pointers sought cover behind pillars of the elevated structure and the Eastmans followed suit. Reinforcements for both gangs arrived. By midnight scores of gunmen, evenly divided between Eastmans and Five Pointers, were blazing away at each other from behind elevated pillars. Three gunmen were slain and many were wounded. Policemen who first appeared at the battle site were forced to retreat in disorder. A short time later, officers from several police stations were rushed to the field of conflict. Several gunmen were arrested and others were driven away. Among those arrested was Monk Eastman, who gave the name of Joseph Morris. When he was arraigned the following morning, a magistrate promptly discharged him. (1983:101)

Reacting to such incidents, even the Tammany politicians agreed that the gangs were out of control and the "Wild West" shootouts had to be stopped. Several efforts to mediate a peace were launched; however, each concluded with a return to hostilities. During one such effort, the two gang leaders agreed to settle their questions of supremacy in the boxing ring. Kelly, once a prizefighter, began with the advantage; however,

Eastman soon compensated with his greater size and ferocity. After more than two hours of fighting, a draw was declared (Peterson, 1983). Alternating cycles of negotiation and battle continued until November 2, 1904, when Eastman, who was by now losing the favor of his important patrons, was arrested attempting to rob a Pinkerton detective. Charged with robbery and assault and unable to block prosecution, Monk Eastman was sentenced to ten years at Sing Sing prison. Even after his release, he was unable to regain his former prominence. After several additional legal skirmishes, on December 26, 1920, Eastman's body was discovered on an East 14th Street sidewalk where, after encroaching on the territory of a Prohibition Enforcement Agent, he had been shot five times.

With Eastman in prison, two of his lieutenants, Kid Twist and Richie Fitzpatrick, assumed leadership. They also inherited the struggle with the Five Pointers. But first, their own command needed to be negotiated. Twist proposed a conference, which Fitzpatrick agreed was necessary. When Fitzpatrick arrived, he discovered that the meeting was a ruse. That knowledge meant little, however, since by the time the police arrived only Fitzpatrick's body remained. Kid Twist could now focus his attention fully on efforts to take over the most prosperous of the Five Pointers' operations. Twist's reign was cut short, however, when barely two years later he was shot to death outside one of the many bars of Coney Island. Although his killer was an ambitious Five Pointer, the cause of his death was an insult over a woman both men had admired. Twist's death badly demoralized the Eastman gang, which broke into factions, many at war with each other (Asbury, 1927).

Meanwhile, Paul Kelly had become preoccupied with a new source of power and wealth—labor unions. Along the waterfronts, Kelly began bringing together unorganized workers to form the Garbage Scow Trimmers Union, which he, of course, agreed to lead. From there, he assumed control of a number of other harbor unions. Next, he organized the rag pickers on the dumps at the East River and 108th Street. Here again, he agreed to serve as business agent. Within only a few months Kelley had this group on strike. Simultaneously, Kelly and his gang began taking commissions from real estate agents seeking to acquire mansions on the Upper East Side. Owners reluctant to sell were subjected to systematic destruction and terrorism until the property was destroyed or the will to resist was weakened (Asbury, 1927). With his now growing successes, Kelly was able to leave the Lower East Side tenements he was from and take up residence in Harlem, a substantial improvement in living conditions.

With Eastman, Fitzpatrick, Kid Twist, and Paul Kelly gone, the gangs fell into disarray. A succession of new leaders stepped forward, yet none seemed able to command the support or demonstrate the vision of their predecessors. The times were different as well. With reform in the wind, even the politicians of Tammany Hall found it difficult to overlook the widespread vice and violence around them. The now increasingly vulnerable gangs grew smaller and less stable, with new groups such as the Red Peppers, the Pearl Buttons, the Parlor Mob, and the Car Barn Gang forming regularly. Prosecution and competition among gangs and gangsters took their toll as well as the gang scene became complex and difficult to follow. Still, Asbury (1927) estimates that by 1913 there were more gangs in New York City than in any other period in history. Each, however, was smaller and less powerful. "The time when a chieftain could muster from five hundred to a thousand men under his command had passed," Asbury wrote. "There were few gang leaders who could take the field with more than thirty or forty thugs" (1927:360). Consequently, where the Eastmans and the Five Pointers had dominated an area before, innumerable small groups now roamed, usually in conflict with each other. Their organizations were more elastic as well. The loyalty that had been characteristic of earlier gangs now appeared absent. In fact, it was not unusual for a gangster to owe allegiance to three or four gangs at once, performing crimes for each. In short, chaos existed among the criminals. A new generation of gang leader, one more in tune with the times, was needed. The time for Arnold Rothstein had arrived.

ARNOLD ROTHSTEIN:
THE ORIGINAL "DON"

Dubbed "The Brain," it was Arnold Rothstein who brought organized crime into the modern era. An Orthodox Jew born to a middle-class family, Rothstein Americanized the gangs of New York, bringing them into the "melting pot" of business coming to life at the time. Rothstein's main accomplishment was to provide organization. His efforts "transformed criminal activity from a haphazard, often spontaneous endeavor into one whose hallmarks—specialized expertise, administrative hierarchy, and organizational procedure—correspond to the classical sociological model of a bureaucracy" (Joselit, 1983:143). As evidence of his success, Rothstein served as the inspiration for the characters Meyer Wolfshein in *The Great Gatsby* and Nathan Detroit in the musical *Guys and Dolls*. Unfortunately, he also inspired an entire generation of organized criminals.

Early on, Rothstein established himself on New York's crime scene as a pool shark. Highly successful as a gambler, he put his profits to work offering usurious loans. For this, he needed assistance, however, so contacts were made with Monk Eastman who agreed to become Rothstein's "collector." As this business grew, Waxey Gordon and "Legs" and Eddie Diamond joined him as well. Soon, Rothstein expanded to dice games and bookmaking, which led to his ownership of established gambling halls. An association with "Big Tim" Sullivan, then the Tammany leader, brought protection from the police. By 1914, Rothstein was a "bookmaker's bookmaker," handling "layoff" bets from other bookmakers. With his relations with the gangs, gamblers, and politicians secure, he expanded into new business territory. Rothstein was virtually the founder of the nation's bootlegging and narcotics traffic. He imported liquor from England and Canada. And he smuggled in diamonds, heroin, and cocaine through an international network he himself had established (Abadinsky, 1985).

Next, Rothstein sent his men into New York's chaotic garment industry. He organized the manufacturers with mass production and marketing techniques not previously tried by the hundreds of small entrepreneurs and tailors dominating the industry. As the workers began to organize their unions, Rothstein offered the owners contract thugs (usually supplied by Eastman and Paul Kelly) as strikebreakers. At other times, however, when the workers were being beaten on the picket lines, Rothstein supplied the unions with toughs to fight off the company goons (Browning & Gerassi, 1980). In either case, a rich tribute was exacted from the clients and a place in the growing garment industry was secured for Rothstein's gangsters, including "Lepke" Buchalter, "Little Augie" Orgen, and "Gurrah" Shapiro. Eventually, Rothstein included bailbonding, stolen securities, insurance, and real estate in his varied lineup of business endeavors. Indeed, Arnold Rothstein loomed large over all that was organized crime.

While Rothstein was rising to his position of preeminence, many other gangsters and gang leaders were also growing in stature. Ironically, it was Rothstein, an Orthodox Jew, who gave impetus to the generation of Italians who would learn from his example and dominate much of New York's organized crime in the years following his death. In fact, young Italians who had grown up in America were especially attracted to Rothstein, who was more interested in talent than heritage as he chose the men to direct his many operations. Among the most prized of these proteges was a young man known as Frank Costello.

Frank Costello

Born Francesco Castiglia in Calabria, Italy, 5-year-old Frank Costello settled in East Harlem with his family in 1896. Already a slum, it was there that Frank and his older brother, Eddie, first became involved in gang warfare and crime. By age 14, Costello registered his first arrest for robbing the landlady of his parent's flat. In 1908 and 1912, he was again charged with assault and robbery. None of these early arrests resulted in prosecution, however, as his well-concocted alibis were accepted by the police. Already showing initiative, the young Costello next turned his talents to rent collecting for absentee landlords in the neighborhood. During September 1914, Costello, age 23, married his best friend's sister. The celebration was short, however, since within only a few months he was arrested once again, this time for carrying a concealed weapon. Noting his local reputation as a "gunman," this time Costello was convicted and sentenced to one year of prison on Welfare Island (Peterson, 1983).

Having learned that small-time crime doesn't pay—or at least not well —after his release, Costello joined Harry Horowitz to form the Horowitz Novelty Company. Manufacturers of punchboards and Kewpie dolls, within a year they were earning over $100,000 annually. Not satisfied, they staged a successful bankruptcy claiming that payments owed them for merchandise sold were uncollectible since the money was owed by "east-side gangsters" (Peterson, 1983:135). They reinvested the profits from this scam in real estate and other punchboard companies. With the advent of Prohibition, however, Frank Costello recognized even greater opportunities for business.

According to George Wolf, Costello's personal attorney, it was Rothstein who served as both tutor and mentor for the emerging Costello. Having met earlier through gambling friends, Costello turned to Rothstein for guidance on organization, cost cutting, and even elimination of competition. More than anyone, it was Rothstein's tutelage that developed Costello into a business brain. And it was Rothstein who backed Costello financially and established the connections he would later need to build and run his considerable criminal enterprise.

Based on gambling, liquor, and narcotics, Costello's criminal and political influence was felt for several decades. In 1951, however, he was called before the Kefauver committee's televised hearings, where his evasive answers and dramatic walkout of the proceedings (as well as his refusal to be televised) led to an 18-month sentence for contempt. In the next year, the government moved against him again, this time for tax evasion. Costello was given a 5-year sentence, but this conviction was overturned in 1956 after Costello's attorney, Edward Bennett Williams, established that illegal wiretaps had been used (Abadinsky, 1985). Following the death of his friend, Albert Anastasia, and a failed attempt on his own life, in 1957 Frank Costello retired from crime to establish an oil leaseholding partnership in Texas with his former allies Frank Erickson (bookmaking and horse racing) and George Uffner (narcotics) (Peterson, 1983). In 1982, Costello died from a heart attack.

Waxey Gordon

Irving Wexler began his career in crime rather unpretentiously by picking pockets on the Lower East Side. As he developed his skills, he advanced himself into the role of a "slugger," working principally in the garment district on matters of labor trouble and violence. There he met Lepke Buchalter and Gurrah Shapiro as they too developed their labor racketeering skills. It took the introduction of Prohibition, however, to bring Waxey Gordon's real talents to the forefront.

Peterson (1983) reports that while Rothstein is credited with making rumrunning the huge industry it became, it was Waxey Gordon who gave him the idea originally. Along with "Big Max" Greenberg of Detroit, Gordon reportedly went to Rothstein for a loan of $175,000 to establish a large rumrunning venture. Rothstein considered their plan and offered a counterproposal instead. Since Rothstein was a difficult man to refuse, they agreed. What they established was an operation to buy liquor by the shipload in England, which they would then transport to the United States for sale. Twenty thousand cases of Scotch whiskey made the maiden voyage. Once offshore, speedboats met the ship to bring the whiskey to Long Island where Rothstein had an agreement with the Coast Guard and the local police. A motorcycle escort provided protection during the last stage of the journey as trucks moved the supply to warehouses in the city. In all, Rothstein's ship made ten crossings under Gordon's leadership before a new Coast Guard commander was dispatched to intervene. Rothstein was tipped off, however, and the venture was brought to a close. Small matter since by then Waxey Gordon was already established.

Making his headquarters in a plush suite of offices on 42nd Street and Broadway, Gordon opened a brewery in New Jersey and a distillery in upstate New York. Additional properties in New Jersey and Philadelphia and nightclubs and gambling casinos in New York were soon added to his enterprises while an expensive apartment on Central Park West, a fleet of luxury cars, and a castle—complete with a moat—on the New Jersey shore became his home. All the while, from 1928 to 1933, Gordon paid an average of only $33 a year in income taxes. Perhaps because of his wealthy lifestyle, but more likely due to a feud with Meyer Lansky, the Internal Revenue Service was informed of Gordon's considerable income, leading the Treasury Department's Special Intelligence Unit to open an investigation. In November 1933, their case was complete, and Gordon was brought to trial for federal income tax evasion. His prosecutor was Thomas E. Dewey, an interim U.S. Attorney for the Southern District of New York. Within weeks, Gordon was convicted and sentenced to ten years imprisonment. Although eventually released from federal custody, subsequent convictions for heroin trafficking led to his reimprisonment; he became ill and died in the prison hospital on June 24, 1952.

The Diamond Brothers, Lepke Buchalter, and Gurrah Shapiro

Jack "Legs" Diamond and his brother Eddie first came to New York from Philadelphia in 1913. Almost at once, Jack joined with a band of thieves on the Lower West Side where he met and was influenced by Monk Eastman, who was by then in decline. Copying Eastman's style, Legs soon abandoned simple theft as a vocation, turning instead to the far more profitable but dangerous business of hijacking. For that he needed both organization and a gang, leading him to ally himself with young but aspiring crime leaders such as Charles "Lucky" Luciano, "Dutch" Schultz, and "Little Augie" Orgen. By 1920, Legs Diamond had become widely known as irresponsible but quite fearless. Equally important, he was also always open to new ideas.

Once Prohibition became a reality, the Diamonds came to the conclusion that it would be a waste of their time and money to make heavy investments in liquor that had to be smuggled into the country for distribution. Far simpler, Legs reasoned, would be to hijack someone else's cargo after it arrived. In effect, they could become wholesalers with virtually no overhead. Better yet, their own "suppliers" would be all but unlimited and quite unable to do anything (at least officially) about their losses. To get started, all they would need was a few trucks, some rented warehouses, and an organization to dispose of the liquor they hijacked—all items Arnold Rothstein was happy to supply.

Meanwhile, industrial racketeering was also becoming an increasingly important source of income for organized criminals. Lepke Buchalter and Gurrah Shapiro, also Rothstein proteges who had been introduced to crime five years earlier as thugs for Little Augie Orgen, had in fact become so influential in the garment district that they owned their own manufacturing firm for clothing. When Little Augie accepted a $50,000 fee to force an end to a painters' strike then in progress, confrontation was inevitable. Buchalter and Shapiro, it seems, stood to profit most from a prolonged strike. Little Augie, on the other hand, was calling on union leaders and threatening them with death unless the strike was called off at once. Labeling their former mentors common thugs unworthy of the complexities of labor racketeering, Buchalter and Shapiro moved to intervene.

On October 15, 1927, the Buchalter–Shapiro forces set out in search of Little Augie. At about eight-thirty they located him and Jack Diamond at

Norfolk and Delancey Streets on the Lower East Side and a gun battle erupted. In the melee that ensued, Orgen was killed and Legs Diamond was wounded several times, including two bullet wounds just below his heart. Diamond recovered, and Buchalter and Shapiro avoided prosecution when all witnesses, including Diamond, refused to identify them as responsible. As a result, they emerged from the event even more powerful than before. That they could commit murder and get away with it was not lost on the garment and related industries; a fact that would help them to gain control of the truckmen's union, most trade associations, jobbers, and many manufacturers (Thompson & Raymond, 1940). Although they suffered some setbacks, most notably in their attempts to seize the fur trade, the garment, leather, baking, and trucking industries soon came almost entirely under their control.

As evidence of their success, by the late 1930s Thomas E. Dewey, the special prosecutor, began action against the pair. Buchalter, by then forced into hiding, responded by ordering a rampage of murder in an effort to remove all possible witnesses against him. In all, as many as 60 to 80 killings may have resulted (Berger, 1940). Rather than cower his opponents, however, the strategy backfired and the efforts against him only intensified. With a $50,000 reward for his capture and a public outcry and demand for his arrest, even his most loyal allies began to wilt under the pressure. Having no place to turn, on August 1, 1937, Buchalter surrendered to Walter Winchell, a well-known columnist, and J. Edgar Hoover, apparently in the belief that a deal had been arranged such that he would stand trial only for federal drug and not state murder charges (Turkus & Feder, 1951). As he expected, on January 2, 1940, he was convicted in federal court for antitrust and narcotics violations and given a 14-year prison sentence. To his surprise, however, he was then turned over to New York authorities for prosecution by Dewey for extortion. For that he received an additional sentence of from 30 years to life in prison. Neither conviction would matter, however, since in 1941, Brooklyn Assistant District Attorney Turkus managed a clean sweep by prosecuting and convicting Buchalter and two of his colleagues for murder. On March 4, 1944, Lepke Buchalter became the only major organized criminal to be executed by the state for his crimes (Abadinsky, 1985).

The Diamond Brothers and Dutch Schultz

Recovering from wounds received in the shootout with Buchalter, Legs Diamond returned his attention to his principal business, bootlegging. Here, too, he found his position under challenge by one of his own proteges—this time Dutch Schultz. Schultz and Joey Noe, close friends, had quietly built a formidable organization of their own in the Bronx and were gradually forcing the Diamonds out of business there. But Jack Diamond had no intention of accepting a second major defeat.

Arthur Flegenheimer, better known as Dutch Schultz, was one of several German-Jewish immigrants from the Lower East Side to turn gangster. Born in 1902, by his early 20s he helped turn the small trucking business where he worked into a beer hauling enterprise. Not satisfied to work for others, however, he and Joey Noe set out on their own and opened a speakeasy they called the Hub Social Club. Before long, other taverns were theirs as was a small fleet of trucks they had bought to deliver their beer. As their organization grew, so did its reliance on violence, ably delivered by emissaries such as Bo Weinberg, Joey Rao, and the Coll brothers, Vincent and Peter. Eventually, as Schultz and Noe expanded throughout the Bronx and into Manhattan, conflict with Legs Diamond was inevitable.

Early on the morning of October 16, 1928, Schultz and Noe were leaving the Swanee Club, one of their favorite haunts located under the Apollo Theater on 125th Street in Harlem. It was dawn, and Schultz was apparently headed to see William "Big Bill" Dwyer, a fellow liquor smuggler and favorite target of the Diamonds' hijacking gang. Joey Noe was on his way to the Chateau Madrid to meet with Diamond himself in an effort to resolve still another of their disputes. The Diamonds had other plans, however, and met Noe on the sidewalk with a barrage of gunfire. Although wearing a bullet-proof vest, several bullets penetrated Noe's lower spine and right breast. Taken to Bellevue Hospital's prison ward, he lingered for over a month and died November 21, 1928 (Peterson, 1983). Even before Noe was dead, the repercussions from the ambush were considerable.

Both Schultz and the police were certain that Diamond was responsible. Days later Arnold Rothstein was in Lindy's Restaurant on Broadway at 50th Street. At about 10:30 he was called by a waiter to the telephone. Following his conversation, Rothstein went outside on Broadway where he announced that he was going to see George McManus in the nearby Park Central Hotel. He would return in about half an hour, he said. Within 15 minutes, however, Rothstein had been shot in the abdomen. Two days later, November 6, 1928, Arnold Rothstein died in the Polyclinic Hospital (Peterson, 1983). Organized crime in New York had lost its mentor and was once again wide open with opportunities.

During the investigation into Rothstein's murder, it was learned that two months earlier he had lost big ($316,000) to several notorious gamblers in a high-stakes poker game. Among them was George McManus. The police believed that Rothstein welshed on his losses, leading McManus to shoot him. When McManus and his colleague Hyman Biller were indicted for the murder, however, a verdict of directed acquittal was handed down due to a lack of credible evidence. Many observers have since agreed with the decision, speculating that it was Rothstein's backing of Legs Diamond that led to his murder in retaliation for the attack on Joey Noe (Thompson & Raymond, 1940).

Regardless of why he was killed, during the two days that Rothstein lingered, many of his personal files were stolen and probably destroyed. What remained established was that he had engineered the infamous 1919 Black Sox loss in the World Series. Also disclosed were relations with Tammany Hall, financial dealings with important political and judicial figures, connections to other important gangsters, and a host of phony corporations created by Rothstein to conceal his worldwide operations and business dealings. Acting on other information found in his files, federal agents seized $2 million in narcotics on December 7, and another ton of narcotics on a Jersey City pier on December 18, 1928. In all, over $7 million in narcotics and a smuggling and distribution trail leading to Boston, Philadelphia, Detroit, Chicago, San Francisco, and several foreign countries were uncovered in the partial files that survived (Peterson, 1983).

With Rothstein dead and Legs Diamond neutralized, Schultz set about removing what remained of his competition. Vincent "Mad Dog" Coll was machine gunned to death as he used a drugstore pay phone. Owen "Ownie the Killer" Madden retired in wealth to Hot Springs, Arkansas, where he married, became involved with charities, and died comfortably of natural causes. Waxey Gordon, as we have already seen, was imprisoned with tax troubles. Dutch Schultz seemed to be having it all his way until he too began to experience the new but increasingly common problem for gangsters—the Internal Revenue Service. Finally, on November 29, 1934, Dutch Schultz, the "Beer Baron of the Bronx," surrendered to authorities to face his own tax charges. Schultz would put up a game fight, however.

First, he succeeded in obtaining a change of venue due to his notoriety in the city. The case was moved upstate to Syracuse, New York, where a "hung jury" produced a mistrial. Next, the trial was moved even further north to Malone, New York. There, Schultz worked the community. Prior to the trial, he made visits to the hospital, bought candy and flowers for children, and held a grand ball for the entire town. After endearing himself to most everyone in town, he was acquitted of the charges against him. Still, his troubles were far from over.

Anticipating some problems, federal prosecutors had held back several counts of the original indictment. Simultaneously, as the first trials progressed, they were busy developing a new series of charges, although most were only misdemeanors. In addition, New York State had prepared its own tax evasion case and was now prepared to proceed as well. Further, it was understood that if Schultz was arrested in New York City, a prohibitive bail would be used to hold him in custody. As a result, Schultz left New York for New Jersey, where he again surrendered to the federal charges against him. Out on bail in New Jersey, he set up headquarters in the Palace Chop House and Tavern in Newark. So far, he had managed a standstill with his legal pursuers. During his now long absence from the city, however, a new, and more deadly, threat had appeared—Charles "Lucky" Luciano.

Apparently expecting Schultz to be convicted and imprisoned, Luciano and his colleagues (among them Lepke Buchalter and Gurrah Shapiro) had begun to move in on Schultz's operations. His acquittal in Malone was a serious setback to their plans. Worse, once in New Jersey, Schultz struck back by murdering one of his own top aides, Bo Weinburg, who was by then cooperating with Luciano. Of greatest concern, however, were the "Dutchman's" threats to kill the special prosecutor, Thomas E. Dewey, a visible and popular figure. The heat such a murder would bring could damage them all. And so, on the evening of October 25, 1935, Luciano and probably Buchalter sent Charles Workman and Emanual "Mendy" Weiss, both professional killers, to the Chop House in Newark to bring the matter to a close.

As the two men entered the tavern, they encountered Schultz's two bodyguards along with Otto "Abbadabba" Berman, the financial brains behind the organization. After shooting all three, Workman went to the men's room where he found and shot Schultz as well (Abadinsky, 1985). Some 27 hours later, Dutch Schultz and the others were dead—to the end, none would identify their killers. Luciano's takeover was complete.

Almost six years later, Workman was tried for the Schultz murder and given a life sentence in prison. In 1964, he was paroled and allowed to return to the city and a job in the garment district. Mendy Weiss, along with Buchalter and Louis Capone (no relation to Al), died in 1944 in the electric chair for an unrelated murder.

CHARLES LUCIANO AND THE
ITALIAN CRIME "FAMILIES"

Like so many of his fellow gangsters, Charles Luciano grew up poor on New York's Lower East Side. Born Salvatore Lucania in western Sicily, the 10-year-old Luciano came to the United States in 1907. In school, Luciano was a chronic truant with a poor academic record. Even as a youth, he gambled regularly, borrowed from loan sharks, and used and sold narcotics. At the age of 14, he dropped out of school, becoming a member of Paul

Kelly's Five Points Gang. By 18, he was sentenced to six months in a refor-matory for selling morphine to a federal narcotics agent (Nelli, 1976). Prag-matic even then, he took the easy way out and became a police informer. For his freedom, Luciano directed agents to 163 Mulberry Street where they found a supply of narcotics (Peterson, 1983).

Early on, Luciano's talent was for organization. His initial boost to crime fame came around 1927 when Giuseppe "Joe the Boss" Masseria asked Luciano to become his number one assistant. Masseria was then battling with Salvatore Maranzano as the two attempted to expand their Prohibition business beyond "Little Italy" into the wider American society. After con-sulting with close associates Meyer Lansky, Frank Costello, Vito Genovese, and Frank Scalise, Luciano accepted Masseria's offer.

The Castellamarese War

Although accounts of this transitional period in Italian organized crime vary greatly, the so-called Castellamarese War appears to have officially begun on February 26, 1930, with the shotgun murder of Gaetano Reina. Reina, it seems, headed a group of Italian gangsters operating within the domain of the more powerful Masseria. Not satisfied with the arrangement, he appar-ently began complaining privately (but not sufficiently so) about Masseria and his manner of business. Unfortunately for Reina, the objections were passed along, and his own career was abruptly brought to an end. After a brief struggle, Salvatore Maranzano seized control of what remained of Reina's organization and the Masseria–Maranzano war was under way.

The Maranzano group consisted mainly of Sicilians, many from the small coastal town of Castellammare del Golfo. Among them were Gaetano "Tommy" Gagliano, Tommy Lucchese, and Joseph Valachi, who would go on to fame as an informant and star of the McClellan committee hearings. Allied with the Masseria forces were, in addition to Luciano, such promi-nent gang leaders as Ciro Terranova, Dutch Schultz, Frank Costello, Vito Genovese, and allegedly Al Capone in Chicago. They, in turn, were allied with Meyer Lansky and Benjamin Siegel. Despite such an impressive line-up, the conflict gradually began to turn against Masseria as several of his top leaders were killed. Valachi, in fact, once boasted that Maranzano forces were achieving an attrition rate of as high as "forty to sixty" to one (U.S. Senate, 1963). More likely, Masseria's significant losses, including Alfred Mineo, Steve Ferrigno, and Joe Aiello, resulted from a combination of the conflict, the internal struggles for power constantly under way, and unre-lated clashes with other criminal groups. Whatever the reason, as the war turned against Masseria, Luciano and several others did likewise.

Perhaps realizing his plight, in the end Masseria reportedly attempted to make peace. Maranzano refused. Finally, on April 15, 1931, Genovese and Luciano lured Masseria to a Coney Island restaurant, telling him that they needed to meet to develop a plan of action. As soon as Masseria was seated, however, he was shot six times in the head and back. According to Valachi, Luciano, Genovese, Terranova, Joe Stretch, and a man called Cheech were all present at the killing. As they fled, Ciro Terranova is said to have become so nervous and shaky that he was unable to put the car keys in the ignition. Because of his fear, he "lost face" and gradually lost most of his power among his associates (U.S. Senate, 1963). With Masseria's death, the Castellammarese War was over; Maranzano declared himself "Boss of all Bosses" while Luciano assumed control of what remained of Masseria's empire. Predictably, the peace was brief and uneasy.

Within only a few months, Valachi reported that Maranzano sent for him with instructions that "we have to go to the mattress again." Maranzano went on to say of his colleagues in crime, "We can't get along." Specifically naming Al Capone, Frank Costello, Vito Genovese, Vincent Mangano, Joe Adonis, Dutch Schultz, and Luciano, Maranzano decided that "we have to get rid of these people." He intended, Valachi added, to use Vincent Coll to kill Luciano and Genovese as they arrived for a meeting in his office that he had arranged for September 10, 1931. His plan was not to be, however.

Having been tipped off to Maranzano's plan, Luciano, apparently with Meyer Lansky's help, sent four men to the meeting in his place. Arriving early, they posed as police, showing badges to others waiting to see the Boss of Bosses. Telling Maranzano that they had business to discuss, at least two of the visitors followed him into his private office. There, he appears to have gotten wise to the ruse and resisted. Sounds of angry voices, struggling, and blows were heard before shots rang out. After his assassins fled, Maranzano was found dead, his body riddled with four gunshot and six knife wounds (Peterson, 1983). Luciano was now the most important of the Italian organized criminals in New York—a status he would enjoy for almost four years.

The Luciano–Genovese "Family"

Ironically, it was one of his least significant ventures that posed the greatest difficulties for "Charley Lucky." In 1935, city police raided the apartment of Polly Adler, one of New York's most notorious madams. As Ms. Adler and several girls and their bookers—the pimps who supplied girls to the brothels—were processed through the legal system, Eunice Carter, at once the only black and the only female on Thomas Dewey's legal staff, began to notice a pattern: Dozens of women represented by the same lawyer were each acquitted during their arraignments. Suspecting organization, Carter convinced Dewey to investigate.

Phones were tapped and conversations intercepted, convincing Dewey that a legal hotline existed to get girls out of jail and back to their brothels. For her part, each prostitute worked an average of 10 to 14 hours a day. At the end of each week, she was paid, with the madam of the house collecting one-half of her earnings immediately. From what remained, each girl then paid $5 a week for medical exams, unspecified amounts for meals during the week, and another $10 to a bond fund. For her money, it was understood that when arrested, a bondsman would arrange for her release and an attorney would appear and coach her through the process. From their investigation, Ms. Carter and her team quickly identified most of the madams, bookers, bondsmen, and enforcers involved in the system. She also learned that most had been independent operators until Luciano forced them into a single combination. Dewey's secretary recalled the special prosecutor's surprise: "Nobody had suspected Luciano. They knew he was in narcotics and every other rotten business, but they didn't know he was in prostitution. They didn't even suspect it" (Short, 1984:152). In fact, however, through his assistants, Little Dave Betillo and Thomas Pennochio, Luciano was believed to control at least 200 madams and over 3,000 prostitutes from whom he extorted an estimated $12 million a year for "protection." "Whores is whores," Luciano declared on one tapped phone conversation. "They can always be handled. They ain't got no guts" (Short, 1984:152).

With case in hand, at midnight, January 31, 1936, Dewey's men quietly took 16 suspects into custody. On the following night they struck again, this time with 160 officers simultaneously raiding 80 houses of prostitution. Although half of these raids were failures (apparently because of tip-offs), hundreds of prostitutes and madams were nonetheless arrested (Peterson, 1983). As one of Dewey's assistants described the evening:

> Starting at nine o'clock that night into the office came hordes of prostitutes, pimps, telephone operators at whorehouses, dope addicts, all kinds of people, venereal and otherwise. We worked throughout the night and the weekend. There were witnesses sprawled all over the floor, having withdrawal symptoms because they weren't getting their drugs—a disgusting scene with disgusting people. In those days we weren't confined to constitutional rights. We were pretty rough. We broke people, we got them to talk. We didn't use violence but in those days they expected to be beaten up. One telephone operator was not co-operating so I got out of the chair to pull the blind down. He recognized this as a sign he was

now going to get his beating so he pulled back cowering and said, "OK, OK, I'll tell you what you want to know." (Short, 1984:151)

One by one, witnesses named the men in charge. Not only did the madams, prostitutes, and phone operators talk, but three of the four major bookers did as well. And consistently, they named Luciano as the top man. With these witnesses, along with others collected at the Barbizon Plaza and Waldorf Towers hotels where Luciano maintained suites as Charles Lane and Charles Ross, Dewey now had enough for a 90-count indictment against Luciano and 15 of his conspirators. Although he fled to Hot Springs, Arkansas, Luciano was arrested and returned to New York where, on June 7, 1936, he and his co-defendants were convicted on 62 counts of compulsory prostitution. While his case was overwhelming, Dewey had left little to chance—as a precaution, he had persuaded the New York State Assembly to enact a special state conspiracy law specifically for this case (Browning & Gerassi, 1980).

With his conviction, Luciano was sentenced to 30 to 50 years in the Clinton State Prison at Dannemora. Dewey had won what was easily his most significant battle against organized crime. In 1942, Luciano's sentence was cut short, however, when U.S. Navy intelligence officers asked that he be moved closer to New York to assist them in their waterfront operations. Luciano, it seems, was still able to effectively gather information on Mussolini as well as help prevent labor unrest that might interfere with important World War II shipping. Ironically, in recognition of his wartime efforts, on January 3, 1946, Luciano was granted executive clemency by then Governor Thomas E. Dewey and deported to Italy. He remained in exile there until his death from a heart attack in 1962. Well before then, however, Frank Costello had assumed control of the Luciano organization and, with it, he became the new Boss of Bosses.

The longevity of Costello's influence is impressive by almost any organizational standards. Once dubbed the "Prime Minister of Crime" for his charm, diplomacy, and political connections, for almost 15 years Costello ran the organization he inherited from Luciano as a shadowy figure about whom little was known. Still, a 1943 revelation that he had caused the nomination of a state supreme court justice (in New York a trial, not an appellate, court), along with his appearances before the Kefauver committee, assured his status as a public figure whose movements were newsworthy. His almost total control over New York crime also assured him the enmity of Vito Genovese.

At the age of 15, Genovese and his family arrived from Naples to New York's Little Italy in Manhattan. Beginning as a petty thief, he quickly graduated in crime to progressively significant positions. Eventually, he become an associate of Luciano. In 1934, however, Genovese's rise in the ranks of crime was sidetracked when a bungled murder (Ferdinand Boccia) forced him to flee to Italy to avoid prosecution. Taking along substantial cash reserves, he reportedly became a friend of the government and a decorated confidant of Mussolini himself. Allegedly, his services for the dictator included the contract murder of Carlo Tresca, the editor of *Martello*, a New York publication for antifascists.

Once the American invasion was under way, Genovese wisely switched sides to become an interpreter for the American military authorities. From that position, he continued as a black marketeer in Italy until 1945 when he was identified as an American fugitive and returned to New York for prosecution for murder. He was little worried, however, since by the time the trial began, Peter LaTempa, a key prosecution witness, had been poisoned as he waited in the Raymond Street Jail for his turn to testify. The charges now unsupported, Genovese was a free man.

For the next 11 years, Genovese served as an assistant to Costello in the organization that he had helped Luciano form. Apparently tired of waiting, he succeeded in deposing Costello in May 1957, after a failed effort to assassinate him led to Costello's decision to step down. With Costello in retirement, Genovese assumed full control for at least the next two years until his own conviction for a narcotics conspiracy and imprisonment in the federal penitentiary in Atlanta. Even then, he continued as the top man in family affairs.

Throughout his long career, Genovese's criminal ventures included narcotics, gambling, loan-sharking, extortion, and murder. A man who took what he wanted, Abadinsky (1985) notes that after Genovese's first wife died in 1931, he announced his plans to remarry to Anna Petillo—the only problem was that she was already married. Twelve days later, after Mr. Petillo had been strangled to death, Genovese and the newly widowed Anna were married as he had predicted.

Along with his other business interests, Genovese also owned several night clubs in New York City, among them the Savannah Club on Third Street, the Groton Village on Eighth Street, the 181 Club on Second Avenue, and the 82 Club on Fourth Street. Additionally, vending machine and jukebox businesses were his as well. Although Genovese unquestionably took the lion's share from each of these enterprises, Valachi once estimated that the organization's reach was so wide that another 40 to 50 members had amassed sufficient wealth to be millionaires (Peterson, 1983).

Joining Genovese in the Atlanta prison were not only Valachi but Genovese associates Joseph and Charles DiPalermo, John Dioguardi, and Mike Coppola. On the outside, Tommy Eboli served as acting boss of the organization on Genovese's behalf. Apparently as a precaution, Eboli's authority was shared with Genovese confidants Gerardo Catena and Michele "Mike" Miranda. The arrangement worked well for nearly a decade until February 14, 1969, when Vito Genovese died of heart failure. Three days later he was buried in the Saint John's Cemetery in Queens, New York. Nearby were the tombs of Lucky Luciano and Joseph Profaci. Three years later, on July 16, 1972, the collapse of the organization's leadership became complete when Tommy Eboli, then 61 years old, was shot to death in Brooklyn's Crown Heights. By then, his apparent successor, Jerry Catena, was already behind bars.

The Anastasia–Gambino "Family"

The second, and probably most well known, of the Italian crime groups to emerge from the Maranzano–Masseria dispute matured in its influence under the direction of Carlo Gambino. In its rise to power, the Gambino family was perhaps the bloodiest of the modern crime syndicates. Indeed, each of Gambino's predecessors lost his position of power by murder. In the end, this colorful yet violent succession managed to rivet the public through the popular media while gaining control of much of New York's organized crime.

The original family bosses, Alfred Mineo and Steve Ferrigno, were the first to be assassinated, on November 5, 1930. Waiting to kill Masseria himself, Maranzano gunmen Joseph Profaci, Nick Capuzzi, and "Buster" of Chicago (whose real identity was never determined) decided that their enemy was not going to show that evening as they were expecting. Instead, they agreed, they would settle for the murders of Mineo and Ferrigno—both allies of Masseria, though far less powerful.

With Mineo's death in particular, the organization languished until the alternating influences of both Masseria and Maranzano were eliminated. In the power vacuum that followed those deaths, Phillip and Vincent Mangano stepped forward, and leadership of the now disorganized gang was transferred to them, some believe as an appeasement to Luciano with whom they were apparently allied (Bonanno, 1983). Whatever their source of support, a general peace accompanied the Mangano brothers' watch until April 19, 1951, when Phillip too was murdered and Vincent, who is presumed dead, disappeared—almost certainly at the direction of Albert Anastasia. Anastasia and his friend Frank Scalise, a man of some influence for several decades, were next in line of succession.

Anastasia, born Umberto Anastasio in Tropea, Italy, is best known as the chief executioner for the infamous Murder, Inc. Coming to the United

States in 1919, Anastasia is reported to have changed his name in 1921 to save his family embarrassment from his arrest for murdering a fellow long-shoreman (Abadinsky, 1985). Surely it was the arrest that bothered him most, however, since although his activities included gambling, narcotics, and extortion, his specialty appears to have been murder. So much did he enjoy his work that he is known to have directed or personally conducted scores of assassinations—shooting, stabbing, or strangling his victims. Operating from Brooklyn, where he and his brother, "Tough Tony," virtually ruled the waterfront, Anastasia and his friend Frank Costello found themselves increasingly in conflict with Vito Genovese. Finally, in 1957, violence erupted once again. Only weeks after Genovese's unsuccessful attempt to assassinate Costello, Frank Scalise was killed by gunmen while in the Bronx. Six months later, on October 25, the "Executioner" himself was murdered by gunmen as he reclined in a barber chair in the Park Sheraton Hotel in Manhattan—the same hotel where Arnold Rothstein was killed almost 30 years earlier. Although several competing motives for the killing are possible, Carlo Gambino, with Vito Genovese's backing, profited most as he became boss of the family.

Gambino, from Palermo, Italy, entered the United States illegally around 1921. Once here, he followed his friend Gaetano Lucchese into organized crime while helping his brothers, Paolo and Giuseppe, follow in his footsteps. Although nominally allied with Masseria, Gambino appears not to have participated in any meaningful way in the Castellamarese War. After Masseria's death, Gambino and Lucchese joined the Maranzano camp. With Maranzano's murder, Gambino moved again, this time to follow Vincent Mangano as he assumed control of Alfred Mineo's organization. By the time Mangano disappeared, Gambino had risen in the organization and earned Anastasia's respect and trust. The family he took from Anastasia may have been the largest and most influential criminal organization in the country.

Gambino's business interests were varied. Valachi, for example, testified to the McClellan committee that "Gambino has been in every kind of business, butcher business, lottery, Italian lottery, shylocking" (Peterson, 1983:183). The New York City police apparently agreed, adding vending machines, gambling, labor racketeering, loan-sharking, and bootlegging to their own list. Additionally, he was suspected of involvement in narcotics trafficking and smuggling aliens. In all, Gambino's record included at least 16 arrests and 6 convictions with an additional indictment in 1970 for conspiracy to hijack an armored car that was never brought to trial because of his failing health. Finally, in addition to his criminal ventures, Gambino was thought to have owned or invested heavily in strategic legal businesses including meat markets, bakeries, nightclubs, linen supply companies, and restaurants—all profitable in their own right and useful for frauds and laundering income from other sources (Peterson, 1983). On October 15, 1975, Carlo Gambino became the first head of this organization to die of natural causes when he did so at his home on Long Island. A relative and his close adviser, Paul Castellano, promptly took his place. Castellano, in turn, returned to tradition a decade later as he and his bodyguard were assassinated, allegedly to make room for John Gotti.

The Profaci–Columbo "Family"

Although a part of the Italian organized crime to emerge from the Castellamarese War, Joseph Profaci's gang was in place prior to the events that shaped so many of the other crime leaders of that day. Perhaps the most legitimate of the era, Profaci has the distinction of never serving a prison sentence in the United States. In addition, he owned a variety of legitimate businesses, was this country's leading importer of olive oil and, in comparison with his associates, lived a modest life in Brooklyn with a second home in Miami Beach (Abadinsky, 1985). A religious person, faithful church goer, and devoted family man, Profaci was also an iron-fisted ruler involved heavily in gambling, bootlegging, narcotics, and murder.

It was Profaci's despotic rule and preferences for tradition, family, and friendships over business that eventually led many of the younger men in his organization to open rebellion. Resenting Profaci's decisions to retain the most lucrative opportunities for his friends and relatives while forcing sizable kickbacks from them, Nicholas Forlano, Carmine Persico, Jr., and the Gallo brothers—Lawrence, Albert, and Joseph—revolted in a bloody fight against the "Old Man." With casualties high, the Gallo–Profaci hostilities were in full swing when Profaci died (of natural causes) and Joseph Magliocco, Profaci's son-in-law, took the reins in 1962.

While he possessed a less powerful personality than Profaci, Magliocco nonetheless pressed on with the conflict. Still, he was an indecisive leader who came to rely on Joseph Bonanno, the head of still another Brooklyn crime family, as he had previously needed Profaci. Convinced, as Profaci had been, that Carlo Gambino and Gaetano Lucchese were, in fact, the inspiration behind the Gallos, Magliocco tried to move boldly by arranging through Bonanno to have both killed. To complete the job, he contracted with Joseph Colombo, Sr., who promptly leaked the scheme to the far more powerful Gambino. Surprisingly, neither he nor Lucchese retaliated. Instead, they forced the already troubled Magliocco from power and named Colombo as his successor. Although no evidence was found during the autopsies (two were conducted), many are convinced from taped phone conversations that Magliocco's fatal heart attack only a few months later was actually caused by poison from Bonanno to prevent him from revealing Bonanno's role in the assassination plot (Talese, 1971).

At age 40, by far the youngest of New York's crime bosses, Joseph Colombo's career in crime was largely unimpressive. A muscle and hitman initially, Colombo progressed to dice games on the waterfront, big time gambling in Brooklyn, loan-sharking in Manhattan, and finally hijacking from the Kennedy International Airport. In addition, he considered himself a real estate dealer (working for Cantalupo Realty) and was an investor in both a flower shop and a funeral home. Considering the struggle with the Gallos, he may have viewed both of these as useful investments.

As Colombo's power peaked, he found himself increasingly harassed by the FBI. With the arrest of his son Joseph, Jr., in 1970 for melting down silver coins, Colombo decided to go on the offensive against the government scrutiny by forming the Italian-American Civil Rights League. Generating considerable publicity, Colombo himself led daily pickets of the New York FBI office and appeared countless times for television interviews and talk shows. Reacting to his attacks on the establishment, his protests won considerable support nationally but especially among working-class Italians in the city. By July 1970, his efforts were having an impact, and Attorney General John Mitchell and New York Governor Nelson Rockefeller were forced to order their employees not to use the terms *Mafia* or *Cosa Nostra* in press releases. The next year, Hollywood responded as well as production for *The Godfather* and the television series "The FBI" were brought to a virtual standstill. *Godfather* producer Al Ruddy told the *Los Angeles Times*, "There were no overt threats but I couldn't get locations. So I called Joe Colombo and I told him I wanted to sit down and talk to him about it and he said, fine" (Short, 1984:320). To resume production, Ruddy agreed to remove all references in his script to either the "Mafia" or "La Cosa Nostra."

Fresh from their successes, Colombo's League called for a Unity Day rally to be held on July 28, 1971, in Columbus Circle. Colombo was the central figure as he mingled with a crowd numbering thousands. Later, as he stood at the podium preparing to speak, Jerome Johnson, a young black photographer, pushed his way through the crowd to fire three shots into Colombo's head and neck. Johnson, too, was then immediately shot and killed by an unknown gunman who disappeared into the crowd. Badly wounded, Colombo was rushed to Roosevelt Hospital where he lingered paralyzed and brain damaged in a semiconscious state for nearly seven years. He finally died on May 22, 1978.

Colombo had many enemies at the time of the shooting. Speculation had it that Johnson was sent by Joseph "Crazy Joe" Gallo to assassinate

Colombo and that Johnson was then killed to ensure that the plot was never revealed. The war between Gallo and Profaci had never ended, after all. Others suspected that Carlo Gambino had ordered the killing to silence Colombo, who had become obsessed with his publicity. He was also being punished, they reasoned, for refusing to share the large sums the league was generating through dues and testimonial dinners. Still others imagined that the FBI may have eliminated Colombo in revenge for the embarrassment he had brought them. Equally plausible, however, is that Johnson was just another crazed loner who had the misfortune of shooting a well-guarded man. Whatever the motive, following the shooting, Colombo's organization came under Gambino's dominance. Gambino's godson, Vinnie Aloi, was put in charge.

Ten months later, in the early morning of April 7, 1972, Joey Gallo, his new wife, her daughter, a bodyguard, and several of their friends were celebrating Gallo's 43rd birthday in Umberto's Clam House in Manhattan's Little Italy. Four gunmen entered the restaurant and emptied their guns into Gallo and the bodyguard. A fighter to the end, Gallo chased his assassins to the street where he collapsed and died.

The Bonanno "Family"

The remaining crime organization to emerge from the era evolved from the Maranzano gang. Headed by Joseph Bonanno, this family was actively involved in gambling, extortion, and racketeering in the "other part of Brooklyn"—the part not controlled by Joseph Profaci (U.S. Senate, 1963).

Bonanno was born in Castellammare del Golfo in 1905. According to his autobiography (Bonanno, 1983), his father, Savatore, was a close friend of Maranzano and was himself involved in Sicilian organized crime. To avoid unspecified criminal charges there, his family left Sicily for the United States in 1908 only to return to the island three years later. Once home, Bonanno's father soon died of a heart attack. In 1924, a 19-year-old Bonanno returned to New York, entering the country illegally through Cuba.

By the 1930s, Bonanno was a man of some wealth. Already part owner of an undertaking business, he became vice president of the Brunswick Laundry in 1934 and part owner of the Morgan Coke Company in 1937. His investment partnership was ended mysteriously, however, when his associate, Philip Rapper, was found dead in a Brooklyn gutter. By 1940, Bonanno's business involvements included the B+D Coke Company and the Hilltop Hotel in Fort Lee, New Jersey. Still an illegal immigrant, according to Talese (1971), Bonanno then left the country only to reenter legally from Canada at Detroit. In 1945, he took advantage of his reentry and was naturalized to become a citizen. By then already a multimillionaire, Bonanno continued to invest heavily in legitimate businesses with money made by his criminal organization.

With the exception of his involvement in the so-called Apalachin meeting of crime bosses, for several decades Bonanno's tenure was uneventful. By 1963, however, internal pressures were building as some members of the organization were becoming increasingly disenchanted with Bonanno's leadership and resentful of his efforts to advance his son Bill at their expense. Externally, he was experiencing opposition as well as the plot against Gambino and Lucchese came to light. Finally, during the fall of 1964, much of the family's leadership was forced into hiding out of fear, both of rival gangs no longer willing to support Bonanno as well as from an internal faction, led by Gaspar DeGregorio, trying to seize control. With little room to maneuver, on October 21, 1964, only hours before he was to appear before a grand jury, it was reported that Joseph Bonanno had been kidnapped at gunpoint in front of an apartment house on New York's Park Avenue. He and his attorney had sought shelter there from the rain. Several weeks later, Simone DeCavalcante, an important colleague of Bonanno's, was overheard saying, "He [Bonanno] pulled that off himself . . . who the hell is he kidding?" (Peterson, 1983:411). Bonanno would remain in hiding for nearly 19 months while his organization battled with itself.

With Bonanno absent and DeGregorio marginally in control, the deterioration of the crime family accelerated. Recognizing the hopelessness, many members simply deserted to other gangs, taking with them not only important contacts but what little legitimacy as a crime power the organization still retained. When Bill Bonanno and other family members still loyal to his father attempted to meet with DeGregorio in January 1966, the meeting to reestablish unity turned into a major gun battle with leaders on both sides narrowly escaping. At last, out of concern that all-out war was near, Carlo Gambino stepped in to make peace. At Gambino's urging, DeGregorio agreed to retire, and Paul Sciacca, a Gambino ally, was installed as the new boss of the family. Just when all appeared to be settled, Joseph Bonanno suddenly reappeared in May.

Claiming that he had been kidnapped by two cousins and held for six weeks in a rural farmhouse, Bonanno reported to federal authorities that he had remained in hiding in Tucson for the remainder of his absence for safety. The government was not convinced, however, believing instead that the whole event had been a hoax to avoid the grand jury's investigation. Nonetheless, after posting a $150,000 bond, Bonanno was released to attempt to regain his authority over his own organization. Unfortunately for Bonanno, he had returned too late. After meeting stiff resistance, he gave up the struggle and again retired to Tucson, Arizona. In 1979, a federal grand jury finally indicted Bonanno for obstruction of justice. Found guilty, he was sentenced in 1983 to a year in the federal prison at Terminal Island.

CONCLUSIONS FROM NEW YORK

Browning and Gerassi (1980) note that two distinct traditions existed in the development of New York's organized crime. First are the Jewish gangsters. With roots traced from Rothstein, Buchalter, and Schultz, these gangsters began with bootlegging but diversified quickly into labor racketeering and manufacturing. All the while, they invested their money in gambling resorts, both legal and illegal. As such, their absorption into the American economy has been subtle but significant.

Equally important are the Italian gangsters. Also rooted in Prohibition bootlegging, these gangsters have remained much more closely tied to their neighborhoods, to the industries (trucking and dock work) where their people traditionally worked, and to the corrupt political machines of their city. While they, too, became financially sophisticated, their focus was directed more inward, causing them to follow much the same path as the Irish before them. As such, during the same few decades, the Italian crime organizations fought for control of vice, the political structures around them, and for consolidation of power rather than diversification. We believe that in the long run, this left them considerably more vulnerable.

In the chapters that follow, we will examine the history and development of organized crime in Chicago and elsewhere.

5

Organized Crime as an Evolving Enterprise:

Crime in Chicago

U nlike New York with its urban ways, dense immigrant concentrations, and reliance on Wall Street economics, by the middle of the 19th century Chicago was a truly American city. Built on the muddy bogs and swamps of Lake Michigan and the Chicago River, the city was central to the country's expanding economic engine. As the transportation hub of the nation, Chicago's packinghouses fed the country's population explosion while its rail lines linked outlying regions to supplies and, increasingly, to manufactured goods. Ironically, with its name derived from the native Indian terms *Chickagou* or *Chegagou*—both references to a bad smell—Chicago would also become known for its corrupt political arrangements and dominance by gangsters.

The city itself actually began as two separate settlements, one at the junction of the north and south branches of the Chicago River (known then as the Forks or Wolf Point), and the second four miles south at a place called Hardscrabble. By 1803, Fort Dearborn was added near the Forks, and within a year, John Kinzie, a silversmith, Indian trader, and the real founder of Chicago, had turned the outpost into perhaps the most important trading post in what was then the northwest (Asbury, 1940). For almost two decades, however, conflict with Indians native to the region slowed the expansion begun by these settlers from the east. It was not until 1827, when Congress authorized construction of a canal to link Lake Michigan and the Mississippi River—a canal that was to begin with construction of a suitable harbor at the mouth of the Chicago River—that the plans and surveying for the town were begun.

Initially proposed by President James Madison in 1814, the canal project was largely ignored for years as visionary and unworkable. Still, for 13 years, Nathaniel Pope and Daniel P. Cook (for whom Cook County is named) kept the proposal alive in Congress. Even after its approval, however, the project remained steeped in controversy as Stephen A. Douglas and Jefferson Davis (then a young army officer) debated where the canal should originate. Douglas, it seems, was insistent that the harbor be constructed at the Calumet River while Davis, the future President of the Confederacy, argued for the Chicago River. By the spring of 1834, Davis had won out and two 500-foot piers were built to create a new channel for the river. On July 11, 1834, when the schooner *Illinois* sailed into the new harbor, Chicago's future as the port and way station west was secure. By then, the city's population numbered no more than 150, and lots 80 by 100 feet sold for $40 to $70 each.

Early Chicago was characterized by historian and geologist William H. Keating, a member of the city's original exploring expedition, as "low, filthy and disgusting, displaying not the least trace of comfort" (Asbury, 1940:7). Charles Butler, a New York lawyer visiting the region in the 1830s, declared that the 100 or so buildings in place were "of the cheapest and most primitive character for human habitation." The city's two hotels (the Green Tree and the Sauganash) and several taverns were described by others as "dirty in the extreme," while one English visitor wrote of the city that "all was in a state of most appalling confusion, filth and racket" (Asbury, 1940:7–13). Indeed, most of Chicago's structures were constructed simply with logs and sheathboard. Few sidewalks and no paving coupled with heavy traffic and frequent rains meant that travel throughout the city, difficult at best, would often become all but impossible. Wagons, stagecoaches, and even horses and pedestrians became mired in mud, where they often remained at length. It was not until 1849 that planking was first laid on selected downtown streets and experiments in street grading were attempted. As most of the early efforts failed, the city council agreed to a herculean public works project to. raise the grade of each city street by at least 12 feet. Started in the 1850s, "the town was a giant jack-in-the-box" (Asbury, 1940:15) for the next ten years as virtually every building in the city was lifted into the air so that the ground beneath it could be filled. Long before work was complete, however, the nation's land rush was under way and Chicago, now ideally located, became the market where speculation and transactions most often took place. Convenient for the immigrants passing through, by 1837 the city had incorporated, extended its limits to almost ten square miles, and grown in population to 4,170. Less than two decades later, Chicago housed 11 railroad trunk lines, 17 branch lines, almost 1,500 businesses, a dozen banks of issue, 60 hotels, 40 newspapers and periodicals, and had become the country's second largest meat-packing center and the world's busiest grain port (Asbury, 1940). With new factories in operation, hundreds of buildings under construction, and a population explosion to 80,000, Chicago, wrote Lloyd Lewis, had become Chicago (Lewis & Smith, 1929).

THE CHARACTER OF THE CITY

Predictably, with such rapid expansion and so dynamic an environment, Chicago was a city of both opportunity and chance—with a considerable dose of disorder. As the fever of speculation took hold, land of all sorts throughout the northwest was sold and resold at an astonishing pace. Buying within the city was even more frenzied as lots on Lake Street near State, overpriced at $300 in 1834, became a bargain at $60,000 in 1836. While fast profits made Chicago a boom town, the necessary risks, along with the willingness to take them, all but guaranteed that gamblers, panderers, thieves, and political parasites would also rush to take advantage of the resulting confusion and instability. And as Peterson (1952) explains, no group thrived more in Chicago than the professional gamblers:

> Gambling was everywhere. Men wagered on horse races, dice, cards, and land. This was a period of insane land speculation, and the general gambling spirit which it generated brought overflowing crowds to Chicago's numerous gambling dens. Fast profits, greatly augmented by expert swindling, attracted blacklegs from other parts of the country. When public uprisings drove the gamblers from Natchez, Vicksburg and other Mississippi River towns, many of them drifted to Chicago. By 1840 only New Orleans and some of the large eastern cities could count more gambling places than Chicago. (p. 6)

Obviously, many of the city's most able businessmen caught the gambling fever. Still, except for periodic downturns, Chicago's future seemed bright and secure. As more and more residents streamed into the city, most found a diversity of jobs readily available. Few cultural outlets existed for recreation (and those that were available attracted little interest), so the gaming tables and saloons became mainstays in what was at once a rough and tough frontier town and bustling metropolis. As gambling profits were boosted by cheating and fraud, many prominent gamblers became fixtures in the social and economic fabrics of the city. As such, George C. Rhodes, "King Cole" Conant, Walt Winchester, and George "One-Lung" Smith maintained close friendships in both the saloons and the private clubs where everyone from laborers, businessmen, professionals, and even judges played high-stakes games of chance. Throughout the 1850s, visiting farm boys, traveling salesmen, and businessmen spread tales of the wild women, countless saloons, and gambling dens they had seen (and used) while in the city. Chicago was well on its way to its well-earned reputation for wickedness. It was not until 1853 that the city's expansion slowed sufficiently for its business and social institutions to begin the process of catching up.

For the first time in Chicago, in August of 1853, laborers staged a two-week strike, stopping most work in protest of worsening working conditions. Although little was accomplished, widespread dissatisfaction was at last becoming apparent. Health and sanitation conditions were deplorable. Smallpox and cholera epidemics occurred regularly, with thousands being stricken and hundreds dying at each interval. Sewage systems, water purification, and hospital construction simply failed to keep pace as railroads and other public works projects arousing greater interest took priority. Finally, as news of the discovery of California gold reached the east, Chicago's workmen and manufacturers were unable to meet the demand for wagons, guns, and provisions, leaving supplies exhausted and driving prices out of reach of all but the most wealthy. When the nation's economy finally slid into the depression of 1857, Chicago was already demoralized and quickly showed the strain. Before the panic ran its course, a total of 117 business firms (including four banks and two major produce firms) failed, taking with them much of the optimism that had become the city's character. Construction throughout the city was halted, and thousands of men were thrown out of work, many having little choice but to roam the streets idle and penniless to loot and search for petty crime. "The city," declared the *Chicago Tribune*, was "at the mercy of the criminal classes" (Peterson, 1952: 25). With the public frightened and law enforcement preoccupied and overwhelmed with other crimes, the gamblers were first in line for recovery.

THE "CHICAGO SYSTEM" OF POLITICS

Among the new settlers in Chicago were immigrants who had only recently come to the United States. As we saw earlier in New York City, foreigners of similar nationality tended to group together in sections of the city where clannishness would preserve their culture and customs. This, along with the help needed to obtain support, jobs, and even naturalization, made them especially vulnerable to manipulation by politicians. In Chicago, this was accomplished easily by the two aldermen elected from each of the city's 36 political districts or wards.

Able to produce votes in neighborhood blocks on demand, Chicago's ward aldermen were (and still are) the basic power brokers needed by the mayor and other city-wide officials. In exchange for their reliable support, the aldermen were granted a virtual lock on the distribution of city contracts, patronage, and public jobs (including the police) within their wards. As a result, as long as their arrangements held, the officials at both levels were assured of continued power and opportunity. To support the system, the saloons and gambling halls throughout the city, the only real gathering points for recreation, served as sites where political alliances and deals could be constructed. In fact, many, if not most, of the city's most prominent aldermen began as barkeepers and gamblers, just as most powerful backroom political bosses were gamblers who now found themselves in charge of local police through payoffs and neighborhood gangs who would assist them on election day (Browning & Gerassi, 1980). For almost four decades starting in 1870, no one mastered this system better than "Big Mike" McDonald.

Destruction, Violence, and the Birth of Machine Politics

In only four decades since its beginning, Chicago evolved from a wilderness settlement into a truly impressive metropolis, the largest and most prominent in the west. An economic powerhouse, the city's physical structure—hotels, residences, railroad terminals, and the rest—was now as impressive as any in the east. So busy had the city's business center become that 27 bridges over the river handled the traffic that streamed daily into the city's core. Despite its growing crime, health, and social problems, as 1871 began to close, Chicago's future appeared nearly unlimited. Much of the optimism would be dashed, however, when on October 8 a small fire broke out in Patrick O'Leary's barn.

Ordinarily, the O'Leary fire would not have been a serious matter. But the city had received only an inch of rain since June, and by October the entire region was as dry as tinder. Within two hours the fire covered over 100 acres, pushed from building to building by a strong wind. In another two hours, it crossed the river, where it raced through what the *Tribune* had described as a city of "pine, shingles, shams, veneers, stucco, and putty." As the flames destroyed the city's business district, Chicago's 200 firemen and 17 fire engines could offer little more than token resistance; indeed, much of the fire equipment was caught early by the fire and destroyed. By three the next morning, the flames crossed the river's main section to the north side where they raced "through that section of seventy-five thousand people as fast as a man could run" (Asbury, 1940:82). Early victims of the fire included the waterworks and pumping station used by firefighters as well as the new Chicago Historical Society where Lincoln's original draft of the Emancipation Proclamation was stored along with other priceless documents (Asbury, 1940). During the morning of the third day, rain began to fall, and the fire was finally extinguished. In its path, at least 300 citizens, 2,024 acres, and 18,000 buildings—including the homes of 100,000—had been destroyed. Among the casualties was the city's jail, requiring the release of the entire population of inmates on an already badly crippled community.

Almost at once, swarms of thieves, robbers, and hoodlums began to loot and riot. They roamed singly and in packs among what little had escaped the fire—snatching from carts, breaking into saloons and stores, and robbing homes. Alexander Frear, a politician visiting from the east, vividly described Chicago's looting for the New York *World*:

> Here, for the first time, I beheld scenes of violence that made my blood boil. . . . I went through the street to Wabash Avenue, and here the thoroughfare was choked with all manner of goods and people. . . . Valuable oil-paintings, books, pet animals, musical instruments, toys, mirrors, and bedding were trampled under foot. Added to this, the goods from the stores had been hauled out and had taken fire; and the crowd, breaking into a liquor establishment, were yelling with the fury of demons, as they brandished champagne and brandy bottles. The brutality and horror of the scene made it sickening. A fellow, standing on a piano, declared that the fire was the friend of the poor man. (Asbury, 1940:85–86)

Reeling from the fire, Chicago's authorities were powerless. Hoodlums from nearby locales moved in to take advantage of the chaos, and martial law was declared. Two thousand special police were appointed, while General P. H. Sheridan responded with six companies of the Illinois militia and four companies of regular army troops. After a week of mayhem and battle, order was at last restored. Evidence of renewed life returned as businesses resumed in temporary structures. The realization quickly set in that the entire city would have to be rebuilt—government offices, schools, police stations, bridges, and even the fire department itself had all been destroyed.

Responding to the opportunity, by year's end carpenters, mechanics, bricklayers, and day laborers rushed to Chicago at a rate of nearly 5,000 a week to take part in construction of more than 10,000 buildings. Fearful of the reckless expansion they had known before, leading citizens and clergy formed the Committee of Seventy to battle crime and disorder and the Committee of Twenty-Five to improve the moral fabric of the city. With work plentiful and wages high, however, probably no segment of Chicago was being rebuilt more quickly than the saloons, brothels, and gambling houses. A battle for the soul of the city was under way. As the citizens' groups pressed their campaign, saloonkeepers and gamblers united for political action of their own. A mass meeting was held, a platform adopted, and by the close of voting on November 4, this coalition had won out by managing the election to mayor of Harvey D. Colvin. Having demonstrated their political power, the gamblers and dive operators were now free to reap the rewards of their victory. No one was better positioned for those rewards than Michael McDonald, the king of Chicago's gamblers and the new mayor's staunchest supporter. Crime in Chicago was, at last, becoming organized in a big way (Peterson, 1952). Figure 5.1 shows the succession of crime bosses in Chicago as organized crime fought for political and economic control of the city.

Michael Cassius McDonald

Much like Boss Tweed in New York, "Big Mike" McDonald ran boss politics in Chicago as if it were an art form. Although he never held office himself, with the election of Mayor Colvin, McDonald managed an effective system of public administration for the next 30 years that was at once powerful, profitable, and able to withstand the city's constant forces for reform. Once a candy vendor, swindler, and petty gambler on trains servicing Chicago, McDonald's real influence and fortune began in 1872 when he and a partner opened a gaming house on State Street. With the profits from the gaming house and those from a West Side saloon he had acquired an interest in, McDonald turned his interests to politics. It was McDonald who organized and financed the People's Party to back his friend Harvey Colvin. Once Colvin was elected, "Big Mike" expanded, opening a resort at Clark and Monroe Streets. Called the Store, this four-story location housed a saloon on the first floor, by far Chicago's largest gaming place on the second, and a boarding house on the third and fourth floors. With every form of gambling known, the Store soon became the sporting center of the city and the favorite gathering place for city officials, politicians, and assorted business and crime leaders. An able substitute for City Hall, from his office on the second floor Michael McDonald ran the city. Although he suffered a brief setback in 1876 when Colvin was defeated for reelection, McDonald was once again firmly in control after his political organization installed

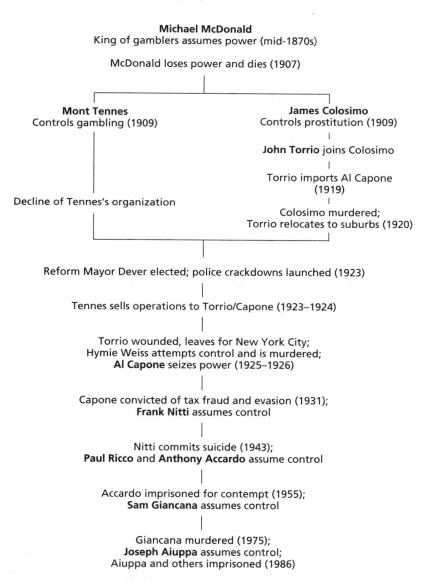

The "Chicago System" of Politics

Michael McDonald
King of gamblers assumes power (mid-1870s)

McDonald loses power and dies (1907)

Mont Tennes
Controls gambling (1909)

James Colosimo
Controls prostitution (1909)

John Torrio joins Colosimo

Torrio imports Al Capone
(1919)

Decline of Tennes's organization

Colosimo murdered;
Torrio relocates to suburbs (1920)

Reform Mayor Dever elected; police crackdowns launched (1923)

Tennes sells operations to Torrio/Capone (1923–1924)

Torrio wounded, leaves for New York City;
Hymie Weiss attempts control and is murdered;
Al Capone seizes power (1925–1926)

Capone convicted of tax fraud and evasion (1931);
Frank Nitti assumes control

Nitti commits suicide (1943);
Paul Ricco and **Anthony Accardo** assume control

Accardo imprisoned for contempt (1955);
Sam Giancana assumes control

Giancana murdered (1975);
Joseph Aiuppa assumes control;
Aiuppa and others imprisoned (1986)

FIGURE 5.1 Organized Crime in Chicago

Carter Harrison as mayor in 1879. McDonald's grip on the city remained firm until his death in 1907.

Off limits to police intent on law enforcement, McDonald periodically submitted to police raids for appearances. Few officers doubted his influence, however, since those who did succumb to a sense of duty without first obtaining his permission were quickly disciplined and usually kicked off the force. When Carter Harrison's first police superintendent, Simon O'Donnell, responded in 1880 to frequent complaints of robberies at the Store, he was immediately demoted to captain and replaced by a detective handpicked by McDonald.

Even after Mayor Harrison was finally defeated by law and order candidate John A. Roche in the 1887 election, McDonald's reign remained intact. As Roche ordered repeated raids on gamblers and confidence men, McDonald simply shifted his focus, turning over daily operation of his more visible enterprises to others. With time on his hands and the fortune he had amassed, he bought the Chicago *Globe,* which he used as a vehicle for even greater prominence. He became treasurer of the Lake Street Elevated Railroad, which he readily bilked, of course, and acquired a quarry from which he sold stone and gravel to the city and county at inflated prices. Less noticeably, McDonald also formed a bookmaking syndicate, gaining control of betting at racetracks throughout Chicago and Indiana (Browning & Gerassi, 1980). By 1893, with help from McDonald, Carter Harrison regained the mayor's office for the fifth time and both set about preparing for the World's Fair and the crowds it would draw.

During his final election campaign, Mayor Harrison had promised to give the World's Fair crowds a wide-open town—a promise he more than kept. Prior to his assassination by a disgruntled city employee, Chicago may have become the most wide-open city in the country with graft and corruption reaching into every department of city government. As the fair approached, McDonald's men worked diligently with police, judges, and city clerks so that crime around the event could be carefully systematized. Pickpockets, hustlers, and con-men were assigned regular corners where they worked as if at the office. For those caught by their victims, beat cops were bribed, fixers chosen, and jury panels rigged. Browning and Gerassi (1980) report one pickpocket's claim: "The arrangement with the police was a regular take weekly of $250. . . . The returns were good. It was a poor week without $1,500 for my end. In the summertime a Sunday alone would net us $500" (p. 304).

Nor were they the only ones who benefited. Kickbacks were common, and tax assessments were openly reduced for those with influence or bribes. During 1887, all of Carter Harrison's holdings were assessed at only $300; his successor, John P. Hopkins, was assessed at $150. The collective property of all 68 aldermen was valued at $1,700, while William Pinkerton, the powerful detective agency owner who protected railroads, banks, mines, and mills, was declared worth only $400 (Browning & Gerassi, 1980). For a brief period after Harrison's death, McDonald's system continued undisturbed, although who wound up with the former mayor's share was never determined.

Gradually, however, a combination of the reformers, a redistribution of the city's immigrant population, and the industrialization of business and crime began to exert their pull. An aging Michael McDonald found his Chicago growing increasingly difficult to control. Still, only his own personal problems would bring about his end.

THE BIRTH OF THE CRIME BOSSES

While McDonald was gaining control of Chicago's politics, gambling, and crime, his marriage to Mary Noonan was slowly beginning to fail. The cause of their problems is unknown, but matters first became public after Noonan ran off with a minstrel singer. Finding her in San Francisco, McDonald brought her back to Chicago. A short time later in 1889 she deserted him again, this time with a Belgian priest—and for good. Nine years later, McDonald, now in his 60s, met 30-year-old Dora Feldman whom he promptly decided to marry. Of course, first he had to finance her divorce from her husband, a professional baseball star. Unfortunately for McDonald, in less than a year his new wife also became close friends with and then the lover of Webster Guerin, a young boy of 16.

The relationship between Guerin and the new Mrs. McDonald continued, apparently undisturbed, until February 21, 1907, when the tenants of the Omaha Building on Van Buren Street heard a gunshot and crashing glass. As they entered room 703, they found Guerin dead from a single gunshot wound. Standing over him with a small pearl-handled revolver was Dora McDonald.

Stunned by the news, McDonald first tried to stop his wife's indictment. Failing that, he hired an experienced attorney for her defense and made known his intention to stand by his wife throughout the ordeal. Before the trial could begin, however, McDonald suffered a complete nervous breakdown and, on August 9, 1907, "Big Mike" McDonald died. Ironically, only five months later, his widow was brought to trial and acquitted of all charges, leaving her free to enjoy the vast wealth that McDonald had accumulated over his years of power and influence.

The day before his death, the *Chicago News* reacted to the end of McDonald's reign:

> Mike McDonald is dying. When the city had a scant half million this man ruled it from his saloon and gambling house by virtue of his political power. . . . Bad government was accepted as a matter of course. Vice sat in the seats of power and patronized virtue with a large and kindly tolerance, asking only that it remain sufficiently humble and not too obtrusive. Gambling was a leading industry. Clark Street was thronged night and day with men going in and out of the wide open gambling resorts. The wretched conditions then prevailing were excused on the theory that vice "made the town lively." Gambling was necessary, it was said, to attract strangers. As for the "king of gamblers" he was a "good fellow." He "always stood by his friends." Boodle aldermen lorded it in the city council. Boodle county commissioners stole everything they could lay their hands on . . . contracts for public works that had thievery written between the lines were let and carried out to the large profit of the conspirators. (Peterson, 1952:86)

With McDonald gone, this editorial and others called for an "awakening of the citizens." Through the combined efforts of independent voters, alert civic organizations, the state's attorney, and the press, it was hoped that good morals and good government could, at last, accompany the city into the future. But even as the editorial writers were writing, bomb-throwing gamblers had begun their campaign for power. Out of the confusion that followed, James "Big Jim" Colosimo and Mont Tennes were the first to emerge as real 20th century Chicago crime bosses.

Mont Tennes

Even before McDonald's death, a gradual transformation in Chicago's gambling was already under way. Where cards, roulette, and faro had been king, many operators were coming to realize that horse races, sports, and other events could be far more inclusive for bettors of all types. No longer was skill at an individual game required; even small-time gamblers could bet on a variety of events at once. Operating out of establishments called "handbooks," McDonald's proteges, with the consent of city officials and the police, were quietly (though probably unknowingly) laying the foundation for the expansion of syndicate crime throughout the nation. In the stockyards district on the South Side, "Big Jim" O'Leary, son of the O'Learys of the great fire, had already formed a string of handbooks with Big Mike's support. On the North Side, Mont Tennes, a saloon owner and part-time dealer in real estate, had begun his rise as well.

Determined to control handbook gambling completely, Tennes was both foresighted and forceful. Realizing that a successful handbook depended on prompt returns on races and games played elsewhere, Tennes understood the potentials offered by John Payne's recently established telegraph service in Cincinnati. Tennes reasoned quite correctly that to control this information service in Chicago was to control gambling in the city. With that in mind, he contracted with the Payne News Agency for sole access; in exchange for $300 a day, no one in Chicago could obtain returns by telephone or telegraph without consent from Tennes. Since the other handbooks had little hope of competing without access to information, the poolroom keepers and bookmakers of the city had no choice but to join the Tennes syndicate to avoid being forced out of business. For only 50 percent of their net daily receipts and a flat monthly fee of from $100 to $200, each operator could receive the wire and be assured of Tennes's growing political protection. While several of the South Side operators tried to strike back with a brief flurry of bombings, by the spring of 1909, O'Leary and the others were forced to concede, leaving Tennes the virtual dictator of the city's racetrack gambling. Two years later, his influence with the police—unparalleled since Michael McDonald—enabled him to extend his reach to dominate the roulette, card, and dice games throughout the city (Asbury, 1940). Tennes had become the absolute master of gambling in Chicago, but he was hardly satisfied.

Pushing outward from Chicago, Tennes formed his own wire service in 1910, the General News Bureau, to compete with Payne. While Payne's complaints of unfair competition were prompting investigations by the Interstate Commerce Commission and the attorneys general of at least three states, Tennes's organization nonetheless began selling racing results throughout the country. As the competition grew bitter, dynamite and arson overcame resistance. Gradually, the Payne system and several others attempting to enter the business collapsed. With no competition remaining and customers in 21 cities from New York to San Francisco, there was little to stop Mont Tennes. With profits reportedly exceeding half a million dollars a day now pouring in from all over the country, Tennes's monopoly on syndicate gambling was nearly complete.

James "Big Jim" Colosimo

While Tennes was consolidating his control over gambling, the city's trade in prostitutes was prospering as well. Largely disorganized and dangerous before 1900, the arrival in Chicago of Minna and Ana Lester pumped life into the industry, added color to the city, and set a string of events in motion that had both far-reaching and long-lasting effects.

Moving from Omaha where they had learned the brothel trade, the Lester sisters took the name Everleigh and opened a spectacular 50-room house on South Dearborn Street. Fitted with a gold-leaf piano, electric fans, oriental rugs, and silk and brocade, patrons paid $10 to enter, $50 for dinner, and considerably more for a soundproof parlor complete with the most professional of the city's highest class prostitutes. Despite the considerable expense, the Everleigh Club had no shortage of clients; by 1911 it was world renowned as the "most splendid whore house on Earth." So famous was it, in fact, that while attending a banquet in another city, Carter Harrison, Jr.—son of the earlier Mayor Harrison and now himself a fifth-term mayor of Chicago—was embarrassed to find a brochure for the club being passed among the guests. Back in town, he ordered the police to close the club, offering his decision as a gesture of his support for the reform movement then under way. Informed of the police plans, the sisters threw a gala farewell, carefully draped the furniture and fixtures with dustcovers, and submitted to the formal raid and closing of their club. Before leaving for a six-month European excursion, however, they were assured by "Hinky Dink" Kenna and "Bathhouse John" Coughlin, both First Ward aldermen, that all would be sorted out by their return so that business could be as usual.

Once they returned to Chicago, however, the Everleigh sisters concluded that conditions were no longer right and decided to close down for good. Feeling that 12 years of payoffs for protection had been a waste, they also revealed that they had given Kenna and Coughlin over $100,000 to avoid raids, get charges against their girls dropped, ensure that their competitors were harassed by police, and block new laws against vice, especially prostitution. In addition, they reported years of bribes to detectives. In all, the sisters estimated that the vice district in the First Ward, widely known as the Levee, had paid Coughlin, Kenna, and their police agents more than $15 million in graft (Short, 1984).

Damaged, but not beaten, Coughlin and Kenna struck back. When Harrison ran for reelection in 1915, the aldermen switched their still considerable support to William Thompson. A Republican and former football player who had little political experience and perhaps even less skill, Thompson campaigned with appeals to patriotism and promises of a wide-open town and flourishing Levee. Finding the platform hard to resist, important Harrison supporters soon abandoned his campaign, and Thompson was left with a sizable majority. While the city's vice was now once again safe, the political damage to Kenna and Coughlin had been considerable. James Colosimo was ready to step forward and take their place.

Only 10 years old when his father brought him to Chicago from Italy, Colosimo began his career in the Levee as a newsboy and bootblack. By 18, he was an accomplished pickpocket and small-time pimp, and by 20 he had added extortion to his repertoire of skills. It was his talent at delivering votes through his influence with the streetcleaners union, however, that brought "Big Jim" to the attention of Hinky Dink Kenna, who would elevate the small-time gangster to precinct captain of the First Ward as reward for his efforts and loyalty. As a power in the First Ward Democratic machine, Colosimo was now all but immune from arrest.

Most likely recognizing an opportunity for business, Colosimo met and married Victoria Moresco in 1908 and took control of her successful brothel almost at once. With steady profits now assured, Colosimo prospered and expanded, adding a chain of whorehouses, numerous restaurants, saloons, and resorts, and the famous Colosimo Cafe on Wabash Avenue that would become the center of Chicago's nightlife for years to come. A wealthy man and the acknowledged king of prostitution on the South Side by 1915, his influence with Italian voters was the real base for Colosimo's power.

With the advent of Prohibition, Colosimo was ideally set to expand his enterprises once again. While many First Ward gangsters found the increased enforcement that accompanied the liquor crusade too much to bear, Colosimo soon had his followers brewing alcohol in their tenement homes. Protected by his influence and armed with a pool of talented young hoodlums to employ as distributors, Colosimo found the profits of bootlegging perfect for his still growing empire. Nor were other risks of much concern either, since years before he had had the foresight to bring Johnny Torrio into his business. A cousin of Victoria Moresco's whose skills were honed with New York's Five Points gang, Torrio had proven himself valuable in response to earlier extortion threats "Big Jim" had received from his competitors. Although physically small and reserved, Torrio soon wiped out the competition, thereby facilitating, if not masterminding, Colosimo's rise (Short, 1984). Despite the potential, as they expanded into alcohol—and more cautiously, into Mont Tennes's world of gambling—"Big Jim" had other things on his mind. His focus was on one of the few respectable women he had ever known.

Reportedly both beautiful and talented, Dale Winter had been stranded in Chicago after her unsuccessful musical-comedy closed. With few other options available, she settled in as a singer in the Colosimo Cafe, where she soon met and fell in love with "Big Jim." Enamored of her as well,

Colosimo divorced his wife Victoria in March 1920 and married Winter only three weeks later.

While Colosimo was becoming a happy, if distracted, man, Johnny Torrio was growing restless. Having learned the city's politics, gained skills at organization and intrigue, and developed the loyalty of a host of skilled gunmen, Torrio had come to dream of a monopoly over vice and crime throughout Chicago and perhaps the nation as well. Colosimo, however, was content and increasingly rejected Torrio's ideas and plans. With bad blood growing between the two, Torrio apparently decided that his future would not include his mentor.

On May 11, 1920, less than a week after his honeymoon, Colosimo left his mansion for work as usual. Torrio had arranged for Jim O'Leary to deliver two truckloads of whiskey to the cafe, and Colosimo had gone to inspect the shipment. After visiting with others in the rear of the restaurant, Colosimo commented on the late arrival of his visitors and went forward to check the lobby. Moments later he was found dead, shot once in the back of the head. Although no one was charged for the murder, most assumed that Frankie Yale, one of Torrio's New York assassins, had completed the job on Torrio's behalf. With "three judges, eight aldermen, an assistant state's attorney, a congressman, a state representative, and leading artists from the Chicago Opera Company" serving as his pallbearers along with gamblers, saloon-keepers, and Hinky Dink Kenna, "Big Jim" Colosimo was no longer in Torrio's way (Browning & Gerassi, 1980:326).

Consolidating Control: Torrio versus Tennes

Following Colosimo's funeral, a gaudy extravaganza, Johnny Torrio wasted little time mourning before assuming full command. Earlier, and with only cursory approval from Colosimo, he had relocated much of the organization's business to Burnham, a small suburban community south of the city. Alert to the growing ownership of automobiles, Torrio had realized that dispersed businesses would be more immune to Chicago's periodic reforms. For its part, Burnham was ideal. It was small enough to avoid media and reform attention, yet close enough for his customers to drive out in their new cars, gamble in the casino, visit the brothel upstairs, and still arrive home in time for dinner with their families. In addition, the town officials in the suburbs were almost all part-time or volunteers. While official control over their much smaller jurisdictions was all but complete and could guarantee a secure base for operations, their price in graft was far lower than that now common in the city (Browning & Gerassi, 1980). Now in charge himself, Torrio's decision to relocate was finally about to pay off in a big way. While his competitors had begun to suffer the weight of repeated raids and escalating payoffs, the empire Torrio built and then inherited was secure. He expanded quickly into Chicago Heights, Stickney, Forest View, Blue Island, Cicero, and a dozen other towns to the south and west of Chicago until he had constructed a network along the city's southern arc. Almost at will, Torrio could safely penetrate the city. He had laid a foundation for the future.

Gradually, Mont Tennes too came to understand. While Torrio was out of reach, the raids against Tennes's enterprises were so numerous that the *Daily News* declared that he had been forced to surrender a large interest in his operations to politicians. Worse yet, the limits of his influence were fully revealed the following year when the Italian candidate he supported lost a bitter and violent fight for election in the 19th Ward. Months later, candidate Anthony D'Andrea, a defrocked priest and convicted counterfeiter, was killed by a shotgun blast to the chest. In contrast, the First Ward's aldermen, Kenna and Coughlin, stayed in office with Torrio's support, and Torrio was by then the primary contributor to Mayor Thompson's successful campaigns. Able to keep police pressure on Tennes, Torrio's influence enabled him to gradually assert control over most of the bookies using the Tennes wire service. Finally, by early 1924, Tennes had had enough and announced that he was selling his poolrooms, handbooks, and even the General News Bureau and retiring. The new owners of the wire service were Jack Lynch, one of the mayor's earliest supporters, and Moe Annenberg, a successful New York publisher. Annenberg's son, Walter, would go on to build upon his father's business, eventually adding *T. V. Guide, Seventeen,* and *The Daily Racing Forum* to the family collection (Browning & Gerassi, 1980).

Although he began as an enforcer, Torrio's real skills were planning and low-key diplomacy, which he used effectively to assemble blocks of power and influence. Having learned well from Paul Kelly in New York, he carried himself neatly and conservatively in contrast to Colosimo and the others of the day. A careful businessman, Torrio sought out cooperative agreements with hot-headed counterparts such as Dion O'Bannion and the Genna brothers while carefully delegating responsibilities to his own men. Gun play, for example, he left to his new protege, a young New York gangster also from the Five Points—Alphonse Capone.

Already a suspect in two New York murders, Capone was only 23 years old when he came to Chicago. Well recommended, Torrio first made him a bouncer in one of his Burnham saloons where his skill and enthusiasm for work were apparent almost at once. So talented was the young newcomer that he was soon brought back to the city to manage the Four Deuces, the organization's headquarters and most profitable club. There he became

Torrio's first lieutenant and primary gunman. Almost an opposite of Torrio, Capone was a crude, brutal, and flashy hoodlum who had been largely obscure in the Torrio organization (Asbury, 1940). Despite their differences, however, Capone's potential showed through, allowing him to rise rapidly under the wing of the boss himself. By late 1923, when the reform mayor William Dever took office, Capone had been remade into a polished criminal, second only to Torrio in power.

The Torrio–Capone organizational arrangement and system of alliances could probably have continued indefinitely had Dever not followed through on his campaign promises. While Mayor Thompson preached the blessings of a wide-open town, organized crime was quickly becoming more powerful than city government. Thompson, however, had not anticipated the public's reaction to the widespread corruption he had permitted, nor was he prepared for the dissension that developed between his administration, the Governor of Illinois, and the state Attorney General over the efforts of each to control the police department, easily the most political branch of city government. As the feud over the police grew in intensity, control of the city seemed to deteriorate until the mayor with ambitions to become president realized that even his reelection in Chicago was unlikely. Deciding late, Thompson stepped aside, leaving his party without a viable candidate and the door open for Dever, a respected judge and a man of character, to be elected mayor. Suddenly, the gangsters and corrupt aldermen found that they no longer had influence with the new administration or police chief (Peterson, 1952). Within days, the old alliances collapsed, leaving Chicago to virtually fall apart at the seams.

The successes of the reformers' campaign against corruption and patronage meant that the only identifiable power brokers were suddenly unable to deliver. As often happens in such power vacuums, open warfare resulted. Where the Thompson administration had permitted an occasional gun battle, full-scale guerrilla warfare now existed. For three years, from September 1923 to October 1926, at least 365 Chicago gangsters and untold bystanders, innocent and not, were killed by each other and the police in the battles for beer control (Asbury, 1940). Among them, Dion O'Bannion was murdered in his flower shop, and Torrio himself was seriously wounded with bullets in the jaw, right arm, abdomen, and chest (Browning & Gerassi, 1980). A quiet man who neither smoked, drank, nor used profanity, Torrio realized that Chicago was out of control and decided that the safest way out was to accept a short prison term for a minor bootlegging charge and retire. After serving his nine-month sentence, Torrio left Chicago for good and returned to the relative safety of New York crime. His wife, who described her marriage to Torrio as "one long, unclouded honeymoon," was almost certainly pleased with his decision (Asbury, 1940:321). Hymie Weiss, a clever Polish gangster allied with Irish West Siders probably shared her enthusiasm.

As he left Chicago, Torrio's organization was impressive by any standard. A portion of his holdings included 25 large brothels scattered throughout Cook County, at least twice as many gambling houses, 65 breweries, several distilleries, and a smuggling operation with fleets of vehicles entering the country from Canada. Newspapers regularly quoted the U.S. District Attorney's estimate that Torrio's take alone averaged $70 million a year (Asbury, 1940). The size of such a legacy and an earlier pledge to avenge O'Bannion's death—a murder that most believed was carried out by Mike Genna at Torrio's request—were simply too much for Weiss to pass up. Almost immediately after O'Bannion's funeral, Weiss assumed leadership of O'Bannion's gang and declared war, first on Torrio and then on Capone and all six of the Genna brothers.

A brutal man who proudly claimed he was kind to his mother, Weiss got his start in crime as a burglar, safe-blower, auto thief, and union thug. With Prohibition's opportunities, he joined forces with O'Bannion to build a North Side booze business second only to Torrio's in size and influence. Then, on January 12, 1925, Weiss made his move against Torrio by attacking his head gunman as Capone's car was parked in front of a restaurant at State and 51st Streets. Weiss and others slowly drove by, riddling the car with bullets as they passed. Surprisingly, only Capone's chauffeur was wounded; Capone had stepped inside the restaurant moments earlier. Two weeks later, Weiss moved on Torrio himself as the crime boss and his wife returned from shopping.

With Torrio wounded and stepping aside, Capone struck back—leaving Chicago's gangs divided, as one English journalist described it, into "Weiss guys" and "Capone guys." Browning and Gerassi (1980) noted that soon enough all but a few of the leaders from both sides were dead guys. First was Angelo Genna, president of the Unione Siciliana, a respectable Italian civic association prior to Genna's tenure. Within six months, two more of the Genna brothers, Mike and Tony, died along with most of their organization's lieutenants and the elder Genna's successor to the presidency of the Unione. Although three brothers survived, the fall of their organization was both sudden and complete.

Capone responded quickly, naming his own man as president of the Unione.

Back and forth the bullets flew, an Irishman here, a Pole there, a Sicilian somewhere else. Chicago became enveloped in death.

Capone's men apparently suffered greater casualties than the others simply because they had been the dominate gang and they provided easier targets to upstart competitors who had much to gain and little to lose. (Browning & Gerassi, 1980:329)

While his casualties may have been high, Capone was nonetheless winning in a war of attrition as Weiss's top men were gradually picked off one by one. Finally, on October 11, 1926, as the 28-year-old Weiss left his car for O'Bannion's old flower shop, he too was torn to shreds by machine gun fire. The beer wars were at last over only feet from where they had begun almost two years before.

Meanwhile, as a city, Chicago was apparently tired of the slaughter and the reform that had precipitated it. By the end of 1926, Mayor Thompson was reelected to still another term on a confused campaign of "America first," opposition to a World Court, and promises of a return to the wide-open Chicago many had known before. With his friend in City Hall and most of his competitors in their graves, the ascension of Capone was now all but complete.

AL "SCARFACE" BROWN

I had respect for Capone. In the Depression he did wonderful work. Before the New Deal got going they set up block restaurants for the unemployed, free food with the complements of the Orga-nization—and you didn't have to listen to any sermons or get up and confess. You sat down and they gave you a real meal with tablecloths on the tables, and no one rescued you. Even the union racketeering wasn't as bad as it's been painted. I knew one racketeer well who ran a hotel worker's union. He ran it with an iron hand, but he also provided a health clinic, a psychiatric department and picnics and social outings. (Allsop, 1961:122)

About few in our history has so much been written, yet so little known as the gangster Alphonse Capone. Born in either Brooklyn, New York, or Naples, Rome, or Castel Amara, Italy, immigration records reveal that Capone came to the United States in 1893, and he and his family settled into the Greenspoint neighborhood of Brooklyn (Abadinsky, 1990). One year old at the time, Capone and his brothers Frank and Ralph remained relatively obscure for the next 25 years.

Even after his move to Chicago, Capone's slow rise in organized crime went largely unnoticed. As late as August 1922, he was so little known that his involvement in an auto accident merited news coverage only on the back pages. Incorrectly referred to as Alfred Caponi by the press, among his fellow gangsters Capone was more commonly known as Al "Scarface" Brown, a surname apparently adopted early on to avoid the discrimination Italians in New York often encountered. (Recall from Chapter 4 that Paul Kelly and others had taken similar steps.) Equally uncomfortable with his nickname, Capone claimed to have received the parallel scars along his left cheek while fighting as a soldier with the 77th Division in France. In fact, although certified in the draft, Capone never entered the military. His well-known scars resulted from a dance hall brawl in Brooklyn (Asbury, 1940). Nevertheless, with Torrio's guidance, Capone soon rose above his inauspicious beginnings to control crime in the second city. He also came to symbolize American organized crime throughout the world.

Commanding as many as 700 to 800 gunmen, Capone was at once a merciless cutthroat and a hero to the masses. So respected were his potency and resourcefulness that to many only he could inherit the mantles of Jesse James and Robin Hood—an outlaw one step ahead of authority who cared deeply for his own people. Still, while it was Capone who gained the notoriety and accumulated the greatest sums of money, Torrio was probably the more accomplished criminal. It was Torrio who built the criminal organization that Capone kept running with occasional replacement parts. Where Torrio maintained peace with strategy and compromise, Capone relied instead on the gun and violence to ensure compliance and eliminate the few competitors Torrio had not driven from the business. While Torrio was seldom armed and often walked the streets alone, his protege was almost never without bodyguards, his bulletproof vest, or his seven-ton armor-plated car. Regardless of their differences, with the advent of Prohibition and the collapse of what little formal authority remained, things changed faster than Torrio could manage them. It was now the more straightforward Capone who was the right man for the times.

Ruling from his headquarters in Cicero, Capone's orders appear to have transcended law. So complete was his control of local officials that once, when Cicero Mayor Klenha failed to do as he had been told, Capone felt no hesitation in kicking him down the steps of City Hall in plain view of a passing police officer. The officer merely strolled by continuing to twirl his nightstick. Later, when the town council dared to pass a measure they had been ordered to defeat, their meeting was disrupted while the trustee who led the defiance was dragged into the street and beaten with a blackjack. Nor were private citizens immune. Arthur St. John, editor of the Berwyn *Tribune*, was kidnapped and shot for editorials attacking Capone's activities in that town. Nearby, his brother and counterpart at the Cicero *Tribune* was badly beaten for interfering with a disciplinary beating being administered to one of his town's policemen. "I own the police," Torrio had once boasted (Asbury, 1940:337). With a combination of military skill, money, and firepower, Capone added sufficiently to the organization's inventory of officials to allow crime, or at least his crimes, to become among the city's most important industries.

By the mid-1920s, an estimated 10,000 professional criminals were at work in Chicago. Because for some, especially Sicilian Italians, crime was the only avenue into respectable society, many made excellent employees for a criminal organization expanding aggressively into racketeering, narcotics, and extortion. Few of those who remained could operate independently of Capone influence; they too contributed to the bottom line, enabling this formerly obscure hoodlum with a disputed birthplace to achieve the highest gross income by a private citizen in a single year (*Guiness Book of Records,* 1930). And enjoy his income he did, reportedly spending lavishly on himself and those depending on his organization. By his own estimate in 1928, Capone had "fooled away" at least $7 million since arriving in Chicago not a decade earlier. Included was a reported $500,000 for a second home in Miami and another $20,000 for his armored car. With a roll of $50,000 constantly in his pocket, it was said that he never gave a hatcheck girl less than $10 or a newsboy less than $5 while his minimum tip to waiters in restaurants was $100. At Christmas, his generosity was unparalleled, with an annual expenditure for gifts exceeding $100,000. He gave diamond-studded belts and solid gold cigarette cases decorated with precious stones to friends. His political henchmen were entertained at elaborate banquets while their cellars were being filled with expensive champagnes. But for the city, particularly the residents of Cicero, Capone was an especially easy mark. In addition to soup kitchens and outreach programs, every winter Cicero coal yards and department stores had carte-blanche orders to supply the poor with coal, clothing, and groceries (Asbury, 1940). Undoubtedly, Capone's largess resulted from his own motives. Many have suggested that by providing food and shelter for the destitute, respectability was promoted, political debts paid, and loyalties ensured—none of which diminishes the fact that the poor were being fed and provided with care. What it also suggests is that behind the romance that was Capone was a very smart businessman who may have underestimated his own significance when he declared that "all I ever did was to supply a demand that was pretty popular" (Browning & Gerassi, 1980:331).

Vagrancy, Public Enemies, and
the Chicago Crime Commission

Despite his popularity and persona, by the early 1930s the expansion of Capone's power had become too much for Chicago to bear. Not content to control liquor, beer, vice, and gambling, Capone had begun to encroach on legitimate businesses as well. Already in control of unions representing plumbers, street sweepers, newsboys, city hall clerks, and marble setters, Capone was maneuvering to establish himself as czar of the city's organized labor. If successful, "businessmen who had to work out union contracts with Capone would be worse off than countries forced to negotiate peace with Mussolini" (Hoffman, 1992:188). Equally frightening were his obvious attempts to build a political machine capable of wresting the power of patronage from the mayor and the aldermen. Already in control of Thompson, Kenna, and Coughlin, Capone was forming alliances with willing businessmen such as Moe Annenberg and Hearst publisher Andy Lawrence, allowing Capone to force appointment of his close companion Daniel Seritella to the posts of city sealer and city superintendent of streets. With these positions, Capone had indirect control of over 3,000 jobs, an annual budget of $7 million, and supervision of more than $5 million a year in street repair work. Indeed, all indications were that Capone was seeking to tighten his grip over the city's political and economic institutions for the future.

In response, Henry Barrett Chamberlin, operating director of the Chicago Crime Commission, proclaimed Capone and 27 lesser gangsters to be "public enemies" and demanded that police "harass gangsters in every way; raid their whorehouses, gambling joints, night clubs and dog tracks" (Hoffman, 1992:192). Declaring that the 28 should be subjected to "vigilant watchfulness and arrest with appropriate court action whenever and as often as possible" (Hoffman, 1992:192), he went further, vowing to personally handle the publicity for this reform blitz so that the light of publicity would remain on the gangsters to the end. Although Chamberlin listed the 28 alphabetically, Capone was the clear target, causing him to branded "Public Enemy Number One," a phrase picked up and popularized throughout the world.

Initially the campaign went nowhere. Despite having a hit list of gangsters thrust under their noses, the police and prosecutors were slow to act. For example, when Myles O'Donnell, one of the 28, killed one woman and injured five other persons in a reckless traffic accident, the case against him was dropped because the police failed to locate a key witness. When told of this, Chamberlin dispatched a private investigator to see for himself. Within

20 minutes, Chamberlin's man easily found several eye witnesses. After a series of such failures demonstrated a lack of police enthusiasm, Chamberlin's friend, Judge John Lyle, proposed an alternative strategy: Why not force the gangsters' arrest by issuing warrants for violating an 1871 vagrancy statute? Once in jail, the judge explained, he could hold them there on high bonds until trial, where several possibilities would present themselves, especially for Capone:

1. Once arrested on the vagrancy charge, if Capone refused to answer questions he could be found guilty and fined.

2. If he did not pay the fine, he could be sentenced to the House of Correction.

3. If he paid the fine, the judge could ask him to explain where the money came from.

4. If he revealed the actual source of his income, a grand jury could be impaneled and he could be indicted for the appropriate crimes.

5. If he claimed legitimate employment, the grand jury could indict him for perjury.

6. If he testified in an effort to defend himself against the vagrancy charge, his testimony could be used against him for tax prosecution. (Hoffman, 1992:201)

In short, Judge Lyle reasoned that with the court's help the Crime Commission would finally have Capone and his colleagues trapped. Chamberlin and Frank Loesch, Crime Commission president, enthusiastically agreed and the plan was approved. Within days Judge Lyle put the plan in motion by publicly signing warrants for 26 of the original "public enemies" (two were believed to have been killed) and directing the few police that could be trusted to personally serve them all.

The Secret Six and the Federal Response

As Henry Chamberlin was considering his options, a special committee of the Chicago Association of Commerce was holding its own meeting to decide what should be done about Al Capone. Chicago, it seems, had reached a crossroads. While a wide-open town had its advantages, the city's reputation was badly soiled as an out-of-control haven for publicity-seeking murderers. As the 1933 World's Fair approached, civic pride and a desire for expanded business connections led several in the association to conclude that a thorough housecleaning was in order. However, given the state of local politics and the ineffectual response of local criminal justice authorities, they reasoned that a bold change in direction would be needed. As such, they gathered secretly to plot a strategy "to accomplish what three thousand police and three hundred prohibition agents had failed to accomplish" (Ness, 1957:11).

According to Eliot Ness, of the now well-known "Untouchables," it was this secret committee of six business leaders who had backed the idea of forming his special unit and had convinced the U.S. Attorney to name him as its head. Willing to gamble their own lives as well, these private citizens had become aroused.

> It was all right when mobsters were merely eliminating themselves but now people realized that the city was no longer safe for decent citizens. This was what aroused the Chicago Association of Commerce, which didn't dare to take open action because nobody was certain who was or wasn't in Capone's pocket, to form the Secret Six. (Ness, 1987:45)

Well connected, this small group, believed to include a former United States Vice President, the director of Colgate-Palmolive, the owner of the *Chicago Tribune*, and both Henry Chamberlin and Frank Loesch of the Crime Commission, was determined to speak and act for all Chicagoans too fearful of Capone to do anything (Hoffman, 1992). Since the root of the city's crime problems could be found in the alliance between gangsters and public officials, they knew that outside help would be required.

Using their influence wherever possible, the committee quietly enlisted federal involvement. On October 18, 1928, President Coolidge responded by authorizing the special intelligence unit of the Internal Revenue Service (IRS) to begin an investigation of Capone's tax affairs. Dwight Green, a former Chicago newspaperman turned IRS attorney, was sent to Chicago as a special prosecutor to assist the U.S. Attorney in building his case. Green was selected because, at least as far as anyone could tell, he was without political affiliations and beyond Capone's temptations. With unlimited support staff promised from both Washington and the secret six committee, Green began his task with simple instructions—send Chicago gangsters to prison.

The End of the Era

The multiple investigations began to take their toll. One after another, the city's newest "vagrants" were arrested, hauled into court, and jailed on high bonds. While often as not the venue would be changed due to court prejudice or charges against the accused would be continued or dropped outright by appellate courts, the message was nonetheless clear—gangsters, especially those designated public enemies, were now vulnerable to criminal justice harassment. When the Chicago Bar Association reacted to Judge Lyle's high bonds and colorful language by labeling him "vigorous and independent, but lacking in judicial temperament," the judge replied to the media:

> If judicial temperament means that I should be lenient with gang-
> sters instead of severe, then I am glad that I am lacking in it. I
> refuse to mollycoddle criminals with lengthy records. (Hoffman,
> 1992:210)

True to his word, when attorneys for Ralph Capone sought to have him put in the custody of a bailiff rather than jail as others before him had been handled, Lyle declared, "What! Courtesy to a Capone! To a man who with his brother heads a gang of criminals the likes of which the world has never known. He'll be handled like any common criminal" (Hoffman, 1992:211). Still, while the arrest totals mounted, Al Capone was nowhere to be found.

While the police may not have been able to locate Capone for warrant service, he continued to surface regularly in the media. In October 1930, the *Chicago Tribune* reported that police detectives were certain he had engineered the machine-gun murder of Joe Aiello, a competitor and bitter foe. The next month, Judge John McGoorty revealed, again to the *Tribune*, that a Capone representative had approached him seeking a compromise with "Al Brown." In return for rights to sell beer unmolested, Brown would end his racketeering activities. McGoorty, of course, reported that he had rejected the deal. Others quickly came forward as well. Stanley Kunz, a Congressman from the 8th Illinois District, for example, blamed his reelection defeat on the gangster, while a California fruit juice distributor claimed that Capone feared him as a competitor and was attempting to disrupt his business. When rumors of Capone's arrival in southern California began to circulate, police there met to develop a plan of action against the "invasion by Chicago gangsters" (Hoffman, 1992:220). By then, however, other sources placed him in New York, where the media speculated he might be hiding out with Johnny Torrio's help.

By December, the U.S. Attorney joined the hunt by issuing a summons for Capone to appear in federal court in Chicago on a two-year-old contempt of court action. Earlier, he had been cited for failing to appear before a federal grand jury investigating a Chicago Heights liquor ring. Capone had requested an indefinite continuance on the grounds that he was too ill to return to Chicago from his Florida home. Noting that he was well enough to attend the Miami dog races daily, attorney George E. Johnson rescheduled the appearance. Should he fail to appear, Johnson predicted that federal agents would be able to find Capone and arrest him.

True to form, on his appointed day in court Capone was not present. Instead, his attorneys arrived and argued that since the contempt charge was only a misdemeanor they could appear on his behalf and enter his plea. Having done so, a trial date in January was agreed upon. As they left the courtroom, three police officers waiting to serve Capone with a vagrancy warrant told reporters that they too would return. When he finally did appear in federal court, Judge Lyle declared, Capone would be arrested on local charges and held long enough to be charged with "Big Jim" Colosimo's murder. "We will send Capone to the electric chair," pledged Lyle (Hoffman, 1992:234).

Eventually, Capone surrendered to the charges that awaited. Appearing in federal court, he was confronted by no less than seven branches of the government including the secret service, the IRS, Prohibition agents, and 15 assistant U.S. Attorneys. After a daylong trial, he was found guilty as expected and sentenced to six months in the county jail. Also as expected, he was released on post-conviction bail to prepare an appeal. A quiet and orderly affair, the most remarkable event was the hundreds of women, mostly federal employees working in the courthouse, who pressed forward, jostling bailiffs, as they strained to catch a glimpse of "Scarface Al."

Within a week, Capone was back in court to face the long promised vagrancy charge. Almost immediately, legal posturing began as defense attorneys challenged the inclusion of Capone's alias "Scarface" on the warrant and demanded that the state produce at least one police witness with personal knowledge of their client's vagrancy. Finding no officers willing to testify against Capone, prosecutors were forced to drop all charges against him. As he left the courthouse, Capone described the affair as the "biggest frame-up I ever knew" (Allsop, 1961:329). Although the Crime Commission had clearly suffered a major and quite public defeat, Henry Chamberlin promised to continue the public enemies campaign, contending that his commission had at least shown that even Capone could be forced to account for himself. As of June 1931, the "scorecard" for the original 28 enemies was:

Incarcerated	5
Convicted and under sentence	4
Convicted and awaiting sentence	1
Ordered extradited	1
Ordered deported	1
Killed	2
Awaiting judgment	1
Fugitives	5
Cleared of charges	8

Chamberlin issued a new enemies list and hailed the program a success.

Meanwhile, the constant efforts of Eliot Ness and his Untouchables and the tedious work of Dwight Green, the IRS special prosecutor, were beginning to pay dividends. Ness began his assault with a telephone tap on Ralph Capone's office at the Montmarte Cafe in Cicero. Once he had discovered the locations of the gang's breweries, he equipped a ten-ton flatbed truck with a steel bumper and battered down the doors of 19 of Capone's distilleries and 6 breweries. In no time, the Untouchables had seized or destroyed more than $1 million worth of the gang's equipment, vehicles, and products (Kobler, 1971).

Sensing the impact, the secret six committee added its support by opening an undercover speakeasy deep in Capone territory where the bartenders, an undercover police officer and his informant, bought information from low-ranking gang members. When Capone learned of the operation in February 1931, he sent Jake Guzik, his right-hand man, to arrange a meeting with Colonel Robert Randolph, the committee's leader. "I have the 'Big Fellow' planted in a hotel near the loop where you can talk to him without being seen," Randolph remembered Guzik asking: "Will you go?" Randolph reported a cordial meeting with Capone, who offered to police the city and end the killings giving it its bad name if Randolph would call off the Untouchables in return. After drinking a couple of beers with his host, Randolph declined the offer and the meeting was over.

As he left Capone's suite, Randolph was intrigued by questions the gangster casually asked about the upcoming mayoral election. Returning to his office, he met with Henry Chamberlin of the Crime Commission where he learned of the roles that Capone associates such as Daniel Seritella played in Mayor Thompson's administration. This too would have to change, he pledged, the secret six would have to enter politics as well.

With prodding from Randolph and the others, businessmen throughout the city began to unite, regardless of party, to ensure a Thompson defeat. Declaring that the new mayor should be a "God-fearing man with a private life above reproach, and public life without stain" (Hoffman, 1992:263), Randolph and his fellow business leaders persuaded lesser candidates to withdraw from the race so as not to split the anti-Thompson vote. Once done, they threw their full support behind Anton Cermak, Thompson's sole remaining challenger. With such backing, Cermak won easily, taking 45 of Chicago's 50 wards. The result, Randolph proclaimed, would tell "the world that we are prepared to regain our business level and restore our good name" (Hoffman, 1992:263).

While the Untouchables were raiding Capone's breweries and Cermak was defeating his ally in office, Green and the IRS continued their work as well. By then, however, Elmer Irey, head of the Treasury Department's Intelligence Unit, had assumed control of the investigation bringing with him agents Frank Wilson (who would later head the Secret Service) and Pat O'Rourke. A genius for detail, Wilson poured over records seized from Capone's gambling joints, whorehouses, and breweries while O'Rourke, using money from the secret six committee, went undercover to join the gang. By early 1930, Wilson reported that the efforts were paying off and that tax cases against Jake Guzik and Frank Nitti, Capone's top enforcer, were ready but that information on Capone himself was proving hard to come by. Hoping that successful prosecutions of a few of the gang's top men might make insiders more cooperative, the agents decided they had little choice but to proceed with what they had. As such, during March of that year, indictments against Guzik and Nitti were handed down.

Almost at once, the strategy proved wise. With Nitti on the run and Guzik on the defense, Dwight Green and the Intelligence Unit's agents soon located Fred Ries, a cashier at a Capone gambling hall called "The Ship." Ries at first refused to cooperate; however, he was later convinced to testify against Capone and the others. By late 1930, he had explained the structure of the organization and provided evidence that more than half of the gang's gambling profits went directly into the pockets of Al Capone himself.

As the agents continued to build their case against Capone, private investigators hired by Randolph and the secret six committee located and seized Nitti, who was hiding out in a Berwyn, Illinois, bungalow. On November 14, 1930, the government's new star witness was presented against Guzik. Ries testified about the enormous gambling profits of the gang and how they were used. With such evidence against him, Guzik was found guilty on three counts of tax evasion and sentenced to 15 years in Leavenworth penitentiary. Nitti, the enforcer, offered far less resistance, pleading guilty to tax evasion just prior to Christmas. His sentence was far lighter but still a substantial 18 months.

For the next year, the agents concentrated almost exclusively on Capone, collecting information on the extent of his considerable expenditures. Once again, Randolph's committee stepped forward to fund agent O'Rourke's covert surveillance and an extended ocean voyage intended to keep Fred Ries—whose testimony would be essential—alive (Hoffman, 1992). Apparently realizing the trouble he was in, Capone began traveling throughout the country seeking a place to retire away from Chicago. Authorities in Los Angeles, the Black Hills of South Dakota, the Bahamas, and Havana all barred him from their jurisdictions, leaving him only his estate in Miami as a refuge. By the summer of 1931, Capone returned to Chicago where he was arrested on October 6 by federal officers. On October 17, 1931, Alphonse Capone was finally convicted in federal court on five felony

tax counts, fined $50,000, and sentenced to 11 years in prison, first in At-
lanta and later in San Francisco's Alcatraz (Asbury, 1940). As he prepared to
be transferred from the local jail, a reporter from Detroit asked the gang
leader who he thought should receive the credit for his downfall. "The Secret Six licked the rackets," he replied. "They licked me. They've made it so
there's no money in the game anymore" (Hoffman, 1992:279). In 1947,
Capone died at his Florida home of pneumonia brought on by an advanced
case of syphilis he had refused to treat for years.

AFTER CAPONE: DISORGANIZING
CRIME IN CHICAGO

With Capone gone, organized crime in Chicago was never quite the same.
Nitti assumed control of what remained, but by 1943, in poor health and
afraid of a pending prosecution for extortion from a local theater chain, he
committed suicide. Following his death, Paul Ricca became boss but
within months was himself imprisoned for his role in Nitti's extortion
scheme. Anthony Accardo stepped forward in Ricca's absence and for a
while stability at least seemed possible. By 1955, however, the Internal
Revenue Service was closing in again, ruling that Accardo's claim that
"gambling and miscellaneous sources" accounted for his income was too
vague. Although his conviction for tax fraud was reversed on appeal,
Accardo and Ricca feared further prosecution and decided to step down.
Sam Giancana was next in line.

According to Abadinsky (1990), by the age of 14 Giancana was already a
school dropout and member of the "42 Gang," a notorious group widely
viewed as crazy. Criminally active, Giancana was arrested at least 50 times
by the time he was 20 years old yet never prosecuted due to sympathetic
judges and disappearing witnesses. By 1929, at the age of 21, his luck finally
ran out when he was both prosecuted and imprisoned for burglary. After
completing his sentence, "Mooney" Giancana was drafted by the army but
rejected for service due to his "inadequate personality and strong anti-social
trends" (Abadinsky, 1990:176). Those same traits would serve him well in
Chicago crime.

Initially a wheelman and bootlegger, Giancana rose rapidly in the organization. Using cunning, deception, and violence, he systematically took
control of the city's numbers rackets, killing competitors who resisted his
advances. Having gained the attention of Accardo and Ricca, Giancana's
profits and organizational skills allowed him to expand his interests until he
was the obvious choice to inherit the organization itself.

A social man, Giancana had something of a flair for the public eye. Romantically connected to one of the popular McGuire Sisters singers, alleged to have shared a girlfriend with President Kennedy, and a publicly acknowledged friend of Frank Sinatra's, Giancana followed the example of Joseph Colombo in New York by openly challenging the FBI's intensive surveillance of his activities. Eventually, he too would encounter legal problems, however, after refusing to testify before a federal grand jury despite being granted immunity from prosecution. In her autobiography, *Mafia Princess*, Giancana's daughter (Giancana & Renner, 1985) reports that in 1966, following his brief imprisonment for contempt, her father was forced into exile in Mexico by his mentors Accardo and Ricca. His attempt to return to Chicago influence in 1975 was not widely supported by those who succeeded him, and on June 19, 1975, Sam Giancana was shot to death at home by someone he apparently knew and trusted. Abadinsky (1990) explains that even in death controversy surrounded Giancana as it was revealed that the Central Intelligence Agency had attempted to enlist his aid to assassinate Cuban President Fidel Castro. With the death of Giancana and the imprisonment a decade later of Joseph Aiuppa, his successor, the decline of the organization that Torrio and Capone had so carefully built was all but complete. As new organizations emerged, now mostly black and Hispanic, Chicago was once again a wide-open town. Organized crime had again become disorganized.

In Chapter 6 we will review the similarities in the economic and governmental conditions in the neighborhoods of New York and Chicago. When efforts to prohibit the use of alcohol and drugs were added to this mix, the combination permitted the rise of organized crime to a position as powerful and dominating as piracy during colonial piracy days.

6

◦⊱═◐ ◑═⊰◦

The Role of Prohibition

Surely most would agree that the earlier gangs, gangsters, and crime fighters we have examined are fascinating characters with exploits rich for storytellers. Blackbeard, Rothstein, Torrio, and their like were daring individuals—bold enough to build empires and seize fortunes. But the lessons from these earlier experiences can be even more valuable as guideposts to the future; observations from the past can help in shaping policies for today. In this light, then, let's review what we know.

With the turn of the 16th century, American colonists were faced with a weak economy, limited employment opportunities, and a threatening and often hostile environment. Exploration of the continent was fraught with risk, and the rewards for the effort were hardly comparable with the hardships regularly endured. Even where success did become possible, the tax and trade laws of the day were enough to ensure that the greatest portion of the spoils went to the colonists' British sponsors—wealthy men who had done little to contribute to the outcome. Until the advent of westward expansion and a manufacturing economy, privateering and piracy were often the only real hope of opportunity for the more enterprising, aggressive, and impatient colonists.

Similarly, a century later in Five Points, New Yorkers suffered in an environment of crushing, dead-end poverty. Jobs were few, health and services poor and deteriorating, and the community rough and violent. Crime on the streets offered one of the few steady sources of income, but even here in the mayhem around them organization was essential for survival. In Chicago and other midwestern cities of the 1800s, the rushes to gold and land brought rapid but uneven expansion. Sanitation was poor and disease routine as alternating cycles of depression and disaster created large pockets of poverty where many had little choice but to roam the streets idle and penniless in search of crime.

Although in each instance the conditions of chaos and depression may have produced environments supportive of crime, the criminal entrepreneurs who emerged in these earlier eras did not do so on their own. Recall that the idea for piracy was first formed by the British Crown and merchant traders who saw crime as an expedient arm of foreign policy. For decades, the privateers they commissioned remained loyal, seizing only ships of the enemy. Eventually, of course, inhibitions were loosened, and what began as a convenience to confront the Spanish became a problem of organized theft and robbery. Even then, however, local support continued from colonists eager to profit from resupply and benefit from the availability of much sought after, but illegal, goods. It was not until the colonists too became the victims of pirate expeditions that the environment ceased to be so supportive.

The early gangs of New York served political purposes as well. Closely tied to their communities, their influence and ability to intimidate were central to the Tammany politicians whose power was built on local voting blocks. Controlled by neighborhood leaders who could extend or withhold protection from the police and city reformers, powerful gangs such as the Five Pointers and the Eastmans became little more than "goon squads" working for their sponsors while training future generations of gangsters. Like the pirates before them, they too outgrew their controls as the evolving national economy turned local gangs into regional mass marketers of crime. Increasingly complex and financially sophisticated, some diversified into a variety of enterprises—many quite legal—to ensure their futures through absorption into the larger American economy. Others, however, such as the more visible Irish gangs and Italian "families," continued their struggle for the control of vice and the political structures around them, leaving themselves vulnerable to competition and the same evolving economic reforms that ended the reign of the pirates before them.

Meanwhile, in Chicago's heady world of expansion, the gamblers and gangsters either were the politicians or controlled them directly. Here, too, however, they found progress difficult as pressure from the secret six and other business sectors forced them from the scene. Later, in Chapter 7, we will explore how some believe that this pattern of unwitting government cooperation has repeated itself during our more recent war on drugs.

Finally, in addition to a nurturing environment to support crime and official tolerance of the organizations that result, for organized crime to flourish some significant opportunity must exist. For the pirates it was the colonists' desire to avoid the costly import taxes imposed by the restrictive navigation and trade acts. Without wholesale theft and fencing, manufactured goods and many raw materials would have been unavailable to most. Two centuries later, Prohibition, the "noble experiment," provided the opportunity for organized crime to flourish.

PROHIBITION AS REFORM

Ushered in with considerable fanfare, national prohibition was saddled from its inception with the great expectations of both proponents and opponents. "At one minute past midnight," boasted the Anti-Saloon League of New York on Prohibition's eve, "a new nation will be born." William Anderson, the league's superintendent, went on to warn drinkers to accept the new reality. "Shake hands with Uncle Sam," he cautioned, "and board his water wagon." Unfortunately for Anderson, within four years he would be serving a prison sentence for forgery instead of participating in what then President Hoover, a Prohibition supporter, would label "a great social and economic experiment, noble in motive and far reaching in purpose" (Kyvig, 1985:4).

Others, such as the writer H. L. Mencken, were less certain of the "experiment's" objectives. Saying it was little more than an effort to "punish the other fellow for having a better time in the world," Mencken (1926:256) viewed the movement as a threat to democracy itself. Hofstadter would later agree, scorning the effort as a "pseudo reform." Prohibition represented "not merely an aversion to drunkenness and to the evils that accompanied it," he concluded, but an aversion "to the immigrant drinking masses, to the pleasures and amenities of city life, and to the well-to-do classes and cultivated men" (Hofstadter, 1955:289). Nonetheless, most, like Colonel Daniel Porter (the supervising revenue agent in charge of enforcement), predicted that the penalties accompanying prohibition in the Volstead Act were so severe that no one would attempt to violate the law. No one, he was sure, would risk a fine of up to $1,000 and imprisonment for up to six months for the sake of a few drinks. "There will not be any violations to speak of," said Porter (Asbury, 1950:142).

Through it all, few observers seemed to realize that the 18th Amendment bringing the nation prohibition was to become perhaps the most significant and radical of constitutional reforms ever adopted. While other amendments adjusted or restricted government powers, clarified individual rights, or extended constitutional coverage to additional classes of citizens, the 18th Amendment departed from this fundamental pattern by destroying private property holdings and established economic arrangements. When John Kramer, the newly appointed Prohibition Commissioner, declared that "the law says that liquor to be used as a beverage must not be manufactured" (Asbury, 1950:143), the nation's brewers and distillers offered hardly a comment. Nor would protest have mattered, as Kramer proclaimed, "We shall see that it is not manufactured. Nor sold, nor given away, nor hauled in anything on the surface of the earth, or in the air" (Asbury, 1950:143). Only the 13th Amendment abolishing slavery so asserted the federal government's power in pursuit of social restructuring. With national prohibition, that assertion brought the direct intervention of federal law into private lives in an effort to restrain individual behavior. That it outlawed one industry and crippled several more mattered little. In short, while some Americans argued about their drinks and others boasted of their enforcement prowess, the balance of power was quietly shifted from the states toward the national arena (Kyvig, 1985).

The Birth of the Movement

The origins of national prohibition can be traced to our revolutionary period and the need for colonists who were both dedicated and sober. While the harmful physical effects of alcohol remained largely unknown at the time, as war approached and men were needed at their best, many churches, several of the colonial legislatures, and even the Continental Congress began to express concerns about the habitual drunkenness of members. Building on their fears throughout the mid-1700s, at least seven colonies, the Methodist Church, various Indian tribes in Pennsylvania, numerous social organizations, and even the commander of the English forces issued complaints about the growing trade in distilled liquors. Most went on to impose restrictions and request punishments for drunkenness. Not content with such individual responses, however, Anthony Benezet and the Society of Friends in Pennsylvania attempted to spread their influence with publication and distribution of a cautionary pamphlet. Advising against the common use of any drink likely "to steal away a man's senses and render him foolish, irascible, uncontrollable and dangerous" (Cherrington, 1920:76), Benezet's efforts didn't appear to have a direct or immediate impact. They undoubtedly did much to shape the debate that followed, however.

Dr. Benjamin Rush is generally recognized as the pioneer in the movement against alcohol use. A noted physician and one of the principal figures behind the Declaration of Independence, Dr. Rush became especially concerned about the effects of intoxication on soldiers. With the Revolutionary War at its height and fearful that independence could be lost, by the late 1700s Dr. Rush began to issue the most uncompromising attacks on distilled liquors ever written. So persuasive were his warnings that they were quickly adopted by the War Board of the Continental Congress and circulated to all troops in the United States Army. The result was the first official appeal by government for abstinence.

While many have credited Dr. Rush for the push for total abstinence, in fact his writings and efforts were limited to distilled liquors. The doctor took an approach concerning them that was somewhat different from those before him. Rather than seeking abstinence for moral reasons, he was the first to speak out from the viewpoint of science. Citing medical opinion for support, he argued widely that hard liquors had no food value and were therefore useless to the diet. Further, they aggravated all diseases and indeed, were the direct cause of many. He claimed that scientific argument demonstrated that even moderate use led inevitably to drunkenness and destruction, and proclaimed that in no case should liquor in any amount be taken other than on the advice of a physician. To prevent and cure intemperance, however, he went on to recommend either wine or beer with a mixture of wine and laudanum or opium for those truly in need of their alcohol. Failure to heed his advice, he warned, would almost certainly lead to burglary and murder, madness and despair, and eventually, the gallows (Asbury, 1950). With science supposedly on his side, Dr. Rush's views were difficult to refute.

If Dr. Rush was the first to employ science, the impact of this argument was quickly realized, and others soon followed suit. By 1790, the College of Physicians of New York presented a memorial to the United States Congress condemning spirits and recommending high tariffs on their importation. They, in turn, were joined by the College of Physicians and Surgeons of Philadelphia, a host of individual physicians and scientists, and eventually the American Medical Association (AMA) itself. In each case, the arguments offered were remarkably similar to those of Dr. Rush—continued use of ardent spirits could only lead to dire results.

Apparently attentive to the warnings, the consumption patterns of Americans shifted dramatically. By the close of the century, the use of distilled liquor fell from an earlier rate of about two and one-half gallons per capita annually to somewhere near one gallon per person. Meanwhile, however, the use of malt liquors rose correspondingly. In fact, with other beverages, such as water, milk, coffee, and tea, either frequently unavailable or prohibitively expensive, beer and cider soon became staples of life. Already the usual mealtime beverage, many farmers and workers sipped beer or cider throughout the day, while group projects, such as church gatherings and harvests, often began with a cask of spirits. While the early reform movement appears to have influenced in what form alcohol was consumed, it left how much largely untouched.

By 1790, per capita consumption of absolute alcohol averaged just under six gallons per year. Between 1800 and 1830, consumption rose to more than seven gallons annually. Since the alcohol content of beer and cider averaged around 10 percent (until about 1840, when it dropped to 5 percent), with wine at 18 percent and distilled liquors at 45 percent, these rates of consumption represented 70 gallons of beer and cider or 39 gallons of wine or nearly 16 gallons of hard liquor per citizen per year. By comparison, during the 1970s, a period known for socially liberal habits, consumption hovered at less than three gallons annually. In short, by the mid-1800s, Americans of all ages were sipping their alcohol literally morning, noon, and night (Kyvig, 1985). Gradually, however, the country was changing.

The Role of Industry and Economics

New York, Chicago, and most of the rest of the country experienced rapid economic development and modernization during the 19th century. Family farms and local shops and stores had been the staple of business, but improved transportation and other developments brought industrialization, commercial agriculture and ranching, and the growth of urban centers. With better roads, shipping, and the addition of rail freight services, mass production and distribution became the business of America. Inevitably, family life too changed as work places and homelife grew increasingly separate and an economy based on wages emerged. As coordinated, continuous production replaced the previous cycles of seasonal work, time became an increasingly valuable commodity (Kyvig, 1985). Schedules had to be kept so that work shifts could be manned and production rates maintained. In this more modern economy, alcohol, which had mattered little before, had the potential to become a serious problem.

Initially, at least, liquor was a way of life in most factories. While it makes sense now that workers should remain drink and drug free, that attitude represents a remarkable change from the past. So much a part of routine life were spirits, in fact, that employers who failed to provide regular rations to their employees faced dissatisfied workers and threats of work stoppages.

By the middle of the century, however, employers were growing more and more hostile to their frequently intoxicated workers. Increasingly, regulations were imposed to require on-the-job abstinence with punishments for violations ranging from warnings in most cases to dismissal in a few. While the newly introduced restrictions were widely attacked as "inconsiderate of the 'individual liberty' of employees," employers nonetheless adopted them overwhelmingly on grounds of safety and as a means to get workers to accept their responsibilities. Among the latter concerns were alertness, reliability and on-time performance, and work quality.

> As more things are done by machinery, as trolley cars supplant
> horse cars, as implements of greater precision and refinement take
> the place of cruder ones, as the speed at which machinery is run is
> increased, as the intensity with which people work becomes
> greater, the necessity of having a clear head during the hours of
> labor becomes imperative, and the very conditions of modern business life necessitate sobriety on the part of the workers. (Feldman,
> 1930:213)

Undoubtedly, some employers were compelled by moral and religious reasons in addition to their concern for their employees' health and well-being.

Regardless of motivation, few denied that alcohol and industry were poor companions. Long before Henry Ford formally introduced the five-day work week, many plants had done so de facto because of worker absences after pay days. "Blue Mondays," with incapacitated workers unable to return from drinking sprees, frequently disrupted production by bringing assembly lines to a standstill. To lessen such troubles, many employers tried changing their pay days from Saturday to other days in an effort to reduce Monday absenteeism. Others adopted Saturday for pay, hoping that their employees would sober up on the Sunday off that followed. Still others tried paying wages less frequently. As one midwestern company explained:

> There was so much drunkenness that many times we were scarcely
> able to operate the plant the following day [after Wednesday pay].
> Absences would run as high as 25 percent. On this account we
> were forced to change our pay day to Saturday in order that we
> might have six full working days. (Feldman, 1930:201)

Nor was absenteeism the only concern. Accidents, employee unreliability, poor workmanship and productivity, and high rates of turnover were increasingly attributed to alcohol and worker intoxication. Although hard evidence was rarely available to support the claims, respected researchers such as Yale economist Irving Fisher (1928) issued varying estimates of alcohol's destructive influence. "It is assumed that alcoholic beverages slow down the human machine," professor Fisher wrote, "so that each daily glass of beer reduces productivity 2 to 4 per cent." From this assumption, he went on to calculate that "productivity of labor would be increased from 10 to 20 per cent by effective Prohibition" (p. 101). Anticipating such gains, one business after another began to press for abstinence both on and off the job as industry joined the ranks of the liquor reformers.

The Coalitions for Change

Early on, the calls for voluntary moderation had an impact. By the 1840s, liquor had come to be widely credited for much of the nation's poverty, crime, and child neglect, leading many to stop drinking altogether. Others reduced their consumption such that by the middle of the decade per capita use had fallen to around three gallons annually. But reformers were not satisfied with successes that they knew had come hard but could be reversed quite easily. Alcohol, after all, was additive they argued. Moderate drinking would inevitably lead to immoderate drinking—the only true temperance was total abstinence. If abolishing liquor was in the common good, then why not legislate its use out of existence? To that end, the anti-alcohol efforts would need to be organized and aimed at grassroots political power and legislation. Begun in Maine in 1851, for the next half century this approach succeeded in at least temporarily installing some form of legal prohibition in 18 states and many more towns, cities, and counties. Despite the apparent successes, however, every advance in the movement was matched with a corresponding retreat as court appeals, referendums, and political treachery reversed most of what had been accomplished. In fact, by 1893, only six states remained under nominal prohibition, and even there the laws were not well enforced. In each of the six, camouflaged drugstores, speakeasies, and greengroceries designed to evade the liquor restrictions were flourishing (Cherrington, 1920). It was in this atmosphere that the Anti-Saloon League of America was organized and took charge of the crusade.

Despite claims that their organization was "born of God," the Anti-Saloon League was, in fact, an offspring of the Women's Crusade. Traced back to the Oberlin Temperance Alliance of 1874, the Women's Crusade and their mass meeting alliance in Oberlin, Ohio, was intended to wage war against saloons while employing "all lawful measures to suppress the traffic in and use of intoxicating liquors." For the next several years the alliance was content with a successful focus on local concerns. During a 1888 struggle to establish a local option law for townships, however, the alliance temporarily expanded statewide to increase their pressure on the Ohio legislature. Successful in their first attempt, on September 5, 1893, the organization was made permanent as the Anti-Saloon League of Ohio. In the first large-scale effort at political pressure, the league then joined forces with 46 other local groups to form the Anti-Saloon League of America. Although they would require nearly a decade to become organized nationally, almost at once this new coalition came to dominate the movement as "the real agency through which the church was directing its fights against the liquor traffic" (Asbury, 1950:95). At last, the liquor industry had a dangerous enemy worthy of their respect. As the *Bonfort's Wine and Spirit Circular* warned:

> The Anti-Saloon League is not a mob of long-haired fanatics, as some of the writers and speakers connected with our business have declared, but it is a strongly centralized organization, officered by men with unusual ability, financiered by capitalists with very long purses, subscribed to by hundreds of thousands of men, women, and children who are solicited by their various churches, advised by well-paid attorneys of great ability, and it is working with definite ideas to guide it in every state, in every county, in every city, in every precinct. (Asbury, 1950:96)

From the beginning, the league's officials recognized the potential for propaganda to influence. With considerable financial backing from individuals, churches, and industry, among their first efforts were the publication and widespread distribution of temperance literature of all types. Farming the work out to commercial firms at first, by the early 1900s they had established their own publishing house, the American Issue Publishing Company. With a newly built plant on donated land near Columbus, Ohio, the league soon became one of the most efficient, if not effective, sources of propaganda in our history. After only three years of operation, they routinely produced 40 tons or about 250 million pages of material a month. According to their own yearbook, by 1916 the output had increased to include 18 different editions of their official paper, the *American Issue*; seven editions of the *New Republic*; one monthly issue each of the *American Patriot* and *Scientific Temperance Journal*; a daily version titled the *National Daily*; seven other minor periodicals; and millions of books, charts, leaflets, tracts, folders, and pamphlets. With expenses estimated by the *New York Times* to be as high as $2.5 million annually (Asbury, 1950), the league could safely boast that their influence reached virtually the entire country.

Although the league took credit for bringing Protestant denominations into politics and officially declared itself "the strongest political organization in the world," the organization remained remarkably free of the entrapments that so often have entangled other causes. Strictly nonpartisan, league officials consistently refused even temporary alliances with any political party out of fear of compromise. Instead, they worked assiduously toward a single goal—drying of the country in steps from the grassroots townships to the nation as a whole. Further, while their critics alleged that the movement's image as agents of the churches engaged in "the Lord's business" allowed them to engage in various unsavory actions, proof of corruption in their methods was never demonstrated.

Unfortunately, their opponents were not so fortunate. As the brewers and their unions attempted to fight back, bungled attempts to bribe politicians and the press, influence elections, and coerce businessmen were regularly exposed. Both the Pennsylvania and the United States Brewers' Associations violated federal and state statutes with their sizable campaign contributions. The *Advertiser* of Montgomery (AL) and the Newark (NJ) *Ledger* were heavily subsidized by brewers, while the Washington *Times* was a target of outright takeover. A stable of well-known writers were paid to produce slanted articles for national magazines. But it was the German–American Alliance, long the principal clearinghouse for antiprohibition work among immigrants, which proved most embarrassing. Following a well-publicized investigation, the U. S. Senate found that the brewers were contributing large sums of money "with a view of using it [the Alliance] for their own political purposes." Unfortunately, the Alliance had its own agenda as well, as the investigation also revealed it as a center for anti-American and pro-German materials while the nation was at war with Germany during World War I. The alliance lost its charter by unanimous Senate vote, several of its leaders were imprisoned for their disloyal acts, and the Anti-Saloon League was delivered a major propaganda coup (Asbury, 1950). Liquor, and its makers, were solidly linked with un-American activities. With that final boost toward prohibition, the liquor industry was given one year to wind up its business while the Volstead Enforcement Act took effect—all beverages with .5 percent alcohol content were outlawed (Kyvig, 1985). On January 16, 1920, national prohibition had arrived.

ENFORCING THE UNENFORCEABLE

Though enforcement began at once, the modest budget for regulation was a clear sign that legislators assumed that Americans would abide by the law voluntarily. After all, support for reform had been considerable. True, no popular vote had been taken and public opinion polling was still in the future, but statewide referendums on prohibition measures had shown impressive public backing. In all, 19 of the 23 states holding such votes in the five years prior to passage of the 18th Amendment had passed antiliquor laws with majorities of between 52 and 76 percent. In addition, although the requirements to amend the Constitution were demanding, nevertheless between 1917 and 1919 the proposed amendment had quickly gained broad legislative approval.

Officially, at least, the expected support and benefits began to appear at once. For example, according to Colvin (1927), who documented the movement for the Prohibition National Commission, compliance during the first year was so widespread "that the results produced were so decisive and the benefits were so extraordinary that they may be described as almost miraculous" (p. 476). With selective comparisons of events of 1917 with those of 1920, his commission noted as proof of the success a 63 percent decrease in arrests for drunkenness in Chicago; decreases in prison populations in many states; reductions in prison admissions in several states; and a drop in some categories of crime (as measured by arrests) in New York City, Chicago, Massachusetts, and Connecticut. Similarly, Cherrington (1920), chief editor of the Anti-Saloon League's publishing company, declared national prohibition a success in its first year and advocated its expansion to accomplish the same worldwide. A more careful examination, however, suggests far more mixed results.

Buoyed with the confidence that society's transformation had begun, the budgets for prohibition enforcement agencies were remarkably small, while responsibilities were spread widely among authorities at all levels. At the federal level, the newly formed Prohibition Bureau (which had been forced upon the Treasury Department) was hurriedly staffed with political appointees. Honesty, ability, and experience were seldom inquired about, only an endorsement from the Anti-Saloon League or a member of Congress was required. While some conscientiously tried to recommend good men, the Wickersham Commission's study of the law estimated that as many as 50 percent of the men hired were "unfit for their position and incompetent as law enforcing officers" (Dobyns, 1940:327). The Assistant Attorney General in charge of all prohibition prosecutions observed:

> I had not been in charge for more than a few months before I realized . . . that hundreds of prohibition agents had been appointed through political pull, and were as devoid of honesty and integrity as the bootlegging fraternity. I found that there were scores of prohibition agents no more fit to be trusted with a commission to enforce the laws of the United States and to carry a gun than the notorious bandit Jesse James. (Asbury, 1950:175)

Predictably, within hours of the law's enactment, confusion began to take hold. While Protestant churches and league chapters celebrated, police throughout the country disagreed over their role. In Boston, officers were stationed in all the well-known drinking places to ensure enforcement the moment prohibition became the law. In San Francisco, however, the *Chronicle* reported that little had changed. "Corks popped and siphons fizzled and glasses clinked long after the legal hour." In New Orleans, nothing out of the ordinary occurred—then and thereafter, New Orleans simply ignored prohibition. And in New York City only the weather prevented a celebration in Times Square billed as the biggest drunk of all time. By far the wettest city in the country, New York's police had already announced that since no state prohibition law existed, they would not enforce the federal statutes. Meanwhile, crime was getting organized in a hurry.

As Chicago's drinkers were cheering their final moments, a gang of six masked men invaded the city's main rail yard to offer a preview of what was to come: After binding and gagging watchmen, trainmen, and the yardmaster, they made off with whiskey worth over $100,000. In the weeks leading up to prohibition, hundreds of thefts of liquor in large quantities from warehouses and trucks had already occurred, leaving investigators with swelling caseloads from the start. In one such case, 61 barrels of bourbon simply disappeared from a government warehouse in Kentucky. If drinkers greeted the news happily, the brewers who still owned the booze did not, since the Prohibition Bureau had imposed a tax of $6.40 a gallon for all liquor withdrawn even though someone else had done so (Asbury, 1950).

By the morning after enactment, newspapers were full of tales of agents seizing trucks full of liquor in New York and Peoria (Illinois), raiding stills in Detroit and Hammond (Indiana), and serving warrants on liquor law violations throughout the country. The first infractions occurred within hours of the "new beginning" and would become increasingly commonplace thereafter. With a jump of 500 percent in the cost of a cocktail, all but the wealthiest of Americans had to become far more creative in their pursuit of a drink. Many who couldn't afford or didn't trust the bootleggers learned to make their own. The procedures could be learned at any good library (ironically, the Department of Agriculture continued to issue pamphlets that explained how liquor could be made from most produce), while most kitchens had the utensils necessary for distilling. Supplies were easy to find from the stores that suddenly opened to meet the new demand for hops, yeast, malt, copper tubing, and other supplies necessary for home brewing.

Those who could afford the price of a drink or a bottle had suppliers available as well. The tiny islands of Saint Pierre and Miquelon off the coast of Newfoundland, for example, imported at least 118,600 gallons of British liquor during 1922 alone. With only 6,000 inhabitants, it is unlikely that more than a small portion was consumed locally. In addition, legally produced industrial alcohol was regularly diverted to beverage use, and California grape growers quadrupled their output as home wine making flourished (Kyvig, 1985). Even the doctors got into the business by writing prescriptions for medicinal liquor, which continued to be quite legal (Dobyns, 1940). And men such as Rothstein, Torrio, Frank Costello, and Al Capone were all too happy to supply the public's demand.

In no time, U.S. Attorneys across the country were devoting nearly one-half of their time to dry-law cases: 90 percent in southern Alabama; at least 70 percent in North Carolina, Kentucky, and West Virginia; and more than 60 percent in Florida and Minnesota. Worse yet, prosecutors noted that the federal courthouses were becoming a "seething mob of bartenders, peddlers, waiters, bond runners, and fixers" while judges complained of the "pollution . . . the air of corruption had even descended into the civil parts of the court" where jurymen were unable to avoid bribe attempts even in the restrooms (Asbury, 1950:170). By 1924, the population of the federal prisons had nearly doubled with the 313,940 suspects arrested during the first six years by federal agents (and untold more by state and local officers). For all the activity in the courts, however, a far more disturbing scene was being played out on city streets.

At the end of the first year of enforcement, officials reported that one agent and one civilian had been killed as a result of federal enforcement efforts. Less than five years later, April 1926, the Bureau of Internal Revenue raised those totals to 89 civilians and 47 federal officers, including two members of the Coast Guard. By 1929, the Treasury Department estimated that civilian deaths had risen to 135, although they counted only 45 federal agents slain in the line of duty. Two years later in 1931, the Wickersham Commission placed the total at 60 agents and 144 civilians despite similar investigations a year earlier claiming 86 agents and 200 civilians slain.

As the varying figures were released, many noted that regardless of what the true count was, they dealt only with the operations of federal agencies—the Prohibition Bureau, Customs, and the Coast Guard. Not included were state and local officials or private citizens or groups acting on their own. In its pamphlet, *Reforming America with a Shotgun,* the Association Against the Prohibition Amendment reported "instances in which ardent prohibitionists, without any official standing whatsoever, have taken it upon themselves to enforce the law." Similarly, the New York *World* told of clergymen in that city raising funds to organize and equip teams of undercover agents to hunt down liquor law violators. In all, Senator Tydings of Maryland estimated the total killed due to prohibition enforcement during the first ten years to be at least 1,365; the Washington *Herald* placed the total at

1,360 (Asbury, 1950). Of course, countless others were wounded or otherwise injured.

Nor was widespread violence the only unintended result. Many in the legal community attacked enforcers for being either too lax or overzealous in their efforts. As such, while District Court Judge Louis Henry (1929) was advocating federal legislation to compel more aggressive action from the states, federal appellate courts regularly reversed convictions and condemned misconduct by officers pursuing violators (Solomon, 1985). Even more troubling, however, were the large numbers of agents actively pursuing their own self-interest. Ten days after the 18th Amendment's enactment, three Chicago agents were indicted for accepting bribes and selling seized liquor back to bootleggers. Two weeks later, two others were arrested in Baltimore on similar grounds. By the end of 1921, more than 100 agents were dismissed in New York for illegally withdrawing liquor seized and stored by the government. Before the end of 1925, a deputy collector of Internal Revenue in New York, the prohibition administrator of Chicago and his assistant, and 58 agents in Cincinnati were convicted for various incidents of conspiracy to violate liquor laws. In Cincinnati, two Pullman railcars were needed to haul officials to the United States Penitentiary in Atlanta, the same prison that would later hold Al Capone. Unfortunately, these convictions represent only a few of the hundreds of officials accused, indicted, arrested, or convicted for profiting illegally from their positions. In fact, during the first four years of prohibition, 141 federal agents were jailed while thousands more were "separated from the service" or "dismissed for cause." Two years later, before a congressional committee in 1926, the Assistant Secretary of the Treasury in charge of prohibition testified that to February of that year, his bureau had required at least 10,000 men to keep 2,200 jobs staffed (Asbury, 1950).

The higher ranks of the service were equally troubled. Four national commissioners of the Prohibition Bureau were hired during the first five years, while the New York City office was administered by four different men in the first 13 months. During the first three years, both New York and Pennsylvania had their state directors indicted for conspiracy. In the Pennsylvania case, T. Henry Walnut, the Assistant U.S. Attorney for Philadelphia, attempted to act as early as 1921 on evidence that the state's first prohibition director was conspiring to illegally withdraw 700,000 gallons of stored whiskey. When he attempted to take his case before a grand jury, however, he was ordered by the Department of Justice to wait, apparently because of the director's backing in both the state and federal senates. After three such attempts, the Attorney General, Harry Daugherty, removed the problem by firing Walnut instead. The resulting public uproar finally forced indictments against the director and 48 others, but before a trial could proceed, the government announced that nearly all of its evidence had disappeared. Quickly, a verdict of acquittal was directed. No other action was ever taken.

Understandably, all of this led to considerable public outrage. As a general spirit of lawlessness spread, no one seemed safe from the violence and corruption. In every large city in the country it was commonly known, or at least assumed, that significant portions of the police were in collusion with the bootleggers. Attitudes of disregard and contempt for law became increasingly common as the machinery of enforcement suffered a progressive breakdown under the weight of the Volstead Act. Naturally, opponents of prohibition did their part, seizing every opportunity to display the law's failures and declare the effort itself at fault. Taking the lessons from the Anti-Saloon League before them, the opponents too set their propaganda at full volume. As one observer complained:

> Every time a crime is committed, they cry prohibition. Every time
> a girl or a boy goes wrong, they shout prohibition. Every time a
> policeman or politician is accused of corruption, they scream pro-
> hibition. As a result, they are gradually building up in the public
> mind the impression that prohibition is a major cause of all the sins
> of society. (Odegard, 1930:180)

It was increasingly clear that something had to be done.

THE RETREAT FROM REFORM

Confronted with a steadily deteriorating society, advocates on both sides were quick to offer analysis and solutions. Supporters of temperance staunchly defended prohibition, insisting that the failures were of administration rather than concept. Federal enforcers were understaffed and incompetent, they noted, while the state level response had been all but nonexistent. As an example they pointed to 1927 when federal funding for enforcement topped $12 million, while the 48 states spent less than $700,000 combined. Utah spent only $160 that year. Further, of the cases that were brought to court, at least two-thirds were settled through plea bargaining with no more punishment than a fine. Emory Buckner, the U.S. Attorney for the Southern District of New York, complained that although those cases counted as technical victories, the records should be changed to read, "Escaped on payment of money" (Asbury, 1950:171).

If the failure was one of resolve and effort, then what was needed was greater toughness. For some, that meant legislation to hold local officials accountable and compel them to act more assertively under threat of their own prosecution for noncompliance. The federal government could then focus more directly on smuggling, manufacturing, and major conspiracies. If such a statute were enacted by Congress, they predicted that "a few prosecutions against violators in the federal courts would immediately put an end to sham enforcement" (Henry, 1929:243).

For others, the solution could be found in a combination of penalties and incentives. Large rewards to be funded with fines and other penalties could be paid to persons assisting law enforcement with amounts varying based upon the capacity of the operation reported. Under one such plan, a special fund would be established for informants under 18 years of age. "School children make splendid operatives" (Custer, 1929:322), the proposers noted. Simultaneously, penalties should be increased sharply (Goodwin, 1929), offenders deprived of their citizenship (Doyle, 1929), private persons empowered to use force when they encounter violations (Lightner, 1929), and schools and churches pressed to teach and reinforce values, morals, and the wisdom of abstinence (Hobson, 1929). Others added plans for military involvement in enforcement (Dibrell, 1929) and reorganization and streamlining of enforcement agencies (Davis, 1929), the prosecutorial process (Dunham, 1929), and our judicial systems (J. Brown, 1929).

To those on the opposite side of the issue, however, the problem was prohibition itself. Far from making a better society, they contended that in only a short time the 18th Amendment and its companion legislation, the Volstead Act, had promoted widespread disrespect for the law and support for lawbreakers. "All I do is supply a public demand," Capone often declared—incorrectly. As we saw earlier, he also murdered, extorted, and engaged in racketeering offenses. It was prohibition, the critics complained, however, that provided the opportunities for the enormous profits he made. When coupled with improvements in transportation and mass production manufacturing, they contended that the temperance movement had also succeeded in expanding the power and reach of what had been local gangs into regional criminal organizations, all the while teaching them the value of organizing well and cooperating with each other.

Despite a growing dislike of the law, the general belief throughout the 1920s was that nothing could be done to alter it because it had been installed in the Constitution. Constitutional amending was regarded as incredibly difficult—removal of a previous amendment was thought to be completely out of the question. To accomplish such a revision, at least one-third of Congress and half of the states would have to reverse their previous positions and withdraw their earlier support. Perhaps enforcement could be abandoned or the definition of intoxicating beverages could be changed to allow beer and wine. But as Senator Morris Sheppard of Texas gloated, there was as much chance of repealing the 18th Amendment as there was "for a hummingbird to fly to the planet Mars with the Washington Monument tied to its tail" (Kyvig, 1985:14).

Nonetheless, with a platform that respect for law and order needed to be rebuilt; that the 18th Amendment placed too much power in the hands of the federal government; and that enforcement expenses, lost taxes, and corruption made prohibition too costly, opponents began to push for a retreat from the decade-old reform. After forming an organization similar to the Anti-Saloon League, the Association Against the Prohibition Amendment (AAPA) called for a return to a limited, socially neutral government in place of the activist, reformist state that had evolved. By the mid 1920s, John Raskob, the Democratic party's national chairman, and the wealthy du Pont brothers joined the effort, bringing with them the organization skills and financing to expand the campaign. Meanwhile, when the Women's Organization for National Prohibition Reform was formed in 1929, its 1.5 million members put to rest the notion that all women supported prohibition and would be active in blocking any change. Finally, when the 1932 election saw voters turn the "dry" President Herbert Hoover out of office for his Democratic opponent, Franklin Roosevelt, Congress interpreted the voter returns as a judgment on prohibition and a mandate for change. Undoubtedly, the unanticipated onset of the Great Depression could explain much of the voter dissatisfaction, but even it had boosted the anti-prohibition cause. After all, if drinking were legal, the excise taxes on liquor—one-third of federal revenues before prohibition— could go far to ease the federal budget crisis that had developed. All that was left now was to determine how the temperance reforms were to be undone.

Most in Congress favored the direct approach used to establish the 18th Amendment, confident that following the 1932 election state legislatures would ratify their action. The AAPA, however, insisted that a Constitutional Convention be held with delegates drawn specifically to reconsider prohibition. No constitutional provision that directly affected the American people should be adopted without their specific approval, they argued. In fact, it appears that many were less worried about the issues of fair representation than that dry pressure and recalcitrance in the legislatures of only a few small, rural states could deny the majority their repeal. As such, while a convention ratification was cumbersome and had not been employed since 1788, this time there should be no question as to popular preference. Eventually, Congress would accede to these demands.

As each state established its convention, voters were offered a clear choice between wet and dry representatives. For almost eight months beginning April 14, 1933, delegates were elected from one state after another and quickly came together to consider whether a 21st Amendment should be passed to repeal the 18th. Most of the state conventions operated smoothly, with no state requiring more than a day of discussion to reach agreement—New Hampshire needed only 17 minutes. By December 5, when Ohio, Pennsylvania, and Utah added their support for repeal, the necessary 36 states for ratification were in place. Of the 37 states to consider the constitutional question, only in South Carolina did the voters prefer to keep the 18th Amendment. In all, delegates supporting repeal were favored by 73 percent of the votes cast (Kyvig, 1985). With a rejection so emphatic, the end of the "noble experiment" with national prohibition was both prompt and decisive. Liquor could now return to its place as an avenue of escape for those feeling the wrath of the Depression.

PROHIBITION AND REPEAL:
WHAT LESSONS FOR TODAY?

Although doubts naturally arose about the extent that the public had supported prohibition in the first place, almost all indications are clear that it was nonetheless successful at its stated goal. A significant reduction in the consumption of alcohol had occurred. Burnham (1968) notes that the medical problems most closely related to alcohol use almost all declined sharply once prohibition began. Further, once the amendment was repealed and more accurate measures again became available, many were surprised to find annual per capita consumption at less than one gallon. Quite clearly, many Americans were by then out of the habit of drinking. For some, the cost of evading the law was undoubtedly too high. The price of a cocktail had risen to nearly $1, while the average family earned less than $2,000 per year. And, of course, not all who could afford to would break the law. In fact, per capita annual consumption did not reach anywhere near pre-prohibition levels again until the 1970s.

Why then was the opposition to and ridicule for the effort so intense? Kyvig (1979, 1985), regarded by many to have authored the most comprehensive study on the politics of repeal, offers several reasons. First is the very nature of law. Although the prohibition effort was apparently quite successful at reducing the overall consumption of liquor, a substantial demand continued to exist.

Law indeed becomes a social contract, and unless most of the members of a society agree to honor the contract, it becomes unenforceable. In the case of prohibition, a very substantial number of people simply refused from the beginning to sign the contract. Drinking was an integral part of the culture of several large, cohesive, urban-centered ethnic groups, including the Irish, Italians, and Jews, and they could not be convinced that there was anything wrong with it. . . . So in sum, the degree of compliance with prohibition, although substantial, was insufficient to the need. (Kyvig, 1985:13)

More complex is the issue of the proper role of government. Known largely as the Progressive Period, to many in the early 1900s society had become not only complex but evil and awash with sin. As a result, moral responsibility rested with society's natural leaders who would create, through law, improved conditions for all. At the same time, however, others felt strongly that it was inappropriate for the government to attempt to control behavior that had no substantial significance beyond self. Hostility toward statism and a commitment to limited government were equally felt. Inevitably, these two forces collided as government expanded its powers to enforce its new constitutional mandate. Many Americans, including some who had initially favored eliminating alcohol, came to resent the law as applied, reasoning that it was at once ineffectual as well as an excessive intrusion into private matters. In the end, private liberties were chosen over public interest.

Finally, while the nation celebrated the repeal of prohibition, few then or since have examined the significance of the change brought by the 21st Amendment. Having declared the liquor industry illegal in 1920, government undertook one of its greatest reversals to become a partner in 1933. Ironically, Elliot Ness, the now well-known head of the prohibition crimefighters, the Untouchables, spent his final days retelling his stories over a beer in a neighborhood tavern he would have closed only a few decades earlier. Such a shift in policy is important not only to those interested in government–industrial relations and the foundations of alcohol-related social problems but is equally significant from policy and enforcement perspectives. For example, as the shift in policy forced the states to respond with their own control mechanisms, it revealed a lack of consensus in the nation on how such control could and should be accomplished. In response, some states created monopolies over the trade, others imposed complex regulations that were often quite difficult to follow, while others left the free market to operate with few restrictions at all. To our knowledge, no effort has been made to measure the utility or the impact of these different approaches (Lender, 1985). Such an effort would be worthwhile given the uncertainty of the efficacy of prohibition, both historically with alcohol and more recently with our current concerns with narcotics and other drugs.

Certainly, national prohibition as provided by the 18th Amendment was an interesting if not noble experiment that both succeeded and failed in important ways. At once, it reduced the consumption of liquor while reducing respect for law, corrupting law enforcement and others, and feeding and enlarging organized crime. While drawing lessons from history is often a tricky business, the lessons from national prohibition can be valuable as we wrestle with our drug problems today.

7

⊹►⇌◉⇐⇌►⊹

Prohibition Today:

Narcotics, Control, and Organized Crime

A   s the momentum for reform built toward Prohibition, the forces for abstinence inevitably widened their nets to include substances other than alcohol. Although a far less significant part of everyday life than the spirits, by the turn of the 19th century, narcotics were readily available and regularly used. A common ingredient in prescriptions and treatments, opium in particular came to be valued for its calming effects when dealing with ailments varying from cholera to parasites. In relatively mild doses, enhanced by frequent use and in combination with alcohol, opium was so diverse in its applications that physicians dispensed it freely. In addition, self-dosing became commonplace. Given that the medical profession's goal was to relieve pain and that its primary focus was on symptoms rather than causes, it should not be "difficult to understand the wide popularity of a drug which either singly or combined so eminently was suited to the needs of so many medical situations" (Terry & Pellins, 1928:58).

As the middle of the century arrived, technological advances in farming increased opium availability while breakthroughs in organic chemistry resulted in new and more potent drugs. At roughly the same time, introduction of the hypodermic permitted direct injections. This, in turn, allowed physicians to seek ever more powerful painkillers. The opiates were a natural, especially morphine. Easy to produce, morphine was especially effective and soon popularized by the scientific journals as completely lacking in negative side effects. With the onslaught of the Civil War and the massive casualties suffered on each side, this cheap, compact, and quite predictable drug was quickly in demand. Indeed, many writers have attributed the growth of addiction in this country directly to the treatment of Civil War battle wounds (Terry & Pellins, 1928; Morgan, 1981). No thorough study of morphine use during the war appears to exist, however, and Musto (1987) and others are skeptical of so convenient a cause. Regardless of its origin, by the war's close a relatively high level of opium consumption had been established in the United States.

Although the practice of excessive use was "peculiarly American" (Wiley, 1912), opium itself was not domestically available to any great extent. Despite the poppy plant's ability to survive under a variety of conditions, even then the process of production was far too labor intensive to be commercially successful in the United States. Instead, distributors found that they could rely on a host of European importers who were both dependable and cost effective. Since no restrictions existed on importation, throughout the remainder of the century consumption rose rapidly as physicians and manufacturers came to realize the effects of the product. By 1870, morphine and cocaine were cheaper than alcohol. Musto (1987) notes that by then drugs had become so popular a part of the lives of Americans that even cures for opium addiction often contained large amounts of opiates. Cough syrups, hay fever remedies, and even Coca-Cola (until 1903) contained cocaine as active ingredients. Still, few regulations existed; given the commercial importance of their products, manufacturers had become remarkably successful at preventing legislation that required disclosure of their drugs in commercial preparations.

Gradually, of course, pressures for moderation began to mount with the early focus directed at opium smoking. Because smoking was strictly a recreational habit, the smokers lacked the elaborate advertising that accompanied morphine and cocaine. In addition, the smokers and their opium dens were symbolically associated with the Chinese, a group actively persecuted and almost totally excluded from immigration. Thus, they lacked any broad-based support among the public. As a result, by 1909 the practice was restricted in the United States.

While the limits on opium served notice that the nation was determined to rid itself of addiction, Musto (1987) and others also note that it served important foreign policy objectives as well. The Chinese had lost two earlier wars (in 1840 and again in 1856) in an attempt to stop British importation of opium. Now the United States was asking to convene the first international meeting to consider trafficking between nations. Taking the lead at least partly to soften Chinese resistance to our own Far East investments, as the conference approached, U.S. officials seemed to discover our own lack of restrictions. To save face, legislation against opium smoking was quickly approved. Ironically, it was American prejudice against the Chinese that aided considerably in our efforts to help China itself.

Beyond these limited federal efforts, by the late 1890s, endeavors to curtail opium usage were already under way at the local level. Now alert to the dangers of addiction, manufacturers stepped up their campaigns to block plans to require disclosure of the contents in their products. The effort was too little and too late, however, as public opinion began to shift, until slowly the demand for opiates and cocaine leveled off. By then, importation of crude opium had risen 430 percent, from less than 12 grains per capita annually in the 1840s to over 52 grains in the 1890s. With perhaps as many as 250,000 known addicts, physicians began to acknowledge that they had overmedicated their patients, and a consensus was formed that narcotics as an additive to patent medicines should be stopped (Musto, 1987). A fear of addiction and addicting drugs had taken hold. As attitudes changed, addicts were increasingly identified with foreigners and minorities, especially the Chinese and blacks, who were already the targets of fear and restraints. In the South, however, it was cocaine that generated a special fear.

Immensely popular at first, this derivative of the coca plant was given freely for everything from hay fever to headaches to addictions to morphine and alcohol. Preferred by intellectuals, cocaine usage was promoted freely by medical journals. Sigmund Freud was an early proponent, as was William Hammond, the Surgeon General of the Army, who seldom enjoyed a meal without it (Musto, 1987). Others praising its benefits included Sarah Bernhardt, John Phillip Sousa, and no less than three popes and 16 heads of state. In 1902, "Peruvian Wine of Coca" was available from Sears and Roebuck; and government reports in 1908 listed more than 40 brands of soft drinks that contained cocaine as a primary ingredient (Abadinsky, 1990). It was only after southern whites began to fear that cocainized blacks might become uncontrollable that the substance fell from favor. Reacting to tales of superhuman strength and cunning, along with stories of cocaine improving blacks' pistol marksmanship while making them all but impervious to .32 caliber bullets, the push for antidrug legislation quickly gained momentum throughout the South. As the police upgraded their weapons to .38 caliber, respected publications fueled the fires by telling of "Negro cocaine fiends" (*New York Times*, February 8, 1914) and explaining how "most of the attacks upon white women in the

South are the direct result of a cocaine-crazed Negro brain" (*Literary Digest*, March 1914). Conveniently, while considering the cocaine–race association, Atlanta's police chief took the opportunity to attribute 70 percent of his city's crime to the problem (Musto, 1987).

As the hype grew, the federal government called a second conference in The Hague to iron out an international agreement. Conference participants chastised the United States for its domestic usage and lack of regulation while committing themselves to enact laws to suppress abuse. Of course, the substances of concern included the opiates and cocaine as well as all drugs prepared or derived from either (International Opium Conference, 1911–1912). After ratifying the agreement in 1913, on December 17, 1914, Congress passed the Harrison Act as a regulatory effort to carry out The Hague Convention provisions. America's drug problem had officially begun.

THE HARRISON NARCOTICS ACT

Sponsored in Congress by Representative Francis Harrison, a Tammany Democrat, the antinarcotics bill was a careful compromise. Strongly backed by reformers, the goal of Harrison's bill was to eliminate narcotics use except for medical purposes. The vehicle was a mild regulatory measure consisting of registration and record-keeping requirements thought sufficient to bring domestic drug traffic into observable channels. In 1919, the act was amended to include a moderate federal tax. Dr. Hamilton Wright, one of the bill's chief supporters, explained the legislative intent:

> It is designed to place the entire interstate traffic in the habit forming drugs under the administration of the Treasury Department.
> It is the opinion of the American Opium Commission that it would bring this whole traffic and the use of these drugs into the light of day and thereby create a public opinion against the use of them that would be more important, perhaps, than the Act itself. (King, 1972:21)

The bill itself was the product of the National Drug Trade Conference, a committee of trade associations with input from the departments of State and Treasury, guidance from Wright, and the backing of President Wilson and Secretary of State William Jennings Bryan. Introduced to Congress by Harrison, the bill required everyone whose vocation involved handling narcotic drugs and cocaine—including importers, manufacturers, wholesalers, druggists, doctors, dentists, and researchers—to register with the Treasury Department and pay a small occupational tax. Each registrant was required to keep records that were to be available for inspection by Treasury agents and law enforcement personnel (King, 1972:22). Far from airtight, the bill's numerous compromises allowed simplified forms for reporting, allowed physicians to dispense drugs under some circumstances without records, and allowed patent medicines to continue to include small amounts of some narcotics for sale in stores and by mail. The 1919 amendment added an excise tax of one cent per ounce on opium, coca leaves, and their derivatives. This tax was to be collected at the point the drug first entered commerce, where a tax stamp would be affixed to its package or container as evidence that all taxes were paid. To facilitate collection, it was made unlawful to purchase, sell, dispense, or distribute drugs except in their original stamped packages.

While many in Congress felt that they had, at last, met the government's international obligations, the act's proponents were worried about its weaknesses from the start. After all, there were no quality, labeling, or packaging standards, and no restrictions were included on who could register and deal in the drugs—so long as the necessary records were kept and the taxes paid (King, 1972). As such, with the Harrison Act now in hand, the debate over its enforcement potentials had just begun.

The Impact on Public Opinion

While the Harrison Act may have had its flaws, it was clearly a success at making the stamp of illegitimacy official on most narcotics use. Where the opiate addicts of the 19th century had been respectable citizens, often females, those of the 20th century were seen as undesirables and members of some underworld. Gradually, as the nation drifted into world war, opiates also came to represent menacing tools in the German grand design for conquest. In its stories and on its editorial pages, no less than the *New York Times* told of the blood-curdling German fiendishness:

> Into well-known German brands of toothpaste and patent medicines—naturally for export only—habit-forming drugs were to be introduced; at first a little, then more, as the habit grew on the non-German victim and his system craved ever-greater quantities. Already the test had been made on natives of Africa, who responded readily . . . in a few years Germany would have fallen upon a world which cried for its German toothpaste and soothing syrup—a world of "cokeys" and "hop fiends" which would have been absolutely helpless when a German embargo shut off the supply of its pet poison. (December 18, 1918)

As estimates of the addict population were adjusted upward, tales of drug peddlers concentrating their efforts on military bases and training centers spread quickly around the country. Further, rumors of enemy agents passing out drug-laced candy near schoolyards were reinforced by official reports that drug usage had shifted overnight to become a threat to our youth. While 70 percent of known addicts were suddenly discovered to be under 25 years of age, schools were allegedly now finding children in their classrooms completely stoned (King, 1972). When coupled with the remaining fears of wild blacks and devious Chinese, stopping the addicts and their drugs picked up a patriotic fervor to become a national imperative. The question was no longer *whether* to control but *how* it should be done. The newly formed Prohibition Bureau, created to enforce the Volstead Act, was ideally suited for the job.

Opening the Opportunities for Crime

Since only three states had followed the federal lead by enacting their own drug-control legislation, the full burden of enforcement fell directly on federal authorities. Unlike with alcohol, however, agents had only the Harrison Act behind them. As such, intimidation would have to serve as a primary tactic. For the public at large, roadblocks, lengthy searches, and inspections of passenger trains and other vehicles would do. For the professionals whose work with narcotics left them with far more to lose, more aggressive tactics were available. By arresting, investigating, and then releasing doctors, pharmacists, and others who dispensed drugs—a widespread tactic—many were coerced into abandoning these quite legal aspects of their practices. In 1918 alone, agents reported that they had *dropped* charges against 14,701 persons registered under the act. In 1919, another 22,595 persons were similarly investigated; in 1920, the number jumped to 47,835 (King, 1972). The message was clear: Violations under the confusing Harrison Act were easy to commit; punishments could be quite severe. In no time, the legal supply of narcotics began to dry up.

Simultaneously, officials at all levels continued to adjust their estimates upward, allowing narcotics to be blamed for a variety of social ills. Prohibition Commissioner Haynes, for example, officially estimated that the United States had at least 1.5 million drug addicts and that no part of the country had been spared. The Secretary of the Treasury reported that as a nation we were consuming 10 to 60 times as much opium per capita as any other nation and that users numbered between 200,000 and 4 million. For the first time, he added, drug dealers had formed an elaborate national organization to distribute their product illegally. New York City's health commissioner worried publicly that with supplies no longer readily available, some 8,000 addicts roaming his city's streets would "break out violently when the narcotic hunger becomes stronger" (King, 1972). Chicago, Denver, El Paso, Rochester, Pittsburgh, and other cities each added their own stories of addict populations gone wild, until finally headlines declared that an estimated 30 percent of all residents in the New York metropolitan area were addicted. Nearly lost in the frenzy was New York City Deputy Police Commissioner Carlton Simon who responded that his department knew of no more than 250,000 current users and that no more than 15 percent of them were of the "criminal class." The Treasury Department, too, contradicted its earlier estimates in its own 1923 study that placed the nation's addict population at no more than 110,000 (King, 1972). Throughout it all, no one bothered to offer the basis for any estimates or an explanation for how so massive a supply of narcotics might be occurring. How, for example, had the illegal distribution network become so much more effective than its legitimate counterpart only a few years earlier?

Initially, at least, the criminal entrepreneurs who would take advantage of this new void in the marketplace were disorganized and unprepared. Lacking the moral stigma and the patriotic passion against it, alcohol possessed a much larger consumer base, making it a safer and potentially more profitable business. In addition, a reliable domestic supply of booze was far easier to establish. Nonetheless, profits could be made, so men like Rothstein, Lansky, and Lucky Luciano quietly stepped forward. In 1923, for example, Vito Genovese brought Charles La Gaipa from California to meet Luciano. La Gaipa asked for $20,000 to finance a heroin shipment from Mexico as the initial step in an international pipeline. The return on the deal was to be $150,000, of which Luciano would get 60 percent. Days later, a careless Luciano was arrested carrying samples of the heroin to Brooklyn for testing (Lupsha, 1987). Nor was this his first venture into the trade. Recall that earlier, as an 18-year-old, Luciano had been arrested for selling morphine to federal agents. La Gaipa remained in the narcotics business until his sudden disappearance in 1944 during a federal investigation. Until then, among his business associates were Vincent Mangano, Albert Anastasia, and several members of the Unione Siciliana, the Italian fraternal organization in Chicago.

Despite such individual opportunities, much has been made of a "no-narcotics" rule that was alleged to have existed among many of the major criminal organizations of the day. According to Valachi, fear of an intense public reaction and law enforcement response led Frank Costello to establish a ban prohibiting any members of his organization from dealing in narcotics. Other groups reportedly followed suit. The Iannis suggest that one member of the Lupollo group they studied was disciplined and sent to Florida because of his association with drug traffickers (Ianni, 1972). Lupsha (1987) writes that the Bonannos were reportedly so opposed to the trade that Joseph Bonanno had vowed to put any of his men so engaged into the ovens of his bakery. Tony Accardo in Chicago was said to have actually paid his employees $200 a week—later raised to $250—to ensure that they remained drug free. Those who took the payments and continued to deal in narcotics were to be killed, an action that Peterson (1983) explains only occurred twice.

Undoubtedly, such policies did much to keep the trafficking in drugs disorganized. With demand for narcotics in a severe decline by the 1930s, even a disorganized supply was sufficient to meet the need, however. Musto (1990) observed that the antinarcotics reaction was so sharp by the 1930s that physicians were reluctant to prescribe drugs, and patients would at times refuse medications that were perfectly safe to use. In the schools, antinarcotics education was integrated with the normal curriculum, and the Motion Picture Association agreed to prohibit any depiction of drugs in any movie filmed. In such an atmosphere, the facade of no involvement could be safely maintained while still leaving room for the more enterprising gangsters to profit on the side. A few, such as Anastasia, were bold enough to simply ignore the rule. Others were said to have paid lip service without enforcement. Still others, like the Brunos, quietly franchised out their operations to local gangs for a fee (Lupsha, 1987). By the late 1960s, however, the social climate, as well as knowledge about and resistance to narcotics use, had changed dramatically. With a renewed demand and vast profits suddenly possible, opportunities for suppliers once again became considerable. As they had each time before, crime and the criminals got organized in a hurry.

A LOOK AT THE PRODUCTS

Since the Harrison Act's enactment, pharmacology and the resulting substances available for use and abuse have each advanced considerably. While cocaine and the opiates (opium, morphine, and to a lesser extent, heroin) were the primary products then, today's criminals have a far more diverse assortment available. Added to the earlier lineup of products are synthetic (and semisynthetic) narcotics, improved coca products, barbiturates, tranquilizers, organic solvents and inhalants, amphetamines, cannabis, and LSD and other hallucinogens. Whereas earlier users primarily smoked or ingested their drugs, today's consumers can more easily prepare their dosages for injection (into veins, muscles, or beneath the skin) or absorption (through the outer skin, anally, vaginally, or sublingually through the tissues under the tongue). Of course, tablets, capsules, pills, tinctures, extracts, and syrups are also available. In short, from a business perspective, few would disagree that organized crime has reacted well to its market.

Table 7.1 outlines the psychoactive drugs of abuse currently available. These drugs are briefly reviewed here, according to their general chemical makeup. While not an exhaustive listing, we have included what we believe to be the major substances of concern. Many of these drugs are available legally by prescription, but others have no legal production or distribution.

Narcotics

Although the term *narcotics* is used generically, pharmacologically narcotics refers only to the natural derivatives of the opium poppy. As such, the range of substances that can properly be called narcotics is quite limited. Typically, narcotics are grouped into three distinct categories: natural narcotics, semi-synthetic narcotics, and synthetic narcotics.

Natural Narcotics All natural narcotics are the product of opium, the purified juice of the green, unripened seed of the white opium poppy. As even casual observers are aware, most of the world's opium supply originates from two general focal points. The first is a vast area of Southeast Asia comprised of sections of Burma, Thailand, and Laos. Known as the Golden Triangle, this area emerged as the world's largest producer of illicit opium in the late 1960s and early 1970s. In all, the area provided an estimated 700 metric tons annually. The second area, known as the Golden Crescent, is an arc of land stretching across Southwest Asia through Pakistan, Iran, and Afghanistan. By the late 1970s, the Golden Crescent surpassed its counterpart by producing a more potent, yet less expensive product. Although production has been affected by conflicts throughout the region, Inciardi (1989) reported that by the mid-1980s more than half the heroin entering the United States originated in Golden Crescent fields. In addition to these areas, Mexico, India, Poland, and portions of the former Soviet Union are also actively involved in opium poppy farming.

Although labor intensive, the cultivation of the opium poppy is quite basic. Crop cycles begin in late summer and within three months the plant with its brightly colored flowers is fully mature. As the petals fall, a seed pod the size and shape of an egg is exposed. Inside, the milky white sap is raw opium.

Table 7.1 Major Categories of Psychoactive Drugs

NARCOTICS

Natural Narcotics
  Opium
  Laudanum
  Morphine
  Codeine
Semisynthetic Narcotics
  Heroin
  Hydromorphone (Dilaudid)
  Oxycodone (Percodan)
  Etorphine
Synthetic Narcotics
  (High Potency)
    Methadone (Dolophine)
    Meperidine (Demerol)
  (Low Potency)
    Propoxyphene (Darvon)
    Pentazocine (Talwin)

COCAINE AND OTHER COCA PRODUCTS

Coca Leaves
Cocaine
Freebase Cocaine
Coca Paste
Crack

BARBITURATES AND OTHER SEDATIVE-HYPNOTICS

Barbiturate Sedative-Hypnotics
  Phenobarbital
  Pentobarbital
  Butabarbital
Nonbarbiturate Sedative-Hypnotics
  Chloral Hydrate
  Glutethimide
  Methyprylon
  Methaqualone (Quaalude)

MINOR TRANQUILIZERS

Diazepam (Valium)
Meprobamate
Chlorodiazepoxide
Chlorodiazepoxide Hydrochloride
  (Librium)
Hydroxyzine Hydrochloride

ORGANIC SOLVENTS AND INHALANTS

Coal Tar Derivatives
  Lacquers and Paint Thinners
  Glues and Cements
  Kerosene and Petroleum
    Products
  Cleaning Fluids
Freon
Nitrous Oxide and Related Nitrates

AMPHETAMINES AND RELATED STIMULANTS

Amphetamine (Dexedrine)
Methamphetamine (Desoxyn)
Phenmetrazine (Preludin)
Methylphenidate (Ritalin)

CANNABIS PRODUCTS

Marijuana
Hashish
Hash Oil

LSD AND OTHER HALLUCINOGENS

LSD
Peyote
Mescaline
Psilocybin
MDA
DMT
PCP

Once the opium is collected, the product is transported to a local refinery where it is converted into morphine, a process preferred by traffickers since the resulting "bricks" are far easier to transport. The conversion itself is simple. The opium is first dissolved in hot water and then mixed with lime fertilizer to separate the morphine molecules. What remains is mixed with concentrated ammonia to form chunky white kernels. The finished product weighs only about 10 percent of the original raw opium from which it was extracted (Inciardi, 1989). This morphine product can be transformed into heroin, codeine, or mixed with alcohol to form laudanum. First isolated in 1803, morphine is still considered the single most effective pain reliever today.

Semisynthetic Narcotics Chief among the semisynthetics is heroin. First isolated in the 1870s by German researchers, heroin was initially hailed by the medical community for its advantages in dealing with bronchial and pulmonary problems. That strength, coupled with the erroneous belief that it was a nonaddicting substitute for morphine, led physicians to aggressively promote the drug in its infancy. Soon, however, it was discovered that although fast acting and delivering more than double the potency of morphine for an equivalent dosage, the overall effects of heroin and its morphine cousin are virtually undistinguishable (King, 1972).

More complex than the natural narcotics, heroin is synthesized from morphine since it cannot be extracted from opium directly. A five-stage transformation results in a kilo-to-kilo transition. Tedious and quite dangerous, the process first requires the chemist to mix the morphine with an equal amount of acetic anhydride, heating the mixture to exactly 185° F for six hours. If the portions of morphine to acetic acid are incorrect or if the temperature is too high or low, an explosion can result.

Next, the solution is treated with water and chloroform to remove any impurities. The resulting heroin is drained off and mixed with sodium carbonate until crude particles begin to form. Filtered out and purified in a solution of alcohol and activated charcoal, the result is again heated until the alcohol begins to evaporate. What remains are granules of almost pure heroin. These are then dissolved in alcohol again, and ether and hydrochloric acid are added. Unfortunately for the careless chemist, great caution is again necessary, since ether gas is highly volatile and can ignite, causing a violent explosion (McCoy, 1972). If mishaps are avoided, tiny white flakes of heroin powder of between 80 and 99 percent purity are produced. Although a similar process was developed in Mexico, fewer impurities are removed in that process, resulting in a brownish discoloration. In either case, the heroin is diluted for street sale using quinine, lactose, or any powdery substance that will dissolve when heated. Packed in cellophane, aluminum foil, or glassine envelopes to keep it dry, the purity of the final product made available to consumers will vary from as little as 3 percent to as much as 14 percent, depending upon availability. According to the Drug Enforcement Administration (DEA), ten kilograms of opium selling for between $500 and $2,000 in either the Golden Triangle or the Golden Crescent can produce one kilogram of heroin with a street value in excess of $2.5 million.

Once on the street, heroin can be smoked, sniffed in its powdered form, or consumed as a tablet or capsule. American soldiers in Vietnam often smoked opium and heroin in combination with either tobacco or marijuana. Others chose snorting in the belief that addiction could occur only by injection. Ironically, users several decades earlier popularized injections in the apparent belief that the opposite was true. Today, those who continue to prefer to smoke their heroin seem to favor "Black Tar," a still gummy version of the product that is not fully processed (Akers, 1992). By far the most common method of administration, however, is by injection. Here, the consumer dissolves a small dosage in water under heat (often using a spoon or bottle cap) and injects the liquid directly into the veins (mainlining), muscles, or beneath the skin (skin popping). As for the users themselves,

> most heroin users use heroin the way social drinkers use alcohol: on weekends, at parties, or at other occasional events that call for relaxation or celebration. Some "chippers," as they are called, use heroin more frequently, or in heavier doses, than others, just as social drinkers differ in how much and how frequently they drink. About one heroin user in ten is an addict, i.e., someone who uses heroin every day—about the same as the ratio of alcoholics to the drinking population. (Silberman, 1978:56)

While similar to alcohol in some respects, heroin reduces anxiety and distress, creates a detachment to psychological stress, and depresses aggressive tendencies by disrupting the normal functions of the body's systems. Far from a "high," the user develops a feeling of warmth, depressed bowel activity, and a sedating effect that causes lethargy and a sense of extreme contentment. Unfortunately, heroin use can also result in complications including pneumonia, secondary infections (from shared needles), malnutrition, and death from respiratory arrest. Since heroin has no accepted medical usage, it is classified as a Schedule I drug, meaning that its mere possession is a violation of federal law.

In addition to heroin, less well known semisynthetic narcotics include hydromorphone, better known as Dilaudid, and oxycodone, known as Percodan. Although shorter acting than morphine, Dilaudid is from two to eight times more potent, making it a highly abusable drug. Similarly, Percodan resembles a far more potent and addicting codeine.

Finally, within the past few decades, more dangerous forms of semi-synthetics have appeared, though usually only briefly. Etorphine, discovered in the early 1960s, has a potency several times that of morphine but no accepted medical use in the United States. A variant, etorphine hydrochloride, is occasionally used by veterinarians to immobilize wild animals. This drug is so potent that only 2 cc can stop an 8,000-pound elephant.

Even worse are the narcotics developed in the 1980s in search of "China White," an allegedly pure strain of Southeast Asian heroin. First appearing in southern California, these designer drugs were actually similar to fentanyl, a narcotic analgesic 80 to 100 times more powerful than morphine though not widely used. Inciardi (1989) explains that the series of semi-synthetics that followed were "designed" by slightly altering the chemical makeup of other illegal substances, usually in an effort to evade prohibition. What resulted were even more potent but often contaminated versions of fentanyl. One version briefly in use was found to destroy brain cells, another produced the symptoms of Parkinson's disease and accelerated aging, while a third paralyzed its users. One especially dangerous variety had a potency 6,000 times that of heroin. Its use caused instant death. Given their power and impact, few of these drugs remained in use for long, although newer and undoubtedly equally dangerous versions will likely appear in their place.

Synthetic Narcotics At the other end of the narcotics spectrum are the synthetic drugs produced entirely in the laboratory. Perhaps less troubling than their more natural relatives, these products emerged from efforts to retain the effects of morphine while avoiding the dangers of dependence. Although pressed into use by consumers when heroin supplies are poor, for the most part these substances have not been as popular among consumers. Probably the best known of the synthetics is methadone.

Synthesized first by German chemists fearful of uncertain supplies of morphine during World War II, methadone was introduced to the United States in 1947. While not derived from the opiates, both methadone and its cousin meperidine (Demerol) offer most of the same effects—including the potential for addiction. Because their withdrawal symptoms are less intense, however, both have been used widely in the treatment of addicts. "Methadone maintenance," in particular, was intended as a substitute for heroin that would permit an addict to gradually reduce his or her dosage to a point where withdrawal could be accomplished with only a minimum of discomfort. Dispensed from federally operated narcotics clinics throughout the early 1970s, proponents of the treatment claimed great successes. Unfortunately, more objective analyses did not support their claims.

It is now clear that methadone failed to stop addicts from using heroin. While it did make the user's habit easier to regulate, some addicts would switch to methadone periodically to get their heroin intake down to a more manageable size. Once done, they then resumed their earlier consumption patterns. Others found that when taken with wine and tranquilizers, methadone would no longer block the effects of heroin but act instead as a stretcher to reduce the amount of heroin needed each day. For these enterprising users, the main problem was one of supply since methadone was dispensed by treatment centers only so long as progress toward treatment of an addiction could be demonstrated. Not surprisingly, many users enrolled in more than one program. In some cities a black market developed for both the drug and testable urine. With "clean" urine, a user could mask a continuing heroin habit; with heroin-dirty urine, those not using the drug could be admitted to treatment where methadone tablets could be obtained for resale (Silberman, 1978). As for the successes the proponents had reported, more careful examinations showed that they had accepted for treatment into their programs only those addicts demonstrating a strong desire to recover from their addictions. Success under those circumstances should hardly be surprising.

Beyond its lack of treatment success, experience with methadone revealed its dangerous side as well. Less intense but longer acting than heroin, methadone was reported in some cities to have become the drug of choice for some consumers. By 1974, in fact, deaths from this synthetic substitute actually exceeded those from the heroin it was intended to replace. In addition, since it was typically taken in combination with other substances, problems of liver cirrhosis and malnutrition became a concern as well. Finally, in a study comparing addicts, the DEA found that "methadone addicts are equally prone to arrest, are more prone to commit property crimes or crimes of assault, and are equally unemployed" (Silberman, 1978:181). Given its dismal performance, most of the treatment programs were discontinued shortly thereafter.

Cocaine and Other Coca Products

Originally discovered by the peoples of South America, the leaves of the coca shrub produce a mild stimulant effect that suppresses hunger. The plant is indigenous to Peru and Bolivia but has been transported to other parts of the continent as well. Its leaves are smooth and oval shaped, growing in groups of seven to a stem. Traditionally, workers throughout the region have placed the leaf inside the cheek or wrapped it around lime for chewing. A legal practice in both Peru and Bolivia, enabling workers and farmers to labor for extended periods of time, the habit is thought to have been common to the continent for more than a thousand years (Inciardi, 1989).

More recently, the process of extracting cocaine from the leaves of the plant emerged. The principal alkaloid of the coca plant, cocaine first came into vogue in the late 1880s. Like the opiates, cocaine quickly became part of the "feel good pharmacology" of the time. After its initial success, however, the product failed to develop a separate following and soon became widely associated with deviants—especially prostitutes and jazz musicians. Just as quickly, it fell from favor, and demand diminished sharply. For several decades until the 1960s, supplies reflected the market for the drug and were both limited and disorganized.

As the nation entered the 1970s and attitudes about recreational drug use became more relaxed, cocaine use was again revived, this time emerging as the drug of choice for the elite. Increasingly, athletes and celebrities came to view its use as somehow chic and daring. As its reputation for producing an intense euphoria grew, cocaine became evermore popular, leading to changes not only in the product but also in its supply. These changes were intended to increase both its potency and marketability in an effort to bring a growing cross section of consumers into the market. Perhaps as significant, by the 1980s the strong demand and high prices for the product brought new suppliers into the trade as well.

The drug itself is a white crystalline powder, leading many to refer to it as "snow." Production begins, of course, with the coca plant. Neatly planted in rows so that the leaves can be carefully picked and dried, from there the coca is transported to a clandestine laboratory for processing. From the jungle, the leaves are sold for little more than $10 to $15 per kilogram.

Once they have arrived for processing, the leaves are pulverized and soaked in an alcohol solution mixed with benzol. Next, the fluid is drained, sulfuric acid is added, and the solution is shaken. As sodium carbonate is mixed into the solution, a solid clump begins to form. This, in turn, is washed with kerosene and chilled until crystals of crude cocaine form as coca paste. While the cocaine content of the leaves is low (less than 1 percent by weight), the drug's concentration in the paste can range from 40 percent to as much as 90 percent. Because the procuring occurs in the mountains and jungles along the Amazon, a region that is difficult to police, the process is all but impossible to stop (Inciardi, 1986).

As soon as it is processed, the coca paste is shipped from the jungles to Colombia where it is further refined with ether, acetone, and hydrochloric acid to form cocaine. Now ranging from 85 to 97 percent pure, the cocaine is moved by air or sea to the United States, either directly or with stops in Central America, Cuba, Mexico, or the Bahamas. Before being passed to the streets for sale, the shipment is processed one last time by mixing it with lactose, quinine, caffeine, or a similar substance until a purity of around 12 percent is reached (Inciardi, 1986). At a 1990 street price of between $100 and $150 per gram, what began as a small investment in coca leaves can quickly become a substantial profit for the cocaine trafficker.

In the hands of the consumer, cocaine is intensely pleasurable. Injected as a liquid, but more often snorted in its powder form, the drug's effect is said to be immediate, enhancing, and intensely vivid. A feeling of excitement that reinforces the user's initiative and achievement is produced as optimism and energy suddenly abound (Dusek & Girdano, 1980). Many add that cocaine also creates or greatly heightens sexual desire and endurance—all without the hangover, physical addiction, or secondary problems such as lung cancer or infections so often caused by other substances. Unfortunately, while the lift can be euphoric, it is also short-lived and almost always followed by a corresponding letdown. With cocaine, it seems that what goes up really must come down. As a result, many users in search of repeated highs become compulsive, with ever-deepening emotional peaks and valleys, until eventually they are plunged into a severe depression from which only the drug can save them. In addition to such "psychic dependence," chronic users often experience hyperstimulation, nausea, digestive disorders and loss of appetite, convulsions, and feelings of paranoia and delusions of persecution. Erosions in the nasal membranes can result from constant contact with the drug, producing the persistent "runny nose" so often associated with regular use. As a sexual aid, users have found that a sprinkle of cocaine on the clitoris or penis can retard the climax, ultimately promoting a more intense orgasm; however, the urethral membranes too can be damaged as a result. Further, since cocaine is absorbed more rapidly through the urethral walls, accidental overdoses have been known to occur (Inciardi, 1989).

Despite the potential dangers, many users continued to seek more regular and intense highs. Intravenous use became more common, and some began to smoke coca paste or to combine cocaine with other substances. Whereas earlier users had concocted "speedballs" or "whizbang" by mixing cocaine and heroin to intensify the effect, by the 1970s cocaine with marijuana began to appear. Eventually, many who preferred to smoke the drug moved on to "freebasing." To create freebase cocaine, volatile chemicals such as ether or ammonia under heat are used to remove all impurities and reduce the cocaine to a pure crystallized form. The crystals can then be crushed and smoked to produce a far more intense high than is available with other methods of use (Akers, 1992). As a trade-off, however, since the high is more intense, the letdown that follows can create a craving for the drug that has led many users to continue freebasing for days until exhaustion of either themselves or their drug supply occurs. In addition, as several well-publicized cases of users being badly burned have shown, the highly flammable chemicals required to freebase mix poorly with the open flame necessary for smoking by a fatigued user suffering from a drug-induced lack of coordination.

Finally, the drug of greatest concern most recently has been "rock" or "crack" cocaine. Produced with a more easily managed technique to reduce the powdered drug to a more smokable form, what results is a less dangerous and far less expensive form of freebasing (although since crack is reduced to its base state without removing the impurities it is not technically freebasing). With its intense high, crack becomes especially problematic since it can be sliced into tiny units (rocks) that are easily concealed and transported and can be sold in small quantities at very cheap prices, typically $10 or less for a single dosage. This means, of course, that the market for cocaine can be greatly expanded since virtually everyone can afford its use or become involved in the trade with very little expense up front. Because the effect of the drug is short-lived, the motivation to smoke more right away becomes strong, leading many to believe that the drug is enslaving and a direct cause of crimes and violence as users seek quick cash to continue their consumption (McBride & Swartz, 1990). According to popular media, the social damage is particularly devastating among the poor, where a "crack nation" has virtually been created for those with insatiable appetites for the drug.

> By mid–1986, *Newsweek* claimed that crack was the biggest story since Vietnam and Watergate. The words "plague," "epidemic," and "crisis" had become routine. In April 1988, an ABC News "Special Report" again termed crack "a plague" that was "eating away at the fabric of America." In a scant 48 minutes of airtime, millions of viewers were told drugs, especially crack, were destroying virtually every institution in American life—jobs, schools, families, national sovereignty, community, law enforcement, and business. In 1988, just as in 1986, crack cocaine was defined as supremely evil—the most important cause of America's troubles. (Reinarman & Levine, 1989:218)

Through it all, few noticed that by the end of the decade, crystalline methamphetamine, known popularly as "ice" or "crank," had begun to arrive and spread throughout the Hawaiian Islands.

Barbiturates and Other Sedative-Hypnotics

The barbiturates, a category of psychoactive drugs, are derived from barbituric acid. Also first synthesized by German chemists, by 1903 these drugs with their sedative properties had been introduced to the medical practice where they were used both alone and in concert with other drugs. In all, about 2,500 variants have been prepared, and a few dozen are currently in use under various brand names.

Lawfully produced, the barbiturates are typically found in capsule or tablet form and are used to induce a general depression of neural and muscular activity. Classified according to the speed at which they are metabolized, fast-acting forms can induce unconsciousness in only minutes and are useful for surgical anesthetics. Perhaps the best known of these is sodium pentothal. In slower acting forms, barbiturates decrease general motor activity and are used to produce drowsiness, sedation, and even hypnosis (Abadinsky, 1990).

Barbiturate abusers often include the emotionally distressed who are seeking to remain in a sedated state. Others, however, have found that after a sufficient tolerance to the drugs has been developed they can actually stimulate rather than depress. Still others combine sedatives with heroin in an effort to stretch their supplies or enhance the intensity of the opiate effect. Finally, some users rely on the barbiturates to induce sleep to allow recovery from the abuse of other substances (Inciardi, 1989). Because they are highly addicting and users develop an extreme tolerance to these drugs, withdrawal from prolonged use can often be especially difficult and even deadly. An overdose with barbiturates is also often preferred as a means of suicide.

Similar to barbiturates in most respects, nonbarbiturate sedatives were introduced in the 1960s as prescription treatments for anxiety and insomnia. Believed safer than the barbiturates, these drugs were widely overprescribed until their dangers became equally evident. Indeed, methaqualone, known mostly by the product name Quaalude, actually produces an even greater loss of motor coordination than does its barbiturate counterpart. Now classified as a Schedule I drug whose mere possession is illegal, the abuse of these sedatives is currently limited to a small supply illegally produced in western Europe and South America. For both forms of sedative, the illegal market remains small and fairly disorganized.

Amphetamines and Related Stimulants

Amphetamines have exactly the opposite effect of barbiturates; rather than sedate, amphetamines stimulate the nervous system to reduce fatigue and increase alertness. Although these drugs were first synthesized in 1887, this adrenalinlike substance did not come into medical use to any real degree until the 1940s when amphetamines became popular in the treatment of psychiatric depression, obesity and weight control, fatigue, and as a vaso-constrictor for inflamed mucosal membranes. By the early 1970s, however, the shortcomings of these drugs became apparent, and their usage was sharply curtailed.

Amphetamines are prescribed in both capsule and tablet form. When taken illicitly, however, many choose instead to crush the tablets so they can be smoked in a powdered form or dissolved in water and injected. In either case, illicit supplies are typically obtained from those willing to divert the drug from the prescription market or from small-scale manufacturing spe-cifically for street sales. Preferences in administration and supply of amphet-amines tend to vary greatly, depending on the nature of the intended abuse.

Three distinct patterns of abuse have been noted, with the first prob-ably the most well known. Here are the truck drivers, students, writers, and others attempting to keep awake and alert for long periods of time without sleep. Benzedrine (bennies), Dexedrine, and various "pep pills" are common to this group trying to push themselves beyond their normal endurance. The second group are those using amphetamines without medical supervision as a shortcut to dieting. Unfortunately, while these substances do appear to act on the hypothalamus to suppress the appetite, most users have found that the effect is brief and that the hunger sup-pressed returns with even greater intensity after the drug has left the sys-tem. For this reason, methamphetamine hydrochloride (Desoxyn) is cur-rently prescribed medically only as a last-resort component of weight reduction programs. For most of the abusers in these first two categories, legal products containing caffeine are now readily available over the counter to meet most of their needs.

The third group are those who make recreational use of amphetamines, either alone or in combination with other drugs. Here, too, methyl-am-phetamines are the products most sought after by those seeking a "rush" of increased alertness, physical strength, and indifference to pain. Commonly referred to as "speed," these drugs were especially popular among "flower-children, bikers, and other counterculture groups of the 1960s" until wide-spread public recognition that "speed kills" suppressed demand (Chaiken, 1993). With the arrival in Oahu, Hawaii, during the late 1980s of a variant known as crystal methamphetamine, many health professionals feared that a resurgence of this drug was under way.

Known widely as "ice" or "crank," one form of "crystal meth" had emerged among many of Oahu's ethnic groups almost a decade earlier but had gained only a marginal foothold of acceptance. As the practice of cocaine smoking became popular on the mainland, however, Hawaiian drug users suddenly found themselves unable to supply a growing demand. As a result, they substituted *pakkalo,* a locally grown marijuana, in its place. By 1985 when pakkalo too was growing short, many altered their practices again, this time turning to *batu,* their local version of crystal methamphetamine. While most of the early preparations were home-cooked, as word spread and recipes were exchanged, fear of a new drug crisis was under way. Before the news media began to report the story in 1988, enterprising drug dealers on Oahu had already begun to tout the product as an inexpensive, hard-to-detect drug that produced better and longer highs than cocaine (Chaiken, 1993). Nonetheless, by 1990, the drug had failed to take hold, and its sales and use appeared to return to the earlier negligible levels.

Cannabis Products

A widow and her four children have been driven insane by eating the Marihuana plant, according to doctors, who say there is no hope of saving the children's lives and that the mother will be insane for the rest of her life. . . .

The mother was without money to buy other food for the children, whose ages range from 3 to 15, so they gathered some herbs and vegetables growing in the yard for their dinner. Two hours after the mother and children had eaten the plants, they were stricken. Neighbors, hearing outbursts of crazed laughter, rushed to the house to find the entire family insane.

Examination revealed that the narcotic marijuana was growing among the garden vegetables. (*New York Times,* July 6, 1927)

Although in no sense a narcotic, marijuana came to popularity in the United States in much the same way as did the opiates. Derived from the Indian hemp plant *Cannabis sativa,* it is tetrahydrocannabinol (THC) that gives cannabis products their hallucinogenic effects. An annual plant that grows best in warm or temperate climates, the drugs produced from this plant's leaves and resin were made popular during the late 1800s when well-known pharmaceutical companies such as Parke-Davis and Squibb offered them for ailments as varied as depression and impotence. Difficult to prescribe orally (dosage standardization is a problem) and impossible to inject, by the time the national mood began to turn against drugs these had already fallen from medicinal favor. With little more than recreational uses, cannabis, like cocaine, soon moved underground to become associated primarily with deviants and the avant-garde.

By the late 1920s, what was referred to in Mexico as marijuana began to appear in border towns and southern cities. As its usage became increasingly apparent among blacks and Hispanics, many whites grew concerned, came to see it as a corrupting influence, and pressed even harder for specific reforms intended to impose its prohibition. With reliable estimates that as many as one of every four southerners had begun to smoke the drug (Musto, 1987), by 1931 nearly one-half of the states had enacted marijuana legislation. In 1937, Congress went even further, passing the Marijuana Tax Act in an effort to put an end to the drug's recreational use. With that, marijuana did not again become an important issue in the United States until the 1960s.

While potent in their effect, none of the products of cannabis requires extensive processing and each is easily administered. Marijuana, for example, is produced by crushing the dried twigs, leaves, and flowers of the plant for smoking. Known by a variety of slang names, most of the domestically grown marijuana is olive green in color and is very weak in THC content. Jamaican and Colombian marijuana is dark brown in color, Panamanian marijuana is a claylike red, and Acapulco Gold is a dull yellow shade. Each of these foreign products is stronger in THC content than the marijuana grown in the United States. Indian *bhang* is similar in both color and potency to our home-grown varieties and has been widely used in India with few health or social concerns (Dusek & Girdano, 1980).

Somewhat more potent than marijuana is hashish, a resinous extract obtained by boiling or scraping the cannabis plant. Called *charas* by the Indians, this resin hardens into brown lumps that can be smoked either directly or after first pounding and rubbing it into a gray-white powder. In the Middle East, hashish has a slightly different meaning in that it contains a mixture of both leaves and resin. In North Africa, this same combination is known as *kif* or *takrouri* while those in central and southern Africa know the same as *dogga* (Inciardi, 1989). Regardless of its name, hashish typically contains a potency of nearly 20 percent THC and can produce euphoria, disinhibition, an alteration of space and time perception, and even hallucinations and psychotic-like symptoms in some. Even more potent (20 percent to 70 percent THC) is hash oil, which is produced by repeated extraction of cannabis materials.

Regardless of its form, the immediate effects of marijuana are much the same as intoxication—a light-headedness referred to as a "high." Overall, however, the drug is less a stimulant than a depressant that reduces nervous system activity. Beyond that, marijuana accelerates the heart rate and can temporarily weaken the contractile strength of the heart, making usage dangerous for people with cardiac conditions. In addition, regular users have also been known to suffer from bronchitis and chronic coughs (Dusek & Girdano, 1980).

Research has shown that marijuana contains at least 426 known chemicals that are transformed to more than 2,000 in number during the smoking process. Of these, 70 are fat-soluble cannabinoids (of which THC is but one) that are deposited in the high-fat body tissues such as the brain, lungs, liver, and reproductive organs. Since the body has a water-based disposal system, these chemicals become trapped in these organs for weeks at a time. As such, a person smoking marijuana as little as a few times monthly not only retains but is building up residue levels in significant organs (Inciardi, 1989); diminished sex drive, respiratory problems, and lung cancer can result. Further, animal studies have demonstrated that overdoses can be deadly to cats and dogs, a potential concern to humans given the increased potency of the more recent drug. California *sinsemilla,* for instance, has a THC potency of around 14 percent. In some areas, this drug can be traded for cocaine on an equal-weight basis. While the role of marijuana as a gateway to other drugs is widely debated, the quick profits to be made and the ease of entry the drug offers into the business of trafficking has clearly made it a gateway for many into organized crime.

LSD and Other Hallucinogens

The last of the major categories of drugs of abuse are the hallucinogens that act on the brain and central nervous system to produce mood and perceptual changes. According to Akers (1992) and others, the actual effects of these drugs depend both on the potency and the size of the dosage as well as the social and physical setting under which they are taken and the user's expectations. This can be easily demonstrated with the more potent hallucinogens that can produce complex alterations in perceptions of light, color, sound, taste, and odor. To some, such changes are a sought-after mind-expanding experience. To others, however, the same effects can be interpreted as a frightening psychosis. Undoubtedly, the best known of the hallucinogens are LSD and PCP.

LSD First synthesized from ergot, a wheat and rye fungus, LSD is comprised of lysergic acid, diethylamine, and trifluoroacetic acid. Tightly controlled, 1 kilogram of lysergic acid will make one-half kilo of LSD, about 5 million 100-microgram doses. Administered orally, the drug is broken down and absorbed into the bloodstream very rapidly. From there it is distributed throughout the body, apparently concentrating in the liver, kidneys, and adrenals. Although as little as 1 percent of the digested dose accumulates in the brain, examinations of monkeys have found that the drug is concentrated in the pituitary and pineal glands, along with the limbic system, the hypothalamus, and the auditory and visual reflex areas. It is in the limbic system that the drug produces electrical storms in its subjects (Dusek & Girdano, 1980). Cohen (1968) reports that with an oral dose of LSD, a delay of about 45 minutes should be expected before the onset of the drug's effects. This time is referred to as the drug's latency period.

LSD-induced activity lasts between 8 and 12 hours, with the most intense changes in mood and perception occurring during the first half of the user's "trip." As the latency ends and the drug's effects take hold, the user often experiences a tingling in the hands and feet, numbness, a flushed appearance and dilation of the pupils, along with sensations of chilliness and nausea. Alterations in the user's mood are the first behavioral changes to occur followed by significant increases in sensory input, feelings of floating, and perceptual distortions. Hallucinations follow shortly after. In addition, "synesthesia" or sensory crossover often occurs among users—colors are heard, sounds tasted, and music seen through colors. For some, "tunnel vision" is also experienced, allowing minute details not seen before to be observed (Inciardi, 1989). Given the influence exerted by the drug over its subject, as the user's trip progresses it can be pleasurable, traumatic, or both, depending largely upon expectations and the suggestions of others during the process. Persons ingesting LSD unknowingly are often terrorized by what occurs.

Regardless of the experience, researchers have found that LSD impairs a user's intellectual processes. Since a tolerance to the drug develops quite rapidly, regular users must either space their trips carefully or take ever increasing dosages for the same effect. While a standard dosage for an average user is 100 micrograms, dosages as high as 2,000 micrograms have been observed. Still, a physical dependence upon the drug does not result, there are no withdrawal symptoms, and, to our knowledge, no deaths have been reported from overdoses in humans. Since LSD is normally produced as a colorless, tasteless, odorless, liquid it can appear and be administered in almost any form. For example, while sugar cubes are often used to carry the drug, reports of it being stored on blotting paper and even the backs of stamps appear regularly in the media. Since demand for the drug is currently low and production both illegal and complex, distribution of LSD is sporadic and disorganized.

PCP Phencyclidine (PCP) is a central nervous system excitant originally produced as an animal tranquilizer and anesthetic. First developed in the 1950s, PCP affects a number of different neurotransmitters allowing it to function variously as a stimulant, a depressant, or an analgesic. Because of its potency, users often experience irrational and disoriented reactions, hallucinations, loss of sensory control, and even terrifying feelings of death. While the user's expectations influence the PCP experience as they do with LSD, in higher dosages convulsions, coma, and death can occur.

In its pure form, PCP is a white crystalline powder that dissolves in water. Originally marketed for a short time by Park, Davis and Company under the trade name Sernyl, manufacturing now is almost always in makeshift laboratories that make little effort to remove impurities. Depending on the extent of the impurities present, the drug as currently sold will often range from white to tan and even to brown. Given its versatility, PCP can be found in both powder and liquid forms as well as in tablets and capsules. Many users prefer to smoke the drug after applying it to marijuana, tobacco, or oregano. At present, the market for PCP is small, with production and distribution being managed primarily by outlaw motorcycle groups.

Other Hallucinogens In addition to PCP and LSD, more naturally occurring hallucinogens exist as well. Peyote, for example, is a spineless cactus found in central and northern Mexico. The top crown of the plant (button) can be dried, then held in the mouth until it softens, and swallowed whole. Three or four such buttons are usually sufficient to produce effects similar to those experienced with LSD.

Mescaline, the principal alkaloid in the peyote cactus, was perhaps the first hallucinogen to be chemically isolated. Still less potent than LSD, this drug can be taken orally, injected, or smoked. Interestingly, confiscated samples of mescaline are often found to be PCP. Similarly, psilocybin is the active ingredient in the *Psilocybe mexicana* mushroom. A white crystalline substance first isolated in 1958, this substance's potency is somewhere between mescaline and LSD. It is, however, the fastest acting of the hallucinogens, with a latency period of only about 15 minutes. Finally, MDA and DMT are both synthetically produced: MDA by modifying the psychoactive components of nutmeg and mace, DMT from the seeds of various South American and West Indian plants (Inciardi, 1989). These substances produce effects similar to LSD, but are much weaker and more short-lived.

PREPARING FOR A WAR ON DRUGS

The return of recreational drug use in the late 1960s is often attributed to a general revolt against the values, mores, and status quo of the times. Conflicts over the war in Vietnam and the civil rights movement may have led the way, but rejection of previously unquestioned ways of living hardly stopped there. Sex, marriage, parenting, and religion each were reassessed as a "generation gap" seemed to open, tearing much of the fabric of society apart. Literature and the mass media reflected the conflicts, while music focused on protest and the arrival of a new, less formal culture. As the focus and belief in self grew stronger, a loss of faith in the established powers—business, government, and authority figures—was unavoidable.

By the early 1970s, much seemed to be out of control. Early in the decade, the Survey Research Center at the University of Michigan found that trust in government had reached all time lows in virtually every segment of the population. When asked, more than half of those surveyed agreed that their government was run by big interests looking out for themselves, a surprising finding given that less than one-half as many felt so less than a decade before. As the *American Political Science Review* summarized the mood, "a widespread, basic discontent and political alienation" seemed to be sweeping the nation. "What is startling and somewhat alarming is the rapid degree of change in this basic attitude over a period of only six years" (Zinn, 1980:530). Just as it seemed that the nadir had been reached, however, five burglars were caught attempting to break into the offices of the Democratic National Committee in the Watergate complex in Washington, D.C. With disclosure of their ties to the White House, what was left of our social contract seemed to all but disappear.

Simultaneously, as Musto (1990, 1987) has observed, the nation's consensus on drugs began to disappear as well. The recipients of school-based antinarcotics educations and an aggressive antidrug campaign by the media and the entertainment industry, the generation born in the 1920s grew to adulthood with little direct knowledge of the substances but a great deal of animosity toward them. Their parents had experienced the peak of drug use in the late 1880s and passed on both their knowledge and fears with conviction. As the problem diminished, however, the antidrug focus disappeared, leaving the next generation to enter the 1960s with little but exaggerations that were easy to dispel. The credibility of those before them was quickly damaged. Apparently, the hope had been that not knowing would be enough to prevent the generations that followed from experimentation. Obviously, it was a false hope.

The Road to Restrictions

By the passage of the 1914 Harrison Narcotics Act, only a few states had even considered the problems of drugs and their regulation. With the exception of San Francisco, whose 1875 ordinance dealt with the spread of opium dens, and New York's Town–Boylan law prohibiting nonmedical trafficking, for the most part the states were content to monitor prescriptions and the contents of patent medicines. And indeed, throughout the 1920s, little local enforcement was necessary. Demand for drugs was low, the professionals who handled narcotics were intimidated, and federal enforcement had been so aggressive that few problems remained to be dealt with. Nonetheless, by 1930, the newly formed federal Narcotics Bureau began to push for supplemental state laws to assist in their efforts. Accordingly, in 1932, the National Conference of Commissioners on Uniform State Laws began drafting a Uniform Narcotic Drug Act to offer a separate set of state criminal penalties as a complement to Harrison Act provisions. Once written, the Uniform Act was offered as a model to states so that a concerted effort would be possible.

With little resistance and an endorsement from the American Bar Association (ABA), one state after another quickly adopted the Uniform Act in whole. Because it was a popular cause with no opposition, even states with no apparent drug problems approved the legislation. In fact, by the end of the decade, only Kansas, Massachusetts, New Hampshire, and Washington had failed in passage, but each of these states had developed equally repressive statutes on their own (King, 1972). With little concern of overlap or jurisdiction, a strict system of licensing and controls was now in place throughout the nation. Meanwhile, the Narcotics Bureau had turned its attention elsewhere.

Having watched repeated attempts throughout the 1920s fail to regulate the possession of heroin and cocaine, adopt international prohibitions on the opiates, and accomplish the prohibition of alcohol, the Narcotics Bureau joined the movement against marijuana rather cautiously at first. To Commissioner Anslinger, the problems caused by the substance were minor compared to heroin and were largely restricted to the southwestern states anyway. In addition, he questioned whether a federal law to prohibit marijuana would be workable or constitutional. Even if it were, he feared that federal enforcement on such a large scale might generate such local resistance as to threaten the existence of his fledgling and underfunded organization. After all, he pointed out in 1936, marijuana grew "like dandelions" (Musto, 1987:222). Still, when the Treasury Department proposed a campaign for a transfer tax similar to one enacted in 1934 to reduce the spread of machine guns, Anslinger and his bureau had little choice but to sign on to promote the cause.

Apparently, the pressure for marijuana control was mostly political. With a shrinking economy and an animosity toward Mexicans growing throughout the southwest, the tales of "dope fiends" committing crimes and molesting children—especially white girls—spread rapidly, forcing a call for action. Police chiefs, governors, Congressmen, and eventually the Treasury Department and the Commissioner of Narcotics were each pushed to search for grounds to support greater restrictions. Responding first, the bureau claimed that only the treaty-making powers of the federal government could justify an antimarijuana statute. When this was attempted but rejected by other nations, the idea of a transfer tax was offered instead.

In Treasury Department conferences and at hearings before Congress, government officials, consultants, and selected medical officials were brought forward to develop a legal definition of marijuana and to testify as to its effects on consumers. Dr. Voegtlin, the National Institutes of Health's pharmacology expert, provided the most powerful testimony when he stated: "I think it is an established fact that prolonged use leads to insanity in certain cases" (Musto, 1987:227). With almost no opposing testimony, Congress was easily persuaded. As such, with little fanfare, the Marijuana Tax Act was signed into law on August 2, 1937. Erroneously classifying marijuana as a narcotic, this substance too was now under the same controls that the Harrison Act had imposed on the opiates and cocaine. For at least the next decade, the tools of prohibition were set.

Following the Lead in the State Houses

Building on the movement to regulate marijuana, Congress went on to add increased penalties for second and subsequent violations. Lawmakers in many states did likewise, but it was not until 1951 when Congressman Hale Boggs, one of Commissioner Anslinger's strongest supporters, sponsored mandatory minimum penalties that the race for get-tough sanctions got under way. While Boggs had proposed mandatory minimums of 2 years for a first offense, 5 for a second, and 10 to 20 for a third (King, 1972), several states responded with even greater vigor. Dubbed "Little Boggs Acts," penalties (in Ohio) of 2 to 15 years (first offense), 5 to 20 (second), and 10 to 30 (subsequent convictions) for mere *possession* in violation of the law were enacted. For sales they got really serious, starting at

10 to 20, then jumping to 30 to life. New Jersey followed with similar terms but added stiff punishments for doctors who failed to report addicts, any person who induced others to use drugs, and even 1 year and a $1,000 fine for simply being an addict. Almost a dozen states quickly followed New Jersey's lead, prohibiting the mere status of addict until the Supreme Court held all such provisions to be unconstitutional (*Robinson v. California*, 1963). In response, New Jersey turned to a novel statute, requiring every person ever convicted of a crime involving narcotics to complete a lengthy registration within 24 hours of being in the state. The registration, along with a photograph and fingerprints, was then circulated widely among police agencies.

Not wanting to appear soft on drugs, in state after state, legislators passed mandatory minimums in the 10- to 40-year category. Some added life imprisonment and a few even proscribed death for the most flagrant violations. In addition, eligibility for parole was routinely eliminated for drug law violators, and a few went so far as to include drug addicts among those suitable for civil commitment. In these states, prosecutors found that they had been blessed with a second, even more powerful, line of attack— if conviction wasn't possible, incarceration might still be possible by involuntary commitment on a noncriminal basis (King, 1972). Even better, under the civil process, the defendant's constitutional protections were less exact, the institutions of confinement were usually the same, and the sentence was indeterminate until the "patient" was cured. In short, by the late 1960s, although little was being done to help addicts, much was occurring to punish them. Still, the arrests continued to mount, prisons filled to capacity, and the costs of enforcement, both social and financial, escalated on a curve that seemed to have no end. Only California and New York offered any serious effort to provide treatment facilities and follow-up for addicts returning to the community.

It was not until the end of the decade that social scientists and legal scholars began to point out the inconsistencies and inequities that had evolved in the drug laws and the negative consequences of so repressive an approach. Only then did the sentiment begin to shift sufficiently to allow a modification in federal policy from an almost total reliance on law enforcement to include something of a focus on rehabilitation. As the trend continued, federal enforcers—now moved to the Department of Justice and reformed as the Drug Enforcement Administration (DEA)—shifted their emphasis from control of the user to the smugglers and dealers who supplied the products now so in demand. Here too, however, they met with considerable frustration and failure.

REGAINING CONTROL
(AND CONFUSION) OF THE
INTERNATIONAL INITIATIVE

While the Narcotics Bureau was having its way domestically, the road to international cooperation was proving a bit more difficult to travel. Congressional delegations to international conferences had failed to win cooperation in 1925 and 1930, finding confusion and even hostility instead. The United States representatives had, in fact, walked out of the 1925 conference in Geneva as a rebuke to what they termed unfair criticism of this country's high opiate consumption. Determined to avoid the earlier fiasco, a more conciliatory tone in 1930 produced little more than criticism at home for being led around (especially by the British) "by the nose." By 1936, the United States found itself protesting that year's conference agenda and, after attempting to change the focus to gain an agreement to suppress marijuana, came home largely empty-handed. With World War II on the horizon, this was the last meaningful effort for several decades. By the time efforts at cooperation were resumed, drug trafficking, demand for the products, and the role of many of the nations involved had changed considerably. Figure 7.1 shows the primary international drug trafficking routes that exist to this day.

Guns, Drugs, and the CIA

As American soldiers fought against communism in Southeast Asia, much of the region was preoccupied with cornering the market on the opiates. With boundaries artificially drawn by the British and French decades earlier during their colonial periods, many of the region's countries were ruled less by central governments than by paramilitary organizations with important backers. As such, throughout Burma, Laos, and Thailand, various armies of tribesmen battled continually for control of land no one seemed to own. Needing allies whenever possible and with a long tradition of opium production, many warlords soon discovered that both their military skills and their narcotics were important commodities for sale.

For their part, the major powers battling for the region often found cooperation more important than firepower. Through local alliances, the Central Intelligence Agency (CIA) and its French counterpart before found that covert missions, enemy monitoring, and even surrogate combat were all quite possible. To win such cooperation, however, something in return was necessary—for decades that something was support for the region's growing opium trade.

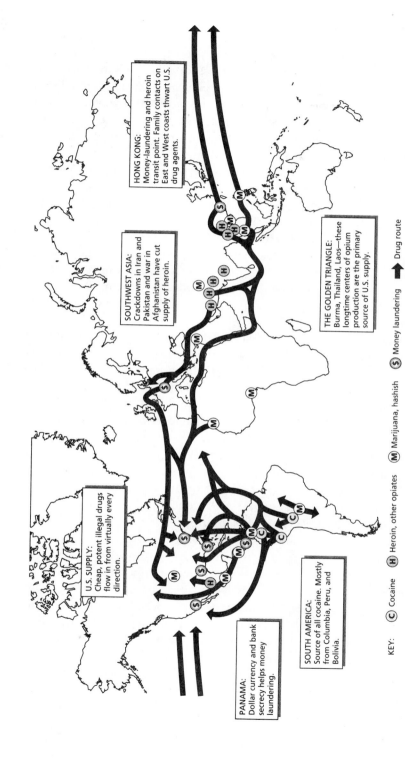

FIGURE 7.1 International Drug Trafficking Routes

With the French, at least, cooperation was straightforward. Tiring of a decade-long occupation of Indochina and lacking the funds to finance their operations, by the 1950s French military intelligence had become directly involved in connecting the Laos supply of narcotics with a growing demand in Saigon. French paratroopers fighting in the northern regions obligingly shipped their allies' opium south to Saigon on military aircraft. There, the drugs were sold by local bandits protected by city officials (who ran the city on their French patrons' behalf). With the arrival of the CIA, however, the picture grew far more complex.

Better funded than the French, CIA operatives nonetheless soon realized that an operational capacity far beyond what their budget could buy was possible. After all, covert operations in such rugged territory had to be conducted almost exclusively by locals. As the war waged on and the casualties mounted, the Hmong tribesmen in the northern regions increasingly demanded added incentives for their continued involvement. The CIA responded by making itself an integral part of the Hmong household economy.

Living basic lives with an agricultural economy centered around rice (for subsistence) and opium (for cash), the Hmong were devastatingly affected by the war. Not only did they suffer disproportionate losses, as their young men died they found the labor needed for crop maintenance diminishing as well. Since they were now unable to feed themselves reliably, the CIA stepped in to fill the need with rice shipments delivered on its proprietary air service, Air America. While this helped to placate the tribesmen, it was not sufficient for their leaders who quickly realized that the planes flew in both directions. Having little direct stake in the war's outcome, the tribal leaders soon added free transport of their opium as their price for continued service as soldiers ("Frontline," 1991; McCoy, 1972). Like the French earlier, the CIA had little choice but to agree.

Although the arrangement was expedient, few in the agency appeared to consider the longer term implications. By the mid-1960s, with CIA complicity, the Laotian drug trade had grown from a small one, meeting the demand in its own cities, to a self-contained industry—feeding chemists in Hong Kong for export throughout the world. With unlimited supplies available from protected laboratories, heroin use among United States soldiers exploded as well. By 1973, in fact, a special White House committee confirmed that at least 34 percent of the GIs stationed in Vietnam had "commonly used" the drug. Still, the CIA was undecided about the response it should take. In reviewing the problem, for example, the agency's Inspector General agreed that "local officials with whom we are in contact . . . have been or may be still involved in one way or another in the drug business." Qualifying that recognition, he added: "What to do about these people is a particularly troublesome problem, in view of its implications for some of our operations, particularly in Laos" (McCoy, 1992:260–261). Despite the benefit of hindsight, nearly a decade later in the 1980s, the agency's indecision in balancing consequences would again appear as the same policymakers undertook similar operations in Central and South America—with nearly identical results. This time, however, cocaine was the drug of choice ("Frontline," 1991; Scott, 1992). In the meantime, President Nixon's "war on heroin" in the Mediterranean produced even more dramatic but unanticipated outcomes.

Political Expediency and the Law of Unintended Consequences

Having successfully campaigned throughout the late 1960s on a "law and order" platform, President Nixon and his administration wasted little time beginning the new decade with a well-publicized "war on heroin." Applauded by James Q. Wilson (1974) and others for its foresight in returning to a more aggressive law enforcement focus, almost at once the administration's sponsors were declaring success. "We have turned the corner on drug abuse," the President himself proclaimed. "The alarming six-year trend of an increasing heroin addiction rate has been reversed," his staff went on to boast (Silberman, 1978:175). While we now know that they were either wrong or deliberately misleading, as the "war of the poppies" pressed on, attention turned international once again in an effort to cut off the opiates at their source. By combining international efforts with strict interdiction at home, the administration felt certain that the "French Connection" could be broken to end the supply of heroin to the east coast.

With the contention that as much as 80 percent of the heroin reaching the United States came from Turkey by way of Beirut and Marseilles, the President took the lead in demanding results. Threatening an end to military and economic aid, by 1971 the Turkish government was persuaded to ban planting of the opium poppy and to work to squash the export of drugs from their end. To offset their losses, the U.S. administration agreed to reimburse Turkish farmers for their lost crops while providing additional help and advice to the government. By 1972, most agreed that the plan appeared to be working. Heroin prices rose and purity dropped, indicating that the drug was becoming more scarce. Turkey had become a less significant source of heroin on American streets.

Unfortunately, what the planners on the President's cabinet-level Strategy Council on Drug Abuse had failed to account for was the ready accessibility of other suppliers of the drug. India, Afghanistan, and Pakistan, as well as Laos, Thailand, and Burma, each produced the poppy on levels comparable to Turkey. Even Iran had resumed production after its own 13-year ban. Since these countries were less likely to respond to pressure, however, only Turkey was chosen as a target. As the initial successes began to develop, it was an easy matter for illicit producers to shift to alternate supplies.

With their preoccupation with the French Connection, the planners had also ignored the fact that the use of heroin was widespread in the West and Southwest as well. With Mexico as their principal source of supply, West Coast traffickers quickly recognized an opportunity and expanded their own operations into the now more open East Coast markets. As "Mexican Brown" flooded eastward and new sources in the Golden Triangle and Golden Crescent opened up, even Turkey resumed its opium planting. Within 18 months of the campaign's start, a new "heroin war" began as distributors battled over once stable markets. Prices plunged, purity increased, and usage spread from the large cities to the small, from men to women, and from minorities to the white middle class. In a short time, the government had managed to accomplish what the dealers alone could not.

As the new supply routes from the west were established, cocaine soon rushed into them as well. "The basic fact that eluded these great geniuses," the Commissioner of Customs reportedly declared, "was that it takes only ten square miles of poppies to feed the entire heroin market, and they grow everywhere" (Silberman, 1978:177). They were also apparently unaware that in the capacity of no more than two ten-ton trucks an entire year's supply of heroin can be smuggled into the United States. In 1970, about the time the interdiction was being attempted, approximately 65 million cars and trucks, 306,000 planes, 157,000 ships, and at least 250 million people entered the country. Finally, even the successes were soon undone when 300 pounds of French Connection heroin seized by the police was stolen from the police property clerk's office and undoubtedly put back into play on New York City's streets (Daley, 1978). As the investigation into this new embarrassment began and frustration throughout the country continued to mount, critics stepped forward and a debate over the policies that ought to be proper got under way.

POLICY OPTIONS TODAY

No one denies that the use and abuse of illicit drugs is among the greatest of public concerns today. People of all political affiliations, rich and poor, regardless of ethnicity or geographical location now consistently rank drugs at the top of the problems facing the nation. Although substantial numbers of Americans report having used drugs themselves—even recently—they are increasingly and overwhelmingly disapproving of others doing so (Inciardi & McBride, 1991). As a result, policymakers today find themselves in something of a catch-22. On the one hand, demand for the products remains high, ensuring that suppliers and a marketplace will continue to exist and that the police may not be able to avoid being overwhelmed in their enforcement efforts. As William Buckley (1992) recently pointed out: "Try to abolish that market and you will find yourself engaged in an endeavor as futile as trying to eliminate war." At the same time, however, in light of the strong disapproval that exists, appearing soft on drugs can be hazardous to a political career. Not only are stiffer penalties favored by most but as many as three-fourths of those recently surveyed offered to surrender important constitutional rights to aid the police in enforcement (see Beck, 1993, for example). "It is discouraging that a fresh approach to the drug problem is so exclusively forbidden to any politicians running for office," Buckley (1992) adds. With the history of our efforts in mind and in light of the conflicts existing in the current context, let's review the basic policy options generally available today.

Increased Law Enforcement

Beginning with President Reagan's administration, the most recent response to illicit drugs has been a return to the preeminence of law enforcement. With a commitment that was "unshakable," the President promised to "do what is necessary to end the drug menace" while crippling "the power of the Mob in America" (Wisotsky, 1991:103). Accordingly, he called for (and got) more than 1,000 additional agents for the DEA; 200 new assistant U.S. Attorneys; a substantial reallocation of funds to law enforcement from prevention, treatment, and research; more stringent laws; and almost 1,300 new beds at 11 federal prisons. In addition, the administration pushed forward to permit military involvement in this new war on drugs. Assault helicopters, AWACS planes, NASA satellites, and "Fat Albert" (a surveillance balloon equipped with sophisticated radar and listening devices) were all brought on-line to give needed help to the forces fighting the smugglers. Finally, the Coast Guard and U.S. Customs Service introduced *Blue Thunder*, a 900-horsepower boat designed to run down the high-performance speedboats widely used by traffickers and made popular on "Miami Vice" (Inciardi, 1991). Armed for battle, by the late 1980s the President's policymakers announced a "zero-tolerance" policy: An antidrug version of the Maginot Line was to be drawn along the entire 96,000 mile border of the country. The nation would, at last, be able to protect against drug smuggling incursions.

From a purely technical standpoint, the effort could boast considerable success. For the first time, a single-minded attack on drugs had set new records in virtually every category of measurement. Seizures, indictments, arrests, convictions, and asset forfeitures all surpassed previous records. The DEA, FBI, and Customs officials seized nearly one-half billion dollars in assets in 1986 alone. DEA arrests doubled, and from 1981 to 1987 nearly 5.3 million kilograms of marijuana were seized. Cocaine seizures increased from 2,000 kilos in 1981 to over 36,000 in 1987. More significantly, the proportion of high-level traffickers among arrestees rose from one-third to one-half as the prison population in federal facilities soared to over 570,000. In addition, by 1987, more than 40 percent of all new prison inmates went in for drug offenses (Wisotsky, 1991). While these successes were being realized, however, the drug enforcers were not alone in boosting their totals.

As if to mock the administration's efforts, while arrests, seizures, and budgets were doubling, the price for the targeted drugs was nonetheless dropping as purity increased significantly. Not only did the domestic cultivation of marijuana skyrocket, the supply of cocaine did as well. Estimated at 40 metric tons in 1980, by 1986 at least 140 tons of cocaine slipped through the now tightened drug net. While the 1980 kilo of cocaine sold for $50,000 delivered in Miami, by 1986 the price had fallen to $20,000; to $14,000 by 1988. During the same period, cocaine-related hospital emergencies increased more than sixfold (Wisotsky, 1991). When taken together, the Office of Technology Assessment was led to conclude that the effort had, in fact, been a failure. "Despite a doubling of Federal expenditures on interdiction over the past five years," they reported, "the quantity of drugs smuggled into the United States is greater than ever" (1987:3).

Unfortunately, some now contend that the effort was more than a failure. Spreading the casualties from the war, many cities came to resemble shooting galleries as gangs and gangsters battled over markets in turmoil. Corruption in some communities was reported to be systematic, and several Latin American and Caribbean countries were effectively seized by the new gangsters. For example, after proudly announcing an extradition treaty with the United States, Colombian officials quickly retreated in response to a wave of assassinations that eventually included one-third of their Supreme Court, at least 60 lower court justices, the nation's Justice Minister, several presidential candidates, and hundreds of police officers and prosecutors. Not surprisingly, many South American officials, media, and citizens have begun to wonder why they should continue to pay so heavy a price for what they see as a North American problem. Figure 7.2 shows the current American drug trafficking routes.

LOS ANGELES:
Here, the "West Side Story" battle between the Bloods and the Crips is a battle over distribution rights. Not since Chicago during Prohibition has a U.S. city experienced so many drive-by shootings.

SAN FRANCISCO:
In 1991 the birthplace of the drug counterculture saw the largest-ever U.S. seizure of "China White" heroin—1,080 pounds, worth up to $4 billion on the street.

SAN ANTONIO:
The federal government says that the Alamo City has one of the largest surplus money supplies in the country. The only explanation is drug profits.

NEW YORK:
The undisputed crack capital. An estimated 80 percent of cocaine is supplied by the Cali cartel, a professional operation that appears to value efficiency over violence.

MIAMI:
Once the prime destination for South American coke smugglers, this southern Florida city has been the most visible target of recent enforcement efforts. As the heat was turned up, many traffickers turned to the Texas–Mexico border.

MEXICO:
Although corruption among authorities appears to be lessening as cooperation with U.S. law enforcement agencies increases, Mexico has become the main route for cocaine into the U.S. and remains the primary grower of the marijuana consumed in the U.S. Its smuggling networks are experienced and are represented on both sides of the border.

CENTRAL AMERICA:
The U.S. Drug Enforcement Administration reportedly has set up office in El Salvador. A new "Guatemalan Mafia" is involved in the shipment of cocaine. Colombian cartels continue to take advantage of Panama's attractive banking system, which is more discreet and far less discerning than that of Switzerland or the Cayman Islands. Convenience counts, too—the banks are right on the travel routes.

COLOMBIA:
Drug cartels threatened to turn this country into a war zone, but a change in government policy ended the extradition of drug dealers and consequently much of the killing and bombing. The government remains beset on one side by drug cartels and on the other by leftist guerrillas.

ECUADOR:
Although the problems of this country are comparatively small, smugglers do use its harbors, and some coca paste is produced near the Peruvian border.

PERU:
About 60 percent of U.S.-bound cocaine comes from the leaves grown in this nation's highlands, the same highlands controlled by the Maoist guerrillas, who receive a cut of the profits.

BOLIVIA:
Bolivia produces 30 percent of the coca that ends up in the U.S. More than a third of its $1.2 billion in foreign exchange comes from cocaine.

FIGURE 7.2 American Drug Trafficking Routes

At home the war on drugs has been costly as well. In addition to the added expenses for enforcement, many are concerned that the courts have eagerly joined the effort and are whittling away at important constitutional guarantees. Not even added penalties, making many drug crimes more severe than crimes of violence, have been enough, however, and more than one official has proposed shooting dealers on sight and blowing suspected drug planes out of the sky. While far-fetched and, hopefully, offered only for effect, the program of "zero tolerance" has produced concrete examples of excess. Using the power of asset forfeiture, in 1988, for example, the Coast Guard boarded and seized the $25 million *Ark Royal* after finding ten marijuana seeds and two stems on board. That same year, the 52-foot *Mindy* was impounded because of cocaine dust found on a rolled up dollar bill. The $80 million research vessel *Atlantis II* was seized after .01 ounce of marijuana was found in a crewman's shaving kit. While the policy was eventually abandoned and each of these ships was returned after payment of heavy fines, Wisotsky concluded that "Americans have significantly less freedom than they did only five or six years ago" (1991: 112). Rather than continue along the same path, many have begun to wonder if the war on drugs is even winnable.

Drugs, Rights, and Legalization

Surprising to many, the earliest interest in repealing the policies of drug prohibition came from the conservative end of the political spectrum. Critical of prohibition tactics and doubtful of the government's right or ability to restrict such personal behavior, by the early 1970s Milton Friedman, Ernest van den Haag, William F. Buckley, and others openly questioned the approach being pursued. Despite the status of such critics, however, for nearly two decades the idea of legalization as a legitimate option failed to gain much ground. But in 1988, with the frustrations of the latest drug war still in mind, the idea emerged on the front pages and on television talk shows to be debated in full view.

The Case for Legalization The basic argument for legalization has changed little over the years. Pragmatically, the proponents of legalization note that the current drug control policies are fundamentally flawed and can do little else but fail. To them, the drug problem is not so much a moral issue as a medical one. Having no difficulty with the idea that adults should be able to use such substances so long as others are not harmed, they note the inconsistencies between drug policies and those dealing with alcohol and tobacco. Equally important, these critics complain that the current approaches are not only failing but are costly and counterproductive. Indeed, many of our drug-related problems are, in fact, a result of our prohibition efforts, they warn. By legalizing the sale of drugs to adults, corruption would be reduced, organized crime would be dealt a crushing blow, and public resources could be diverted to far more meaningful education and treatment programs. By driving up drug prices, they argue, our current efforts are subsidizing rather than waging war on drug traffickers (Dennis, 1990).

Far from being a single voice, the proponents of legalization actually offer a range of policy choices. At one end are the libertarians whose vision includes the end of virtually all government restraints. Except for minor restrictions such as those prohibiting sales to children, these advocates embrace Milton Friedman's (Friedman & Friedman, 1984) earlier view that as a matter of principle the government has no right to place such limits on its citizens. At the opposite extreme are those seeking total government control over the production and sale of such products. With most drugs available through prescription, where distribution is carefully monitored and controlled, these proponents seem to seek a return to the stated goals of the original Harrison Act. By moving our problems of addiction into more observable channels, they suggest, the powers of government to seek a remedy can be employed.

In the broad middle are a range of proposals attempting to draw from the arguments of both extremes. Here, government steps out of the marketplace, making most of the now prohibited substances legally available to competent adults. By maintaining regulatory powers over production and sales, however, drug usage can be monitored and heavily taxed. With the funds produced, both treatment programs and drug education can be made available to all who need them, especially to children. From the reductions in enforcement costs and with the proceeds from taxes, these policy advocates argue that our drug problems can be more competently addressed while we contribute substantially to public treasuries (Trebach, 1987; Nadelmann, 1989, 1991; Dennis, 1990).

Although plausible to many, public opinion and political consensus have remained opposed to each of these positions supporting legalization (Inciardi, 1991). Despite increased funding from sources such as the ACLU and the Drug Policy Foundation, proponents of legalization have had little success repealing current laws or passing new ones. In addition, they have been aggressively attacked by federal officials, rejected by others such as the Conference of Mayors, and criticized heavily by a host of scholars and researchers (Wilson, 1990; Inciardi & McBride, 1990; Inciardi, 1991; Akers, 1992).

The Case against Legalization While the case for legalization rests largely on the failures of the present system of drug control, those opposed see the option as little more than an unconditional surrender to the criminals. To legalize drugs, they argue, would be to imply approval. By most standards of measurement, the drug problem in this country is less widespread than only a decade ago (Akers, 1992) and now is not the time for complacency, they contend. Despite the admitted failures and the reforms that may be needed, to move in a totally opposite direction risks undoing the fragile headway made during the 1980s.

In addition, the opponents note that the social costs of legalization are both unknown and potentially devastating. Since research has demonstrated that drug use is disproportionately concentrated in the inner cities, a free market system puts our most marginal communities at the greatest potential risk. Inciardi and McBride (1990) note that for unknown reasons, as a group, women appear to develop a dependence on drugs more readily than do men. Since this is especially so for crack, and since a great many inner-city families are headed by women, legalization of drugs may further increase the problems of child abuse, neglect, and the growing occurrence of "crack babies." Further, since recent research also suggests that drug addiction may intensify criminal careers, opponents fear that legalization runs the risk of bringing about the chemical destruction of an entire urban generation. Finally, these advocates note that contrary to many expectations, addicts coerced into treatment by the criminal justice system appear to do better than voluntary patients. The key factor related to success, it appears, is the length of stay in treatment, and those coerced stay longer than those who are not. In short, those opposed to legalization contend that legalization attempts too much too soon and is a reflection of our cultural tendency to seek immediate solutions to complex problems. Logic, they add, argues against it.

THE SEARCH FOR ALTERNATIVES:
A FEW CONCLUDING THOUGHTS

If increased enforcement hasn't worked and legalization isn't acceptable—then what? It appears that we are now at a point where the credibility of previous solutions to our drug problems are sufficiently low that much of the public no longer believes viable answers are possible. Confidence in the system is so low that in late 1985 more than 800 Miami police officers felt compelled to volunteer for drug testing in a move to demonstrate their integrity. Further, despite the considerable costs so far, no one can be sure if we have actually made progress, if we have struggled but failed, or if our drug problems are the result of our efforts. In such a mood, the tendency has been to oversimplify the problems while narrowing rather than broadening the options available for consideration. In so doing, fatigue and frustration have become the two most powerful forces driving policy.

The answers to these issues ultimately involve judgment calls, where the costs and benefits of action (or inaction) are balanced. As we proceed from here we offer the following thoughts for consideration.

1. We should carefully define the problem. While this may seem obvious, since 1914 a consensus has yet to emerge on exactly what the drug problem in the United States may be. Are we referring to the use of any prohibited drugs or only the abuse of substances that lead to physical or psychological harm? Is it drug-induced misbehavior that most concerns us or only drug trafficking and the vast amounts of money it generates? Such confusion in the statement of the problem necessarily leads to confusion in solving it.

2. Because we have limited resources available, future policies should establish realistic goals. Policies that promise quick and simple solutions offer incentives for abuse and are most often frustrating in their failure. Since "zero tolerance" is probably beyond our reach, it is both logical and necessary to make distinctions based on principle and the importance of a concern. For example, should we focus most sharply on (a) drug use by children or by adults, (b) public use of drugs or private use at home, or (c) recreational consumption or addiction and drug impairment? In discussing these concerns, Wisotsky (1991) recommends specific goals intended to protect children, public safety and order, public health, and the value of individual liberty and responsibility.

3. We should resist the temptation to blame others for what is largely a domestic problem. The willingness to do so in the past has led to massive interventions that are costly and often counterproductive and that almost certainly interfere with other important policy goals. For example, if the naval blockade some have proposed would be effective at stopping the flow of drugs from South American countries, why hasn't it worked to stop Hawaiian marijuana? "If we cannot stop the flow of a relatively bulky drug from a small remote set of islands we control," Weisheit (1990a) recently asked, "how can we realistically expect to stop the flow of drugs from South America?" Similarly, if crop substitution will work in foreign countries, why won't it work in Kentucky where as many as 40 percent of the citizens in

some counties are believed to be actively involved in growing marijuana for profit?

4. Finally, if we have learned anything from our earlier experiences, it is that enforcement alone cannot work—to be effective, we must also reduce the demand for drugs. Here too, however, the issues are far from simple. For example, for many, demand reduction is synonymous with the provision of more treatment for addicts. In attacking current policy, these critics contend that solutions can be found only through increased funding of treatment facilities. What they fail to note is that many find drug use an intensely enjoyable experience for which treatment is not desired. As we saw with methadone, even when they are addicted, many users are interested in treatment programs as a means of stretching their supplies or to get them over the immediate hump until their habits are again more manageable. For them, treatment may ease the suffering but it will not "cure" them of their problems.

Beyond offering help to those who need it, Musto's (1987, 1990) analyses suggest that peer pressure may be the key to demand reduction. Awareness of the dangers of abuse, negative images of addicts and addiction, and intensive school-based programs had a significant impact on an entire generation. As drug use declined, however, drug education sank with it, leaving a generation of young people in the 1960s poorly prepared and with little first-hand knowledge upon which decisions could be made. As the current trends in smoking and drug use make clear, considerable knowledge has again been accumulated—mostly by experience. We should put it to work and ensure that it is passed on to those who follow us.

8

Gambling, Loans, and the Other Businesses of Organized Crime

Mark Haller argues that a "central goal in the study of the organized underworld . . . should be an understanding of the economics of loan-sharking, numbers gambling, drug dealing, labor racketeering, and the numerous other illegal ventures that are often classified as part of the organized underworld" (1992:8). According to Haller, such understanding comes from looking at the economic factors that shape illicit enterprises, the geographical factors that bear on the locations of enterprises, and the law enforcement policies that help structure the environment in which the enterprises are carried out. This is what we will be doing in this chapter.

GAMBLING

If Prohibition and, later, drugs provided impetus for the expansion of organized crime, it was gambling that first necessitated a structural framework. In fact, by the early 1800s, gambling was a well-established profession supporting talented individuals willing to take risks. We saw earlier that dynamic characters such as Arnold Rothstein in New York and Mont Tennes in Chicago had the skill and ambition to build criminal organizations from the individual games they organized. Before them, however, were the "blacklegs," who had a rich tradition of card playing and horse racing against the English in the early South. The first jockey clubs were organized in Virginia while card games such as euchre and poker were popular throughout the region. Even the French and Spanish contributed to the rise of professional gambling in New Orleans where games of chance were considered among the prerogatives of gentlemen. As hundreds of businessmen traveled the Mississippi, innovations such as faro, craps, and variants of poker offered opportunities for profit for those with sufficient skill and the wits to use them (Johnson, 1992).

As the lure of growing business centers spread, the mobility of the blacklegs transformed gambling into the primary recreation for many cities throughout the nation. By the middle of the century, faro houses had appeared as far north as Philadelphia and Boston. Ostensibly offering a bettor the fairest chance of winning, "gambling hells" had been set up on the second floors of many downtown saloons by the 1850s. Here saloon keepers and gamblers developed close relationships for their mutual benefit. Acting as landlord and bondsman in cases of arrest, the saloon keepers soon realized that their tenants' games attracted an inexhaustible supply of customers. The rewards from such an arrangement required some degree of permanency however, which in turn implied a fixed location and ties to the local community. In addition, since gambling was usually illegal, arrangements with local authorities were necessary for protection.

Beyond their attraction for the saloon keepers, the gamblers and their gambling houses needed employees of their own. A faro dealer, two assistants, and a doorkeeper were common for even smaller banks, while more successful operations included cooks, waiters, and "ropers" who worked hotel lobbies, restaurants, and other public places scouting out visitors seeking a game. With staffs ranging from 4 to around 30, hundreds of houses spread throughout most major cities, and gambling became a major employer in many communities. By 1870, some estimate that as many as 3,000 New Yorkers depended upon gambling for their salaries. And with incomes often reaching $100 per week, even the lowest paid employees earned far more than the customers who played and the police who monitored their games (Johnson, 1992). With such opportunities available, as the 19th century drew to a close, the life of a gambler increasingly became one to be envied and a model for those who aspired to succeed.

Eventually, of course, as the profits mounted, the casual ways of the riverboat gamblers gave way to consistency. Originally, old gambling pros had held the crucial positions, but the more successful faro backers came to prefer more reliable workers who could be counted on to show up regularly—and sober. After all, interruptions in business were difficult enough to control and could be quite costly. In addition, as the competition for customers grew, the sites for gambling "hells" moved steadily downtown to be nearer the major hotels, rail depots, and entertainment centers. These locations brought the gamblers into closer contact with the more respectable citizens and saloon keepers. As these downtown building owners grew dependent on the high rents they could charge, the gamblers soon found themselves to be a central component of the economic life of many communities. Expanding from faro alone to become crucial backers of most professional sports and other entertainment, the more successful operators quickly realized the opportunities before them. Haller (1992) notes that by the early 1900s the takeover in many neighborhoods was nearly complete. It was not so much that the gamblers influenced local politics, he explains, but rather that they increasingly had become the political organizations. Beyond that, their money and influence allowed them to have a broad impact on most other aspects of urban life as well. Although this was not a healthy situation from the start, with the arrival of bootlegging, these arrangements proved even more dangerous in many important cities.

Organizing the Gamblers

Although the organization and control of gambling were significantly altered as ghettos emerged and access to national racing wires and telephones spread, it was the rise of bootlegging in the 1920s that brought the most immediate influence. As we described in Chapter 6, with the passage of the Volstead Act, legitimate distributors of liquor largely abandoned the business altogether. At the same time, established gamblers (who were happy living by their gambling skills) tended to remain on the sidelines. Taken together, the business of bootlegging was left to ambitious newcomers. Young and tough, most who were successful were graduates of the juvenile gangs in urban slums. In addition, almost all were identified with particular ethnic groups, since Prohibition arrived just as the first generation Jewish and Italian Americans reached maturity. Some 50 percent of the major bootleggers were Jewish, 25 percent Italian, and the rest primarily Irish and Polish (Haller, 1992). By 1933 when Prohibition ended, most who survived were still young and ambitious and in need of opportunities where their wealth and connections could be used. Their influence would be felt for decades.

Aside from the profits to be made, gambling was a natural for gangsters in other ways as well. Risk takers by definition, many of the early hoodlums and aspirants were ardent sports fans with an appreciation for competition and conflict. Their wealth and influence gave them ringside seats at boxing matches, from which many also bet often and heavily. As they expanded their businesses to include other activities, the money, power, and relations they had established with politicians and police instantly transformed them into formidable rivals if not exactly welcome partners. One by one, the bootleggers supplanted the old-time gamblers, either outright or through partnership arrangements, bringing their resources and the gamblers' skills together. Although most of these partnerships appear to have been arrangements of convenience, Haller (1992) notes that the relationships continued to develop well into the 1940s and 1950s. By then, of course, gambling had become an important mainstay of organized crime.

The Rise of the Lotteries

A simple, painless and honorable way for the U.S. Government to earn at least $10,000,000,000 a year lies within the reach of Congress. Congress can create a national lottery, and states could legalize off-track betting and bingo . . . carefully supervised and controlled, would provide a harmless release for man's gambling instinct and collect desperately needed funds for useful public welfare activities. (Fino, 1955)

While Congressman Fino was probably not aware of it, his proposal marked a return to a debate several centuries old over the recreations that ought to be proper in a society. Apparently concerned that our "modern life with security built in" offered too few "opportunities for daring," Congressman Fino appeared to be siding with those who viewed gambling as proper—a basic or natural instinct over which government ought to have only limited powers of regulation and control.

Others, however, argued that "it is not fit that every man that will cheat every man that would be cheated." Describing gambling's promise of easy profit as a tax upon "unfortunate self-conceited fools," as early as the 17th century these reformers insisted that "it is ordained that the Sovereign should have guard of these fools, even as in the case of lunatics and idiots" (Ezell, 1960:1). Regardless of one's view, the issues and policies concerned with gambling today have evolved from a long tradition of established lottery play.

Fueled at first by war and westward expansion, and later by industrialization and urbanization, lotteries—used to raise revenues without taxes and to raffle land or goods—became entrenched in the economy and habits of the American people. Ever-expanding needs led to cycles of even more ambitious lottery drawings. Soon few communities were considered to be sufficiently large and wealthy to support all the sales of lottery tickets for all the many schemes for which they were being used. As a result, the wealth of neighboring communities, an entire state, or even an entire region were often necessary to support the projects undertaken. As they grew, however, games became increasingly complex and time consuming until eventually, full-time ticket brokers and contractors were necessary in what was becoming an industry of lottery gambling. By 1825, even small towns had their middlemen who, for personal gain, would skillfully buy up blocks of tickets for resale to players who might otherwise be left out. This, in turn, required full-time managers to control and direct the games. Slowly, these new entrepreneurs absorbed most of the functions previously performed by volunteers. All the while, of course, they spread the game's reach to virtually every corner of the country. Although this evolution stimulated many of the marketing and promotional techniques in use by businesses today, the rapid, largely unregulated growth it produced caused important problems as well.

The Birth of Policy Gambling As the lottery merchants worked to expand their customer base, what began as a means to finance noble causes quickly lost any semblance of control. With brokers' shares often reaching as high as 20 or 25 percent, increasingly only the wealthy could afford tickets that rose in price to as much as $60 each. (At the time, family incomes seldom reached $1,000 per year, and laborers earned 40 cents a day.) As the cost of tickets soared out of reach, the more enterprising brokers responded by selling partial tickets, developing installment plans, and even renting tickets for the day. This latter practice was possible since several days (sometimes weeks or months) were usually required to draw the thousands of tickets in even the smaller games. As such, the renter could lease the ticket for the day at a sliding rate that varied according to the number of tickets remaining to be drawn. If the rented number was selected, the prize went to the temporary holder; if not, the ticket was returned for the next day.

Among the more creative adjustments by the lottery brokers was the practice of "insurance" or "policy." Rather than buy or rent all or a portion of a lottery ticket, players with limited funds could bet that a particular number would be drawn on a specified day. Of course, their guesses paid off only in the unlikely event that they were correct. Not part of the actual lottery, all winnings were paid from the betting pool with a formula determined by the odds on that given day (calculated by the number of tickets to be drawn from among those remaining). With these small bets now possible, the game quickly became popular as "policy shops" opened to accommodate players seeking a game.

Out of fear of abuse and perhaps recognizing that the lure of policy could damage the profits of the lottery system upon which it was based, by the 1820s modifications were introduced in the lottery system. If all tickets could be drawn in a single day, the sponsors reasoned, policy betting would no longer occur. As such, rather than selecting numbers individually, projects began using tickets carrying a combination of three numbers each, usually from 1 to 78. Using only these 78 numbers, at least 76,076 different combinations (tickets) could be issued. On the day of the drawing, 78 ballots (each numbered consecutively) would be prepared; only 12 of which would then actually be drawn. The ticket bearing the first three numbers drawn received the first prize, the next three numbers selected the second, and so on. In all, 12 three-number winners were possible. Smaller prizes were then awarded to those tickets with two numbers drawn and, finally, to those with only one. In so doing, in the 15 minutes required to select 12 numbered ballots, 30,316 winners could be determined. The remaining players, of course, received nothing for their tickets (Ezell, 1960).

Despite the added complexity, the now more complicated lotteries succeeded only in changing the form of the popular policy games. Players could now bet that from one to four numbers would be drawn in various sequences. Although illegal by then in most states, policy watchers would routinely attend a drawing where they would take down numbers as they were selected. From there, they would report back with runners. The typical bet was seldom more than 6 cents, while a winning pick might pay as much as $2.50. By the early 1820s, policy betting was widespread in most major cities, including New York, where one legislative investigation revealed that in one three-day period a single policy shop had made $31,000.

Throughout the 1830s the games developed an importance all their own as neighborhood shops sprang up, especially in the inner wards where the poor and working classes could be found. With 600 to 1,000 such shops each in New York and Philadelphia, and countless more in other cities, anyone desiring to play had little trouble finding a game. By 1845, betting as little as 3 cents per number had become possible. Even so, by the early 1850s, the income in New York's shops averaged between $6,000 and $8,000 per day (Johnson, 1992). So profitable were the prospects that Benjamin Wood, Zachariah Simmons, and others began to organize the operators. As alliances among those in control shifted back and forth, however, local brokers in many neighborhoods began to turn instead to a new game—a game they controlled—called numbers.

The End of Lottery's Dominance Despite oversaturating the market and causing a brief lull around the 1790s, lotteries stimulated and fed the insatiable American appetite for gambling. Still, opposition was quietly growing. The Quakers had maintained their objections throughout, and gradually others joined the cause. Publications such as the *Massachusetts Missionary Magazine*, *Evening Fireside*, and the *Monthly Anthology* told stories of family destruction caused by the lure of easy money and called for abolition of the lotteries. For the most part, these warnings were ignored by a nation where everyone felt compelled to better themselves—and quickly. Ambition was everywhere, and the desire for success generated its own momentum. While unauthorized ventures and the spreading policy games were a concern, for many in power the lotteries remained an effective means of voluntary taxation. In short, there was little to cause change until the failures of supervision and management became apparent.

Having already lost heavily on one collapsed scheme, New York acted in 1813 to shore up the supervision of its state-appointed lottery management. It was too little, too late. By 1818, concerns had reached such proportions that in September the *Republican Chronicle* felt compelled to run a blasting editorial telling of corruption in the state-sponsored drawings. As a result, an immediate investigation was demanded. A week later the charges were repeated, this time adding that the fraud was both systematic and continuing. As the directors of the lottery reacted angrily to the charges, their response only made matters worse. Rather than let the allegations lie and likely be forgotten, the directors decided to sue for libel.

Once in court, the *Chronicle*'s attorneys singled out John H. Sickles, the state's acting lottery manager, as the most culpable of those responsible. They proved that prior to one drawing he had given assurances that specific tickets would not be chosen. Further, he had been seen withholding tickets from several other drawings and had a personal interest in a winning ticket that had paid $35,000. As the evidence was presented, the case against Sickles was overwhelming, leaving the court little to deliberate as it ruled in the *Chronicle*'s favor. The actual outcome was of secondary importance, however.

Once the evidence of such widespread fraud was made public, both players and officials demanded action. A special committee was appointed to find solutions, though the chairman expressed little hope that any might be workable. The system, the committee noted, might be beyond repair. Salesmen were paid handsome commissions to "entice women, children, apprentices, servants, Negroes, and the poorest and most ignorant" into playing (Ezell, 1960:200). In addition, the state's losses through failure and fraud had mounted to at least $109,000. In fact, the only positive thing they could find was the "cheerfulness" with which the players turned over their money.

As the bad news leaked out, similar problems in Pennsylvania, Massachusetts, and the District of Columbia were revealed, producing an avalanche of concern and a growing movement for reform. While much of the public played on, seemingly oblivious to the controversy around them, a slow decline in sales at Yates and McIntyre, New York's leading broker, revealed the seriousness of the situation. Where they had succeeded in selling at least 93 percent of the tickets they were assigned in 1826, by the end of the decade that had fallen to no more than 38 percent (Ezell, 1960). This situation continued for the next several decades as reformers seized upon every lottery failure to demand that the promoters be forced from business. Finally, near the end of the century, the Louisiana Lottery collapsed, dragging others throughout the country down with it.

The Rise of the Numbers Operators

With the close of World War I, blacks from throughout the South began to migrate to the northern cities in search of economic opportunities. Once there, however, much like the Irish, Jews, and Italians before them, they were quickly confronted with social and residential segregation, giving rise to still another wave of ghettoization. Also like their predecessors, they responded by developing local political organizations to organize voting, exert influence, and spread economic growth (Osofsky, 1966). Unlike those before them, however, as the entrepreneurial class began to establish itself, many turned to numbers gambling as an opportunity for quick profit.

In almost any variation, numbers games are easy to establish and operate. The earliest versions required players to select a three-digit number from 000 to 999. Bets from as little as one cent were then placed in the hopes that the number chosen would match the game's official winner. Early on, many games were based on the last three digits of the daily Treasury Balance; stock market sales, horse track attendance, and a variety of other easily established statistics were often used as well. With Bolita, a numbers variation popular among Hispanics in Florida, winning numbers were often determined with numbered balls drawn from a bag. Using this method, dishonest operators could easily ensure that numbers carrying little betting money were chosen by filling the bag with balls containing only that number or by first refrigerating the desired ball so that the person drawing could identify it by touch (Jones, 1973). Regardless of the variation used, although the odds against winning are 1,000 to 1, payoff odds are normally limited to 500 or 600 to 1 ($25 or $30 paid for a nickel bet) to ensure the profit advantage to the games' backers. To increase interest in their games, some operators offer additional, though smaller, payoffs for mutations of the number (such as a reverse sequence) or for the appearance of two of the chosen digits (King, 1969).

Given the small amounts that could be bet, numbers games have a natural appeal in poorer communities. In addition, since betting occurs at established locations such as newsstands, bars, factories, or from cab drivers, close daily contact at the neighborhood level is required. Further, since an operation requires only a modest bankroll and almost no upfront investment, many local community leaders found the system hard to resist. Even better, while many banks were attractive to big-time competitors such as Dutch Schultz, Al Capone, and their successors, even they soon realized that partnerships were the best that could be readily managed. While neighborhood operators might share their profits to avoid violence, since street-level runners are essential and competing games so easy to establish, outright takeovers were seldom successful. As such, then and now, it is believed that the largest share of numbers games are backed by smaller local operators (King, 1969). Even so, they continue to employ thousands of people while circulating millions of dollars through local economies. Although a significant source of small-time but systematic corruption, these widely popular and profitable games are dismissed by many observers who underestimate their importance. Later, we will look at the problems that numbers pose for enforcement.

Horse Racing, Bookmaking, and the Parimutuel Bet

Although numbers may be the backbone of illegal gambling, its profits always seemed to exceed its prestige. At the opposite end of the prestige scale, gambling on horses offered not only excitement but both social acceptance and a high rate of return on the gambling dollar. Always popular, horse racing grew steadily from only 39 tracks in the early 1800s to over 123 in 1865. Still, only a few of these rated as major establishments. Most were informal arrangements where horsemen arranged their own races. Interestingly, among the earliest promoters of the sport were the railroads, which regarded the mass transportation needs of racing fans as an important source of income (Johnson, 1992). By the latter half of the 19th century, major tracks at Saratoga (New York), Monmouth Park (New Jersey), the New Orleans Fair Grounds, Pimlico (Baltimore), and Churchill Downs (Kentucky) had all opened, giving rise to a more organized and exciting form of gambling.

While horse owners and race fans justified their sport as vital to improved breeding, in reality it was usually the betting that became the central attraction. At first, a horse's owner and his friends made private wagers where the only guarantee of a payoff was a gentleman's pledge. Where doubts existed, a neutral party would hold all bets until the end of the race. With the spread of racing in the 1860s, however, this system of "stakeholders" became increasingly inadequate. It seems that the gentlemen of racing had less honor than had previously been thought. As a result, most of the major tracks turned to a European scheme of pool betting.

With the auction pool, a track auctioneer accepted the highest bid placed on each horse as the official bet. He then held the total of all bets placed in a pool until a winner was declared. After deducting a commission or takeout of from 3 to 5 percent for expenses, the stakes for the winning horse's ticket holder were paid by the track. Since reforms were needed to ensure more honest betting and the pools offered a more consistent income for the tracks, by the late 1860s pool betting had become the officially recognized procedure at virtually all major tracks. Ironically, Johnson (1992) notes that it was this and subsequent betting reforms that opened the way for professional gamblers and organized criminals to become an integral part of racing. And New York's John Morrissey was among the early pioneers.

While Morrissey and others opened the country's leading tracks, they also began a system of off-track betting. Where pool selling had become part of the sport's normal routine, it occurred only on the day of the race and required the bettor to actually be present. By expanding their services to hotels and other sites nearby, the number of bidders per horse could be increased. This, in turn, led to ever bigger pools and commissions. In no time, "poolrooms" began to appear in cities throughout the country. With the advent of wire services such as John Payne's in Cincinnati, betting was soon diversified to include sporting and other events as well. Still, since the pools continued to limit betting to the wealthy by accepting only one bet per horse per race, a few enterprising gamblers looked again to the Europeans for a means of making the action more broadbased. The results of their efforts brought parimutuel wagering and bookmaking to the United States during the 1870s.

After touring France in 1871, Leonard Jerome (the founder of Jerome Park in Westchester County, New York) returned with a device touted as "a poor man's auction pool." Invented only a few years earlier, the Paris mutuel machine allowed a bettor to purchase a ticket on a horse of his choice. The machine both issued the ticket and recorded all bets placed on that horse. Following the race, the track could then divide the total money wagered on the race by the number of persons holding winning tickets to determine how much each bettor was due. A commission based on the "handle," the total amount bet, was first taken to cover track expenses. Invented in Paris, these mutuel machines had quickly become a centerpiece to French betting (Johnson, 1992). Here, however, where the devices were expensive and infrequently available, they would catch on far less quickly.

Meanwhile, as the introduction of mutuel betting allowed the less afflu-ent to play, the American Jockey Club began to promote the English system of bookmaking as still another alternative. In its version, the club reserved a room at its Jerome Park clubhouse where the right to "make book" was leased to a few important gamblers. Players paying a special club fee were permitted to enter the room where they could wager safely in a controlled environment. In effect, the club had become a more formalized version of the stakeholder. In this system, however, not only the track but the book-maker as well extracted a commission from the handle. Once again, only the affluent could afford to participate.

Both systems caught on and spread slowly among horse tracks and pool rooms, but the final blow to pool betting arrived with the 1876 U.S. presidential election. Acting as stakeholder for pools worth over $350,000, John Morrissey decided that the race between presidential candidates Hayes and Tilden was too close to call and too complex to sort out. As a result, he suddenly called off all bets and returned the money bet to his players, minus his 2 percent commission. As other stakeholders did like-wise, a storm of controversy erupted. Facing demands that they take ac-tion, the New York state legislature simply outlawed all pool selling in the state. After unsuccessfully seeking exemptions for their horses, the tracks at Jerome Park, Saratoga, and elsewhere had little choice. Lacking mutuel machines and having few other options, they installed bookmakers to handle the action. This time, however, the process was altered to accom-modate the mass market appetite for gambling. It was not until the 1920s that the cost and availability of mutuel machines allowed their widespread adoption. Long before then, of course, bookmaking had moved off-track to replace the now obsolete poolrooms.

Gambling Today

With the recent return of state lotteries and the proliferation of casinos, the picture of gambling in the United States has become considerably more confused. As Congressman Fino urged decades earlier, one jurisdiction after another has returned to the tradition of funding public projects with the proceeds of gamblers. Not only could education and other worthwhile projects be benefited, proponents argued, but as the demand for gambling was filled through legitimate means, organized crime and corruption would be dealt a serious blow as well. With that logic, by 1993 gambling in some form had been legalized in 47 states and the District of Columbia. Through these legitimate outlets alone, some $330 billion was wagered in 1992 (Mullen, 1993).

Curiously, while the debate about the benefits of legalized gambling remains unresolved, recent trends do suggest changes in bettor preferences. For example, although nearly 81 cents of every $1 bet was wagered in the casinos of Las Vegas, Reno, and Atlantic City, it was opportunities closer to home that fueled most of the $26 billion increase in betting over 1991. Even there, though, it was the casinos run by Indian tribes and the return of riverboat casinos in Iowa, Illinois, and Mississippi where the most dramatic gains occurred. Indeed, much of the 8.4 percent increase from the previous year appears to have come at the expense of horse and dog racing, jai alai, legal bookmaking, and the table games in Nevada and New Jersey. Meanwhile, riverboat casinos experienced increases in betting of some 566 percent, casinos in Deadwood (South Dakota) and the Colorado mining towns were up 299 percent, and the casinos operated by Indian tribes were estimated to have taken in at least $14 billion in bets, an increase of 240 percent. While some of the gains may have been the result of greater access and availability, it would appear that "casinos are the one type of gaming where demand still exceeds supply" (Mullen, 1993:1). Unfortunately for the casino's competitors, the same apparently cannot be said. Although it is likely that the illegal games have been affected similarly, as we will see there are important reasons why these games may be somewhat more resistant to the spreading opportunities to gamble than are their legitimate counterparts.

The Role of Numbers Despite public access to state-run lotteries since the 1960s, numbers gambling has retained much of its popularity. Although still primarily associated with minorities in the older cities, especially in the east and midwest, numbers gambling has been adopted by the poor in other communities as well. By 1977, Light (1992) estimated that at least 70 to 80 percent of numbers gambling occurred in communities that were mostly nonblack. Regardless of the players' ethnicity, however, most observers agree that the amounts wagered on these games are considerable. Warner and Junker (1941) estimated that by 1938 at least 5,000 people were employed in various capacities by numbers banks on Chicago's mostly black South Side. They estimated the total annual gross to be around $18 million. If correct, an average of $64 was being bet for every resident of the community—$256 for each family of four. With the median city-wide family income then $1,463, participation at that level meant that numbers gambling accounted for an amazing 17.5 percent of family income on the city's South Side.

Three decades later, the Fund for the City of New York (1972) estimated that the proportion of family income spent on numbers in that city was a relatively low 5 percent. Ed Brown, the Director for Political Affairs for the Congress of Racial Equality (CORE) disagreed with this estimate, however. He estimated that by the mid-1970s at least $300 million to $500 million was bet on numbers by residents of Harlem alone (E. Brown, 1973). Even his lowest estimate translates to almost 16 percent of family income. During the same period, Lasswell and McKenna (1972) estimated that between 2.5 and 5.1 percent of family income was being spent on the numbers by the residents of New York's Bedford-Stuyvesant community. While the estimates vary widely, there is agreement that numbers gambling has consumed a significant portion of the income in many communities, even after the return of state-run lotteries in states where numbers are played. As earlier research suggested, it appears that the more difficult the economy becomes, the more willing a community's residents are to participate in the numbers games (Light, 1992).

Given the amount invested and the odds against winning, many have wondered why so many play. Early explanations of the popularity of numbers centered on the games' ethnic beginnings in black and Hispanic neighborhoods. McCall (1963) noted that religious traditions and superstitions as well as mysticism are involved in the selection of numbers to be played. In effect, he suggested that a symbiotic relationship existed between the two. CORE's Brown (1973), on the other hand, evoked heritage as he reminded his readers of the early role of blacks in the development of the game. Something of a "soul" preoccupation with numbers existed, he suggested. While interesting, each of these views overlooks the fact that most players have more traditional religious backgrounds and that the vast majority of numbers players are white.

A more straightforward explanation emerges from the research of Lasswell and McKenna (1972) in Bedford-Stuyvesant. Bed-Stuy, as New Yorkers often refer to the neighborhood, is a Brooklyn community of 280,000 people, 82 percent black and mostly poor. Although the community contains about 3.4 percent of New York's population, during the 1970s they produced less than 1.2 percent of its income. Predictably, numbers gambling is popular among the residents. In fact, during 1970, 5 identifiable numbers banks servicing 12 different regular operations with a handle of nearly $37 million were known to be operating there. To illustrate their success, Lasswell and McKenna observed that in the eight years they studied the community (1963–1970) the profits of the known numbers and narcotics organizations operating in Bedford-Stuyvesant increased from 2.2 percent to more than 9 percent of the annual per capita income. Explained another way, organized crime took a larger cut of the incomes of these residents than did the Internal Revenue Service. Of those profits, over $11 million, or 20 percent, was traceable directly to the five banks studied.

While the games as entertainment were clearly deeply rooted in the community, the authors noted that they were important to the neighborhood in more subtle ways as well.

Numbers as a Financial Institution With over 1,345 runners and collectors and another 76 controllers employed in Bedford-Stuyvesant in 1970, the payroll for the numbers organizations made them the largest private employers in the community. Equally important, many of those employed were otherwise unskilled and uneducated, leaving them otherwise unemployable in the neighborhood's depressed economic environment. Those who did join an organization were rewarded with relative wealth, some degree of power, and considerable respect. In fact, since the 1,345 participants shared to some extent in almost $13 million, to their neighbors whose average annual income including welfare and other payments was less than $1,900, the runner's position was a sign of upward mobility.

Beyond their economic status, Silberman (1978) observed that numbers runners also play an important social role in their communities. Given the informal nature of transactions, players usually choose to deal with runners they know and can trust. As he makes his daily rounds or his customers stop by the local hangout where bets are placed, the runner becomes a source of information about the neighborhood. Newcomers must be introduced, and bettors have a chance to chat with each other, store owners, and whoever else might be around. When someone actually wins, these relationships are solidified further since it is customary to share the celebration with friends and neighbors. As Silberman retells the enthusiasm of one resident: "A number runner is something like Santa Claus, and any day you hit the number is Christmas" (1978:101).

For their part, the individuals who play often refer to their bets as investments in the belief that the games are their only means of personal savings. "The dime or quarter which one bets is scarcely missed, but when one hits the pay-off is a chunk of money large enough to be really useful to the winner" (Light, 1992:582). Serving a role to the poor not unlike a bank's Christmas Club, from the bettor's view if the game is played consistently enough, eventually small change that might otherwise be frittered away can be converted into sums of a substantial amount. And win they occasionally do. Lasswell and McKenna (1972) note that on an average day the betting public can expect to receive half of its total wager back in winnings.

Finally, in many neighborhoods the proceeds from gambling provide the basis for what is often the only credit available. Most obvious are the runners who provide direct loans to their customers. Some allow customers to play on credit and, in fact, in New York at least 18 percent of all players in the Fund for New York's study (1972) acknowledged doing so. Of those players regularly betting a dollar or more a day, 23 percent had played on credit. Beyond their gambling, however, another 9 percent of customers reported borrowing from their numbers runner for other purposes; among the dollar bettors, 15 percent. While the problems of loan-sharking will be discussed later, it is interesting to note that the percentages using this credit source are roughly comparable to those among the working poor who use credit unions (Light, 1992).

A second source of credit from numbers gambling benefits the businesses and business investments in the communities where the gamblers operate. Not only are the numbers bankers known to donate freely to churches, athletic leagues, and at holiday events, but they are often the largest investors in ghetto businesses. Beyond that, with their proceeds from collecting numbers bets, many small businesses serving as part-time runners or as legitimate hosts for operators are able to extend credit to their own customers.

The Problems for Enforcers All of this suggests that the problems confronting those who would stop these criminal enterprises are considerable. While there is no doubt that organized gamblers take far more from a community than they return, they nonetheless perform several important functions residents may not be able to meet legitimately. So interwoven with the community is this form of organized crime that Lasswell and McKenna suggest that their futures may be tied to each other. Each one dollar increase in business profits, they estimated, would lead to a 10-cent increase in gambling volume. In turn, for each additional million dollars of betting, another 30 residents would be recruited as employees. With so refined an interaction, it is unlikely that traditional tactics of added police or harassment of suppliers will be met with much support locally or result in any lasting impact. Nor is it likely that legal alternatives will replace the demand for numbers gambling. In short, as we have seen with other forms of organized crime, gambling succeeds largely because the communities where it does want it to.

LOANS AND LOAN-SHARKING

To enforce a debt, they will go very far—I have known them to go as far as hanging a man out of a window by his feet, fifteen stories—he got the money up in one hour—after you are frightened, you will come up with it—the only time a man gets killed is when he has defied their law completely—when he has it and just doesn't want to pay it—then it pays to make an example of him. (New York State Commission of Investigation, 1991:35)

In 1935, New York's special prosecutor Thomas Dewey announced that his ongoing investigation of organized crime would begin to include loan-sharking activities in Manhattan's financial district. The decision was offered with little fanfare, since at the time Dewey was apparently unsure of the extent of the problem and had little to suggest that more than small-time hoods were involved in any significant way. Still, salary lending had been around for several decades and current events, though not directly related, indicated that important changes might be under way. What had prompted his concern was an incident two weeks earlier in which a young Wall Street clerk had been badly beaten while at work. The clerk, it seems, had failed to make a $6 interest payment on a $10 loan. Although such loans were not unusual, Dewey knew that the use of violence as a collection technique marked a significant change in operating style. To him, this change implied involvement of the gangsters he had been pursuing for years.

While the announcement was largely forgotten on the back pages of the papers, by year's end Dewey's efforts began to pay off. As arrest totals grew, New York's other law enforcement agencies began their own probes as well. Simultaneously, internal investigations of city government, of special city projects, and in the Post Office were opened with each producing evidence of illegal lending. Although combined arrests would reach nearly 100 by 1937, Dewey was never successful in providing proof of the connection he had set out to establish.

The Transition from Salary Lending

Although loan-sharking as we think of it today first appeared quite recently in New York (during the 1930s), salary lending at usurious rates has been around much longer. Probably developed in the 1870s, the practice of lending against future salaries had at least an appearance of legality. Seldom violent, these lenders usually operated out of an office, investigated borrowers to determine their employment standing, and required complicated loan forms be signed before money actually exchanged hands. When payments weren't met on time, collection seldom required more than threats to inform the borrower's employer, although harassment and even lawsuits were occasionally necessary. In extreme cases, a lender might employ a stern-voiced woman, known as a "bawler-out," to visit the delinquent borrower's work place or neighborhood and berate him for his dishonesty in refusing to pay his debts. Embarrassed and afraid of being fired because of the public display, the borrower was generally eager to seek a settlement (Haller and Alvitti, 1992).

As for the borrowers, most were married men who had steady jobs and legitimate reasons for seeking a loan. Regular employees of large organizations, these civil servants, railroad workers, and insurance clerks had generally encountered an unexpected illness in the family, costs for moving, or needed money for vacations or Christmas. In one New York study, an estimated 2,000 police, 2,500 firemen, and 75,000 railroad clerks and mercantile house employees were customers. In a second study, one salary lender alone was found to have over 1,500 accounts with city employees (Haller and Alvitti, 1992). While only a small number of these borrowers needed loans for reasons such as gambling debts, ruinous rates of repayment were nevertheless usually required.

For the most part, lenders tended to be small operators, offering $5 to $50 loans from limited capital. Usually located near downtown office buildings, they advertised as all businesses must, and often competed for customers by varying rates or terms. As their businesses prospered, most preferred to open new companies rather than expand—a preference that allowed a few to develop regional chains. Daniel Tolman, who was recognized as the "King of Loan Sharks" around the turn of the century, saw his empire grow to include branches in more than 60 cities nationwide. Large or small, however, almost all were exploitive, often tricked or manipulated their customers, and were frequent targets of lawsuits and prosecutions.

Haller and Alvitti (1992) report that despite differing state laws concerning lending, the procedures for securing a loan seldom varied among lenders or from city to city. Once a customer had been steered their way, an application was generally the first step, followed by a background investigation to ensure a prospective borrower's creditworthiness. As loans were approved, applicants were next required to sign a series of complicated forms. In an effort to avoid conflict with usury laws, these forms shaped the transaction into the language of an investment. In other words, for a specified amount, the borrower agreed to assign rights to a portion of his future salary to the lender. For some, relatives were also required to sign, often unknowingly pledging their own wages as well. Worse yet, many forms included powers of attorney permitting the lender to impose fees, fines, and otherwise alter the terms of the agreement on his own. Of course, if a transaction wound up in court for collection, the lender, with power of attorney in hand, could simply appear and request judgment. Generally ignorant of what they were agreeing to, countless men were ruined by unscrupulous lenders who slowly bled them dry. While reformers launched campaigns against the loan sharks on several fronts, with the close of Prohibition and the expansion by the former bootleggers into loan-sharking, conditions only grew worse.

Racketeer Lending

Today's loan shark runs a surprisingly simple business that is not only profitable but an avenue to other opportunities as well. While it is true that individual entrepreneurs can operate on their own as loan sharks, individuals tied to organized crime groups have much more credible and diverse threats to enforce repayment.

Requiring a considerable up-front investment, the loan-sharking process usually occurs in a distinct hierarchy, with the funds in play flowing downward for protection. At the top is an initial investor who serves as the original source of the money to be loaned. In larger operations this individual may be a major organized crime figure (although not necessarily so) who is able to commit millions of dollars on short notice. In other cases, a consortium of smaller investors may pool their money so that each buys a stake in the process. Either way, few others are aware of this person's involvement, making it difficult for law enforcement to connect him to the lending process. Of course, it is precisely this connection that Thomas Dewey was attempting to establish years earlier.

At the second level of the operation are the money middlemen. These people are entrusted to distribute the investor's funds to the actual lenders. Generally independent contractors, the amounts made available to these wholesalers are usually determined by their stature, past performance, and capabilities. For their role, these middlemen pay a vigorish, or interest, of about 1 percent per week on the money they receive for distribution. In exchange, they have absolute responsibility for its use. On rare occasions, especially large loans may be handled directly at this level.

More often, the middlemen distribute the money in their charge to a third level in the process where the loans will actually take place. To protect the initial investors, the lenders at this third level seldom know the origin of the money available to them. For its use, however, an additional vigorish varying from 1 to 2.5 percent must be paid to their distributor. In turn, they are free themselves to make loans to borrowers at whatever rate the market will bear, with 5 percent to as much as 20 percent being common. Sometimes known as five-percenters, these lenders too have strict responsibility for the funds in their care.

Unlike the earlier salary lending, today's borrowers come to loan sharks with a variety of needs, both short and long term. Drug dealers and bookies arranging quick deals, for example, have a reliable source of short-term financing not otherwise available. Convenience and ready access to unlimited funds more than offsets the high costs of these loans, especially since the most favorable terms are often available to such regular and reliable customers. This is so because repayment is guaranteed, since these borrowers will seek to protect a source they may need to rely upon again soon. Gangsters from Lucky Luciano to Joey Gallo have been regular customers of this type.

At the opposite extreme are borrowers desperate for money with no other source available. Referred to loan sharks by finders, these borrowers are often businessmen in economic difficulty. Soon they find themselves encumbered for the long term with weekly "vig" payments they can hardly manage. Struggling to pay their interest alone, many of these customers are slowly bled dry without ever reducing their debt. In such cases, in fact, the loan shark is seldom interested in repayment of the principal preferring instead to continue to collect interest indefinitely. Eventually the loan is settled or the resources of the borrower completely disappear, leaving the borrower unable to continue payment. Alternative arrangements then become necessary.

Collecting Delinquent Debts Although violence, or at least a believable threat, is an obvious part of loan-sharking, we should remember that these lenders are in business to make money. Borrowers who are dead or seriously injured are of little use; indeed, they are a serious liability to a lender who must account for the money he has put into play. As a result, unless the delinquent borrower is openly defying his loan shark, force is usually a last, and least preferred, option.

Instead, the lenders might choose to establish a "sit-down." Here, the parties meet with a mediator who is typically an influential member in the loan process—often a representative of the initial investor. The claim against the borrower can then be adjudicated with the mediator establishing a "fair" payment to settle the obligation. In a sense, the hearing is not unlike those in a bankruptcy proceeding. Fairness, however, has little to do with the process in which the loan shark is never required to accept less than the original loan (New York State Commission of Investigation, 1991). In those instances where the borrower's resources are insufficient to support a settlement, some additional service can be agreed upon to satisfy at least partial payment.

Racketeers have always looked to loan-sharking as a vehicle of convenience. For example, in an effort to clear or legitimize their money, vigorish payments in the form of salary checks may be required. While appearing to work as an outside salesman or consultant, the lender on a borrower's payroll is able to claim legitimate employment for tax protection. In other examples, industrial secrets may be compromised for payment, insider information provided, or sports events rigged. The New York State Commission of Investigation (1991) uncovered several creative settlements such as the hairdresser who "fingered" wealthy clients and occupied them in his salon while burglars entered their homes or businesses. Other examples included a prominent sports announcer who steered high rollers to crooked gambling games and a trucking firm forced to ship and store stolen property. In some instances, a complete takeover of the borrower's business may be arranged if other options are not available. While the terms of such settlements may be harsh, to the beleaguered borrower they are usually considered preferable to the violent alternatives he and his family believe they face.

How Big Is the Business? However the loans are satisfied, it is clear that loan-sharking has become one of organized crime's most profitable enterprises. In 1967, Lawrence Kaplan and Salvatore Matters made estimates based on expert opinion that the industry-wide income ranged from $1 billion to $2 billion per year. Although such informal estimates are risky at best, the results compare favorably with the view offered by an Assistant District Attorney in testimony before the New York State Commission of Investigation in 1965.

> COMMISSIONER LANE: Mr. Rogers, can you give us an estimate in dollars and cents of this loan-sharking operation in the United States? I know that it is an estimate. Could you give us one for the United States?
>
> WITNESS: It is very hard to say, Commissioner Lane. I can give you an idea from one particular loan shark that I was very familiar with. Perhaps you could get it from this.
>
> From reliable information we know that in approximately 1959 and in 1960, there was made available by the lender to his chief subordinates approximately a half a million dollars, $500,000. Again, from reliable information, from the best accounting we could obtain of this, we now believe that $500,000 has been pyramided to seven and a half million dollars.
>
> COMMISSIONER SARACHAN: Seven and a half million dollars?
>
> WITNESS: Yes.
>
> COMMISSIONER LANE: It is reasonable to expect, there is roughly five hundred million to one billion dollars.
>
> WITNESS: That would be very easy sir. Here in New York City, in New York County, there is at least ten men who are comparable to him. A loan shark that we know of lent a million dollars in the morning and a million dollars in the afternoon.

COMMISSIONER LANE: So it would sound as if were in the billion dollar class, if you take the entire United States.

WITNESS: Yes, very easily.

(New York State Commission of Investigation, 1991:37)

During the mid-1970s, Carl Simon and Anne Witte used a more complex analysis to estimate that revenues from loan-sharking could have increased to as much as $6.5 billion per year. Less than a decade later, James Cook somewhat arbitrarily raised the figure to $20 billion (Fishman, Rodenrys, & Schink, 1986).

While each of these estimates is variously flawed by unreliable methods or questionable assumptions, loan-sharking is big business. With interest rates ranging from 250 to 1,000 percent per year for loans paid on time (interest is compounded, and therefore higher for delinquent loans), a ready supply of borrowers in need, and reliable methods of collection, it would be difficult to assume otherwise. Although it may not be possible to estimate profits with precision, perhaps the best evidence of the potential for loan-sharking was offered by an associate of Philadelphia's Bruno crime family when he explained that "the safest and best business is loan-sharking. Borrowers don't complain, usually pay their loans back, and are always coming back for more" (Pennsylvania Crime Commission, 1990:72).

BUSINESS, LABOR, AND

ORGANIZED CRIME

The activities of organized crime are difficult to measure, leaving debate about the actual extent of its involvement and profits. Different researchers and experts have produced widely varying estimates, almost all of which are suspect given the problems of definition and measurement that accompany them. For example, in 1982 James Cook asserted that organized crime had become a large and growing part of the U.S. economy with revenues in excess of $150 billion per year. Of that total, narcotics ($63 billion), gambling ($22 billion), and loan-sharking ($20 billion) made up at least 70 percent of the activities producing illicit revenues. If correct, Cook's assumptions would make organized crime the nation's second largest industry. Others, however, are far more conservative. Years after Cook's often cited work, Fishman and colleagues (1986) at the Wharton Econometric Forecasting Associates produced an estimate of $47 billion for all activities, a figure based on their own work and analyses of that of others. While much lower than the previous estimate, their estimate of organized crime's revenue still equals 1.13 percent of the nation's gross national product, making it larger than the paper or tire and rubber industries. In all, they concluded that organized crime employs at least 281,487 people directly, while producing as many as 500,000 related jobs.

Whatever the correct totals may be, there is agreement that the activities of organized crime have a direct impact on other segments of the economy. Among the industries most heavily influenced, law enforcement agencies surveyed (President's Commission, 1967) singled out several as showing the greatest vulnerability. These included

- construction,
- waste removal,
- garments,
- real estate,
- banking, and
- hotels, bars, entertainment, and legal gambling.

In fact, only manufacturing and mining were considered free of significant organized crime influence. Among the concerns engendered by such penetration of legitimate business is the fear that beyond its immediate profits, the intimidation so freely used by organized crime limits competition, produces higher prices, lowers wages, and reduces legitimate employment. In addition, using even their lowest estimate of income, Fishman and colleagues (1986) added that lost taxes on organized crime profits were probably somewhere in excess of $6.5 billion. It would appear then that the impact of organized crime may go far beyond the provision of the well-publicized vices. Therefore, for the remainder of this chapter, we will explore the involvement of organized crime in the business of business and labor, which might be termed the infiltration of the upperworld by the underworld.

The Business of Labor

In late 1975, the mysterious disappearance of former Teamster President Jimmy Hoffa, coupled with standing complaints concerning many of the union's activities, led the Department of Labor to open an investigation of the union's Central States Pension Fund. Created in 1955, by 1979 the fund served a membership of about 500,000 active and retired union members, with assets of nearly $2.2 billion. This was and is an impressive money machine; annual contributions in 1979 totaled $586 million, while pension payments paid out were less than $323 million (U.S. Senate, 1991).

Almost from the start, controversy surrounded the pension fund and its management. Critics contended that its trustees had fallen under the influence of organized crime and accused mobsters of making the fund little more than their private bank. As proof, they noted the regularity of fund investments in risky real estate ventures, many of which became bankrupt almost at once. By one estimate, in fact, over 30 percent of the loans issued by the fund were in default. In many instances, the critics' suspicions that the money had been lost to organized crime were confirmed by law enforcement. With Hoffa's disappearance and the successful prosecutions of several high-ranking union officials, many believed as the 1990s dawned that the glare of public attention would at last bring real reform to the union.

Labor Racketeering on a National Scale The power and eventual corruption of the Teamsters can be traced to the transformation of the country's industry following World War II. The federal government's decision to construct an interstate highway system had the effect of expanding trucking while speeding the decline of the railroads—all as the quantity of goods to be shipped was increasing dramatically. With labor plentiful, manufacturers soon found that no towns were too remote, thus enabling the trucks and their drivers to dominate transportation. A national strike meant industrial paralysis. As membership swelled to over 1.6 million, in no time the union became the nation's largest (Browning & Gerassi, 1980). Meanwhile, with help from Anthony Provenzano, reportedly a ranking member of the Genovese crime organization, Jimmy Hoffa became president in 1957. As a forewarning of what was to come, Hoffa's rise was made possible by the conviction of then union president Dave Beck for embezzling union funds.

In the years that followed Hoffa's rise, one bad investment after another occurred. As it began its investigation, the Labor Department produced an initial list of eight loan recipients for real estate purchases that were bankrupt. Ranging from Lake Tahoe to Detroit to Savannah, Georgia, these eight represented nearly $52 million of lost pension funds. Nor, unfortunately, were they a complete listing of the fund's failed loans. In addition to the complete failures, another $138 million in loans was committed to back Las Vegas casinos, including the Stardust Hotel ($75 million), Circus Circus ($22 million), and Caesar's Palace ($20 million). Further, Morris Shenker, a well-known St. Louis attorney, informed the Nevada Gaming Control Board that the Central States Fund had promised him at least $17 million to finance a takeover of the Dunes Hotel and Casino. In most instances, "finder's fees" averaging 10 percent of each loan were paid by loan recipients to union "consultants"—a practice that eventually resulted in several prosecutions for kickbacks (U.S. Senate, 1991). Eventually, of course, Hoffa himself was prosecuted—first for bribery, later for illegally wiretapping the phones of Teamster officials, and finally, in 1962, for a technical violation of the Taft-Hartley Act (a misdemeanor). Although he defeated each of the charges against him, Hoffa was additionally charged with jury tampering in 1962. Two years later he was convicted and sentenced to eight years' imprisonment. Before completing his sentence, however, the former Teamster leader was granted executive clemency by President Nixon, and by 1975 he was actively seeking a return to the union's presidency. Ironically, among his primary campaign tactics was criticism of the man who had succeeded him as being a tool of organized crime. On July 30, 1975, Hoffa's campaign was cut short when he mysteriously disappeared after arriving at "a meet" with Provenzano to iron out their differences (Abadinsky, 1990). After much investigation, he was officially declared murdered. Although his body was never found, rumors placed his remains under the newly constructed grandstands at New Jersey's Giants Stadium. In 1978, Anthony "Tony Pro" Provenzano followed the path of his union predecessors when he too was convicted and imprisoned for racketeering and the murder of Anthony Castellito, still another rival for control of the Teamsters. In 1987, the International Brotherhood of Teamsters was readmitted to the AFL–CIO as part of a compromise to avoid a motion to place the union under a court appointed trusteeship.

The Labor Rackets Locally Beginning with Paul Kelly of the Five Pointers gang, organized crime has profited handsomely from its involvement in union activities on the local level as well. Kelly graduated from theft and regular gang battles with the Eastmans over turf to the waterfront, where he organized garbage scow trimmers, rag pickers, and others. By manipulating labor peace, he found that the opportunities for extortion were sufficient to leave the gang life and the Lower East Side tenements he was from and move uptown to Harlem. Nearly a half century later, Hoffa, Provenzano, and others nearly perfected the system Kelly and the gangsters that followed him had begun.

In 1941, as he rose to the top of Detroit's Teamster Local 299, Jimmy Hoffa first turned to friends in that city's Meli crime organization to drive back the competing CIO union representatives. By year's end, his strategy had worked: "Considering the new players on Hoffa's team," one observer noted, "it was a miracle that the CIO survived at all in Detroit" (Moldea, 1978:38). Years later, his formula for success continued. In exchange for support when it was needed, now Teamster president Hoffa generously rewarded his friends with lucrative contracts and consulting opportunities; in a few instances, he even appointed them head of important locals. Allen Dorfman, for example, was awarded much of the Teamster's insurance business. Eventually, he became a consultant to the pension fund's trustees, overseeing the theft of millions through investment fraud and kickback schemes. The Provenzano family was given a virtual license to embezzle from New Jersey's Local 560. By 1963, Anthony Provenzano's salary of $113,000 for local duties made him the highest paid union official in the world. That same year, however, he was convicted of extorting $17,000 from the Dorn Trucking Company to end its labor troubles. While in prison, his brothers Salvatore and Nunzio continued operations on his behalf. Following a subsequent conviction in 1978, Nunzio returned as local president until he too was convicted of extortion in 1981. For the next three years, Salvatore took charge until his own conviction. The three still remained active through Josephine Provenzano, Tony Pro's daughter, who remained as secretary-treasurer. Finally, after invoking civil RICO proceedings, federal authorities ended the reign by forcing the local into a court approved trusteeship (see Chapter 13). Although Local 560 had been saved, the Provenzanos' hold over Local 84 in Fort Lee (New Jersey) and Local 522 in Queens remained.

Beyond the direct benefits of union leadership, control over labor offers other advantages as well. In his memorandum to the court asking for RICO action against the Teamsters, Rudolph Giuliani (1991), former U.S. Attorney for New York's Southern District, outlined an assortment of abuses. For example, the Genovese organization controlled concrete contractors with threats that Local 282 would disrupt ongoing work unless payments were made. The Bonannos' control of Local 814 allowed similar extortion from moving and storage companies. Since they owned several companies themselves, their control of labor also kept their competitors out of jobs (see also, "Mob Trial Prompts Review of Contracts," *New York Times,* June 4, 1992). That these were not isolated instances is reflected in other examples involving air freight, construction, and moving and trucking in Cleveland, Philadelphia, and elsewhere. Others have observed organized crime using labor influence to arrange cargo thefts, fencing operations, prostitution, gambling, and loan-sharking at truck terminals. From one New Jersey investigation, the theft of cargo by labor controlled by organized crime was said to be "so common that some dockmen are called shoppers." In addition, more sophisticated operations have included rigged bankruptcies, fraud through overbilling ("Indictment Details Fraud by Mafia Family," *New York Times,* July 8, 1992), and complex schemes to seize property and occasionally entire businesses from their owners (Browning & Gerassi, 1980). Finally, union members may be undercut by their own officials who withhold them from jobs while supplying nonunion, contract workers for less. In such cases, kickbacks are almost always paid, usually by both the employer and the contract workers.

The Business of Business

The possibilities for profit from labor are considerable. Equally important, however, are opportunities available to organized criminals in other realms of business. From their case studies, Reuter, Rubinstein, and Wynn (1983) observed that organized crime's involvement in business can be direct, openly operating businesses in essentially the same manner as their legitimate counterparts. In other cases, continuing conspiracies are operated by acting in more peripheral roles. While not controlling or dominating participants directly in these businesses, organized criminals perform services for the industry that help to maintain and support the illegal arrangements they have often instigated themselves. While legal involvement may indicate only a recognition of a good opportunity, the second approach often suggests a desire to seize control of the industry itself. Historically, such involvement has occurred in response to an invitation by an industry association; however self-initiated action does occur.

Where control is sought, both Reuter (1983) and Albanese (1987) note that industry conditions play an important role in the outcome. For successful infiltration, an industry's market should have strong incentives to create and support a cartel arrangement but sufficient impediments to limit formation of competing groups. As such, while participation in a cartel that fixed prices for a service such as waste removal would almost certainly raise costs, a consumer's trash must still be removed. Within limits then, demand in such industries is largely inelastic, while alternative suppliers are unavailable. In addition, lower status industries with unskilled and poorly educated entrepreneurs less often possess industry standards and preventive controls. This means, of course, that locally controlled, family-based enterprises are more readily influenced than are either the professions or industries involving high technology or domination by large corporations.

Once entrenched in an industry, a range of services, including licensing arrangements, bid-rigging schemes, and customer allocation agreements, become possible. Each puts the conspirators in a position to dominate important business arrangements, which, in turn, brings influence beyond that of any individual participant. In the end, the system becomes self-perpetuating, since rumors of criminal involvement make competitors reluctant to enter the business and customers frightened about complaining aggressively. This eventually renders the industry less efficient and more costly to maintain. Perhaps the best example of such an arrangement can be found in the waste hauling industry.

Waste Hauling in Yonkers The introduction of organized crime into Yonkers' carting industry began in 1949 after the city's Common Council passed an ordinance removing the city from commercial and industrial garbage collection. The most lucrative parts of the business (all but residential pickups) were to be turned over to private haulers—a decision that opened a series of conflicts among competing companies and the unions that represented them. While the Teamsters' Local 456 was the first involved, at the subsequent request of Alfred Rattenni of the Westchester Carting Company, Local 27, which had well-established criminal connections, intervened and arranged the signing of a contract. A box and paper union out of New York City, Local 27 soon splintered, forming Local 813 to handle the expanding Yonkers' companies. Meanwhile, Rattenni's primary competitor was murdered, leaving Rattenni the dominant force in the Yonkers' industry (P. Miller, McFarland-Benedict, & Salzman, 1986). Quiet for the next several decades, it was not until 1986 that the New York State Commission of Investigation uncovered the extent of corruption in the city's operation.

By that time, solid wastes in Yonkers were routinely disposed of through city-owned incinerators. Although operated at city expense, the incinerators were available for garbage collected inside the city limits by private carters as well. In all, that included 11 additional companies, 6 of which were industrial firms disposing only of their own garbage. For the use of city incinerator service, a nominal fee of less than $1 per ton was established, even though the city's Budget Committee declared the cost to the taxpayers to be many times greater (New York State Commission, 1971).

Unfortunately, by the 1970s, Yonkers' incinerating capacity had been stretched to the breaking point. Nonetheless, efforts to adjust the fee schedule or place limits on the amounts of waste dumped there were effectively blocked by Rattenni and his friends in city government. The city was left with little choice but to cart much of the residential garbage it collected to the Croton dump 23 miles away. However, since the city had insufficient trucks to handle the transport, additional contracts with private firms were required. As a result:

> The city thus found itself in the absurd position of having to pay $8 to $10 per ton to private carters to transport its garbage to Croton, while Rattenni and the other private carters were paying only $1 per ton to use the city incinerator. In addition, the SIC reported that more than half the payments made by the city to private carters went to Rattenni-owned companies. (P. Miller et al., 1986:32)

Nor were these companies confined to the Yonkers' city limits. By the late 1980s, similar arrangements were in place in 35 cities throughout the county (P. Miller et al., 1986). While Alfred Rattenni was but one player in the system, the waste hauling empire he engineered and passed on to his sons eventually reached well beyond Yonkers and Westchester County into Connecticut and other counties in the Mid-Hudson Valley. While impressive, this is but one example of a criminal involvement that has been observed in dozens of industries throughout the nation.

Organized Crime as a Legitimate Enterprise In addition to their illegal activities, some people otherwise involved in organized crime also operate legitimate enterprises. As Maltz (1990) points out, both business and nonbusiness pressures may motivate organized crime groups to become involved in legitimate business. In some cases, involvement may constitute little more than a good opportunity. Just as members of organized crime choose their offenses for profit, legitimate employment may at times be the most attractive option available.

Similarly, some may seek out legal avenues as a means of diversification. After all, except for recent efforts at asset forfeiture, a legitimate business is less often a target for law enforcement or fellow gangsters. In addition, as with other industries, the extent of organized crime is generally dependent upon the levels of consumer demand. Thus, it may not always be possible to reinvest profits in an illegal activity unless a significant expansion of the market or market share can be achieved.

As an added feature, a legitimate business investment can provide a tax cover to account for illicit income as well as a front through which friends or members needing to demonstrate employment can pass. Thus, the business can be used to launder money or otherwise serve as a front. "Stolen merchandise can be 'laundered' by commingling it with legally purchased merchandise. . . . This has the advantage of cutting business costs, giving the business an unfair advantage over its competitors" (Maltz, 1992:13).

Finally, like most of us, many in organized crime may want a legacy that can be passed along to their children. According to Maltz (1976), this goal is not unlike that of the early robber barons such as Vanderbilt, Rockefeller, or Jay Gould, who left great family fortunes to posterity. A desire to gain respectability, to ascend the "queer ladder of social mobility" (Bell, 1953), can also be a factor behind organized crime's infiltration of legitimate business.

The bottom line here may be one of balanced risks. Will the resources and methods of organized crime destroy the industries it infiltrates, or is the risk worthwhile to avoid the greater harm that would result from further illicit investments? Do such investments signal legalizing of former gangsters, or are organized crime groups simply expanding their portfolios to pose an even greater risk to society? Whatever the answers, it is clear that from its early beginnings the business of organized crime has evolved dramatically, increasingly becoming interwoven with the fabric of our economy. As new criminal methods and opportunities have proliferated, interactions between the legal and illegal sectors have grown in their complexity. At the same time, the difficult task of detecting business infiltration by organized crime and keeping it from being profitable has become considerably more difficult.

CONCLUSION

In previous chapters we noted the well-known significance of alcohol and narcotics prohibition in the growth and wealth of organized crime. Less known, but equally significant, however, are the "backbone" industries of gambling, illegal lending, labor racketeering, and even legitimate business ventures. First came manipulation of the legal lotteries. When that was no longer possible, creation of policy and numbers operations provided steady income and an avenue of upward mobility for many. Given the multiple roles these games play in many neighborhoods, that they have survived and prospered despite law enforcement efforts and legal competition should hardly be surprising.

Similarly, with the close of Prohibition, gangsters invested heavily in bookmaking and off-track betting as well as in complex arrangements of investment and lending. Content to draw high rates of interest on open-ended loans, we saw estimates of industry-wide loan-sharking revenues vary from $2 billion to $20 billion per year.

Finally, more direct than their other operations, organized crime has succeeded in muscling in on legitimate industries and labor where pension funds, contracts, kickbacks, and price fixing have all offered opportunities for enormous profits. Taken together, these varied activities have allowed organized crime to become central to many communities and a large and growing part of the overall U.S. economy. In the chapters that follow, we will explore the organizations themselves and the policies and methods used to confront them.

9

Myths and
Organized Crime:

Is There a Mafia, and
Does It Really Matter?

Before we attempt to deal with the possible relationship between myth and organized crime, we first must understand what a myth is and why myths are important. This is a difficult but necessary task because of the significant connections claimed to exist between the mythology of organized crime and the law enforcement policies for dealing with it.

When you think about the word *myth*, a number of ideas probably come to mind—the mythology of Greek and Roman gods and goddesses, biblical stories, fables, old wives' tales. The diversity of ideas about myths, and the overlapping definition of myth with the definitions of beliefs, values, and ideologies makes a clear definition difficult. Nevertheless, myths play a critical role in explaining wonders that cannot be fully explained through rational, empirical means, that is, through facts and evidence. One such wonder has been said to be organized crime.

Patrick Gerster and Nicholas Cords (1977) defined myth as "false belief"—as something mistakenly taken to be true and real. The belief is said to be false because it has no foundation in fact. An example is the "false belief" that American Indians were bloodthirsty savages who were a menace and a peril to the 19th century white settlers whose destiny was to subdue and eliminate barbarism on the western frontier of the United States (Gerster & Cords, 1977). An example from the arena of crime and criminal justice might be the false belief that most crime in the United States is violent crime.

Gerster and Cords' definition of myth is, however, too narrow. It does not encompass all myths, only one type of myth. A myth may be a false belief, but it is not always and necessarily so. On the contrary, a myth may be at least partially true. Myths that are approximations of fact, that have some truth to them, actually work best to explain the otherwise unexplainable because they are more believable. For instance, some Indians did in fact attack and slaughter some white settlers. It is only the belief that all Indians were doing this to innocent settlers on some kind of mass scale that was false. Nevertheless, this belief—this myth—was used to help explain (and to rationalize) why it was necessary for our white government to do all the terrible things it did to the Indians.

False beliefs held out of simple ignorance or misunderstanding and readily refutable with factual information, such as the violent crime example, are not true myths. It is relatively easy to show that most crime in the United States is not violent crime. True myths are much more complex than that. They are deeply held, basic beliefs concerned with good and evil and right and wrong. The Indian example fits this latter requirement because Indians were portrayed as being evil—as atheistic, savage subhumans who required conquering and salvation by the "good," God-fearing, white settlers.

The basic beliefs that compose myths are formed from jumbles of images that come from a wide variety of sources—stories, books, personal experiences, the press, television, advertising, movies, cultural, and athletic events—over a lifetime. The jumbles are made up of combinations of facts, prejudices, values, pictures, memories, and projections (Nimmo & Combs, 1980). A better way to think about myth is not simply as false belief but rather as "a gnarled thicket of dubious ideas that don't yield readily to contrary evidence" (Fantel, 1988:24).

An example of a myth about crime and punishment is the fundamental belief of many Americans that it is punishment (specifically severe punishment) and the fear of such punishment that deters people from violating the law. Is this true for some potential offenders? Undoubtedly so! Thus, the belief is at least partially true. But it is a "gnarled thicket of dubious ideas" because it fails to take account of the many and complex reasons people do or do not commit crimes (for example, morals and values, opportunity), and it puts undue faith in the idea that we can deliver the swift and sure punishment necessary for deterrence. The continued support for long prison terms and the death penalty as deterrents to crime in the absence of evidence that they have any such effects also demonstrates the general unwillingness to "yield to contrary evidence."

Myths serve to reduce complex problems to simple terms and propositions. Myths also help give meaning and direction to reality. Once we buy into the myth, we tend to accept, modify, or reject new information depending upon how well it fits with our myth. Thus, new knowledge or empirical evidence will not necessarily dispel belief in a particular myth. In sum, myths have at least three purposes:

1. to explain some bothersome and threatening phenomenon that cannot be explained otherwise,

2. to reconcile new information with our preexisting actions and beliefs, and

3. to help interpret new facts or new knowledge so as to perpetuate our preexisting understanding.

Perhaps the most negative view about the risks of myth-based thinking is the concern that "at best, myths are simplistic and distorted beliefs based upon emotion rather than rigorous analysis; at worst, myths are dangerous falsifications" (Nimmo & Combs, 1980:9). A much more benign view is that of anthropologist Claude Levi-Strauss (1963), who argued that myths simply help people live with uncertainty and ambivalence. Because it is impossible for us to hold up every idea or image to scientific scrutiny, myths help resolve that which is otherwise unresolveable, and they get rid of what Levi-Strauss called "unwelcome contradictions."

But in all events, the danger is that once the myth is believed, skepticism disappears and the myth becomes fact. As such, myth becomes the basis for action. Why is this dangerous? Myth-based public policies—policies intended to solve social problems such as the problem of crime—have been shown to be much more likely to "go bust" than policies based on rational, empirical evidence. It is nearly impossible (except perhaps by accident) to solve problems that are ill-defined and ill-understood or misunderstood. In their book, *Myths that Rule America*, London and Weeks (1981) point out that numerous policies are developed on the basis of myth, and that "in many instances the policies are unsuccessful because they are ill-conceived in the first place. They are ill-conceived because they rely so heavily on erroneous assumptions" (p. ix). Policies based on incorrect assumptions as to what is causing a particular problem and on inaccurate definitions of the problem are policies ripe for failure.

If our government's policies for dealing with organized crime have been founded upon myth, as some people have charged, then certain conclusions are obvious:

- these policies will have been more symbolic than real;
- these policies will be more concerned with how things appear than with whether they actually accomplish anything; and
- the result will have been a considerable waste and misdirection of law enforcement time and resources and, ultimately, much failure and frustration.

It is to this issue that we now turn, beginning with the contention that a myth of a Mafia mystique has in fact been foisted on the American people.

Not everyone considers this to be an important issue. Charles Silberman has written widely on social problems and criticizes what he called "a heated, at times acrimonious, and often downright silly debate about the Mafia: whether or not the Mafia really exists; whether it is called the Mafia or La Cosa Nostra; whether it is limited to Italian-Americans or includes members of other ethnic groups; whether or not there is a national syndicate, or 'crime confederation,' that controls organized crime throughout the United States; and whether or not that syndicate is controlled, in turn, by the Mafia" (1978:97). Similarly, Annelise Graebner Anderson dismisses the question of whether a national syndicate controls organized crime throughout the country as being a "strawman." She says that "politicians and law enforcement officials can be expected to make extreme and unqualified statements about the extent and dangers of organized crime: it gives them visibility, it develops public support for an increase in the law enforcement budget, it may discourage the citizenry from purchasing illegal goods and services" (1979:12–13).

Suffice it to say that we do not consider the debate to be silly, nor do we consider it to be simply a strawman argument. Rather, this debate has serious policy implications. President John F. Kennedy once observed, "The great enemy of the truth is very often not the lie—deliberate, contrived, and dishonest—but the myth—persistent, persuasive, and unrealistic" (Silberman, 1978:313). Is there a Mafia myth that has been the enemy of the truth? Let's see if we can begin to sort this out.

THE BIRTH OF THE MAFIA MYTH

A U.S. Senate Committee, chaired by Senator Estes Kefauver of Tennessee, conducted a sweeping examination of organized crime in the United States in 1950–1951. This was not literally the first time a criminal organization loosely called the Mafia was acknowledged in the United States; the Mafia had been recognized as a part of American organized crime as early as the late 1800s. But it was the Kefauver committee and its investigations that first put Mafia figures (so-called mafiosi) on national television. It was the Kefauver committee that made the Mafia and organized crime one and the same thing in the minds of the American public.

Television viewers were fascinated by the confrontation of good and evil. "Good" was personified by the meek, almost schoolmaster looks of Estes Kefauver. The drawling, coonskin-capped Tennessean was the common man as hero, a kind of Gary Cooper. He stood to do battle with "evil" personified by a bunch of swarthy Italians and Sicilians named Costello, Adonis, Moretti, Luciano, Genovese, Profaci, and Anastasia, and some Jewish hoodlums named Longie Zwillman and Meyer Lansky. White, Anglo-Saxon, protestant, middle America was going to the mat with some dark-skinned foreigners who had brought an evil conspiracy to our shores.

All of the elements of good drama—and of myth—were there. Viewers watched the nervously clenching and unclenching hands of Frank Costello, who refused to permit his face to be televised. He also refused, in a rasping and barely audible voice, to answer questions on advice of counsel. In the minds of the committee members and, of course, in the minds of the public, this confirmed his complicity in the things about which he was being questioned. America, or at least a big part of America, reveled in the spectacle of these sweating, fidgeting gangsters professing shocked surprise at being called and questioned, feigning ignorance of any wrongdoing, sometimes being sullenly silent, sometimes refusing to answer, and sometimes evading the questions. These were mafiosi, the masters of the underworld. This was organized crime—or so it seemed.

Senator Kefauver wanted answers to such questions as whether a nationwide crime syndicate existed. If so, where did its sources of power lie? To get these answers, the committee held their televised hearings in various cities around the country. These hearings brought to light a number of attributes and acts associated with organized crime: gambling (determined to be the principal source of support for big-time racketeering and gangsterism), narcotics, infiltration of legitimate business, corruption, and violence. The committee stressed the important part played by the Mafia in binding together into a national association the major criminal gangs and individual hoodlums from around the country. The Mafia was said to be dominant because it used "muscle and murder" and because it was willing and in fact did ruthlessly eliminate anyone who stood in the way of its success (Kefauver, 1951).

The influence of the Kefauver committee in defining organized crime is confirmed by a study by John F. Galliher and James A. Cain titled, "Citation Support for the Mafia Myth in Criminology Textbooks." The study examined 20 criminology textbooks with chapters or sections on organized crime that were published in the United States between 1950 and 1972. The most frequently cited source for information about organized crime in these books was the Kefauver committee report, cited in over half the texts, followed by Kefauver's book based on the investigation (Galliher & Cain, 1974). Thus, the image and understanding of organized crime conveyed to students through these textbooks was in large part the image and understanding promulgated by Senator Kefauver and his committee.

This image, the belief fostered by Kefauver that the Mafia and organized crime are synonymous, was first attacked as being false—as being a myth—by sociologist Daniel Bell (1953). Bell identified the enforcement of public morals in America as one of the core stimuli promulgating what he criticized as being a myth. The existence of a Mafia helps resolve the "unwelcome contradiction" between our straight-laced conventional morality on the one hand and our desire for the "forbidden fruits" on the other, he said. These forbidden fruits include drugs, gambling, and sex. In other words, we are not hypocrites but are instead the victims of an alien, sinister force. Here we see an example of the scapegoating function of myth. Myths sometimes find villains to be blamed for complicated or undesirable circumstances. These ready explanations are popular because they offer an outlet for anger or guilt, and they absolve us of responsibility. We prefer to believe that organized crime is being imposed upon American society by a group of immoral men engaged in an alien conspiracy rather than that it is simply an indigenous product of the way American society operates—and the result of our own human weaknesses.

Senator Kefauver asserted that a "nationwide crime syndicate does exist in the United States, despite the protestations of a strangely assorted company of criminals, self-serving politicians, plain blind fools, and others who may be honestly misguided, that there is no such combine. . . . Unfortunately," says Bell, "for a good story—and the existence of the Mafia would be a whale of a story—neither the Senate Crime Committee in its testimony, nor Kefauver in his book, presented any real evidence that the Mafia exists as a functioning organization" (1953:219).

Why would Kefauver and his committee push so hard for their theory of the Mafia? Why would they, in Bell's words, be "taken in by [their] own myth of an omnipotent Mafia and a despotic Costello"? Bell says it was because they may have been misled by their own hearsay.

> Senator Kefauver had begun the investigation with the attitude that with so much smoke there must be a raging fire. But smoke can also mean a smoke screen. . . .

There is, as well, in the American temper, a feeling that "some-where," "somebody" is pulling all the complicated strings to which this jumbled world dances. . . . In the field of crime, the side-of-the-mouth low-down was "Costello." (Bell, 1953:219)

Another critic of the "myth-making" by the Kefauver committee is historian William Moore (1974). Moore charged the committee with dramatizing organized crime more than investigating it. He says, "particularly in the case of the Mafia, the senators lacked adequate evidence for their conclusions." He accuses them of making "overblown and unfounded statements" (p. 134). These statements and conclusions were seemingly accepted by the public because they fit with their preconceived notions about organized crime.

[T]he popular myths and misunderstandings grew stronger, buttressed by the "proofs" of the Kefauver Committee. Sensational journalists and publishers enjoyed a field day, explaining and enlarging upon the Committee's work; gangster movies and television programs dramatized variations of the same theme. . . . Even after the initial shock and novelty of the Kefauver findings had lifted and critics began to question the more sweeping Committee statements, the public at large continued to hold to the older conspiracy view, thus making more difficult an intelligent appraisal of organized crime. (Moore, 1974: 134)

Here is an example of the complicating role of the partial truth in myth. Italian-American men were leading characters in much of the mob and gangster activity in the country. They were involved in gambling, prostitution, and narcotics. But the tendency of the media to emphasize a few sensational gangsters who fit the Mafia image gave an illusion that domination of organized crime by mafiosi was much greater than was seemingly warranted by the facts.

THE MCCLELLAN COMMITTEE AND ITS STAR WITNESS: JOSEPH VALACHI

A second Senate committee, the Permanent Subcommittee on Investigations, of the Senate Committee on Government Operations, chaired by Senator John L. McClellan of Arkansas, also conducted hearings on organized crime and narcotics in 1963 and 1964. This same group had looked into organized crime and gambling two years earlier. In his opening statement before the second investigation, Senator McClellan laid out his perception of what had come to be known as La Cosa Nostra, which was loosely translated as meaning "Our Thing":

> The existence of such a criminal organization as Cosa Nostra is frightening. . . . [It] attempts to be a form of government unto itself. . . . Murder has often been ordered for a variety of reasons: a grab for power, the code of vengeance, gangland rivalries, infidelity to the organization or even for suspicions of derelictions. (U.S. Senate, 1963:1)

The featured witness before the committee was a convicted heroin trafficker named Joseph Valachi. Valachi, who was said to be the first member of La Cosa Nostra to ever testify publicly about the nature of the organization, talked for five days about his personal knowledge of the history of organized crime in New York and about his experiences as a member of the Vito Genovese crime family. Why was he willing to break the so-called code of silence and to talk to the committee and to law enforcement officials?—because he believed he had been marked for death for "ratting" to the Federal Bureau of Narcotics. After killing a fellow inmate of the federal prison in Atlanta, Georgia, whom he believed was going to kill him, Valachi negotiated a deal with federal officials to talk to them about what he knew in return for being allowed to plead guilty to the lesser charge of murder in the second degree.

Prior to his appearance before the Senate committee, Valachi had been talking to the FBI for almost a year, so the law enforcement value of his information had already been pretty much maximized. Testimony before the committee was the forum for having Valachi go public. As with the earlier Kefauver hearings, the press, the public, and the committee members found the witness to be a fascinating figure. His descriptions of the so-called Castellamarese War (which we will turn to momentarily) and of being initiated into a fraternal-like organization through a secret ritual (which we will also get to later on) were particularly captivating. Needless to say, these descriptions tended to fit the preconceived stereotypes the public and the senators held about the Mafia. Suspect and tenuous evidence is not a problem if we truly want to believe. Myths are not subject to ready refutation by contrary evidence. Gordon Hawkins (1969) contends that whereas acknowledgment of membership in the Mafia appeared to be accepted at face value, as in the case of Valachi, denials of such membership (as had occurred before the Kefauver committee) were taken as evidence that the Mafia was in fact a secret society and that violation of this secrecy would be met by Mafia killings.

The McClellan committee findings, and in particular its reliance upon Valachi's testimony, met with mixed reviews. The committee itself accepted Valachi's story of organized crime and of the character of La Cosa Nostra. Attorney General Robert F. Kennedy, the other principal witness before the committee, pointed to the importance of the intelligence information obtained from Valachi in the latter's interrogation by the FBI:

> We know that Cosa Nostra is run by a commission, and that the leaders of Cosa Nostra in most cities are responsible to the commission. . . . It is an organization. It is Mafia. It is the Cosa Nostra. There are other names for it, but it all refers to the same organization. . . . The members of the commission, the top members, or even their chief lieutenants, have insulated themselves from the crime itself; if they want to have somebody knocked off, for instance, the top man will speak to somebody who will speak to somebody else who will speak to somebody else and order it. The man who actually does the gun work . . . does not know who ordered it. To trace that back is virtually impossible . . . there have been large numbers of very brutal murders which have been committed by those in organized crime just over a period of the last two years. Certainly not a week goes by that somewhere in the United States an individual is not killed or murdered in some kind of gangland battle or a witness is not garroted and killed. (U.S. Senate, 1963:6–31)

Attorney General Kennedy called Valachi's testimony a significant intelligence breakthrough that enabled the Department of Justice "to prove conclusively" the existence of the nationwide organization known as Cosa Nostra. Likewise, Ralph Salerno, a noted expert on organized crime from the New York City Police Department, said that Valachi's confessions should be ranked next to Apalachin (a 1957 incident in upstate New York in which 65 alleged mafiosi were discovered in what was called a high-level conference on organized crime) "as the greatest single blow ever delivered to organized crime in the United States" (Salerno & Thompson, 1969:312).

Writer Peter Maas (1968), on the other hand, in his quasi-biography of Valachi called *The Valachi Papers*, said Valachi's televised appearances before the committee were a disaster. This was because, according to Maas, the senators wanted to use the hearings for political purposes rather than for conducting a thorough investigation into organized crime. The testimony of Valachi has been even more heavily criticized by Bell, and by a number of others for its contributions to continuing the myth of the Mafia.

In a 1963 article called "The Myth of the Cosa Nostra," Bell wrote:

It is a vivid demonstration of the power of the mass media, the gullibility of the American audience, and the deceit of certain public officials that the phrase Cosa Nostra has passed so quickly and so uncritically into the lexicon. . . .

Yet the hard fact is that there is no such thing as the Cosa Nostra, at least not in the sweeping sense in which the phrase is generally used. Nor is there a nationwide "syndicate" or "crime cartel," such as the press has identified with the Cosa Nostra. And as a result of these misconceptions the complex nature of organized crime in the United States—which does exist—has been seriously oversimplified and distorted, thus making it much harder to conduct an intelligent fight against it.

The phrase Cosa Nostra comes, of course, from Joe Valachi, the gravel-voiced, self-confessed murderer who appeared on the national television screens . . . while testifying before the McClellan Committee. Valachi was a natural. His mangling of the English language, his Brooklynese, and the unalloyed casualness with which he told his gory tales, in contrast with the stiff but credulous moralizing of the Committee Chairman, delightfully fitted the imagination of an older generation raised on Nick Carter and a younger one fed by Elliot Ness. (p. 12)

Bell's comments are pertinent to our earlier observations about myths and their effects on policy. Myths oversimplify and distort reality—Bell claims that La Cosa Nostra is an oversimplified and distorted picture of organized crime. Myths reflect deep-seated beliefs about such things as good and evil—in this case "good" is personified by Senator McClellan and "evil" by gangster Valachi. Myth-based policies against organized crime are likely to fail—Bell claims that whole areas of organized criminal activity have not received proper attention and focus because of this misplaced emphasis. Bell challenged Valachi's testimony as being "old hat." He questioned why no one in law enforcement had ever heard of Cosa Nostra before the Senate investigation (assuming it was as big and powerful as Valachi said it was). This same question is also raised by Gordon Hawkins (1969). Finally, Bell concluded that no new evidence was presented by Valachi—a very different view from that of Kennedy and McClellan.

Who was responsible for promulgating this myth? According to Bell, "the myth of the Mafia has been spread for years by a single agency of the United States government, the Bureau of Narcotics" (1963:14). Why?

Because this bureau "has had to contend with a highly organized international racket" and could blame its lack of success on the racket being controlled by the Mafia (Bell, 1963:14). So, the Mafia myth could serve the useful and fairly typical purpose of explaining the otherwise unexplainable; narcotics were continuing to come into the United States despite the hard (and as the bureau would tell it, excellent) work of the bureau because narcotics were controlled by this omnipotent international organization called the Mafia, or now, La Cosa Nostra. Further, the belief in Mafia drug pushing helps resolve the "unwelcome contradiction" that there might be demand pressures in this country that kept the drug trade flourishing.

Bell also contends that the Justice Department and Attorney General Kennedy wanted to exploit Valachi and heighten public fears to gain support for new legislation to legalize wiretapping. This, too, is fairly typical of how myths may be used to influence public policy.

Influenced by Valachi's testimony, historian Alan Block (1978) has looked into beliefs about the so-called Castellamarese War. The name Castellamarese came from the Sicilian town of Castellammare del Golfo, from which New York Mafia boss Salvatore Maranzano and many of his followers came. It was this 1930/31 war involving the Maranzano crime family and a rival faction headed by Giuseppe Masseria that some authorities claim established the basic framework for the current structure of organized crime in the United States. Maranzano was executed in 1931, and some large number of his allies, old-style Mafia leaders called "Mustaches," were supposedly purged—murdered. Block refers to this story as an example of historical naivete. We might go further and examine it as a demonstration of myth-making.

> While all the believers in purge day cite figures of from 30 to 90
> men executed, and while all believers cite or refer to Valachi for or
> as evidence, Valachi only testified about four or five murders.
> (Block, 1978:457)

"Clearly," says Block, "what has been done is to use the popular story of Valachi as a primary source in the reconstruction of the history of organized crime" (1978:457). Valachi not only did not say what some people apparently heard, or at least wanted to hear him say, but the story of the war and the mass killings had, according to Block, been around since the 1930s. It was therefore not new information.

As an empirical test of the hypothesis that the Maranzano purge was a myth, Block surveyed newspapers in selected cities (where the killings allegedly took place) for two weeks prior and two weeks after Maranzano's death. Block writes about his search:

> I looked for any stories of gangland murders that could be con-
> nected, even remotely, with the Maranzano case. . . . While I found
> various accounts of the Maranzano murder, I could locate only
> three other murders that might have been connected. . . .
>
> The killing of four or five men does not make a purge, and cer-
> tainly the killing of three of four men in the New York Metropoli-
> tan area and one man in Pittsburgh does not make a national ven-
> detta. It is also significant that all the names turned up in our survey
> . . . have been accounted for. Left out are only the fictional mem-
> bers of the Mafia's legion of the damned—those unnamed and
> more importantly, unfound gang leaders whose massacre signaled
> the end of one criminal era and the beginning of another.
> (1978:460)

If the purge story is a myth rather than a reality, was it consciously invented? Was it a deliberate lie? According to Block, the answer is no. He
concludes that the people who told the story actually believed it. His reasoning provides another fascinating glimpse into the function of myth. The
death of Maranzano

> was a momentous event that both could have and should have sig-
> naled increased violence. Certainly the level of anxiety, along with
> the need for a comprehensible framework, was high. When in-
> creased violence did not follow Maranzano's death, a comprehen-
> sible framework was established, not out of whole cloth, but out of
> the bits and pieces of events that were transformed as they were
> transmitted. The suggestion, therefore, is that the purge story per-
> formed the function of reducing anxiety by magically wiping out
> Maranzano's followers—those who would have been expected to
> revenge their leader's death. (Block, 1978:461)

Valachi's testimony was interpreted as bearing witness to a story, to a preexisting belief that was generally accepted and that served an explanatory
purpose.

This case example, as well as others, points to the difficulty of testing assumptions and theories about organized crime with rational empirical evidence. Evidence testing the existence or nonexistence of Mafia-style organized crime is not readily obtained nor unambiguously interpretable. We are
dependent on informers (such as Valachi), infiltrators who act as participant-
observers, wiretaps or eavesdrops, and newspaper accounts (such as those
used by Block). Each of these sources has considerable problems of reliability and validity.

In part because of these limitations, research into organized crime has "displayed a strong affinity with the 'ideological preconceptions' of the creators of the popular works" (Block, 1978:464). The distinction between fact and fiction has become blurred. As a result, these popular accounts have been taken up by the social scientists "where they have fueled further flights of fantasy" (Block, 1978:467). (We will deal with the Mafia myth in popular culture in a later section.)

What are the consequences of this interweaving of myth and science? "Reliance on the unsubstantiated accounts of informers and the ideological preconceptions of lawmen has mired down the study of organized crime in the bog of conspiracy allowing the term to be carelessly transformed to stand for the monolithic organization of criminals" (Block, 1978:470). Again, the suggestion is that there are implications from inadequately defining and focusing the problem. Perhaps the outstanding example of becoming mired in this "bog of conspiracy" is the criticism of the work of Donald Cressey and its influence on the Organized Crime Task Force of the 1967 President's Commission on Law Enforcement and Administration of Justice.

CRESSEY AND THE
TASK FORCE REPORT

In Chapter 1 we briefly described the work of the President's Commission Task Force on Organized Crime and the contributions to this work made by commission consultant Donald Cressey, looking at both the commission's and Cressey's definitions of organized crime. Cressey, perhaps more so than any other authority on organized crime, has been criticized for making the Mafia into a myth synonymous with organized crime.

Donald Cressey was the principal consultant to the Task Force on Organized Crime and wrote an extremely influential appendix to their final report entitled, "The Functions and Structure of Criminal Syndicates" (President's Commission, 1967). In this paper, Cressey argued his belief that there is a nationwide cartel and confederation that operates the principal illegal businesses in the United States. He said that this cartel came into being in 1931, at the time of the Castellamarese War, when organized crime units across the country formed monopolistic corporations.

Relying principally on data given him by the government, which included police data and the results of FBI interrogations of Joseph Valachi, and upon Valachi's testimony before the McClellan committee, Cressey described organized crime as a bureaucratically structured organization. This organization had a hierarchy of ranks, a code of conduct for its members and, most important, functioned as a secret society. Of Valachi, Cressey wrote: "The McClellan Committee and a nation-wide television audience in 1963 heard Mr. Joseph Valachi, an active member of the confederation, describe the skeleton of the structure of the organization, its operations, and its membership" (President's Commission, 1967:32–33).

The importance Cressey attached to Valachi's information is evident in these examples of Cressey's analysis:

> Especially since the McClellan Committee hearings, law-enforcement officers have shown conclusively that "families" of criminals of Italian and Sicilian descent either operate or control the operation of most of the illicit businesses—including gambling, usury, and the wholesaling of narcotics—in large American cities, and that these "families" are linked together in a nationwide cartel and confederation. Nevertheless, some officials, and some plain citizens, remain unconvinced. (President's Commission, 1967:33)

> Many issues were at stake in the 1930–1931 war. . . . It is relevant to note, however, that after joining together in what outsiders called "The Italian Society," Sicilian and other Italians seized territories formerly controlled by other criminal groups, especially Irish and Jewish groups. Almost simultaneously the members of the new alliance started fighting each other. . . . The war extended across the nation, and in one forty-eight hour period thirty to forty leaders of the existing Sicilian and Italian groups were killed. Most of them were men of the older generation, called "greaseballs," "handlebars," and "moustaches." (President's Commission, 1967:37–38)

The "war" referred to by Cressey is the Castellamarese War.

Donald Cressey painted a frightening picture of a malevolent and sinister national force run by Italians and Sicilians that, in his words, was undermining basic economic and political traditions and institutions in the United States. Others since then have accused Cressey of buying into a false or overblown image they say the government wished to exploit to justify extreme law enforcement measures such as extensive wiretapping. Let us turn to the work of others who have considered Cressey's conclusions and looked at the larger question of the mythology of organized crime.

One critic of this myth-making is Gordon Hawkins (1969), whose article "God and the Mafia" attempts to draw an analogy between assertions about the existence of the Mafia and about the existence of God. "In neither case," Hawkins says, "is it clear what would be regarded as constituting significant counterevidence" (1969:26). Hawkins accused Cressey of reaching unfounded conclusions based on limited and very questionable information. He does not, said Hawkins, demonstrate or prove the existence of a nationwide criminal confederation called La Cosa Nostra. But Hawkins does suggest why the mythology about organized crime persists:

> It is important to recognize that, quite apart from the evidence
> available, the notion that behind the diverse phenomena of crime
> there exists a single mysterious omnipotent organization that is
> responsible for much of it, is one that has long exerted a powerful
> influence on the minds not only of journalists, but also of law en-
> forcement agents and serious students of crime. . . . Much of the
> literature on the subject consists of myths and folktales. . . . When-
> ever alarm and uneasiness are induced by an apparently chaotic
> upsurge of crime and lawlessness, or whenever explanation in terms
> of anonymous and intangible "social forces" is found unsatisfying, it
> is likely that the attribution of responsibility to a group of identifi-
> able human agents for a large proportion of the disturbing happen-
> ings could be both intellectually and emotionally reassuring. . . . In
> the field of crime, the national crime syndicate provides a specific
> focus or target for fear and discontent. (1969:30–32)

A Mafia myth helps us deal with a fundamental conflict between good and evil, one of the principal purposes of "true" myths. It also may help to preserve the morality of its believers—"we" are good and moral; "they" (the Mafia) are evil and immoral. They will seek to undermine us, and sometimes in our weakness they may even succeed. Therefore, we must be ever strong and vigilant; and (an implication for crime policy) we must support those who carry the battle against evil on our behalf, for example, the FBI, G-men, and the Untouchables.

Dwight Smith (1975), who, if he didn't coin the phrase "Mafia mystique," at least did more than anyone else to insert it into the realm of research and writing on organized crime has also evaluated Cressey's role in promulgating the myth. Smith describes what he calls the "alien-parasite" perspective as follows:

> It all boils down to a question of perspective. Cressey had bought
> one that assumed "organized crime" and "Mafia" to be synony-
> mous labels for a real-world phenomenon. It gave him a way of
> viewing a set of circumstances associated with organized crime, of
> seeing certain characteristics in them and ignoring (or dismissing)
> others, of interpreting what it allowed him to see, and of categoriz-
> ing the results into a logical description of organized crime. The

perspective was based on assumptions about how the real world "ought" to look.

It is a narrow perspective, bounded on one side by a limited view of human events and on the other by a set of pejorative, stereotypical labels that reinforced a moral imperative behind the initial assumption that "Mafia" and "organized crime" are the same. Organized crime was to be described not simply as a "different" way of responding to real-world circumstances, but as the result of having a group of criminally minded persons appear, insisting on imposing their crimes on a society ill equipped—except for what the forces of law might be permitted to do—to withstand them. Its origins were traceable to the turn of the century; its principal characteristics were violence and aggressive intimidation. If we would get rid of that group (or at least reduce its threat), we would solve the problem of organized crime. It is not a perspective that encourages new questions.

Cressey did his best to justify that perspective. (1975:311)

The Mafia as organized crime, and only the Mafia, provides an acceptable and believable explanation for those illicit activities we cannot or do not wish to explain otherwise. It fits the us and them, good and evil, notion. It helps maintain our moral imperative. It also provides a rationale for taking actions we might not take otherwise. If "they" are evil, are different from us, are sinister-looking, dark-skinned, dangerous foreigners, then the ends of control and elimination might justify any means. (Remember the American Indian example?) This is where some policy implications arise.

In a eulogistic piece remembering Donald Cressey, Joseph L. Albini (1988) assessed Cressey's contributions to the study of organized crime. Cressey "was captivated by [the] secretive aspect of the government's conception of Mafia and Cosa Nostra" (Albini 1988:341). Cressey adopted the model of organized crime that portrayed it as being in the hands of a secret, national bureaucratic cartel made up of rational criminal entrepreneurs. According to Albini, Cressey failed to be sensitive to what Alan Block later warned about—namely, that informants, whether they be from the underworld (like Valachi) or from law enforcement, have their own specific and limited descriptions, understandings, and interpretations. Valachi was only a low-ranking member of the Genovese crime family. His observation point was limited. Much of what he testified to was based on hearsay or on a very fuzzy recollection of events that may have occurred as much as 30 years before. Beyond that, as we illustrated earlier, some people heard Valachi say what they wanted him to say. They even heard things he didn't say.

A further problem, according to Albini and others, was that the McClellan committee called before it only those witnesses who would "fit" the stereotype of Cosa Nostra membership. "It certainly appears obvious that this subcommittee, along with Attorney General Robert Kennedy, was seeking to develop and portray a more vivid stereotype of the 'slippery label' created earlier by Senator Kefauver" (Albini, 1988:348). The political purpose of this exercise was seemingly to create and garner support for a particular policy agenda.

Donald Cressey and the Organized Crime Task Force gave researchers and investigators an explicit model of organized crime. Much, although not all, of the research since then has failed to find support for this highly structured, hierarchical, centrally controlled model. Nevertheless, as a research model, it still has great value. But as a foundation for organized crime control policy, it has been problematic.

POPULAR CULTURE AND
THE MAFIA MYTH

Crime in general, and organized crime stories in particular, are popular fare in newspapers, magazines, movies, and novels. Crime stories abound in television news and entertainment programming. Most of the public, most of the time, gets most of its information about organized crime through some combination of these sources. From early radio shows like "Gangbusters" to gangster novels such as those of Mickey Spillane to gangster movies like *Prizzi's Honor*, to TV shows like "The Untouchables" and "Wiseguy," there has been considerable public interest in the exploits of gangsters and racketeers over the years. But there has been nothing before or since to rival the impact of Mario Puzo's 1969 novel *The Godfather*—and the three movies derived from it. The book, and the first movie, featuring Marlon Brando as the Godfather Don Vito Corleone, were the public "proof" of the Mafia's or Cosa Nostra's existence and structure. This is what organized crime was like; this is the way mobsters looked, talked, acted, and lived. *The Godfather* had more influence on the public mind and the minds of many public officials than did any library filled with scholarly works that argued for the true nature of organized crime. Scholarly work that purports to show that the Mafia as a secret society does not and has never existed, such debunking work, according to Albini and Bajon, has "had virtually little impact in changing the thinking of the American public. This public still prefers to believe a fictionalized version of truth—*The Godfather*" (Albini & Bajon, 1978:292).

Smith, who read literally hundreds of gangster novels in researching *The Mafia Mystique*, puts Mario Puzo's book at the center of those fictionalized accounts of organized crime that have had the effect of making this kind of crime interchangeable with the Mafia in the public's perception. *The Godfather* was a true saga, in this case a saga of a gangster hero. There had been other gangster heroes in books and movies before but "it was not until Puzo in 1969 that the ethnic traits of 'Mafia' became a permanent part of the basic stereotype patterns that had been established nearly forty years earlier" (Smith, 1975:254). *The Godfather*, Smith said, laid to rest any doubts about the power of ethnicity as the principal character trait for gangsters. Before this, fictional gangsters came in various ethnic varieties; but after it, the only really authentic big-time mobster had to be Italian or Sicilian. "The public," says Smith, "was ripe for a book that would demonstrate the 'reality' of the twenty-year campaign of the law-enforcement community to depict organized crime as an evil, alien, conspiratorial entity comprised of Italians bearing the 'Mafia' label" (1975:277).

To further illustrate the power of *The Godfather*, after its publication and popular acclaim, it was "virtually impossible . . . to find a book concerned with gangsters that does not identify them as members of the Mafia or Cosa Nostra" (Smith, 1975:302). In less than ten years after its publication, there were more than 150 "Sons of the Godfather," that is, books using the Mafia theme and following the Puzo format. This literary deluge reinforced "the concept that narcotics agents and others wished to convey of an alien, parasitic, and violent group" (Smith, 1975:305). Now that we have peaked your interest, let us look at a few excerpts from *The Godfather* to get an idea of just how it depicted organized crime and the Mafia.

In this first excerpt, Vito Corleone (the Godfather) is meeting with a man who has come seeking revenge on a couple of young punks who have brutally attacked his daughter. It will give you some sense of what being the Godfather means and how he and the Mafia operate outside the normal rules and laws of the larger society—or at least how this occurs in Mario Puzo's imagination.

> Don Corleone was gentle, patient. "Why do you fear to give your first allegiance to me?" he said. "You go to the law courts and wait for months. You spend money on lawyers who know full well you are to be made a fool of. You accept judgment from a judge who sells himself like the worst whore in the streets. Years gone by, when you needed money, you went to the banks and paid ruinous interest, waited hat in hand like a beggar while they sniffed around, poked their noses up your very asshole to make sure you could pay them back." The Don paused, his voice became sterner.

"But if you had come to me, my purse would have been yours. If you had come to me for justice those scum who ruined your daughter would be weeping bitter tears this day. If by some misfortune an honest man like yourself made enemies they would become my enemies"—the Don raised his arm, finger pointing at Bonasera—"and then, believe me, they would fear you." (Puzo, 1969:32–33)

The second excerpt illustrates the role of the consigliori or counselor, a kind of legal adviser to the boss. It also tells you something about how the Mafia is allegedly structured into hierarchical layers with buffers in between.

The Consigliori was always a full-blooded Sicilian. . . . It was a question of blood. Only a Sicilian born to the ways of omerta, the law of silence, could be trusted in the key post of Consigliori.

Between the head of the family, Don Corleone, who dictated policy, and the operating level of men who actually carried out the orders of the Don, there were three layers, or buffers. In that way nothing could be traced to the top. Unless the Consigliore turned traitor. (Puzo, 1969:48–49)

The movie *The Godfather* (1972) was the biggest money-maker in movie history to that time. Given that more of the American public sees movies than reads books, and given that there were sequels starring Al Pacino, the movies probably had even more effect than the book.

A contemporary of *The Godfather*, as both a book and a movie, was *The Valachi Papers*. One principal difference was that one was fiction and the other ostensibly nonfiction. Author Peter Maas published his biographical diary about Joseph Valachi in 1968. The movie came out in 1972. Although it did not make nearly the splash of *The Godfather*, the book was probably at least as widely read among connoisseurs of organized crime. In this excerpt, Joseph Valachi describes being made, that is, being initiated into what he called La Cosa Nostra:

I'd say about forty guys were sitting at the table, and everybody gets up when I come in. The Castellammarese. . . .

I was led to the other end of the table past them, and the other guy with me said, "Joe, meet Don Salvatore Maranzano. He is going to be the boss for all of us throughout the whole trouble we are having." This was the first time I ever saw him. Gee, he looked just like a banker. You'd never guess in a million years that he was a racketeer.

Now Mr. Maranzano said to everybody around the table, "This is Joe Cago," which I must explain is what most of the guys know me by. Then he tells me to sit down in an empty chair on his right. When I sit down, so does the whole table. Someone put a gun and a knife on the table in front of me. I remember the gun was a .38, and the knife was what you would call a dagger. After that, Maranzano motions us up again, and we all hold hands and he says some words in Italian, and talks about the gun and the knife. "This represents that you live by the gun and the knife," he says, "and you die by the gun and the knife." Next he asked me, "Which finger do you shoot with?"

I said, "This one," and I hold up my right forefinger.

I was still wondering what he meant by this when he told me to make a cup out of my hands. Then he put a piece of paper in them and lit it with a match and told me to say after him . . . "This is the way I will burn if I betray the secret of this Cosa Nostra." All of this was in Italian. In English Cosa Nostra would mean "this thing of ours." It comes before everything—our blood family, our religion, our country.

After that Mr. Maranzano says . . . "Here are the two most important things you have to remember. . . . The first is that to betray the secret of Cosa Nostra means death without trial. Second, to violate any member's wife means death without trial. . . .

[After describing how Joe Bonanno, aka Joe Bananas, was chosen as his "gombah" or kind of godfather to be responsible for him, Valachi adds this finishing touch.]

So Joe Bananas laughs too, and comes to me and says, "Give me that finger you shoot with." I hand him the finger, and he pricks the end of it with a pin and squeezes until the blood comes out.

When that happens, Mr. Maranzano says, "This blood means that we are now one Family." In other words, we are all tied up. (Maas, 1968:94–97)

In addition to making entertaining reading, this passage helps confirm the stereotype of the secret blood cult, sworn to silence on pain of death. But was it true? Did these kinds of rituals actually take place? According to one of Valachi's colleagues, Vincent Teresa, who was allegedly a high-ranking member of the Mafia, Valachi's story was an exaggeration, a dim memory of the past. How much of Valachi's stories were true, partially true, or created out of whole cloth? It is impossible to say. But we do know they contained the stuff of myth, in this case, the Mafia myth. For many, these insider stories confirmed their preconceived notions about the Mafia. *The Valachi Papers* movie starring Charles Bronson as Valachi simply added to the aura and the mystique.

Now, a generation later, TV series, movies, and books still feature organized crime–type criminals with Italian names. Despite the efforts of many
prominent Italian-Americans (including Governor Mario Cuomo of New
York) to disassociate being Italian-American from being Mafia, the perception persists, in part because it has some truth to it and in part because it
fills the need for explanation, resolution, and reconciliation that all myths
fill. We turn next to a case example of the policy effects of the Mafia myth.

A CASE STUDY OF THE MYTHOLOGY
OF ORGANIZED CRIME: PHILADELPHIA

Philip Jenkins and Gary Potter (1987) have recently looked at organized
crime in Philadelphia and at the role of the Mafia or Cosa Nostra in that
city. They start with the premise that organized crime, in general, clearly
exists and, further, that there is also clearly a strong Italian-American component to it. "In Philadelphia . . . it is easy to find examples of powerful organized criminals of Italian origin; thus, speaking of the 'Mafia Myth' does
not suggest that Italian criminals are nonexistent or negligible. . . . Clearly,
Italian organized crime as such is no myth. . . . However, they are not the
only group and not [even] the most powerful" (Jenkins & Potter, 1987:474).
Jenkins and Potter's second premise is that, in the face of historical evidence
to the contrary, "both the existence and the history of the Philadelphia
'Cosa Nostra' largely represent the work of myth-makers" (p. 475).

Jenkins and Potter present historical evidence to show that the criminal
elite in Philadelphia has historically been made up of all the major ethnic
groups in the city. These included Irish, Jews, and Italians, but also blacks,
Greeks, and Latin Americans. Organized crime has never been, they say,
monopolized by any one ethnic group. The "remarkably consistent pattern"
operating through the first half of the century is one in which "gangsters
were drawn from a variety of ethnic groups and held power in alliance with
police and politicians" (pp. 478–479). The latter is important because it suggests the importance of the ties existing between the organized crime
groups and the powerful political machines operating in many cities. These
machines were so powerful in some cities that they controlled organized
crime rather than vice versa. The vice trades and the rackets were a lucrative
source of income for machine politicians and for the police, either through
skimming or payoffs.

In contrast to the history Jenkins and Potter lay out, a history in which
Italians "played a small but active role," there is "an 'official' history of organized crime in Philadelphia, which omits virtually every fact not per-

taining to Italian activity and any interpretation contrary to the Mafia theory" (Jenkins & Potter, 1987:479). This official history is said to be the work of the Pennsylvania Crime Commission (PCC). "The PCC believes that the key component of the state's organized crime structure is the Cosa Nostra . . . . [Their] analysis has provided the basis for much law enforcement activity and for the essential scheme of interpretation used by the FBI, DEA, and other federal and local agencies" (p. 479).

This official version, which has significant implications for policy-making, as Jenkins and Potter point out, is said to be wrong on several counts: First, the belief that organized crime and the Mafia are synonymous is wrong because organized crime predated Italian immigration into Philadelphia; second, this version ignores the powerful role of other ethnic groups in organized crime, for example, the Irish and the Jews; and third, it ignores the link between the various organized crime groups and the police and the politicians. One implication of the PCC historical model is that it "confirms that law enforcement agencies should choose the Mafia as their primary target" (Jenkins & Potter, 1987:480).

Why was this new mythology of a sovereign Cosa Nostra in Philadelphia created? Jenkins and Potter describe it this way:

> In 1963, Valachi's crucial testimony had said that Bruno [Angelo Bruno, the alleged organized crime boss of Philadelphia] had a hundred men in his family. . . ; Cressey's books described an elaborate corporate structure; a burgeoning literature was describing a myth/history of the Mafia more consistent and romantic than that of most states. Could Pennsylvania be different? It would be embarrassing not to find a Mafia. Indeed, this could even lead to allegations (unfounded, of course) that the Commission had been bribed or threatened by the Cosa Nostra, that the Commission members were naive dupes, that they were unfamiliar with the criminological literature.
>
> So the Cosa Nostra had to be invented. . . . The fiction began to flourish in the 1960s, and it rapidly took hold. . . . State authorities . . . found a Mafia and preserved their credibility. (1987:482–483)

One of the principal results of this myth-making was an almost exclusive law enforcement focus on the alleged Bruno crime family. Although the PCC described the operations of three loan-sharking rings in Philadelphia in 1970, only the one associated with Bruno received law enforcement attention. "Immense time and effort has been devoted to the detection and prevention of illegal activities by the 'family' and their friends, while a more significant criminality on the part of other ethnic groups has received only passing notice" (Jenkins & Potter, 1987:483).

Jenkins and Potter conclude that the "rise" of the Mafia in the 1960s (we would take it back even further to the 1950s) did not represent any real change in the power or composition of organized crime. "Rather," they say, "it reflected the use of a new perspective by official agencies responding to urgent bureaucratic needs" (1987:483). Was this unique to Philadelphia? We don't really know, but there is good reason to suspect not. We concur, however, with this final comment: "The discovery of the Mafia in the 1950s began a fruitful period of myth-making. Only when the myth is recognized for what it is can a real understanding of the nature of organized crime past and present be developed" (Jenkins & Potter, 1987:483–484).

DOES IT MATTER AFTER ALL?

The myth of the Mafia or La Cosa Nostra, or the Mafia mystique, does exist. We will close by reiterating why such a myth exists, that is, what its social and law enforcement benefits are and its implications for organized crime control policy.

Galliher and Cain (1974)—along with Bell (1963), Hawkins (1969), Smith (1975), and others, claim that the Mafia is a scapegoat that can be blamed for a lot of our crime problems. This is a social benefit. It helps get rid of some of the anxiety attendant in dealing with an unknown. What is causing our crime problem, our drug problem, our corruption? Why, the Mafia! Belief in this myth also helps relieve our sense of responsibility and guilt for availing ourselves of illicit goods and services and for the fact that we have corrupt public officials.

One law enforcement benefit is that "extreme measures are easily justified when people believe they are facing a widespread conspiratorial threat" (Galliher & Cain, 1974:74). Extensive use of wiretapping, eavesdropping, and other forms of surveillance that might otherwise be looked at askance from a civil liberties point of view become more acceptable when we are facing the "enemy within." Wiretapping is one of those law enforcement tools whose value in crime control effectiveness must be weighed against the due process concerns raised by the invasion of privacy. The same kinds of justifications and reservations can be made about the practice of seizing assets—government confiscation of houses, cars, boats, and so on determined to be the fruits of crime—permitted under the RICO statutes but which can be taken to unconstitutional extremes. This is also true of the use of scams that can tread dangerously close to entrapment, defined as inducing or encouraging criminality. In a somewhat different vein, the habit of denigrating the criminal defense lawyers that work on organized crime cases as being "mob lawyers" or "mouthpieces for the mob" or worse fails to fully recognize that even the worst criminals in our society have a constitutional right to be represented by legal counsel.

Albini and Bajon claim that the power of the Mafia myth is shown in the functions it serves:

> They are to blame for all types of crime. The Mafia has been cited as responsible for controlling the American economy, for controlling unions and major corporations, for starting race riots in various American cities during the 60s and indeed for controlling the very government of the United States which it has supposedly corrupted. . . .
>
> Yet it is the simplicity of the belief that makes the Mafia myth so appealing. Rather than having to accept the fact that syndicates in the U.S. have been operated by people from all types of ethnic and racial backgrounds, that syndicates exist because the American public has and continues to demand illicit goods, and that syndicates openly operate only because they receive protection from American police and public officials, belief in [the] Mafia allows the American public to cast its attention away from such harsh realities and place the blame on the mysterious group called Mafiosi. But we must remember that such a belief allows this public to feel more safe and comfortable. Why? Because by focalizing the blame on the Mafia there is the belief that it and its members can always be controlled. It is just a matter of time before the secret will become known, its membership-list will be revealed and at last we will crush the Mafia and all crime will disappear. Does this sound too simple? Yes. But is not the belief in a myth just that—a simple answer to a complex reality? (1978:292)

This mythical belief has led numerous government agencies, commissions, committees, prosecutors, and the police to conduct numerous hearings and investigations, and to produce volumes of reports and other information—much of it for nought. As Smith says: "At the heart of my concern is a distinction between what is real and what we think is real and the importance of that distinction in our response to 'pictures' of organized crime. . . . Our 'pictures' of organized crime have failed to recognize [its] complexity, and we are at the mercy of preconceptions that prevent us from fully understanding the problem at hand" (1975:8, 23).

Not understanding the problem, you will recall, is one of the principal dangers of adopting a myth-based explanation. Further, not understanding the problem or, worse yet, thinking we understand the problem when in fact we don't generally sets us up for failure. Have our efforts against organized crime been a failure? Here are the observations of two law enforcement officials in positions to know. The fact that these opinions were expressed nearly 20 years apart gives us an interesting time perspective on how the Mafia myth has affected organized crime policy. First, from a police official in 1966:

> It's because the public and some policemen themselves have bought this crap about the Mafia that makes our work twice as tough. They figure since they're organized, all we have to do is go out, get a couple of the big guys and the castle will come tumbling down. (Albini, 1976:35)

Next, in the words of Justin Dintino, a member of President Reagan's Commission on Organized Crime and a member of the New Jersey State Police, in 1986:

> The attention given to La Cosa Nostra is fogging over the following realities: the fact that 30% of all labor racketeering is not investigated because the participants are not defined or labeled as members of La Cosa Nostra; the fact that La Cosa Nostra is made to appear the major organized crime menace to the country whereas its involvement in organized crime represents only .001 of the total of all organized crime in America; that, instead of Cosa Nostra, the number one problem in American organized crime consists of the Colombians and their involvement in cocaine distribution. (Albini, 1988:352)

These comments should not be taken to mean that law enforcement has been ineffective against those upon whom it has chosen to focus its efforts. The .001 of the total to which Dintino refers (and we should take that figure with a grain of salt, as hyperbole) has been severely disrupted by the work of such prosecutors as Rudolph Giuliani, former U.S. Attorney for the Southern District of New York, and Samuel A. Alito, Jr., former U.S. Attorney for New Jersey. The latter, for example, obtained convictions of a man described as "the most powerful member of the Genovese crime family in New Jersey" and two of his associates. They were convicted of plotting to kill John and Gene Gotti, reputed heads of the rival Gambino crime family in New York City. The plot allegedly arose out of a struggle for control of organized crime in the New York metropolitan area (*New York Times*, June 27, 1989).

What is relevant from our point of view is this comment made by the first assistant U.S. Attorney following the convictions: "With these convictions, we have a hope of making organized crime a historic relic rather than something that preys on people year in and year out" (*New York Times*, June 27, 1989:B1). They might make Italian-dominated syndicated crime a relic, but organized crime?—hardly. The real policy question is whether all this effort had any significant effect on the larger entity of organized crime.

Is there organized crime? Unquestionably. Are Italian-Americans and Sicilian-Americans involved in organized crime in the United States? Plenty of evidence suggests that these groups have been extensively involved. But are racketeers of Italian and Sicilian descent the only ones in organized crime? Clearly not. Are they as well organized, as bureaucratically structured, as nationally powerful as Kefauver, McClellan, Kennedy, and Cressey seemed to believe? In our opinion, no, no, no. So, is there a Mafia myth, and does it matter? Yes—and yes!

10

Ethnic and International Organized Crime

In this chapter, we will describe and compare some of the newer faces on the American organized crime scene. These are not all the groups we might have looked at, but simply those we believe are most important and most interesting. They are particularly illustrative of how immigrant communities can spawn organized criminality that then victimizes the communities themselves. Calling these various bands of criminals emerging groups or nontraditional newer groups does not necessarily mean they are new. Some of them have been around for a long time. This is certainly true, for example, of what some are calling the "Chinese Mafia."

CHINESE TRIADS, TONGS, AND STREET GANGS

Four different but overlapping kinds of groups fall under the broad umbrella of Chinese organized crime. These four are Triads, Tongs, Chinese street gangs, and some other loosely defined but fairly commonly recognized organized crime groups. We will begin by defining these different phenomena, stressing that they are not by any means mutually exclusive categories. On the contrary, these groups are very intertwined and entangled.

Triads

Triads are secret societies, originally formed in China in the early 17th century as resistance groups to the Ching Dynasty. They are patriotic and nationalistic organizations formed for various reasons, for example, as religious groups, peasant rebellion groups, and political groups. But some also exist mainly as criminal groups in Hong Kong and Tawain. Two of the principal Triads are the Green Pang and the Hung Pang (Chin, 1986). According to Chin (1986), the criminal variety triads include the Hong Kong–based 14 K and Wo groups. Some law enforcement authorities and other experts consider the origin, evolution, rituals, and practices of the Triads to be very similar to those of the Sicilian Mafia (Keene, 1989). The President's Commission on Organized Crime said that "Triad-like crime groups" have been formed in major American cities "and are active in drug trafficking, illegal gambling, and loan-sharking, among other sophisticated criminal offenses" (President's Commission, 1986:81). It appears that some of these groups engage in organized crime in the United States. But some who have closely examined the different and multifarious organizations stress that the Chinese Triads and the domestic organized crime groups are not synonymous.

Tongs

The word *tong* refers to a hall or gathering place. The groups called Tongs function as benevolent associations, business associations, ethnic societies, and centers of local politics in Chinese communities in the United States. They engage in a number of activities, including political activities and some protest activities (flowing from the fact that they are sometimes alienated from more legitimate organizations). In some instances, Tongs also engage in criminal activities. According to the FBI "several of the tongs are used as fronts for vicious Chinese organized crime groups that prey mainly on Chinese immigrants and Chinese Americans . . . while the economic mainstay of the criminally involved tongs is illegal gambling, some members have been known to direct gang enterprises that include extortion, drug trafficking, robbery and 'protection' schemes for prostitution and pornography" (Keene, 1989:14).

Chinese Organized Crime

Many people consider Triads, Tongs, and Chinese organized crime to be pretty much identical. But Chin (1986), who has made one of the few in-depth studies of the similarities and differences among these groups, reaches a somewhat different conclusion. He limits the definition of organized crime to those criminal groups in Hong Kong and Tawain that "have [only] emulated the structure and ideology of the Chinese Triad societies" (Chin, 1986:98). He says that the organized crime groups copy the structure, the initiating ceremony, and the spirit of the Hung Pang Triad society, which is the main Triad, but that the major difference is that the principal purpose of the crime groups "is to exploit the societies in which they reside to make money for themselves" (Chin, 1986:332). Like the Triads, these criminal syndicates are located mainly in Hong Kong and Taiwan, and their connections with domestic U.S. organized crime are ambiguous.

Chinese Street Gangs

Chinese street gangs are a special case of the American urban street gang. These gangs, which operate in the Chinatowns of major American cities, were affiliated with the Tongs in the early 1970s. They were a kind of paraprofessional criminal organization that acted to guard the gambling dens run by the Tongs. But in the mid-1970s, well-armed gang members became so powerful that the Tongs could no longer control them. "When the street youths emerged as powerful street gangs through the financial and moral support of the tongs, the gangs overran the tongs and indulged in their own criminal activities such as extortion, robbery, and murder" (Chin, 1986: 279). Chin indicates that the gangs are exclusively male, ages 13 to 37, and are mostly immigrants from Hong Kong or China. Their criminal activities include protection rackets, extortion of legitimate Chinese-owned businesses, robbery of exclusively Chinese victims, prostitution run out of massage parlors, drug trafficking, and gang warfare. The President's Commission on Organized Crime observed that given the complexity of their criminal enterprises, the term *street gang* is a misnomer when applied to "the *Tong*-directed Chinese crime groups" (President's Commission, 1986:86).

A recent government report concluded that the extent to which the foreign-based Triads and the Triad-like organized crime groups are involved in organized crime in the United States is largely unknown. The American groups, that is, the Tongs and the gangs, appear "to be different in structure and composition than their foreign-based counterparts" (U.S. General Accounting Office, 1989a:36).

The Tongs and street gangs possess many of the characteristics we have used to define organized crime groups. They are involved in laundering drug profits, which are then invested in legitimate businesses. They practice formal ceremonial rites of initiation and maintain the strong group loyalty associated with bonding. They also enforce strict secrecy through the use of internal discipline. Their organizational structure is often a tight hierarchy that insulates the top leadership from the group's criminal activities. Violence is used to enforce the extortionate activities employed against Chinese businesses. And finally, there is evidence of their corruption of police and local officials in Hong Kong and elsewhere.

The disagreement over definitions of these groups and the portrayal of what has been called "the new Mafia" are similar to the Mafia myth notion discussed earlier. Chin, a conservative debunker here, makes the following observations in this regard:

> Depending upon who the "enemy" or "outsider" is, a Triad-emu-lating tong organization in the United States may be labeled either as a patriotic political group or as an organized crime group . . . the assumption that there is a world-wide conspiracy among the groups to dominate the international crime scene is considered unwarranted and misleading for the time being. . . . We may conclude tentatively that up to the present there has never been any such group as the Chinese Mafia on either the national or international level. Furthermore, the dissimilarities between the Chinese crime groups and the Italian crime groups are more significant than their similarities. (1986:330, 334, 350)

On the other hand, Gerald Posner (1988), who uses the term *Chinese Mafia*, says of the Triads: "These criminal syndicates, with branches spread around the world, are the Asian equivalents of the Sicilian Mafia. . . . The Triads control the heroin trade in the United States, and they are slowly challenging traditional organized crime for dominance of the underworld in both Europe and America" (p. xvi). He quotes a California police chief who says, referring to Chinese Triads: "Asian organized crime will end up being the number one organized crime problem in North America in the next five years. . . . They'll make the Sicilian Mafia look like a bunch of Sunday-school kids" (Posner, 1988:261). Posner concludes that so far this prediction is "right on target."

The Chinese Mafia might be just another appearance of the alien conspiracy theory—the Mafia myth all over again. But there is a very real concern that with reversion of the British colony of Hong Kong to the control of mainland China in 1997 the United States will experience a massive influx of Chinese organized crime in all its sizes and shapes. Given that the Chinese are already involved in armed robberies, arms dealing, auto theft, contract murder, extortion, gambling, and racketeering and are said to totally control importation of Southeast Asian heroin into the United States (New Jersey State Commission of Investigation, 1989), any expansion of their criminal activities is certainly not a happy prospect.

Based on their recent examination of Chinese organized crime in New York City, Kelly, Chin, and Fagan (1993) concluded that the Chinese criminal groups they studied illustrated the universality of the phenomenon of organized criminality. Organized crime, as the history of Chinese criminal groups illustrates, is not solely a Mediterranean cultural trait but is instead a response to a historical combination of social, economic, and legal conditions (Kelly et al., 1993). The pernicious effects of immigrant, ethnic-organized crime on the immigrant community and the larger surrounding community are illustrated very well by the Chinese. Kelly and his colleagues argue that extortion, more than prostitution, narcotics handling, or dealing in stolen goods, is especially damaging to its victims and potential victims. And it is extortion at which the Chinese have proven to be particularly adept.

THE JAPANESE YAKUZA

Yakuza is actually the collective name for some 2,500 different crime groups operating in Japan and elsewhere, including Hawaii and the U.S. West Coast. The Japanese word *Yakuza* is said to describe a worthless hand in a card game. Thus, the Yakuza call themselves "worthless persons and social outcasts." The Japanese National Police, on the other hand, refer to them as *Boryokudan*, or the "violent ones" (New Jersey State Commission of Investigation, 1989). The estimated 110,000 or more members in these gangs make the Yakuza the largest organized crime group in the world. The largest of the gangs is the Yamaguchi Gumi, which has an estimated 11,000 members. The history of the Yakuza goes back even further than that of the Chinese Triads—back to seventh century Japan (Iwai, 1986). The multitude of gangs can be categorized into three basic types: gamblers, drug dealers, and "violent entrepreneurs and power brokers" (Iwai, 1986:214).

All the gangs possess certain distinctive group structures, behavior patterns, codes, value orientations, and a certain jargon. They are highly structured and are based on hierarchical systems of elders and younger brothers in a kind of familial paternalism. Hiroaki Iwai, who has studied the Yakuza extensively, indicates that they share many of the cultural folkways and mores of feudal Japanese society. As a result, great emphasis is placed on ritual, including ceremonial initiations (involving rice, fish, salt, and sake), body tattooing, and finger cutting as a form of self-mutilation. A member who has angered a supervisor may apologize by amputating a finger or finger joint and presenting it to the offended supervisor.

Yakuza members are said to be involved in fairly extensive weapons trafficking between the United States and Japan. Because gun control laws are extremely strict in Japan and guns are in short supply, there is a lucrative Japanese market for guns (especially handguns) illegally imported from the U. S. Handguns valued at $100 to $200 in the United States can be sold in Japan for $1,000 or more. A similar business is conducted in methamphetamines trafficking from the United States to Japan. In addition, the Yakuza are involved in heroin trafficking, murder, gambling, extortion, blackmail, pornography, loan-sharking, bookmaking, and prostitution. They even carry on a kind of white slave trade between the two countries; young women are lured to Japan with promises of jobs and careers as entertainers but end up working as topless dancers or prostitutes.

Besides these fairly typical criminal enterprises, the Yakuza are also involved in business enterprises that are somewhat unusual for organized crime. Their business activities include banking, real estate, and corporate takeovers (Delfs, 1991). This type of involvement is believed to relate to the unique centrality of organized crime in Japan and, according to Delfs, "the extent to which the underworld plays various essential and tacitly acknowledged economic and political roles at all levels of society" (p. 28). The total annual revenues for Yakuza have been estimated at $32 billion (Bureau of Organized Crime and Criminal Intelligence, 1987).

The FBI believes that Yakuza activity in the United States has increased in the last 15 years because we are a source of weapons, because we serve as an excellent investment source for the excess capital generated by the drug business, and because of the tourist business, particularly in Hawaii and California where the Yakuza active in the United States are located (Keene, 1989). The Yakuza have been especially active in southern California, in the San Francisco area, and in Nevada, where they have invested illegal earnings in restaurants, commercial real estate. and import-export firms. Another prevalent Yakuza criminal activity is blackmailing United States–based Japanese company employees who are in financial or personal trouble.

In their book, *Yakuza,* Kaplan and Dubro (1986) described the multitude of criminal and legitimate enterprises this criminal conglomerate is involved in:

> Like the American mob, the yakuza service the covert vices: prostitution, pornography, drugs, gambling. . . .
>
> The Japanese gangs share other similarities with their American equivalents: large chunks of the construction and entertainment industries lie under their control, including movie studios, night-

clubs, and professional sports. Half the Japanese mob's sizable income comes from drug dealing, say police, particularly in amphetamines. . . . The yakuza portfolio also includes loan sharking, trucking, and an array of strong-arm, smuggling, and extortion rackets. (p. 6)

Historically closely associated with Japanese business interests and with political figures at the highest levels of the Japanese government, this latter association was particularly evident in post-World War II Japan. One of the old Yakuza principals was entangled, along with high Japanese officials, in the Lockheed bribery case in 1984. Yakuza enforcers are routinely used by corporate boards in Japan to maintain order at stockholder meetings, and they sometimes employ violence to accomplish this objective. This suggests that they have a degree of acceptance and, strange as it may appear, even a degree of legitimacy in Japanese society not attained by La Cosa Nostra in the United States. The unusual relationship between the upperworlds and underworlds in Japan may derive from the Yakuza's historical roots in revered feudal ceremony and ritual. It may also be the reason Japanese gangs are relatively open and accessible.

The National Police Agency in Japan reports that the Yakuza control over 25,000 legitimate businesses there in addition to their countless illegal ones. In the United States, the President's Commission on Organized Crime (1986) found that the Yakuza had financial interests in legitimate import-export businesses, real estate, oil, nightclubs, gift shops, and tour agencies. One Yakuza entity, the Rondan Doyuki Company, was said to own shares in General Motors, Bank of America, Atlantic Richfield, Chase Manhattan, Citicorp, IBM, Sperry, and Dow Chemical. The commission indicated that Yakuza members attended stockholders' meetings of these corporations.

The Yakuza is obviously a very sophisticated, highly structured, well-disciplined, and complex criminal organization that uses violence, corruption, diversity of activities, money laundering, and infiltration of legitimate businesses to carry out a broad array of licit and illicit enterprises. It is unquestionably organized crime on an international scale. But in a curious way, the Yakuza too feeds the old alien conspiracy theory for Americans who are looking for a scapegoat to explain some "bad thing" they need explained. Like the Chinese, the Japanese Yakuza can, and seemingly do, conjure up images of the old "yellow peril" supposedly invading the West Coast. Kaplan and Dubro point out how "archaic racist stereotypes" attach to what is referred to as Japan's latest threat to America, namely, their version of the Mafia (1986:9). Deja vu?

COLOMBIAN DRUG TRAFFICKING ORGANIZATIONS: THE MEDELLIN AND CALI CARTELS

The dominance of the South American country of Colombia over the enterprise of cocaine trafficking has been facilitated by a number of factors characteristic of that country. According to a report by the Pennsylvania Crime Commission (1991), these factors are geographical, demographic, cultural, and historical. "The cultural and historical tradition[s] are particularly important," according to the commission.

> With a socio-historical background paralleling that of Southern Italy, the cultural ethos underpinning the Colombian "narco-mafia"—the traditions of violence, the strong family ties, the long history of social banditry and extortion, the distrust of government, and the combination of criminal and entrepreneurial skills—resembles those of the Sicilian Mafia and La Cosa Nostra. Also, as has been true of Sicily, Colombia provides a friendly refuge for launching or incubating organized crime. (p. 255)

In the early 1970s, drug traffickers from Colombia were suppliers of cocaine for such established criminal groups as La Cosa Nostra and various Mexican and Cuban gangs. Later, when the cocaine business became so hugely profitable, a number of these traffickers decided to get in on the profits directly by running their own smuggling and distribution operations. As a result, they formed what are known as drug cartels. These are defined by the U. S. Drug Enforcement Administration as independent trafficking organizations that have pooled their resources. Of these cartels, the Medellin cartel (named for the city in Colombia that is its home base) has been considered, until recently, to be the largest and most powerful.

The Medellin cartel and the Cali cartel (from Cali, Colombia) that rivals it are said to control over 80 percent of the cocaine sent to the United States. Both groups are strongly entrenched in New York and New Jersey and have extensive networks in Miami, Los Angeles, and Houston as well. These cartels are organized into complex infrastructures employing thousands of people—one estimate puts the figure at 24,000. These include those who deal directly with the illicit product, that is, growers of coca, smugglers, small-time distributors, and street pushers, and those who are said to nurture and tend the structure—accountants, chemists, lawyers, paid politicians, and corrupt customs officials.

The Colombian cartels exhibit many of the characteristics of other organized crime groups. They control prices of drugs; they eliminate competition; they avoid prosecution through the use of violence and corruption; and they use other criminal activities and legitimate businesses to hide and launder their huge drug profits. According to Florez and Boyce (1990), the cartels' use of violence is evidenced by the fact that they have murdered rival group members, informants, and witnesses. More than a hundred people were killed during the "cocaine wars" of 1979. Drug money is used to bribe law enforcement officials, judges, politicians, and lawyers and as is the case with other organized crime groups, bribery cripples legitimate law enforcement efforts aimed at combating the cartels.

Those most directly involved in the cartels' activities are limited to Colombians and are usually members of the same family. They value skills and loyalty, but "unlike the LCN, Colombian drug traffickers have no lengthy organizational heritage and often include women in leadership positions" (U.S. General Accounting Office 1989a:11). A Department of Justice study described the cartel as having an "onion-like layering of organizational power, with kingpins at the center, directing operations but insulated by layer upon layer of protective subordinate operatives" (U.S. Department of Justice, 1989:17).

Besides their sophistication and organizational structure and their use of violence, the Medellin and Cali cartels have other organized crime characteristics, including the extensive use of corruption. They have corrupted government officials in South, Central, and North America. One example is the U.S. prosecution of Panamanian strongman General Manuel Antonio Noriega for accepting payoffs from the cartels. Prior to Noriega's arrest, Panama was considered to be the primary money-laundering haven for the Colombia cartels. Millions of so-called narco-dollars moved out of the United States and into various Panamanian bank accounts controlled by the cartels.

Public officials, business and community leaders, journalists, and others who cannot be bought are subjected to intimidation, threats of violence, or assassination. A Colombian presidential candidate, an Attorney General, numerous judges, prosecutors, police officials, and others have been assassinated over the last several years. The cartels' reputation for violence and retribution is such that the Department of Justice report concluded: "Colombian cartel operations in the United States have been characterized by a propensity for violence that has not been seen in the American underworld since the bootleg days of prohibition in the 1920s and early 1930s" (1989:20). The traffickers have shown a willingness to kill anyone who turns against them or who moves against them and have even smuggled Colombians into the United States for use as contract killers.

The cartels' involvement in multiple criminal enterprises is limited pretty much to those activities associated with their drug business. Their main criminal enterprise is the production, distribution, and sale of illicit drugs but that limitation does not restrict their income. They have also been involved in counterfeiting money, passports, and other legal documents. One criminal investigation into the Medellin cartel completed in 1989 found that sophisticated techniques had been used to conceal over $1 billion in drug money over a two-year period. The drug money coming into Colombia alone is said to rival in size the legal economy of that country. The cartels infiltrate legitimate businesses by laundering money through United States and European banks, import-export companies, electronic retail outlets, shopping centers, and landholdings in Tennessee, Kentucky, and elsewhere (U.S. General Accounting Office, 1989a).

With the exceptions of continuity and involvement in multiple criminal enterprises, the cartels meet our criteria for organized crime groups. Most important, few, if any, groups anywhere can rival the Colombian drug cartels in sheer financial resources—and the power and control that that gives them.

VIETNAMESE GANGS

Vietnamese gangs are, in many ways the most obscure of this lot. Because relatively little is known about what may be an emergent form of organized crime, it is not yet possible to classify and define Vietnamese gangs according to the criteria we have been using. We nevertheless include them because they demonstrate in a most incipient form the manner in which immigrants interact with their social, economic, and political environments and how organized crime has historically been born and has thrived.

Unlike Chinese and Japanese organized crime discussed earlier, the thousands of Vietnamese who came to the United States in the late 1970s and 1980s did not come from a country with a tradition of organized crime. To a great extent, their involvement in organized crime in the United States developed out of their experiences as immigrants here. It was, however, very much shaped by who they were and where they had come from.

A number of the Vietnamese refugees had collaborated with the U.S. military during the war in Vietnam. Some, including high-ranking officers, had been in the Vietnamese military forces. Others had been government officials at various levels. One of the unfortunate characteristics of both the

South Vietnamese government and the military at that time was that they were riddled with corruption. Therefore, although they did not have the experience of organized criminal involvement, many Vietnamese refugees did have extensive experience with bribery, corruption, extortion, and violence.

Admittedly, Vietnamese organized crime in the United States is not a problem on a scale with that of other ethnic groups. It is, however, of particular interest in part because there is a Chinese connection; Vietnamese gangs have frequently been very closely linked to Chinese organized crime. One of these links is in the form of the use, by the Chinese, of young Vietnamese immigrants as enforcers in their extortion and protection rackets.

The Vietnamese are also of interest because they are considered by some to be the "most vicious and ruthless of the Asian criminal groups" (New Jersey State Commission of Investigation, 1989:46). The New Jersey State Commission of Investigation observed that the Vietnamese are even more violent than the Chinese gangs, and it is their violence that makes them a matter of special national concern.

Some of the principal criminal activities engaged in by the Vietnamese include extortion, armed robbery, prostitution, auto theft, arson, and gambling. They have also been involved in various property crimes and murder. The gangs are highly mobile and move around the country from one Vietnamese community to another. Their victims are mainly other Vietnamese immigrants. The New Jersey State Commission of Investigation noted that both New York and Philadelphia had several Vietnamese gangs and that there was gang activity in Chicago, Houston, New Orleans, Boston, Los Angeles, and Washington, D.C., as well.

The Pennsylvania Crime Commission, which has also examined Vietnamese gang activity, described their practices in the city of Philadelphia as follows:

> In Philadelphia, the primary criminal activities of members of Vietnamese gangs include extortion, residential burglary, robbery, auto theft, narcotics trafficking, and assaults. . . . Gang members use "direct" and "indirect" methods to extort from Asian-owned businesses in Philadelphia. Using the direct method, gang members approach merchants, demand payments, and threaten violence or property damage if their demands are not met. Using the indirect method, gang members, with no intention of repaying, repeatedly "borrow" money from merchants. The affected merchants realize that the loans will not be repaid but comply to avoid violence. Sometimes gang members repeatedly run up "tabs" in restaurants and then leave without paying their bills. (1991:303)

One last example of the willingness to use violence among the Vietnamese was the bizarre attack on mourners at the July 1990 funeral of a gang member from a Vietnamese gang called Born to Kill. This gang member, Vinh Vuu, had been shot to death in New York City's Chinatown. Gunmen posing as mourners opened fire with automatic weapons during burial services at a cemetery in New Jersey, wounding seven persons. It is believed by law enforcement sources that the murder and the shootings were part of an ongoing feud between the Born to Kill gang and other Asian gangs for control of organized crime in New York's Chinese community.

The Vietnamese are not now a major crime problem, being limited in numbers and mainly operating in small pockets in widely scattered places around the country. Their range of victims is relatively narrow and restricted to Vietnamese or other Asians. As the Vietnam War generation of immigrants dies off or at least ages out of criminal behavior and other Vietnamese find legitimate means of upward mobility, these gangs may disappear and never become a full-blown form of organized crime.

JAMAICAN POSSES

The Jamaican posses are among the country's youngest and most violent organized criminal groups. Born in the poverty and political turmoil of Kingston, Jamaica, individual Jamaican criminal gangs adopted the name *posse* because of their fondness for American western films and because the word connotes the use of violence to enforce political will. These gangs or posses have moved out of Jamaica, beginning their migration to the United States during the early 1970s, and are now based in New York City and other major cities throughout the United States. In addition to New York, they have a presence in Miami, Philadelphia, Washington, D.C., Chicago, Detroit, Houston, Dallas, Los Angeles, San Francisco, and Hartford.

The two largest, most violent and best established of the posses are the Shower Posse and the Spangler Posse. The former group is said to have more than 5,000 members, and the latter nearly 5,000. The Shower Posse is believed to have gotten its name from its willingness to shower its enemies and rivals with bullets. There are approximately 40 posses altogether in the United States, with an estimated total membership of some 22,000 individuals.

If we look at the Jamaican posses in terms of the characteristics we have used to define organized crime, we see that they conform to most of our criteria. They use violence; they have multiple criminal enterprises; they infiltrate legitimate businesses; they have a hierarchical structure; they are nonideological; and their criminal operations are sophisticated.

Law enforcement officials interviewed by the General Accounting Office (GAO) in its investigation of nontraditional organized crime considered the Jamaicans to be among the most violent criminal gangs confronting American law enforcement (U.S. General Accounting Office, 1989a). They are said to be preoccupied with firearms and violence and to display a willingness to use torture that is rare even among gangsters. Between 1985 and 1989, the posses were said to have been involved in at least 2,125 drug-related homicides. The Pennsylvania Crime Commission also concluded that the Jamaicans "are heavily involved with firearms, and they have a well-deserved reputation for brutal violence, even by the standards of an unusually violent business" (1991:243). The commission offered two causal explanations for this propensity for violence: (1) that their brutality "stems in part from cultural tradition and in part from their belief that violence is an occupational necessity"; and (2) that they seem to "equate violence with personal power and prowess, and they are fascinated with firearms of high quality and power" (p. 243).

The GAO study concluded that the posses were trafficking in large quantities of firearms and were heavily involved in cocaine and crack distribution as well as being engaged in money laundering, fraud, robberies, kidnapping, auto theft, and homicides. The frauds include insurance frauds, bank kiting, falsification of documents, and passport and visa fraud. The Jamaicans' cocaine business has become their principal criminal enterprise, largely supplanting smuggling and distribution of marijuana, which had been their primary criminal activity. It is estimated that they control 30 to 40 percent of the U.S. crack trade as well as 20 percent of the marijuana operation (U.S. Department of Justice, 1990, 1991). The New Jersey State Commission of Investigation (1991b) adds to the Jamaicans' list of criminal enterprises, home invasions and alien smuggling.

The U. S. Department of Justice concluded that whereas in the past the Jamaican posses were sending most of their illicit profits home to Jamaica, more recently they are laundering their money and investing it in commercial property such as record stores, restaurants, auto body shops, travel agencies, video stores, and trucking companies (1990, 1991). Given the size of the profits to be made from the cocaine and crack business, these investments and the amount of control they engender can be very substantial.

The GAO report (1989a) describes the posses as having a three-tiered structure. At the top is a leader (or leaders) who controls the posse. This individual is usually somewhat insulated from the street-level activity. The second tier is composed of subleaders or lieutenants who transport drugs, guns, and money to the leaders. They also smuggle illegal aliens into the United States. The bottom tier is made up of street-level drug dealers who often get involved in violent incidents resulting from drug disputes. The overall structure is subdivided into a substructure of cells, each with its own leader. The top leaders are usually Jamaican nationals who have lived in the United States since the 1970s and have legal status here. It is estimated that roughly 70 percent of the bottom tier are illegal aliens.

The Jamaican gangs have a political underpinning that makes them somewhat different from other organized criminal groups. The Jamaican street gangs from which they evolved were politically oriented. Members of the Shower Posse, for example, were avid supporters of the Jamaican Labor Party, whereas Spangler Posse members were behind the opposition Peoples' National Party. Not only were these gangs aligned with political nationalism in Jamaica, but they were often also linked to the Rastafarian movement. Some sources believe that the posses first came to the United States to make money and to purchase weapons that could be used to influence political developments in Jamaica. Today, however, the political connection is thought to be overstated. Most Jamaican organized crime groups are now concerned only with making money, and most of their membership is made up of nonideological career criminals.

The Department of Justice (1990, 1991) concluded that the Jamaicans possessed considerable management skills. They are able to control large shipments of cocaine from its original purchase in the Caribbean through its distribution in gram-sized street sales. Their marketing structure is said to result in unusually high profit margins per dosage unit. The posses are also adept at obtaining phony drivers licenses, birth certificates, passports, citizenship cards, and naturalization certificates. These are good indicators that there is a degree of sophistication in the operation of their criminal enterprises.

What is the outlook for the Jamaican posses? The message from the various law enforcement bodies that have investigated them is somewhat mixed. The prevailing view of investigators and other experts is that the posses have come "farther faster" than any other organized criminal group now active in the United States. The fact that they maintain close ties with the Colombian drug cartels and are also expanding their contacts with American street gangs like the Crips suggests that the Jamaicans are highly likely to be a continuing problem. Table 10.1 reviews the defining characteristics of the Jamaican posses and other ethnic-based organized crime groups in the United States. Table 10.2 on pages 272–273 provides a summary of the various groups' activities and notable characteristics. Both tables include one final group that we will look at next—the Russians.

Table 10.1 Defining Ethnic/International Groups as Organized Crime

GROUP TYPE	CORRUPTION	VIOLENCE	CONTINUITY	MULTIPLE CRIMINAL ENTERPRISES	STRUCTURE	INVOLVING LEGITIMATE BUSINESSES	SOPHISTICATION	DISCIPLINE	BONDING
Chinese Tongs and Triads	X	X	X	X	X	X	X	X	X
Japanese Yakuza	X	X	X	X	X	X	X	X	X
Colombian (drug) cartels	X	X	X		X		X		
Vietnamese gangs	X	X		X				X	X
Jamaican posses		X		X	X	X	X		
Russian Mafia	X	X	X	X	X	X	X		

Note: Definitional criteria adapted from M. Maltz (1985), "Towards Defining Organized Crime," in H. Alexander and G. Caiden (eds.) , *The Politics and Economics of Organized Crime*, Lexington, MA: D.C. Heath.

THE RUSSIAN MAFIA: A CASE STUDY

The remainder of this chapter is devoted to an extended, in-depth look at one of the most enigmatic of the ethnic varieties of American organized crime. In its own way, organized crime among emigres from the former Soviet Union is somewhat typical of how organized crime originated and developed in our immigrant communities; but at the same time, it has been uniquely shaped by the culture, history, and traditions of Russians and other Soviet peoples.

The Source

Our task is to examine the Russian version of American organized crime. To do that, it is appropriate to begin with the Russian connection. The term *Russian* is used here in a generic sense to describe all Soviet emigres. This reflects how Soviet emigres to the United States have generally characterized themselves. One of the issues that must be considered in any examination of Soviet emigre crime is to try to understand what role, if any, specific ethnic identities (for example, Chechen or Ukrainian) play in defining Soviet organized crime networks. This is especially pertinent because in addition to the traditional role of ethnicity in defining American organized crime, current indications suggest a rise in the number of organized crime groups based on ethnicity inside the former Soviet Union (Serio, 1993).

Organized crime in the former Soviet Union and its accompaniments—corruption, the shadow economy, and the black market—first flourished because of the peculiarities of the Soviet economy and Soviet politics. Both the economy and the politics have changed dramatically in recent years, but the foundation for the export of the seeds of Russian organized crime was set under the old system.

Because of the unique confluence of circumstances and characteristics, the U.S.S.R. produced a people uniquely socialized to facilitate their involvement (both as clients and victims) in organized crime. Rosner, for one, reached such a conclusion:

> The new Russian immigrant [to the United States] arrived on these shores already steeped in a criminal system . . . and with certain skills already in place. It is the conclusion of this study that these immigrants did not change their behavior to ascend the American social ladder. Rather, they continued patterns of behavior that were ingrained after a lifetime in a social system where extralegal values were stressed. (1986:132–133)

Table 10.2 A Comparison of Ethnic/International Organized Crime Factions

ETHNIC GROUP	ORIGINS	EXEMPLARS	NOTABLE ILLICIT ACTIVITIES	NORTH AMERICAN LOCALES	COMMENTS (UNIQUE OR NOTABLE CHARACTERISTICS)
Chinese (Tongs, Triads, street gangs)	17th century China	Wo, 14 K	Gambling, extortion, drug trafficking, robbery, prostitution, murder, arms dealing, racketeering	California, New York	▪ Tongs and street gangs possess many of the characteristics we used to define organized crime groups
Japanese Yakuza	7th century Japan	Yamaguchi Gumi	Weapons trafficking (to Japan), methamphetamines trafficking (to Japan), murder, gambling, extortion, bookmaking	California, Hawaii	▪ All Yakuza gangs are highly structured/hierarchical ▪ Legitimate activities include banking and real estate ▪ Annual revenue estimated to be $32 billion
Colombian drug traffickers	Colombia has a long history of social banditry	Medellin and Cali cartels	Cocaine trafficking	New York area, Miami, Los Angeles, Houston	▪ Complex infrastructures employ about 24,000 according to one estimate ▪ Criminal activities limited to those associated with the drug trade
Vietnamese gangs	Arrival of immigrants in U.S. in the 1970s	Born to Kill	Extortion, prostitution, auto theft, arson, gambling, armed robbery	Chicago, New Orleans, Houston Washington, DC, Los Angeles, Boston	▪ Not a major problem compared to other ethnic organized crime groups ▪ Closely linked to Chinese organized crime ▪ Considered to be the most ruthless of Asian groups

Table 10.2 (continued)

ETHNIC GROUP	ORIGINS	EXEMPLARS	NOTABLE ILLICIT ACTIVITIES	NORTH AMERICAN LOCALES	COMMENTS (UNIQUE OR NOTABLE CHARACTERISTICS)
Jamaican posses	Kingston, Jamaica. Came to U.S. in mid-1970s	Shower Posse, Spangler Posse	Cocaine (crack distribution), firearms trafficking, money laundering, fraud, robbery, kidnapping, murder, auto theft	New York, Miami, Los Angeles, San Francisco, Detroit, Philadelphia, Dallas, Washington, DC, Chicago, Houston	■ One of the most violent organized crime groups in the country ■ 40 posses in the U.S. have 22,000 members ■ Control 30 to 40 percent of U.S. crack trade
Russian Mafia	Emigres arrived in large numbers in the 1970s	Odessa Malina, Organizatsiya	Marketing illegal goods (drugs, weapons, stolen cars), extortion, forgery, loan-sharking, racketeering, gasoline bootlegging (#1 activity)	New York, New Jersey, Philadelphia, Los Angeles, Chicago, Baltimore, Dallas, Cleveland, Phoenix, Toronto	■ Perestroika reforms coupled with economic mayhem fueled a tremendous growth in new forms of organized crime

Rosner divided Russian emigres into survivors and connivers; then further subdivided them into necessary criminals, criminals, and system beaters. Necessary criminals were those who were forced by circumstances in the U.S.S.R. into criminal behavior there. System beaters are those who violate U.S. law in dealing with bureaucratic agencies here. Some Soviets arrived in the United States, steeped in criminal methods and values, and undoubtedly some have used this training to continue their criminality and to become sophisticated, organized criminals.

All the emigres from the former Soviet Union share a common heritage—a state-run, centrally planned Soviet command economy that produced massive shortages as well as widespread bribery and thievery. No area of life in the Soviet Union was exempt from pervasive, universal corruption. Scarce goods and services unavailable through normal channels could usually be gotten through *blat* (connections) or *na levo* (on the left). An illegal second or shadow economy arose to operate in tandem with the official economy.

The notorious Soviet black market was a component of the shadow economy, marketing a wide variety of products from western consumer items to stolen goods, drugs, bootleg liquor, and cigarettes. Because goods were priced much higher on the black market, there was also incentive to siphon off goods from the official market for sale on the black market. Considerable evidence suggests that this practice has not only not ended but has expanded greatly. The nature of the goods being marketed has become much more sophisticated, the consumer market itself has become much more international, and the money involved is much greater. The range of illegal goods being marketed today through multinational links includes antiques, drugs, stolen cars, weapons (including nuclear weapons materials), and metals. It is projected that organized crime in the former U.S.S.R. may quickly move into such things as video piracy, crack refining, and computer crime (Galeotti, 1992).

The *perestroika* reforms of the late 1980s, outlawing the Communist Party, and the demise of the U.S.S.R. itself in 1991—followed by the horrendous economic problems of the past several years—have all fed an enormous growth of new forms of organized crime. Under these conditions, some of the traditional staples of western organized crime (mostly unknown in the old Soviet Union), such as drug trafficking and prostitution, but especially extortion of new companies, businesses, and restaurants, have become among the more prevalent forms of current criminal enterprises in Moscow and other former Soviet cities.

The old Soviet political and socioeconomic system bred illegality and corruption on a scale matched by few countries (Simis, 1982). In *USSR:*

The Corrupt Society, Konstantin Simis described the pervasiveness of Soviet corruption and its links to the shadow economy:

> Underground enterprise is a positive tumor of corruption. Like a drop of water, it reflects the whole world of Soviet improbity. Just as the human body cannot live without air; underground enterprise could not survive except for the fact that the Soviet state and society alike are rotten with corruption from the top to bottom. (1982:179)

Although the "partyocracy" of the Communist Party that engendered this kind of corruption is gone, there is every indication that so far at least the crime and corruption have only gotten worse (Galeotti, 1992; Handelman, 1993; Timofeyev, 1992).

Unlike traditional explanations of the relationships among culture, immigration, and crime, in the case of emigres from the former Soviet Union, their particular culture of origin may play an especially powerful and even unique role in stimulating and facilitating crime in general (and organized crime in particular) in new settings.

Odessa by the Sea:
Russian Organized Crime
Grows in Brooklyn

Brighton Beach in Brooklyn contains the largest Russian immigrant community in the United States. Most of the members of this community are Jewish emigres who were able to leave the Soviet Union and come to the United States under a grant of refugee status as politically oppressed peoples. The exact size of the emigre population in Brighton Beach, and for that matter elsewhere in the United States, is impossible to discern. Large numbers of illegal immigrants either entered the United States illegally or have overstayed their visas. Illegal Russian immigrants are estimated to number as many as 30,000. The U. S. Immigration and Naturalization Service believes, however, that most Russian criminals in the United States are legal aliens, having entered under refugee status (personal communication).

Many of the residents of Brighton Beach came from Odessa (a Black Sea port in Ukraine), and consequently, many of the Soviet refugees suspected of involvement in criminal activity in the United States are believed to have come from Odessa. Odessa has long had a thriving black market. And not unlike many other seaports, it also has a well-developed criminal subculture dating back to the times of the pirates. The Odessukuya Vory, or Odessa

Thieves, according to Russian sources, were in fact the most notorious of all the thieves in Russia.

The possibility is raised that not only have Soviet emigres come generally from a society heavily imbued with crime and corruption but that many of them have come specifically from a city considered to have one of the richest criminal traditions in the former Soviet Union. The FBI reportedly believes that former members of the Odessa underworld—referred to by some as the "Malina" (literally, raspberry), a slang term for underground or underworld—are trying to establish themselves in New York, Atlantic City, Philadelphia, Los Angeles, and other cities, having brought crime as a trade from home (Burstein, 1983). Further, many sources believe that a considerable number of the Soviet emigres involved in crime here came out of Soviet prisons (Adams, 1992; R. Friedman, 1993). At present there is no firm evidence for either of these allegations.

But Is It Organized Crime?

The definition of organized crime is clearly an issue that must be raised in considering the current Russian crime situation in the United States. The characteristics identified by Hagan (1983) and Maltz (1985, 1990), presented in Chapter 1, are particularly appropriate for creating a classification schema that can be applied to the Soviet emigre target group of criminals.

This classification is tied to the integrated (ethnicity, conspiracy, enterprise) framework previously layed out. How well the former Soviets fit these criteria will determine how appropriate it is to classify them as a form of organized crime. There is already evidence available of the applicability of certain of these definitional criteria, for example, the use of violence and involvement in multiple criminal enterprises. A Los Angeles journalist reported that Russian loan sharks threatened to cut out the tongue and eyes of a California businessman, burn his skin with acid, shut down his business, and kill his family (A. Mitchell, 1992). The businessman paid $475,000. In January 1992, also in California, sheriff's deputies found two men from the former Soviet Union dismembering the bodies of two murdered emigres. They were apparently connected to a fraud ring that had been importing Russians to buy computers with bad checks (A. Mitchell, 1992). Since 1991, four persons associated with Russian organized crime have been shot to death in New York. In fact, the number of unsolved homicides in and around Brighton Beach stretching back several years attests to a level of violence surpassing that of La Cosa Nostra.

The Incipient Soviet Emigre Mafia

Because of their relative newness and a general absence of reliable and valid information, it is not possible to completely classify and define Russian organized crime according to the Maltz criteria. This classification problem is compounded because of the mystery, the romanticism, and the sensationalistic reporting surrounding it. There is something particularly exotic about new gangsters coming directly from the former "evil empire." This mystique, of course, is not unique to the Russians. It is difficult to judge the accuracy of what is known about this purportedly emergent form of organized crime because a great deal of the available information comes from the popular media. And the media, in turn, seem to get their stories from each other or from a few law enforcement sources who often cite stories in the media or about each other. Further, because arrests and convictions of Russian emigre criminals have been rare, information that normally comes from such actions is sparse. With those caveats in mind, indications are that the Russians demonstrate, in incipient form, many of the characteristics historically associated with the growth and development of organized crime in the United States. For this reason we focus on the Russians as a prime example of an international, ethnic-based organized criminal network.

There is sketchy evidence of a number of organized crime networks made up of Soviets, principally in the Brighton Beach community, but also in Philadelphia and other urban areas. Los Angeles, Baltimore, Chicago, Cleveland, Dallas, Phoenix, and Toronto also report such a presence. The tri-state area of New Jersey, New York, and Pennsylvania ranks in the top ten areas in the country in terms of Soviet relocations, and it is in these areas, not surprisingly, that Russian organized crime is believed to be most prevalent.

The exact number and size of these groups are unknown. California authorities estimated that there are 150 hard-core members and another 200 to 300 associates nationwide (Bureau of Organized Crime and Criminal Intelligence, 1987). Federal agents, on the other hand, have reported that there are a dozen Russian organized crime groups in New York alone, with an estimated total membership of 400 to 500 members. Similarly, the New York City Police Department listed about 500 suspected Soviet gang members. They are said to merge in shifting, rather unstructured networks that know each other and that use each other. Some sources refer to them as a confederacy of groups—ruthless, totally lacking in loyalty, and greedy—willing to do anything and everything for a dollar. Their sole purpose is to make money. Sources indicate that they appear to be without the codes of conduct and secrecy or the hierarchical, crime family structures of La Cosa Nostra. Members range from street corner thugs to educated professionals. A number of sources refer to them as educated and smart, and even as perhaps the most intelligent and sophisticated form of organized crime currently in the United States. One popular publication, drawing on limited anecdotal law enforcement descriptions described the Russians this way:

> The Russian Malina today is almost a case study of where the Mafia was then [a century ago]. There's only one significant difference—most members of the Malina, far from being poor, ignorant immigrants, are highly educated survivors, skilled in all sorts of hi-tech gadgetry, familiar with outwitting the KGB itself. A number of them are veterans of the Soviet Army, and many are already involved in sophisticated white-collar criminal stings. (Mallewe, 1983:147)

The criminal activities attributed to these groups include extortion, forgery, counterfeiting, confidence schemes, insurance and medical fraud, drug trafficking, gasoline bootlegging, loan-sharking, racketeering, gun running, money laundering, murder, burglary, theft, and arson. Two Russians and their associates were indicted in Los Angeles not long ago in a health insurance fraud case involving $1 billion in fraudulent billings—one of the largest insurance swindles in American history. The United States has also become one of the endpoints of drug trafficking from the former Soviet Union. In April 1992, federal agents arrested 11 Russians and two Italians allegedly linked to a wholesale heroin operation using the New York La Cosa Nostra drug distribution network in the United States.

In one of the few serious studies of Russian organized crime in the United States, Rosner (1986) examined what was going on in Brighton Beach. Based on interviews with Russian emigres and with the police, Rosner concluded that there were groups of "interconnected criminals acting both in organized and in informal conjunction with others" and that "a vast amount of at least informally organized crime" existed there (pp. 113, 116). A Philadelphia Police Department report claimed: "It is evident that an organized criminal group exists within the Russian Immigrant community. Members of this group refer to themselves as the 'Russian Mafia.' It is a present and growing threat to our nation. Their obvious sophistication far exceeds that of La Cosa Nostra in its infant state. The 'Russian Mafia' has perpetrated a series of crimes rivaling any of those perpetrated by existing organized criminal groups" (Rosner, 1986:116).

Preliminary research suggests that various criminal justice agencies, independent experts, and researchers believe that a Russian organized criminal entity, variously known as the Malina, the Soviet-Jewish Mafia, and the Russian Mafia, exists as a nontraditional organized crime enterprise. Agencies holding this view include the FBI, U.S. Customs, the New York State Police, the Pennsylvania Crime Commission, and the Philadelphia and New York City police departments.

Two explanations are offered by law enforcement sources for the emergence of this alleged Russian organized crime in the United States. The first is that during the late 1970s the Soviet government released criminals from its prisons and commingled them with emigres leaving the U.S.S.R. The second explanation is that members of Soviet organized criminal groups smuggled themselves out of the country, concealed themselves in Israel or various European cities, and later emigrated to the United States. If the latter is true, it could mean that international underground networks exist that were, and possibly still are, accessible to these criminals.

As indicated earlier, most suspected members of Russian organized crime have Russian-Jewish backgrounds. Other Soviet criminals, some of whom are not Jewish, are said to have acquired the identities of either dead or jailed Russian Jews in the Soviet Union. Some Federal Bureau of Investigation agents involved with foreign intelligence suggested the possibility that the KGB had placed agents or cooperatives in the U.S. crime operation for both criminal and political purposes.

There are two general ideas about the possible organizational structure of Russian organized crime. One is that Russian organized crime is a unitary but loose-knit organization without divisions. The other is that Russian organized crime is a confederation of gangs based upon geographic origins in the former U.S.S.R.: the Odessa Gang, the Kiev Gang, the Moscow Gang, the Leningrad (now St. Petersburg) Gang, and the more widely dispersed Gypsy Gangs. These groups range in size from 5 to 20 members. They are said to be fluid—coming together for a number of criminal operations for a period of time—and then combining with other criminals (A. Mitchell, 1992).

Suspected members of Russian organized crime have demonstrated mobility in their criminal pursuits. For example, police documents indicate that various crimes in the northeast section of Philadelphia have been committed by Russian residents of Brighton Beach. Suspected Russian criminals from Philadelphia have been involved in credit card and insurance frauds in Los Angeles. U.S. Customs has noted that casinos in Atlantic City, New Jersey, have been the targets of Russian criminal activity (passing counterfeit money and stolen travelers' checks, and laundering money) by Soviet emigres residing in Toronto, Canada.

Some alleged members of Russian organized crime have apparently allied themselves with the Scarfo, Colombo, Luchese, and Genovose crime families of La Cosa Nostra. Seven Russians were indicted in the U.S. District Court for the District of New Jersey, along with members of the Gambino crime family, for operating a racketeering enterprise involving bootleg motor fuel. In both New York and New Jersey, Russians and La Cosa Nostra families have combined to control "no brand" fuel distribution and retail sales. Circumvention of taxes by these enterprises has resulted in evasion of hundreds of millions of dollars in state and federal excise taxes.

In Philadelphia, Russians were said to have enlisted the aid of a Scarfo associate (Joseph Kahana) to commit arson on several businesses. Criminal convictions in New York and Florida also provide strong evidence that suspect Russians have associated and conspired with traditional La Cosa Nostra organized crime.

The Criminal Justice System Response
to Russian Crime Networks

Despite the concerns expressed in the media and elsewhere, very few law enforcement agencies have intelligence units actively monitoring the Russian activity. A 1990 *Washington Post* article concluded that "since the Justice Department does not consider the Russian mob to be organized crime, it doesn't treat it with the seriousness that it reserves for more VIP criminals" (Rosenthal, 1990). Rosenthal, an investigative reporter and freelance writer, argues that the federal government does not view Russian criminal activity as meeting the RICO criteria for defining a criminal enterprise. Therefore, he says, federal agencies are not aggressively pursuing the problem. Neither the FBI nor the New York City Police Department are doing anything about it, according to Rosenthal (personal communication). A *New York Times* article similarly concluded that the Russians were not a law enforcement priority because their numbers are small and because their violence has been largely confined to gangland-style executions (A. Mitchell, 1992). The Washington-based organized crime unit of the FBI concedes that it knows relatively little about the Russian organized crime problem in the United States, but expresses a great interest in learning more (personal communication). A 1991 strategic assessment by the Immigration and Naturalization Service consisted mostly of information gleaned from the *New York Times*.

There are many indications, however, that contradict the assertions that law enforcement is not doing anything to combat Russian emigre organized crime. One is a 1991 RICO prosecution of a defendant named Boris

Goldberg. Goldberg was indicted in the U.S. District Court for the Eastern District of New York as the head of a criminal enterprise called the "Goldberg crime group." This racketeering enterprise was charged with trafficking in cocaine, attempted murder, armed robbery and extortion, fraud, illegal dealings with weapons and explosives, and using violence. Goldberg plead guilty to these charges in early 1992.

Among the racketeering counts in the Goldberg indictment was one charging conspiracy to murder one Evsei Agron. The indictment alleged that in early 1983, Goldberg and other members of the Goldberg crime group discussed murdering Agron, and then carried out a surveillance to that end. On January 24, 1984, Agron was shot and seriously wounded. But this was not the end of the matter.

Evsei Agron is said to have been a sort of self-styled "godfather" of Russian organized crime in New York in the early 1980s. One account provided by an independent journalist described Agron and his activities as follows:

> He [Agron] made his reputation through several years spent in Soviet jails, and claimed to be an experienced killer. . . . [According to one source], "Agron was supposedly one of the top people. When he came to this country he must have picked up with some of his old cronies."
>
> Like most real-life mobsters, Agron was a low-life thug. . . . He kept an electric cattle-prod in his car, and specialized in extortion and blackmail. . . . In his prime, he opened up the gasoline racket that would net millions, possibly billions of dollars for the Russians. He made contacts with emigre criminals in Europe. . . .
>
> In May 1985 . . . Agron was shot dead by two assassins posing as joggers. Like most mob murders, this one remains unsolved years later. An Agron lieutenant may have ordered the killing. Other suspects include one of the five crime families in New York's Mafia. (Cornwell, 1992)

Whether Agron and Goldberg and some others who have been labeled leaders give support to the notion that a structured hierarchy exists in the Russian operation is open to question. What is not to be doubted, however, is the obvious willingness to use violence. Further, the indictment suggests multiple and sophisticated criminal enterprises operated through a substantial conspiracy.

By far the most sophisticated and the most lucrative enterprise of the former Soviets is the fuel tax fraud. Its investigation by law enforcement agencies in New York, the U.S. Department of Justice, and the New Jersey

State Commission of Investigation indicates that law enforcement has not been dormant. The nature of the criminal enterprise here is federal and state tax evasion. The estimated tax loss nationally is more than $1 billion annually; and the estimate of annual tax loss for New Jersey is approximately $40 million. This is a huge money-making operation. It exploits the fact that diesel fuel (which is taxable as motor fuel) and home heating oil (which is not taxed) are basically the same product. The tax in this instance acts as a market control, creating the opportunity to illegally market an otherwise legal commodity.

What then is the present state of our knowledge of Soviet emigre organized crime networks? We know that they are probably not homogeneous entities. At least some of these networks are very sophisticated, use violence, have multiple criminal enterprises, may have some degree of structure, and may employ corruption. We do not know much about the continuity of the various networks, nor about their internal structures. We do not know whether they are hierarchical, how large they are, how members become members, whether membership is restricted and if so to whom, what kinds of internal discipline are employed, or, whether there are codes of behavior and secrecy.

There is evidence that some of the conditions Menachim Amir said favored Soviet Georgian emigre involvement in organized crime in Israel in the 1970s may also be present in the United States. All of these emigres came from a society in which they had been socialized into a system in which corruption and deviance were practically the norm. How this affects their actual involvement in organized crime as they become acculturated in American society is not clear. Some of the criminals identified here may have also been criminals, even organized criminals, in the Soviet Union and may have been in prisons there. However, the reliability of existing evidence of this is unknown.

For some of these emigres, here as in Israel, entry into and participation in the underworld has been comparatively easy. Beyond the fuel tax scam, however, there is limited evidence of other collaborative criminal ventures, although the Russian drug smugglers are also believed to have connections with other organized crime groups. Law enforcement has paid relatively little attention to Russian organized crime networks, and no scholarly research has been done. Thus, most of what is generally known about the phenomenon comes from the media. Unfortunately, the media's coverage of the so-called Organizatsiya, relying as it does mostly on anecdotal information, has portrayed Russian organized crime as a unified Russian criminal conspiracy. There is no systematic evidence to support this. That evidence will be produced only through painstakingly thorough investigation and examination of the interconnections among Russian criminals and within the various criminal networks. We believe that the problem warrants serious attention and that both a law enforcement and a research focus on organized crime among Soviet emigres are more than justified.

CONCLUSION

We have attempted to broaden and expand the scope of what is meant by organized crime. Through case examples, we have illustrated the factors that help to define this unique form of crime. We can also observe the gaps in existing theoretical explanations and the areas where new theorizing appears to be necessary. Organized crime is obviously more than the Mafia and it is not unique to the United States. While organized crime clearly comes in many forms, shapes, sizes, and varieties, they all share similar characteristics and a similar objective—to make money. Some of our organized crime, as we will see particularly in the next chapter, is homegrown (for example, street gangs and motorcycle gangs), and some of it is imported (for example, the Colombian drug cartels, the Chinese, and the Russians). This expanded scope points up the growing magnitude of the problem and alerts us to the dangers of being too narrowly focused by a belief in the old Mafia myth. Organized crime in America today wears many faces.

11

⭈⭇⭆

Urban Gangs,
Motorcycle Gangs,
and Hate Groups:

Other Forms of Domestic
Organized Crime?

nyone who has paid even the most casual attention to newspapers, newsmagazines, and television news and documentary coverage over the last five years is bound to be familiar with the nature and magnitude of what is at the same time both an old and a new problem—urban street gangs. They are as old as the gangs studied by Thrasher (1927) in the 1920s and those portrayed in *West Side Story* in the 1950s and as new as crack and gang violence carried out with modern weapons of war. It is estimated that between 60,000 and 70,000 gang members belong to 75 to 100 gangs in Los Angeles alone, and most of these gangs display a high level of street violence (Lyman, 1989).

The crack gangs and the other street gangs that have received so much media attention (and law enforcement attention as well) are often involved in varied criminality and are certainly organized. But are they really and truly a form of organized crime? And are they as serious a problem as the media coverage would have us believe? Recent research has demonstrated that gangs have developed into new, often violent organizational forms. But some scholars criticize the news media for carrying distorted accounts of drug gangs, Jamaican posses, drive-by shootings, and other gang-related

284

phenomena (Huff, 1989). The reality of the street gang problem in the United States and the form and substance of these gangs are the principal issues we will explore in this discussion.

Our working definition of organized crime includes the following characteristics: a self-perpetuating, organized hierarchy that exists to profit from providing illicit goods and services, uses violence in carrying out its criminal activities, and corrupts public officials to immunize itself from law enforcement. Before we apply this definition to the urban street gang, let's see just what an urban street gang is.

Malcolm Klein has studied street gangs extensively over many years and described them this way:

> We shall use the term [street gang] to refer to any denotable . . . group [of adolescents or young adults] who (a) are generally perceived as a distinct aggregation by others in the neighborhood, (b) recognize themselves as a denotable group (almost invariably with a group name), and (c) have been involved in a sufficient number of [illegal] incidents to call forth a consistent negative response from neighborhood residents and/or enforcement agencies. (1971:13)

More recently, Curry and Spergel defined gang crime as

> law-violating behavior committed both by juveniles and adults in or related to groups that are complexly organized although sometimes diffuse, sometimes cohesive with established leadership and membership rules. The gang also engages in a range of crime but significantly more violence within a framework of norms and values in respect to mutual support, conflict relations with other gangs, and a tradition often of turf, colors, signs, and symbols. (1988:382).

These definitions contain some elements common to our working definition of organized crime, for example, organized hierarchy and use of violence, but they contain unique elements as well. The particular focus on the name of the gang—and on colors, signs, and other symbols that identify the gang—seem to make gangs different from what we have called more traditional organized crime groups. The Italian-Sicilian Mafia, for example, had a specific name for itself in only the most vague way. Some members or alleged members in fact indicated that they had never heard the terms *Mafia* or *La Cosa Nostra* used to refer to any criminal organization. Nor did they go out of their way to advertise their organization by wearing distinctive clothes or colors unless, of course, you count the popular image of the gangster in black shirt, white tie, felt hat, and perhaps carrying a violin case. We believe that these differences have a great deal to do with the critical differences in the motives for joining an urban street gang as opposed to another kind of criminal organization and in the objectives of the organization itself. We will deal with these motives shortly.

URBAN GANGS AND TRADITIONAL ORGANIZED CRIME

Corruption, violence, continuity, and involvement in multiple enterprises are characteristics associated with virtually all organized crime groups (Maltz, 1985). Thus, to be considered a valid form of organized crime, gangs should have these characteristics. Structure (of some kind) is necessary, and involvement in legitimate businesses is also characteristic of almost all organized crime groups. Sophistication, discipline, and bonding may be characteristic of some organized crime groups, but these attributes are neither necessary nor typical (Maltz, 1985).

Corruption

We know of no evidence at present to indicate that the typical street gangs considered here systematically engage in paying off public officials to nullify law enforcement. This may be because it doesn't happen, because it happens only rarely and then only at the lowest levels, or simply because no attention has been paid to the issue and therefore we don't know about it. We do know that gangs engage in street crimes that bring them into direct, visible, confrontational and often violent contact with law enforcement authorities. Their activities are frequently not of the more subtle, sophisticated, behind-the-scenes variety that can be readily protected with payoffs. But given that drug dealing is a major activity of some of these gangs, and given that drugs produce enormous profits, corruption is certainly possible and clearly a high risk. We have been told that the New York City Police Department, for example, routinely rotates officers in and out of Chinatown, ostensibly to protect against corruption.

Violence

Violence (or at least the threat of violence) is always present in an organized crime group. One of the dominant characteristics of today's street gangs about which there is little disagreement is that they engage in sudden, often inexplicable and brutal eruptions of violence. California (particularly the

Los Angeles area), is home to the most extensive urban street gang network in the country and is a classic example of this potential for violence. The Bureau of Organized Crime and Criminal Intelligence, California Department of Justice, reported in 1987 that domestic street gangs were being transformed into "huge, violent networks with major drug connections" (1987:1). According to Los Angeles Police Department estimates, half of the 2,000 people killed in Los Angeles in gang-related violence in a ten-year period were innocent bystanders. Gang-related homicides in Los Angeles County rose 83 percent between 1984 and 1987. Weapons confiscated from California gang members have included handguns, semi-automatics, AK-47 assault rifles, sawed-off shotguns, and Uzi machine guns. Fagan (1988) concluded that "serious and violent behaviors occur among a majority of the gangs" (p. 28) he studied. Most street gangs thus clearly meet the violence criterion.

Continuity

Continuity is also a characteristic of many of these gangs. Theirs is not a one-shot, noncontinuous operation, in part because these gangs serve a variety of other functions. In addition to being criminal organizations they also function as social and party groups and, in some cases, these may be their principal functions. Only certain urban street gangs have continuity. Klein and Maxson (1987) remarked on the transience and generally weak cohesiveness of some gangs, noting that these groups form spontaneously, exist for relatively short periods, and disintegrate quickly. Less like criminal gangs, these groups are called "social gangs" and "party gangs" by Fagan (1988), and "hedonistic gangs" by Huff (1989). So only some urban street gangs can be characterized as having continuity.

Multiple Enterprises

Drugs are the principal (only) business enterprise for urban street gangs operating at a high level of criminal activity. They may engage in other crimes, such as property crimes, robberies, street muggings, and crimes of opportunity, but they do not have organized illegal business enterprises providing illicit goods and services such as gambling, prostitution, and loans. No urban street gangs that we know of control commercial vice in their territories.

Structure and Involvement in Legitimate Businesses

Some structural form is necessary if an organized crime group is to maintain a sophisticated, continuous operation. Structure in this case refers to a division of labor into roles and positions. Do urban street gangs have this kind of structure? Yes, it appears that many of them do. Klein and Maxson (1987) contrast gang structures made up of horizontal alliances having different affiliated divisions of gangs with vertical or "area" gangs made up of memberships that are intergenerational and intrafamilial and that are concentrated in one ethnic group or neighborhood. According to Klein and Maxson, neighborhood gangs probably account for most gang crime. Fagan concluded that "gangs have a natural social structure, are well stratified, and appear to undergo developmental sequences not unlike other social groups or organizations" (1988:9). Two types of gangs, the "serious delinquents" and the "young organizations" have, said Fagan, the highest degree of formal organizational structure, including established leaders, rules or codes, formal roles, age stratification for roles, and roles for girls.

For various reasons—the socioeconomic, geographic, and ethnic backgrounds of most gang members, their youth, the motives for getting involved in gangs in the first place, and the money made in drug dealing—there appears to be very little branching out of urban gangs into legitimate businesses.

Sophistication, Discipline, and Bonding

Maltz used the term *sophistication* to describe such activities as speaking in code on the telephone, keeping the principal operators from direct involvement in handling illegal goods, creating dummy corporations, and creating elaborate paper trails. A few street gangs employ some of these techniques, but most do not. Lyman (1989) indicates that OGs (old gangsters) in the Crips street gang manage their crack operations while staying well insulated from the street. The California report on gangs referred to earlier said that these gangs show "increasing sophistication," but most are not particularly sophisticated—or at least not yet anyway.

Discipline, which Maltz (1985) contends is not essential for defining organized crime, is nevertheless a factor in the operations of many urban gangs. The need for discipline seems to be most prevalent in those gangs heavily engaged in the drug business. Fagan (1988) indicates that violence is sometimes used to enforce discipline in drug-dealing gangs. Likewise, in studies of Chinese street gangs in New York City, Chin (1986) found that the gangs were hierarchically organized with strict codes and violent sanctions for members who violated the rules.

Last is bonding. Maltz suggests that "many organized crime groups have rituals that appear to be a combination of mysticism, fraternity initiation rites, and the process of being made a partner in a law firm" (1985:32). This kind of bonding and ritual seem to be a big part of the character of many street gangs. These gangs are often an alternative form of social grouping filling a vacuum left by the disintegration of families in lower-class urban areas. As such, they provide psychic rewards and status and informal social control over members. Bonding ensures some social cohesion, attachment, and commitment to the gang. Lyman provides this example of the use of ritual: "The recruitment, or initiation process will commonly require the recruit to perform a criminal act on behalf of the gang so the members can observe the recruit's street-worthiness" (1989:98).

TYPES OF URBAN STREET GANGS

Fagan (1988) studied gangs in South Central Los Angeles, San Diego, and Chicago, interviewing gang members. Approximately 150 interviews yielded four types of gangs:

Type 1. The *social gang*. This type of gang engages in relatively few delinquent activities and little drug use (other than alcohol and marijuana). These gangs also have relatively low involvement in drug sales.

Type 2. The *party gang*. This type of gang also has a relatively low involvement in criminal behavior. They do commit acts of vandalism, principally graffiti. They also show extensive involvement in drug use. Gang cohesion seems to be based on mutually supportive patterns of drug use and dealing to support group and individual drug use. Their drug dealing is not an organized criminal enterprise.

Type 3. The *serious delinquents*. This is the largest group. Serious delinquents have extensive involvement in several types of delinquent acts but lower involvement in drug sales than Type 4 groups. Their crimes include serious and violent offenses. These gangs have a much more formal organizational structure than the social or party gangs. They are also more violent and engage in more organized criminality and, thus, they much more closely resemble an organized crime group.

Type 4. The *young organizations*. The second largest group, these gangs show an extensive involvement in serious drug use and a high rate of drug sales. Their drug use seems to be systematically related to other criminal acts in that there is a strong relationship among their acts of violence, serious crime, drug use, and drug dealing. These groups are highly cohesive and organized. They are probably at the highest risk of becoming a more formal criminal organization.

Huff (1989) made a two-year study of youth gangs in Ohio, principally in Cleveland and Columbus, and identified three types of gangs. The first he called informal "hedonistic" gangs. Gang members of this type were mainly interested in getting high and in having a good time. They committed some minor property crimes but no violent personal crimes. Hedonistic gangs seem to correspond with Fagan's social and party gang types. Huff's second type, so-called instrumental gangs, committed a high volume of property crimes. Although individual gang members sold drugs, this was not an organized gang activity.

Huff labeled the third type of street gang "predatory" gangs. They committed robberies, street muggings, and other crimes of opportunity. "Members of these gangs are more likely to use highly addictive drugs such as 'crack' cocaine, and these drugs contribute significantly to their . . . assaultive behavior. Members of these gangs may also sell drugs to finance the purchase of more sophisticated weapons. Although this study produced no hard evidence that any of these gangs is currently a 'drug distribution network,' they represent a ready-made 'target of exploitation' for organized crime or other criminal groups" (Huff, 1989:529).

The observation that some gangs are easy targets for exploitation by organized crime groups seeking new drug markets is reinforced by others who have studied urban street gangs. For example, California's Bureau of Organized Crime and Criminal Intelligence observed that "sophisticated organized crime groups often recruit from among street gang members—a process that can quickly transform neophyte gang members into hardened felons" (1987:2). The implication of this is that although the gangs themselves may not be a full-blown form of organized crime, they provide fertile ground for exploitation by, recruitment into, and linkages to organized crime groups. But even standing on their own, at least one type of urban street gang—whether it is called serious delinquents, or young organizations, or predatory—has many of the characteristics and engages in many of the activities associated with organized crime.

Curry and Spergel (1988), take a somewhat different perspective, arguing that it may not be criminal organization and conspiracy that best explain the recent growth and spread of gangs in many parts of the country. Social disorganization and poverty, they say, are better explanations:

> Gangs are residual social subsystems often characterized by competition for status and, more recently, income opportunity through drug sales. They are organizations concerned with territoriality, status, and controlling human behavior. For disadvantaged youths, uncertain in the face of the unstable urban social world, the gang is responsive and provides quasi-stable, efficient, meaningful social, and perhaps economic, structures. In gang membership, there is opportunity to obtain the psychic rewards of personal identity and

minimal standards of acceptable status and sometimes the material benefits of criminal income. (pp. 400–401)

This is not meant to deny that urban gangs engage in forms of organized criminality, but simply to indicate that crime is usually not the initial stimulus that motivates youths to join street gangs.

A CASE EXAMPLE: THE CRIPS
AND THE BLOODS

One of the best-known urban street gangs in the country, the Crips, was formed in 1969/70 in South Central Los Angeles. This gang has gained a particular reputation for dangerousness and violence and reportedly now has branches in Chicago, Kansas City, New York, and other cities. "The structure of the Crips is not as organized . . . as other gangs but a chain of command concept is generally used" (Lyman, 1989:98). According to Lyman, there are three levels of membership in the Crips: Baby Crips or Peewees, who are 11 to 13 years old; Junior Crips (Bangers or Gangsters) who are 13 to 15 years old; and, Crips (Gangsters, OGs, or Rollers), who are 15 to 30 years old. The Crips identifying color is blue.

The principal rivals of the Crips are the Bloods. Their base of operation is in Compton, California, although it is estimated that there are approximately 75 Bloods gangs in the United States. The Bloods identifying color is red. Both Crips and Bloods wear expensive jewelry and drive luxury cars purchased from the fruits of their drug sales. Crack cocaine is the top money maker for both gangs, in part because it is cheap (to make and to buy), easily concealable, and provides a short duration and addicting high, which creates repeat business for the dealer. Both gangs use extreme violence to protect their drug sales turf and to discourage competition. This violence may be directed at each other, at other gangs, at rival organized crime groups, and sometimes at innocent bystanders, referred to as "mushrooms" (Lyman, 1989). Columnist George F. Will, writing in *Newsweek* magazine, described their violence this way:

Crips, who wear blue accessories, would slaughter on sight Bloods wearing any of their trademark red. Why? No reason is required. Atavism often is a sufficient explanation for the random "drive by" shootings that are a favorite mode of self-expression. There is, of course, the traditional territorial imperative, the gangs' struggle for "turf." What is new is the killing for commerce, for market shares in the cocaine and crack business. (March 28, 1988:76)

The Crips and the Bloods are increasingly organized and have established elaborate and extensive crime networks, are among the most violent of the black street gangs, and are a major force in crack trafficking. "These gangs showed more and more of the sophisticated tactics and structure characteristic of traditional organized crime groups" (Bureau of Organized Crime and Criminal Intelligence, 1987:4).

OUTLAW MOTORCYCLE GANGS

Outlaw motorcycle gangs (OMGs) came into being during the period following World War II. "Groups of young men, many newly-returned soldiers, formed motorcycle clubs and rejected normal civilian lifestyles. In the next several years their behavior became not so much boisterous as surly, less rebellious than openly criminal" (President's Commission, 1986:58). The term *outlaw motorcycle gang* seems to have first been used in 1946 after a motorcycle gang riot in Holister, California.

A certain mythology developed during the 1950s and 1960s around motorcycle riders and motorcycle clubs promulgated by such films as *The Wild Ones, Easy Rider,* and *Angels on Wheels.* Marlon Brando and Peter Fonda personified a myth of rebellion, of freedom to do your own thing, of being antiestablishment. However, this perception of motorcycle gangs has changed over the last two decades. "Outlaw" motorcyclists have become much less romantic figures and are more likely to be viewed today as common criminals or worse.

It is estimated that there are somewhere between 800 and 900 motorcycle gangs in the United States ranging from small, loosely organized, single chapters to highly sophisticated, multiple chapter gangs with branches both here and in other countries. The largest of the gangs engage in a multitude of crimes, including murder, extortion, kidnapping, arson, robbery, bombings, receiving stolen property, drug manufacture, and drug trafficking. Drug trafficking is, in fact, their principal source of income. Some gangs are also believed to cooperate with other organized crime groups on occasion.

The structure of the gangs is hierarchical, with rules of conduct set forth in club charters and constitutions. The symbol of membership in a gang is usually the gang "colors." These are considered to be one of the proudest possessions of gang members. Colors are "usually a sleeveless denim or leather jacket with embroidered patches sewn on the back. The patches display a gang logo, sometimes slogans or initials; there may also be 'rockers' that identify the name of the gang and the home city of the chapter. The colors . . . represent the foremost commitment of his life—his commitment to the gang and its criminal lifestyle" (President's Commission, 1986:60).

Four gangs have gained national or international stature, and these will be the focus of our attention here. These four are the Hells Angels, the Outlaws, the Pagans, and the Bandidos. They are recognized as the largest and most powerful of the OMGs because of their membership and degree of criminal involvement. Together they are estimated to have more than 3,000 members—a membership exceeding that of the traditional organized crime families of the United States. Altogether, in all OMGs, there are an estimated 7,000 gang members, 4,000 male hangers-on, and 8,000 female associates (U.S. Senate, 1983). This represents the largest criminal organization in the country today.

The Hells Angels

The Hells Angels are considered to be the wealthiest and most powerful of the motorcycle gangs. In addition to their membership in the United States, they have chapters in Brazil, Canada, Colombia, Australia, New Zealand, Japan, and seven western European countries. In testimony during the 1983 U.S. Senate hearings on organized crime, an agent from the Bureau of Alcohol, Tobacco and Firearms said, "We believe collectively that the Hells Angels motorcycle club is by far the most dangerous outlaw motorcycle gang in the United States and poses the greatest propensity for violence" (U.S. Senate, 1983:365). According to Lyman (1989): "[The] 20 year transformation [from 'Pissed Off Bastards of Bloomington'] has changed the Hells Angels from a rowdy unorganized group of troublemakers to a modern, sophisticated organized crime organization" (p. 79). The Pissed Off Bastards of Bloomington (POBOB) was the original name of the Hells Angels, and it was they who were involved in the aforementioned Hollister, California, incident. That incident revolved around the attempt by some POBOB members to free a fellow member from the local jail in Hollister. This biker had been arrested during a fight at a series of motorcycle races held over the Fourth of July weekend in 1946.

The Hells Angels have sophisticated and extensive counterintelligence efforts to protect themselves from arrest and prosecution. The President's Commission on Organized Crime reported that some clubhouses "are fortified with elaborate electronic and physical security systems. Gang members do extensive background checks on prospective members, often using female associates who have been placed in positions with public utilities, government services, and law enforcement agencies to assist them" (1986:65). Hells Angels also have extensive networks of limousine companies, motorcycle shops, catering operations, bars and restaurants, antique stores, and landscaping operations used to launder their illegal drug money.

The Outlaws

The Outlaws are also an international organization. They are generally considered to be less sophisticated but even more violent than the Hells Angels. They have some 1,500 members spread over the United States, Canada, and Australia. Like the Hells Angels, the Outlaws are heavily involved in the production and distribution of methamphetamines. Also like the Hells Angels, they have a number of legitimate businesses—pornographic bookstores, massage parlors, marine sales and storage, and others.

The Bandidos

The Bandidos have an estimated membership of approximately 600 and are located principally in Texas. The Bandidos are involved in an array of crimes —murder, arson, larceny, weapons offenses, armed robbery, illegal use of dynamite and other explosives—and in the manufacture of methamphetamines and the distribution of both meth and cocaine. Massage parlors and escort services are said to be favored legitimate business enterprises.

The Pagans

Only the Pagans, of the four major OMGs, have no international connections. They have a total membership estimated at about 900, with 400 alone in Pennsylvania. According to the President's Commission on Organized Crime, the Pagans are considered "second only to the Hells Angels in criminal sophistication, and the strength of their internal structure is unmatched by any of the other three major gangs" (President's Commission, 1986:72). They are also said to have the closest ties to traditional organized crime. Members of the Pagans are thought to be used as hitmen and enforcers by organized crime groups (McGuire, 1986).

THE PHILOSOPHY OF OUTLAW MOTORCYCLE GANGS

Bikers originally strove to live lives totally unlike those of others in the community. They did not want to live as normal citizens. Therefore, they rejected generally accepted norms and instead adopted their own morals, ethics, and norms. The latter are reflected in their dress, mannerisms, and criminal lifestyle—much of which is considered to be repulsive, offensive, shocking, and disgusting by the rest of society. The OMG philosophy has been summed up in this way. " 'Fuck the World' (FTW) is their motto and reflects the arrogant attitude adopted by this sub-culture in pursuit of its goals and objectives. The members have opted out of society; they do not wish to be like normal citizens or dress like them; that is why they are eager to perform shocking and disgusting acts. Their policy on retribution is 'an eye for an eye' and they enforce their distinctive code of honor strictly. . . . The second priority in the biker's life, after his club colors, is his motor-cycle. . . . The biker's third priority is either his dog or his woman. . . . An-other of the basic philosophies of motorcycle gangs reflects certain racist theories [many bikers are said to be white supremacists with beliefs parallel-ing those of the Ku Klux Klan]. . . . Finally, loyalty—not only to the club but to all its members—is one of the rules that is strictly enforced" (Report of Interpol General Secretariat, 1984:173).

The outlaw motorcycle gangs, especially the big four, clearly seem to espouse a philosophy that incorporates the organized crime attributes of violence and discipline. For example, the charters and rules for the gangs spell out the penalties for rules infractions—penalties that include burning off club tattoos and assassination.

Bonding is also characteristic of these gangs. It begins with the initia-tion process into the gang. A former Hells Angel described their initiation process to the Senate committee holding hearings on organized crime. Potential members, he said, must have a good motorcycle (a Harley-Davidson), be white, and be 21 or older. During the initial probationary period, called a hang around, the candidate must do a lot of fighting. There is also a lot of flunky work. Next, the candidate becomes a prospect. This is done by vote of the membership. Prospects also do flunky work—clean bikes, work on bikes, keep watch in the clubhouse, and stay on 24-hour call. Finally, they can be voted in as members. Then, they have to "roll their bones," that is, they have to kill someone. If they fail to do this, according to this witness, they themselves will be killed because by this time they know too much (U.S. Senate, 1983:414–416).

CRIMINAL ACTIVITIES OF OUTLAW
MOTORCYCLE GANGS:
MULTIPLE ENTERPRISES AND CORRUPTION

Outlaw motorcycle gangs seem willing to do virtually anything to make money. Their multiple criminal enterprises include motorcycle thefts in which the stolen bikes are sold in whole or in part through gang-operated repair shops. The gangs also provide prostitution services in which female associate members perform in club-owned massage parlors, bars, and night-clubs. Gangs deal in the transportation and sale of stolen weapons, including explosives and even antitank weapons. Other crimes for profit include contract murder, extortion, burglary, forgery, counterfeiting, fraud, loan-sharking, bombings, gambling, kidnapping, international white slavery, assaults, and arson. But their single biggest money maker is the drug business.

The gangs manufacture LSD, PCP, and methamphetamines. They market these manufactured drugs along with other drugs such as cocaine, heroin, and marijuana. The fact that they manufacture their own products means that they increase their profit margin. It has been estimated by the Drug Enforcement Administration that OMGs control at least 40 percent of the entire United States methamphetamine supply. The illegal drug business has made millionaires out of some gang members. In fact, the President's Commission on Organized Crime cited reports that gang members were "abandoning their outlaw image, wearing business suits and driving luxury cars: in essence, becoming an outlaw motorcycle gang without motor-cycles" (President's Commission, 1986:65).

California's Bureau of Organized Crime and Criminal Intelligence (1987) reported that many OMGs in that state run their operations on a continuing basis as highly profitable, criminal enterprises. The report cites examples of criminal cases involving the Hells Angels that illustrate the scope of their criminal activities:

> In November [1987], a massive sweep by federal and state law enforcement investigators resulted in the arrests of 39 members of the Hells Angels. . . . They were charged with various federal offenses including conspiracy to murder members of a rival club, racketeering, and drug, explosives, and weapons violations. . . . Altogether, agents seized $3 million in cash, 30 pounds of methamphetamine, 25 pounds of gold, one drug lab, and numerous weapons and explosives in the culmination of the two-year investigation. (1987:30).

OMGs share with traditional organized crime groups a willingness to use violence and a willingness to use corruption—the former as a method of controlling competition, the latter as a method of preventing detection, arrest, and prosecution. Testimony concerning OMG corruption of police and other public officials was offered by former Hells Angel "Butch," at the U.S. Senate hearings:

> SENATOR GRASSLEY: In your experience as a Hells Angel, were you aware of any public officials that they were able to contact in order to obtain information not normally available to the public?

BUTCH: Yes; police officers in a couple of towns that provided a lot of information, movements of clubs. . . .

THE CHAIRMAN: Do you have firsthand information about these police officials?

BUTCH: Yes; I do.

THE CHAIRMAN: Without divulging the names of the policemen, could you tell us just what they did to cooperate with or assist the Hells Angels?

BUTCH: Yes; there was a telephone installed in a clubhouse, and one police official had this number, and it was call forwarding.

This phone was installed in the closet upstairs. No one was supposed to touch it. It was for specific phone calls from this one police official that he would call in case there was any word that he had to give us on indictments or anything that pertained to any club member.

It was a call forwarding type thing, that you called it, and then it went on out to someone else's house, to the president's house. He had the number and another policeman had the number. (U.S. Senate, 1983:417–418)

ORGANIZATIONAL STRUCTURE OF
OUTLAW MOTORCYCLE GANGS

Outlaw motorcycle gangs display a continuity and sophistication in their operations that qualifies them as an organized crime group. The California report on organized crime said that like their counterparts in La Cosa Nostra, for example, these groups "are often structured to shield their leaders from investigation and prosecution; are involved in continuing criminal enterprises, such as narcotics trafficking; and use violence to achieve their ends" (Bureau of Organized Crime and Criminal Intelligence, 1987:28). Likewise, the executive director of the Chicago Crime Commission concluded that motorcycle gangs have many similarities to the generally accepted structure of organized crime. Some, he said, are even incorporated in various states as not-for-profit organizations. And they have a degree of sophistication that enlarges their sphere of influence, extending it into legitimate businesses (Healy, 1984). The larger of the gangs use a portion of their profits from criminal activity to invest in legitimate enterprises.

Two officials from the Bureau of Alcohol, Tobacco, and Firearms who testified before the U.S. Senate hearings on organized crime spoke of the similarities and links between outlaw motorcycle gangs and what we have called traditional Mafia-type organized crime. The first was acting director Stephen E. Higgins, who said:

> It can be argued that all of these segments of organized crime in America have much in common. They are largely formed around an ethnic base, and while accommodations have been made among the groups, ultimately the core of each group adheres to a sense of cultural or racial brotherhood. Most adhere to bizarre initiation rituals and oaths, including the commission of felonious acts by prospective members. (U.S. Senate, 1983:304)

Assistant Director McGuire offered this assessment of OMGs as bona fide organized groups in his testimony:

> THE CHAIRMAN: You go further to state that outlaw motorcyclists have made the grade in bigtime crime. In your opinion, would you consider outlaw motorcycle groups to be as powerful as the LCN?
>
> MR. MCGUIRE: Well, in terms of numbers, I would definitely say yes, and also in terms of the propensity for violence, I would say yes. In terms of wealth and their ability to penetrate legitimate society, I do not think they have at this time, and part of the reason is their inability to work with each other as the LCN has been able to do. . . .
>
> THE CHAIRMAN: Mr. McGuire, do you consider outlaw motorcyclists to be more violent than the LCN?
>
> MR. MCGUIRE: Definitely, I do. If you look at the roots of these gangs and their antisocial attitudes and the enclaves that they came out of years ago, there is no question that they have a tremendous propensity for violence. That has never lessened and that is really the leverage that they have used in many areas to get a hold of the criminal organizations in the past. . . .
>
> THE CHAIRMAN: Mr. McGuire, does ATF have any evidence of traditional organized criminal groups using outlaw motorcycle gang members as hit men or enforcers?
>
> MR. MCGUIRE: Yes, sir, we know for a fact that outlaw motorcyclists have performed bombings and arsons for the more traditional organized crime groups. Additionally, at the time of the death of Phil Testa up in the Philadelphia area and when Nicodemo Scarfo took over the organized crime family there, there was certainly evidence that the Pagans were involved in the death of Phil Testa.

THE CHAIRMAN: Mr. McGuire, the outlaw motorcycle gangs comprise the largest criminal group in the United States today and are the best armed. Why are they not taking over control of all LCN enterprises?

MR. MCGUIRE: Well, as I mentioned earlier, the gangs do not really have the national cooperation that the LCN does. . . . They probably lack the ambition or desire to challenge the LCN at this time, but that does not mean that they will not be better prepared in the future. And if all of the different gangs in the United States ever got together, I think that they could probably take on the LCN. (U.S. Senate, 1983:341–342)

McGuire went on to describe how the OMGs have cooperated with traditional organized crime in the drug manufacture and distribution business. The gangs, he said, "acquire the precursor chemicals for the manufacture of these drugs oftentimes from the more traditional LCN members." And, "they also acquire the hard narcotics that must be imported internationally from the more traditional LCN" (U.S. Senate, 1983:342).

Outlaw motorcycle gangs have an organized hierarchy, sophisticated operations, and internal discipline and bonding. They are extremely violent; they have multiple criminal enterprises providing illegal goods and services such as drugs, prostitution, gambling, and guns and other weapons; they corrupt the police and perhaps other public officials to immunize themselves from law enforcement; and they invest their ill-gotten gains in a host of legitimate businesses. Are they a true form of organized crime? It would certainly seem so.

PRISON GANGS AND ASSORTED HATE GROUPS

In his testimony during the 1983 U.S. Senate hearings on organized crime, then Attorney General William French Smith described several different forms of nontraditional organized crime groups. One of these was prison gangs. Prison gangs have been defined as close-knit, disruptive groups of prison inmates whose organization varies from loosely to tightly structured and whose direction ranges "from informal word-of-mouth slogans and rules to formal and written creeds and regulations" (U.S. Senate, 1983:11). The gangs are normally secretive and exclusive. Their purposes range from mutual caretaking of members to large profit-making enterprises. Their activities deviate from typical inmate behavior, and they are disruptive of normal prison operations (Camp & Camp, 1985).

These gangs, said Attorney General Smith, "were first established as a result of associations developed in the California State Prison system over the past 20 years. Today, they operate both inside and outside prison. They remain predominantly a west coast phenomenon, but there is evidence that they are spreading" (U.S. Senate, 1983:11). Likewise, then FBI Director Webster referred to "prison-spawned gangs" as follows:

> The prison-spawned gangs developed inside the California State Prison System in the 1960's. They . . . are quasi-military, violence-prone, highly structured criminal enterprises whose influence now extends well beyond prison walls. They engage in a wide range of criminal activities including narcotics and weapons trafficking, extortion, robbery, and murder. These gangs include the Mexican Mafia, La Nuestra Familia, the Aryan Brotherhood and the Black Guerilla Family. (U.S. Senate, 1983:54)

Not everyone would agree that prison gangs are a valid form of organized crime. This disagreement is based largely on the unique and limited environment of the gangs, that is, the prison environment. But in fact, they seem to fit in very well with some of the criteria defining organized crime groups—for example, their use of violence, disciplining of members, and engaging in multiple enterprises. They meet some criteria in a somewhat different form—using corruption to nullify law enforcement, for example, must be limited to prison officials. And on some criteria, they do not seem to meet the requirements at all, for example, engaging in legitimate businesses. However, some of these gangs have fairly major operations outside of prison, and it just might be that some of the outside operations involves infiltration or operation of ostensibly legal businesses.

One characteristic of many prison gangs (and most particularly of all the so-called hate groups we will also look at here) that causes an additional problem in classifying them as organized crime groups is that they are ideological. Not all prison gangs are organized for purely criminal purposes; a number of them have a political or cultural agenda as well. And all the hate groups have a very definite political agenda, and their criminal acts are almost exclusively carried out in the service of that agenda.

Why is this a problem? Our working definition of organized crime proposed that the organization should be nonideological. Including this element in the definition of organized crime excludes groups whose criminality is only peripheral or instrumental to their main purposes. We will examine the issue of ideology as we describe the groups in this section.

WHAT ARE PRISON GANGS?

Prison gangs, of the kind we are discussing here, are not found in every prison in the country, nor does every inmate belong to a gang. On the contrary, a survey done for the U.S. Department of Justice in 1985 identified 114 different gangs with approximately 13,000 members (the total prison population is about three-quarters of a million inmates). Nevertheless, prison gangs play a significant role in drug trafficking both inside and outside the prisons where they operate. And they are heavily involved in weapons trafficking, extortion, robbery, and murder. Thus, they present a serious problem.

As part of their cultural and political ideologies, many of the gangs have adopted racial superiority considerations as integral to their basic philosophies. Their bonding and their use of discipline and violence are reflected in initiation rites that require commission of a violent act (either murder or drawing blood of another inmate or of a prison employee); in their codes of conduct; in their requirements for blind loyalty and discipline ensured through intimidation, threats of violence, and actual violence; and, through established codes of secrecy. A number of these gangs are particularly violent. Their organizational structure is generally characterized by an established system of leadership and a chain of command. In some cases, this organizational structure closely resembles that of more traditional organized crime groups.

Perhaps the most extensive national survey of prison gangs was the one done for the Department of Justice in 1985 (Camp & Camp, 1985). It surveyed state and federal prison officials across the country and conducted intensive case studies in a number of states. The Camps concluded that geography and ethnicity were the two most important criteria in determining different gang types:

> Membership is based first on race, and is usually connected with racial superiority beliefs. Second, prior affiliation or association with members in a close-to home location can strongly influence membership. Next in importance is the sharing of strong beliefs, political and/or religious. Finally, sharing a lifestyle of motorcycle machoism influences membership. (pp. 30–31)

Many prison gangs have counterpart gangs on the streets. Their principal criminal activities—enterprises operated both inside and outside—include extortion, contract murder, drugs, homosexual prostitution, gambling, and protection. Some of the gangs clearly have multiple criminal enterprises. Like their organized crime counterparts elsewhere, the gangs provide essential goods and services, protect their members and exploit others, and acquire and distribute goods (primarily drugs) in the prison.

> Without exception, violence or the threat of violence is the most prevalent and powerful factor in the maintenance of the gang. . . . All gangs share some common values which can be expressed in terms of their emphasis on power and prestige [which are measured in terms of control of other inmates and prison activities]. . . . The pursuit of ganghood is analogous to the lifestyle of the career criminal. The gang member is completely immersed in being a career prison gangster, leaving little time and less inclination for other than asocial behavior. (Camp & Camp, 1985:39, 41, 42-43)

Survey respondents in some jurisdictions indicated that there was evidence that prison gangs used the prison as a base for crime in the community. California authorities, for example, reported the following on gang connections to the outside:

> All of the gangs have connections to the outside. The Department says that they [the gangs] have expanded their criminal operations into the communities and have evolved into a major organized crime enterprise. Officials are aware of sharing of information, but not of orders being issued from the inside of the walls. The history of murders outside the prisons that have resulted from prison gang activities is staggering. The estimate of homicides from 1975 to 1984 stood at 372.
>
> There has been evidence of contacts between organized crime figures and prison gang figures. Officials also know that there is inter-organizational activity between prisons in California and between prisons and the California Youth Authority institutions for purposes of recruitment. Nevada, Arizona, Missouri, and the [Federal] Bureau of Prisons have reported . . . that there has been contact between their gang members and California gang members. (Camp & Camp, 1985:107–108)

Illinois officials reported that "the outside and the inside" are divided only by the prison barrier, and business is transacted freely across that barrier.

The President's Commission on Organized Crime reported that members released from prison remain in the gang and that they often provide support and enforcement for the organization inside. The commission concluded that several of these prison gangs "are sophisticated, self-perpetuating, and involved in illegal acts for power and profit with operations outside the prison" (President's Commission, 1986:74). Five gangs, according to the commission, meet the criteria for being classified as organized crime groups. It is to these five that we next turn.

MAJOR PRISON GANGS

The Mexican Mafia

The Mexican Mafia is one of the oldest of the prison gangs. It is principally composed of Mexican-Americans from southern California. The gang has some 350 members and associates in California but also has branches in seven other states. The organization's leadership structure is said to be very similar to that of La Cosa Nostra. It controls homosexual prostitution, gambling, and narcotics in certain prisons. The gang is involved in burglary, assault, robberies, extortion, drug trafficking, and contract killings both inside and outside of prison.

La Nuestra Familia

La Nuestra Familia was originally established in California's Soledad Prison in 1967. It has approximately 300 members and associates and has established "regiments" outside prison. As an example of its outside operations (and the similarity of these operations to more traditional organized crime), La Nuestra Familia runs a protection racket in which it harasses small, local businessmen through vandalism, theft, and robbery and then offer them protection against such acts in the future.

The Texas Syndicate

This group emerged as a violent prison gang in California's Folsom Prison in 1974. It is made up of Mexican-American inmates who originally came from around El Paso and San Antonio, Texas. It has gained a reputation in the prison system as being one of the most violent gangs of all. According to the President's Commission on Organized Crime, the Texas Syndicate is the largest gang in the Texas prison system and is active in drug trafficking, contract murders, assaults, and intimidation. It also operates in federal prisons. Its criminal involvement encompasses extensive illegal activities outside the prison, including contract killings, narcotics trafficking, and importation of aliens.

The Black Guerilla Family

This prison gang was founded by black activist prison inmate George Jackson at San Quentin Prison in 1966. It is politically oriented and has as its principal goals the cultural unity and protection of black prison inmates. There are approximately 500 members and associates in California, and offshoot gangs in Nevada and in federal prisons. The gang is said to be closely aligned with the Crips street gang.

The Aryan Brotherhood

This motorcycle-oriented, white supremacist gang was formed in San Quentin Prison in the 1960s. Most of its members are or have been members of outlaw motorcycle gangs. Its membership is limited to whites, and it focuses its aggression on blacks. The gang's criminal activities include extortion and robberies of inmates' families outside prison, protection schemes, drug trafficking, intimidation and violence, and contract murder. The gang has about 300 members and associates in California, with other operations in Kentucky, Missouri, and the federal prisons.

These latter two gangs, in particular are examples of ideologically oriented groups. The Black Guerilla Family is said to be the most politically oriented of the prison gangs and to have adopted a Maoist philosophy. It is associated with the Black Liberation Army. Young black inmates are encouraged to join the Black Guerilla Family to survive the efforts of the white power structure, which is said to be using the prison system as a tool to destroy them. At the other extreme, the Aryan Brotherhood is associated with the Ku Klux Klan and other right-wing hate groups. Neo-Nazi recruiters from the Aryan Brotherhood and other like groups tell white prisoners that they are actually prisoners of war, incarcerated by a Jewish-dominated system that favors blacks and other minorities. It is to these groups that we turn last in this section.

SURVIVALISTS AND OTHER HATE GROUPS

The so-called Survival Right groups are complex in ideology and tend to be more dangerous in practice than other dissident or criminal organizations that have emerged in this country. Not merely a problem of isolated hate groups, right-wing extremists can be found in every region and every state in the country.

Reporter James Coates, who has studied and written about them, says this about the Survival Right groups:

> Armed to the teeth and demonstrably erratic, they . . . are a dangerously active domestic network of terrorists who continue to pose the threat of political assassination, racial violence, and virtually any type of armed mayhem one can conjure. . . . Survivalist groups throughout the country have been linked to sophisticated counterfeiting schemes, terrorist bombings, masterful loan fraud operations, daring armored car robberies, theft rings, a raft of murders, and thousands of federal firearms and explosives violations. (1987:11–15)

Given their sophistication, their structure and organization, the careful degree of planning that goes into their varied crimes, and their willingness to use violence, we should examine this movement more carefully. Four of the best known right-wing extremist groups are discussed below. Poland (1988), Mullins (1988), and others have described at least 30 other organizations that, although smaller and less visible, share common goals and a similar willingness to use crime and violence to accomplish their goals.

The Aryan Nations

Probably the largest and almost certainly the most violent of the right-wing organizations, the Aryan Nations was founded in the late 1970s as the Church of Jesus Christ Christian. While they espouse elimination of all minorities and Jews, members have stockpiled weapons and sought to unify the radical right in an effort to establish a "white homeland" in the northwest (Barker, 1985; Sapp, 1987). Urging immediate violent action, this group has claimed responsibility for numerous bombings in the Hayden Lake and Coeur D'Alene regions of Idaho and is thought to have plans to bomb bridges, sewers, and utility systems; sabotage highways and water supplies; and assassinate police and public officials. The Aryan Nations is reported to have developed international contacts with the Syrian government to obtain finances and weapons (Mullins, 1988). Unfortunately, little independent information about its structure and membership is available.

The Order

In the belief that the group was not sufficiently violent, some members of the Aryan Nations separated in the early 1980s to form a splinter group known alternately as the Order, the White American Bastion, the Aryan Resistance Movement, and the White American Army of National Liberation for the Aryan Nations (Sapp, 1987). Believing themselves to be "God's

Army," and that all activities are done in God's name, the Order is known to consider law enforcement personnel as agents of Satan needing elimination. Following a raid by the FBI in 1984, police learned that this group had prepared an enemies list of federal judges, prosecutors, law enforcement officials, and civil rights leaders who were presumably to be targeted for assassination. In addition to stockpiles of weapons and extensive intelligence files, officers also discovered members' plans to bomb the Boundry Bridge in Seattle, rob the Brinks terminal in San Francisco, poison water supplies in several municipalities, and disrupt shipping in the Puget Sound with LAW rockets (Mullins, 1988). Successful campaigns include:

- December 20, 1983—robbery of City Bank in Seattle
- April 23, 1984—robbery of Continental Armed Transport in Seattle, netting $500,000
- April 29, 1984—bombing of a Jewish Synagogue in Boise, Idaho
- June 18, 1984—assassination of Denver radio talk-show host Alan Berg
- July 19, 1984—robbery of Brinks armed truck in Ukiah, California, netting $3 million
- October 18, 1984—shootout with FBI at Sandpoint, Idaho
- November 24, 1984—shootout with FBI at Portland, Oregon
- December 8, 1984—shootout with FBI at Whidbey Island, Washington
- April 15, 1985—shootout with Missouri State Police (Mullins, 1988)

The Ku Klux Klan (KKK)

Born out of the post–Civil War turmoil, the Klan was intended as a vigilante organization in response to the bitter Reconstruction era of carpetbaggers and fear of a violent backlash by black freed men. With an original charter that spoke of its desire to defend the weak, the defenseless, and the oppressed as well as to uphold the law, including the Constitution, the early Klan drew into its order some of the best men of the South. Many are surprised to learn that as late as the 1920s, the Klan's membership included such notables as Harry Truman (who withdrew after a brief membership), Supreme Court Justice Edward White, and the distinguished justice and civil libertarian Hugo Black. Black, who was a member for two years, went so far as to publicly thank Klansmen for making his election to the United States Senate possible (Johnson, 1967). Unfortunately, once the carpetbaggers were driven from the South after the Civil War and the feared black backlash failed to materialize, most of the better members dropped out, leaving a core membership of poor, ignorant whites who felt resentment and feared economic competition. Violence became such a cause in itself that within only a few years the founders of the original "Invisible Empire" attempted to disband the organization and destroy all of its records. The Klan, according to its early and ardent supporters, had become perverted from its original purpose and had "fallen into low and violent hands" (Johnson, 1967:10). Membership in the Klan, with its focus on patriotism and nationalism, has deteriorated from almost 500,000 members at the organization's height in the 1920s to roughly 10,000 thought now to belong to one of three major factions and a variety of splinter groups. The three major factions of the Ku Klux Klan are the Invisible Empire, the Knights of the Ku Klux Klan, and the United Klans of America. Table 11.1 lists the splinter groups linked to the Klan.

Table 11.1 Splinter Groups Linked to the Ku Klux Klan

California	Invisible Empire, Knights of the White Rose California Knights of the Ku Klux Klan White Heritage Knights of the Ku Klux Klan
Georgia	New Order Knights of the Ku Klux Klan
Iowa	White Knights of the Ku Klux Klan
Michigan	White Ku Klux Klan
Missouri	Confederation of Independent Orders Knights of the Ku Klux Klan National Knights of the Ku Klux Klan New Order Ku Klux Klan
North Carolina	Carolina Ku Klux Klan Federated Knights of the Ku Klux Klan New Empire Ku Klux Klan White Knights of the Ku Klux Klan
Ohio	Independent Invisible Knights Ohio Knights of the Ku Klux Klan
Pennsylvania	United Empire Knights of the Ku Klux Klan
Tennessee	Justice Knights of the Ku Klux Klan United Empire Knights of the Ku Klux Klan
Texas	Knights of the White Camellia

Source: W. Mullins (1988), *Terrorist Organizations in the United States.* Springfield, IL: Charles C Thomas.

The Covenant, the Sword, and
the Arm of the Lord (CSA)

Like most white supremacist organizations, the CSA harbors a deep hatred of communists and Jews and believes that whites are God's chosen race. Founded in 1970 in Arkansas, the CSA is known to conduct extensive paramilitary and survivalist training at the Endtime Overcomer Survival Training School, an Arkansas compound maintained by the organization. The CSA's preparation for the future it envisions became obvious during a 1985 raid where police and FBI agents discovered:

- Kruggerands, other gold, and silver,
- LAW rockets,
- 94 rifles of varying calibers,
- 30 handguns,
- 35 automatic rifles,
- varied sawed-off shotguns,
- 2 land mines,
- 25 explosive devices,
- 40 hand grenades,
- 50 sticks of dynamite,
- 38 sticks of kinetic explosives,
- 3.5 blocks of C-4 explosive,
- smoke grenades, and
- thousands of rounds of ammunition.

Although small in numbers with an estimated membership of no more than 50, the CSA has been active. James Ellison, the group's founder and leader, has been charged several times with various crimes, including arson for profit (1980) in the burning of his sister's house, arson (1983) of a church for homosexuals, arson (1983) of a Jewish community center, and bombing (1983) a natural gas pipeline. In 1985, another eight members received prison sentences under the RICO statutes. And in 1984, CSA member Richard Snell shot and killed an Arkansas State Trooper (Mullins, 1988).

IDEOLOGIES OF RIGHT-WING EXTREMISM

Three ideological belief systems can be identified for American right-wing organizations. These are: Christian conservatism, white supremacy, and patriotism-survival. Each of the extreme right-wing organizations known to be operating in the United States is believed to subscribe to at least one, and often all three, of these value systems.

The Christian Conservative Identity Movement

It is safe to argue that Christian conservatism was the underlying force most prevalent in right-wing extremism in the United States during the past decade. Religion serves to strengthen beliefs and to provide a rationale and justification for behaviors and actions. Unfortunately, it also has the capacity to serve as a unifying factor among diverse groups having otherwise different values and opinions. The primary religious motive for the crimes of these groups is the "identity" movement, based on a theology that features racial and national pride.

Racial identity seeks to divide the world's population into four primary groups: Enosh, Man, Jews, and Mongrels. Enosh, meaning non-men who are descended from animals, is a reference reserved for blacks. Jews, on the other hand, are said to be directly descended from Cain who was born to Eve after she was seduced by Satan in the form of a serpent. Cain was thus "the spawn of Satan" who then bred with the Enosh to start the Jewish "race." Man, made in the image of God, descended from Adam and Eve and became the white or Aryan race. Other races and people of color are said to be "mongrels" resulting from breeding Jews, Enosh, and "race mixing" whites. Racial purity is an all-important concept and race mixing is unforgivable and deserving of death. Race traitors, those who support mixing the races in any way, are also to be put to death (Kenney, Ginger, Sapp, and McNamara, 1990).

National identity denies Jews as Israelites and teaches that the lost tribes were Aryans who found their way to western Europe, the British Isles, and North America and created the Aryan nations. The United States is the "Promised Land," intended by God for whites and only whites. Additionally, those supporting these concepts believe that whites in the United States must purify the promised land by removing or eliminating all Jews and non-whites to prepare for the Second Coming of Christ. Thus, identity theology promotes white supremacy and both justifies and encourages violence against Jews and non-whites in the name of God (Holden, 1985; Sapp, 1987; Mullins, 1988).

The actual plan of action to implement their beliefs is offered to the Christian conservatives in the form of the *Turner Diaries*, a 1980 novel by William Pierce (under the pseudonym Andrew McDonald). Here, law enforcement officers at all levels are described as Jewish agents of the "Zionist

Occupational Government" (ZOG) who must be removed as obstacles. As such, a plan for survival and domination that includes destruction of police facilities, assassinations of non-Aryans and other "race criminals," and other criminal acts is offered. Further, the *Diaries* call for eliminating Jews by nuclear strikes against Tel Aviv and New York and hanging Jews, blacks, Catholics, and other minorities and religious groups nationwide (Mullins, 1988). In short, these extremists consider terror and political violence to be a moral imperative.

White Supremacy

Many right-wing extremists not associated with the identity churches are nonetheless driven to achieve white supremacy. The Ku Klux Klan and the more recently emerging skinhead groups believe that whites are genetically, intellectually, and morally superior to nonwhites. Jews become targets of these groups as well, since they are believed to control the economy and are thought to favor and support nonwhites over whites. While similar in many respects to the religious radicals, these groups are motivated to violence through hatred alone rather than by religious beliefs. Many skinheads, in fact, are anti-Christian as well, believing that Christianity is actually a "Jewish conspiracy" to control non-Jews.

Patriotism–Survival

These groups base their values and belief systems on a love of America and the "American way of life." Tending to be ultraconservative and fiercely anticommunist, many believe that war with communism is inevitable. They have been taught to fear nuclear attacks on major cities with the survivors of those attacks left to swarm over the rural countryside raping, murdering, and stealing food from the rural populace. Others are convinced that large-scale urban riots will have similar effects to nuclear war. To protect themselves and their families, many have established safe areas where they stockpile weapons, ammunition, food, and other survival necessities.

RIGHT-WING EXTREMISM AS ORGANIZED CRIME?

Are these groups organized? Yes, or at least most of them are after a fashion. Do they engage in criminal behavior as a group? Yes, very definitely. But are they an organized crime group? We think not. They are rather what the Bureau of Organized Crime and Criminal Intelligence (1987)

Table 11.2 Defining Domestic Groups as Organized Crime

GROUP TYPE	CORRUPTION	VIOLENCE	CONTINUITY	MULTIPLE CRIMINAL ENTERPRISES	STRUCTURE	INVOLVING LEGITIMATE BUSINESSES	SOPHISTICATION	DISCIPLINE	BONDING
Street gangs		X	X		X		X		X
Outlaw motorcycle gangs	X	X	X	X	X	X	X	X	X
Prison gangs		X	X	X	X			X	
Survivalists	X		X	X		X			
Hate groups		X	X		X		X	X	X

Note: Definitional criteria adapted from M. Maltz (1985), "Towards Defining Organized Crime." In H. Alexander and G. Caiden (eds.), *The Politics and Economics of Organized Crime*. Lexington, MA: D.C. Heath.

called "criminal extremists." That is, they are a group of people who form an alliance and commit crimes to advance their causes or beliefs. Their ideology and seeking political as opposed to economic power puts them in a different category from other groups we have discussed. They do not exist to profit from providing illicit goods and services in public demand. They do not conduct multiple criminal enterprises toward the end of making a profit. They do not engage in corruption of public officials. They do not infiltrate, set up, or otherwise exploit legitimate businesses to achieve their ends. The survivalists are driven by an ideology—political, religious, or cultural—and their criminality is only a means to an end, not the end itself. Thus, they are not a form of organized crime.

CONCLUSION

Among the various groups described here, the outlaw motorcycle gangs best meet the criteria of organized crime groups (see Table 11.2 on page 311). Their organized hierarchical structure, use of violence and corruption, multiple criminal enterprises, infiltration of legitimate businesses, and so on undoubtedly qualify them for the label "organized crime." Next come the more sophisticated of the urban gangs, like the Crips and the Bloods. We would include them as an evolving form of organized crime. The prison gangs, limited by the peculiarities of their prison environment, still nevertheless seem to meet the requirements for organized crime. But the survivalists and other hate groups do not qualify as a form of organized crime.

Having defined the nature of problem, its causes and etiology, looked at its history, and explored its complexity and varieties, in the final chapters we respond to the problem of organized crime. What has been done about it? How successful have our efforts at prevention and control been? What else might be done?

12

⊸⟫⟦⟷⟧⟪⊷

Methods of Combating Organized Crime

A number of investigative and prosecutorial tools have been and are being employed to combat organized crime. In this chapter we will examine some of these tools, describe their use, look at case examples that illustrate their application, and offer an assessment of their effectiveness.

We will begin by looking at that branch of the U.S. Treasury Department known as the Internal Revenue Service (IRS). All of us who pay income taxes have some familiarity with the IRS, but what we may not be so familiar with is how it gets involved in going after organized crime. The IRS has not been a bit player in the organized crime business by any means. To the contrary, through enforcement of the nation's tax laws, it has been a major force in bringing mobsters, racketeers, and assorted organized criminals to justice. Perhaps its most famous case was the campaign against Al Capone. Despite the fact that Capone was alleged to have been involved in a lengthy and sordid list of criminal activities ranging from bootlegging to murder, the only convictions against Capone were five counts of felony tax evasion. Thus, the IRS got Capone when no one else could.

THE IRS GOES AFTER THE MONEY

All income, unless otherwise sheltered or excluded from taxation, is subject to taxation. This includes illegal as well as legal income. When the principal or sole source of income is illegal (for example, drugs, gambling, extortion, loan-sharking, or prostitution), special problems are encountered in reporting that income, and incentives abound to try to evade taxation. Therefore, the laws against income tax evasion are frequently used against organized crime figures. More than 60 percent of all convictions of leaders of organized crime in the years 1960 to 1965 originated from tax investigations (Rhodes, 1984).

Given the myriad of federal and state tax and banking laws and regulations requiring compliance, criminals need to convert illegal income into legal income, or at least disguise its illegality. Further, because hard cash is the preferred medium of exchange among criminals, as well as between criminal entrepreneurs and their clients, hoards of cash must be dispersed or converted (that is, deposited into foreign bank accounts, converted into foreign currency, or converted into treasury or bank checks, money orders, or stocks and bonds). This process is called *money laundering*. As the name suggests, it implies a process of turning dirty money into clean money and it is in the development of strategies to control money laundering that the Internal Revenue Service assumes a particularly prominent role in attacking organized crime. In a study by the Police Executive Research Forum (Karchmer & Ruch, 1992), the authors argue that money laundering provides the essential link between the underworld and "virtually limitless commercial and financial options in the legitimate sector" (p. 2). The enforcement strategies employed by the IRS (and other law enforcement agencies dealing with this problem) include: (1) gathering intelligence and making analyses; (2) analyzing money transactions, such as those at currency exchanges and check-cashing services; and (3) detecting completed laundering transactions. Developing intelligence information involves getting financial institutions to report large cash transactions and investigating assets acquired with large amounts of cash (for example, purchasing a home for half a million or a million dollars in cash).

Detecting completed laundering transactions is possible because the federal government requires that currency transactions larger than $10,000 made through financial institutions must be recorded on federal Currency Transaction Report (CTR) forms. Further, currency or monetary instruments exceeding $5,000 being taken out of the United States must be recorded and filed, and anyone having $5,000 or more in a foreign bank account must report it. Karchmer and Ruch (1992) describe how racketeers try to evade the CTR requirements by concealing or misrepresenting the ownership of the funds or by providing false IDs, or by trying to corrupt or bribe bank employees to prevent the CTRs from being forwarded to the U.S. Treasury Department. A technique known as *smurfing* is also employed. Smurfing—itself now illegal under federal law—refers to breaking large amounts of money into amounts smaller than $10,000 to avoid CTR reporting.

IRS agents have special capabilities in financial auditing and accounting. One investigative technique used is known as the "net worth" method. Establishing net worth helps "investigators document discrepancies between the amounts of income and other assets accumulated by suspects compared with the reported amounts that can be verified through records of legitimate employment" (Karchmer & Ruch, 1992:5). Mobsters often, although not always, have lifestyles that could not realistically be supported by the legitimate "jobs" they allegedly have. For example, Gambino crime family boss John Gotti is unlikely to have been able to afford the thousand dollar–plus suits of which he was so fond from his supposed "job" as a plumbing supply salesman. In addition to investigative accounting, the Internal Revenue Service employs undercover and sting operations and electronic surveillance in its investigations.

From the mid–1960s until roughly 1990, IRS actions against organized crime were frequently carried out as a member agency of the 14 federal strike forces created to investigate and prosecute organized crime. These strike forces combined the skills and resources of investigative agencies, such as the IRS and federal prosecutors, in teams to focus on organized crime in specific geographic areas. Other federal investigative agencies participating in the strike forces were the FBI, the Department of Labor, the Bureau of Alcohol, Tobacco, and Firearms, the Drug Enforcement Administration, the U.S. Customs Service, the Immigration and Naturalization Service, the Securities and Exchange Commission, the U.S. Postal Service, the U.S. Marshals Service, and the U.S. Secret Service. For a variety of reasons, some political, some jurisdictional, and some having to do with concerns about duplication of efforts, the strike force concept was discarded by the U.S. Department of Justice at the beginning of 1990. The fruits of IRS investigations into tax matters involving organized crime are now turned over to any of the 94 U.S. Attorneys for prosecution.

The following depicts a scenario that captures the essence of a typical organized crime case in which the IRS might be involved. Some racketeers have a lot of drug or gambling money they need to launder. They deposit this dirty money to an account in a so-called friendly bank. (Friendly means that not too many questions are asked nor is too much attention paid to the paperwork—deposits and withdrawals are expedited.) This money is then wired to a foreign account (for example, in the Bahamas) that may or may not be registered in the names of the people making the deposit, but the account is controlled by them. The money is then loaned back to a U.S. company that is also controlled by these same people. The returning money is now clean. The tasks for the investigators include constructing the paper trail linking the individuals to the accounts, tracing the movement of the money, and building the evidence to show that banking and tax laws are being violated and taxes are being evaded. "Operation Tradewinds" was one such IRS investigation.

Alan Block (1991) tells the story of Operation Tradewinds. According to Block's account, this IRS project was conceived and set in motion in the period 1963-1965. It developed information on American racketeers among others who took money made illegally to the Bahamas and invested it there. Some of this illegal money was skimmed from gambling casinos in Nevada. Because of a combination of absent laws and regulations and lax enforcement and a local desire to encourage investment and tourism, the Bahamas became a tax haven for various kinds of tax scams. Organized crime was not the only beneficiary of the favorable criminal opportunities to be found there; a variety of shady businesspeople and politicians also took advantage of the ripe pickings.

Tradewinds was a huge, complex investigation that sometimes tread into dangerous political waters. It was subject to a considerable amount of jurisdictional infighting within the IRS itself and between the IRS and other federal agencies. It even occasionally got entangled in foreign policy affairs. Operation Tradewinds lasted approximately ten years. Was it ultimately successful? Block (1991) made this assessment: "Although woefully underfunded, the project always produced substantial money for the government. At the end of 1971, it was estimated that Tradewinds had produced $25 million in taxes and penalties since its inception, and had initiated thirteen full-scale investigations ending in recommendations for criminal proceedings. It was an inexpensive deal for the government. [And] some of the information gathered was of critical significance" (p. 125). Not surprising in the case of something as politically controversial as Tradewinds, not everyone involved with or knowledgeable about it considers it to have been a shining success.

As with other methods for investigating and prosecuting organized crime, using the IRS as it was used in part in Operation Tradewinds raises serious questions about the violation of rights of privacy. Most of us would agree that income and personal investment information is private. Privacy and confidentiality, we believe, ought to cover how much money we have, where we have it, and what investments we have. However, there is a trade-off. For the Internal Revenue Service to be maximally efficient and effective in investigating money laundering and tax evasion by organized crime, this right to privacy has to be breached. Once it is breached, it is breached for all of us. As Rhodes points out, "the ready access of the IRS to the personal income data of all Americans makes it a supersensitive agency. . . . Every American's telephone is not tapped, but every American's income is reviewed by the IRS" (1984:73,74).

RICO AND THE CONSPIRACY STATUTES

American criminal law and criminal procedure focus on discrete crimes and individual criminals. For any particular person to be arrested, charged, and prosecuted, there must be reason to believe that a specific crime has been committed and that this specific individual committed it—in other words, there must be *probable cause*. This system of justice has many important advantages in terms of due process and fairness, but it has distinct disadvantages when it comes to combating organized crime. It is often difficult, if not impossible, to directly connect those in the upper echelons of organized crime hierarchies to distinct crimes. They plan and direct these crimes, and they receive the rewards from their commission, but they do not usually commit the crimes themselves. They are surrounded by a protective buffer, and they avoid getting their hands dirty. Therefore, there is no legal basis for arresting and prosecuting them. This has been a source of great frustration to law enforcement. Even more important, as exemplified by the income tax evasion case against Al Capone, respect for the law is not fostered when the justice system focuses on isolated, perhaps minor, offenses of individuals whose entire lives have been devoted to a career of serious, organized criminality.

One historical exception to this general rule of defining crimes as particular acts by individuals has been the conspiracy statutes. Conspiracy statutes outlaw agreements to commit a crime or crimes by two or more individuals. The American Law Institute's Model Penal Code (1985) defines criminal conspiracy as the act of one person agreeing with one or more other persons to commit a crime, or agreeing to attempt or agreeing to solicit the commission of a crime. The crime of conspiracy might include agreement to aid in planning or commission of the crime or in its attempt or solicitation. Conspiracy also applies if you know that a person with whom you are conspiring has also conspired with others to commit the same crime. In that instance, you are guilty of conspiring with these other persons as well, even if you have had no contact with them and do not even know them.

Organized crime is, by definition, a type of conspiratorial crime. Organized criminal enterprises can only exist to the extent that their members have agreed to form them. The illegal acts that make up organized crime are planned, solicited, and committed through the agreed upon participation of two or more persons—co-conspirators. Thus, for many years the laws against conspiracy were the only tools available for prosecuting organized crime participants who could not be tied to specific crimes. The conspiracy statutes permit prosecution of continuing crimes and connecting crimes, meaning that the conspiracy involves committing a series of crimes over time. They also make all members of an organized crime group equally liable for the crime of conspiracy itself.

Unfortunately, this approach to organized crime has limitations. Defining conspiracy as a criminal partnership in which each member of the conspiracy joins in the same criminal scheme, former U.S. Attorney Rudolph Giuliani (1987) says: "An organized crime case involves a multiplicity of diverse crimes committed by specialists supported by 'thousands of criminals working within structures as large as any corporation.' In the past prosecutors have had to approach their task with a narrow and shortsighted focus, convicting organized crime members either one at a time or in single conspiracy groups for specific criminal activity" (p. 104). Giuliani calls this approach "utterly futile" because when using this traditional model of attacking organized crime, "the conviction and temporary incapacitation of the heads of a crime family for discrete crimes—has not greatly diminished the family's power and ability to survive." The result, he concludes, is an "unenviable record of short term success in prosecuting the leaders while leaving intact the infrastructure of organized crime" (p. 104). It was frustration at this unenviable record that led Congress to enact the Racketeer Influenced and Corrupt Organizations Act (RICO) on October 15, 1970.

Writing in the 1967 Task Force Report on Organized Crime, Notre Dame law professor G. Robert Blakey concluded that "there is no question that existing conspiracy theory is equal to the challenge of organized crime" (Blakey, 1967:82). He was shortly to be convinced otherwise however, and subsequently became the principal author (some call him the father) of the RICO statute. This statute, which is one part (Title IX) of the Organized Crime Control Act of 1970, is considered to be the most dramatic and revolutionary change in the investigation and prosecution of organized crime in the last 25 years. The Pennsylvania Crime Commission (1991) calls it "the single most important piece of legislation ever enacted against organized crime" (p. 17). Because of its importance, we will examine this law in considerable detail, including its purpose and major provisions, its use against organized crime, some of the controversies surrounding it, its effectiveness, and its future.

WHAT IS RICO?

The purpose of the Organized Crime Control Act (OCCA) is:

> To seek the eradication of organized crime in the United States by strengthening the legal tools in the evidence-gathering process, by establishing new penal prohibitions, and by providing enhanced sanctions and new remedies to deal with the unlawful activities of those engaged in organized crime. (*Congressional Record,* 116th Cong., 1970:602)

Congress created RICO with the specific intention of combating the infiltration of organized crime into legitimate business enterprises. It is not, however, limited to organized crime, but rather extends to all forms of "enterprise" criminality. RICO is a major advancement on conspiracy law because the operation of an enterprise (a criminal group) through a pattern of racketeering (a succession of separate crimes) is defined as a single offense. Thus, the rules of evidence that confine the nature of the traditional trial by focusing on the individual offense are suddenly off (Lynch, 1990).

RICO's reach extends to crimes of violence, provision of illegal goods and services, corruption, and criminal fraud. It provides a wide range of criminal and civil sanctions to control these offenses: imprisonment of up to 20 years or life (where the initial or so-called predicate offense authorizes life), fines ranging from $25,000 to $500,000 or twice the gain or loss, and forfeitures, injunctions, and treble damage relief. (The latter are civil sanctions and will be discussed in the next chapter.) Our focus here will be on the criminal applications and penalties.

Three powerful and controversial concepts outlined by Lynch (1990) form the heart of RICO:

1. *Enterprise.* An enterprise is any business, labor union, association, or government bureau that organized crime can infiltrate. It may or may not be a legal entity. A criminal enterprise is one in which the members of the enterprise are engaging in a pattern of racketeering

activity. "Allegations of Mafia membership can be introduced in RICO trials because the defendant's membership in the criminal enterprise is an element of the offense" (p. 787).

2. *Pattern of racketeering activity.* Racketeering activity encompasses any crimes spelled out in state or federal law as felonies or indictable offenses. These include acts or threats involving murder, gambling, or extortion. A "pattern" of racketeering activity refers to the commission of two such acts in a ten-year period. The first of these two is called the predicate offense.

3. *Mandatory forfeiture of the interest in the enterprise.* It is unlawful for a person who has income from a pattern of racketeering activity to invest that income in an enterprise. The criminal penalty upon conviction under RICO is to forfeit that investment interest. Forfeiture is of illicit proceeds, related property, or any interest in an enterprise. It is this provision that permits the government to take over the cars, boats, houses, and airplanes of drug dealers convicted under RICO, on the grounds that these properties were instrumental to or are the fruits of the criminal enterprise.

In sum, the substantive elements of RICO are that a defendant through the commission of two or more acts constituting a "pattern" of "racketeering activity" invests, or maintains an interest, or participates in an "enterprise." Said elements make said defendant a RICO target.

RICO Use Against Organized Crime

Congress intended RICO to address the infiltration of legitimate business by organized crime; although, as previously indicated, it is not limited to organized crime. In *Russello v. United States* (464 U.S. 1983, 26), the United States Supreme Court decided that the "legislative history [of RICO] clearly demonstrates that . . . [it] was intended to provide new weapons of unprecedented scope for an assault upon organized crime and its economic roots" (Blakey, 1990:879). Earlier, in 1981, the Supreme Court had determined that "the organized crime family itself is an enterprise—a group of individuals associated in fact—and anyone who conducts such an enterprise through a pattern of crimes . . . violates RICO" (*United States v. Turkette*, 452 U.S., 1981:576).

Use in combating organized crime has been assessed as stunning and dramatic. "Organized crime has obviously been the central target . . . of RICO. RICO indictments and convictions have increased the effectiveness of our nation's battle against the 'mafia' by an order of magnitude. The stunning success of RICO in convicting the 'Bosses' of the 'Five Families' in New York City prompted former U.S. Attorney Rudolph Giuliani to say 'the mafia is a dying organization and will cease to be a major threat within ten years'" (*Notre Dame Law Review*, 1990:1162). Allowing for some hyperbole and overoptimism in such statements, RICO has nevertheless been used very successfully against organized crime. In view of this success, and in view of the legislative intent, it might seem curious that there is nothing in the original statute aimed specifically at punishing membership in organized crime. The statute says nothing about the Mafia; nor are the crimes included under racketeering activity necessarily "organized" in any particular sense. The reason for the silence on membership and singling out the Mafia issues would seem to be that lawmakers wished to avoid the problem of appearing to try to punish people because of their status (which would be unconstitutional), rather than because of their behavior. Although significantly expanding traditional conspiracy law, RICO still retains a focus on criminal acts (patterns of racketeering activity) and conspiratorial agreements to commit those acts and the predicate crimes that can form the racketeering pattern are those thought to be characteristic of organized crime.

The following case example illustrates the use of RICO against a traditional organized crime group based in Philadelphia.

RICO Attack on Scarfo LCN

The indictment charged 19 defendants who were named either as leaders or members of the Bruno/Scarfo Family of La Cosa Nostra. In setting forth the "enterprise," the indictment identified the "Boss" . . . of the Family, the "Underboss" . . ., and three "Capos" . . . who were all charged with supervising and protecting the criminal activities of the subordinates of the Family. The leadership, as well as the lower ranking members, [were] included within the Family "enterprise" as a group of individual[s] associated in fact. The ongoing nature of the enterprise was demonstrated by the fact that the Family: selected leaders . . . proposed new members, conducted ritual initiation ceremonies "making" new members, and promoted some members to positions of authority or demoted them from these positions. Reliance entirely upon traditional conspiracy law without RICO would not have enabled the government to include all of these individuals within a single prosecution or to identify each of their specific roles within the enterprise.

In addition, RICO's requirement of proving "a pattern of racketeering activity" and its broad definition of "racketeering activity" allowed the prosecution to join in a single indictment the widely diverse state and federal crimes in which the Scarfo Family has engaged over the past 15 years. Thus, the indictment included charges that the Family had engaged in murder, gambling, loansharking, extortion, and drug trafficking. The prosecution was also able to include as predicate acts of racketeering the prior federal extortion convictions of two defendants. . . . In addition, because RICO allows for prosecution of offenses for which individuals were previously acquitted as part of a broader racketeering conspiracy, the prosecution was able to include as predicate offenses, the prior murder charges of three of the defendants. . . .

Finally, because of RICO's broad definition of a pattern of racketeering activity it was possible for the prosecutors to include predicate offenses in which the criminal conduct occurred at a time beyond the statute of limitations. In this regard, all that RICO requires is that one act of racketeering occurred within ten years of a prior act of racketeering. Given these provisions, the prosecution was permitted to charge a 1976 gambling violation as well as extortion that took place in the late 1970s. (Pennsylvania Crime Commission, 1991:20)

Controversies and Criticisms Surrounding RICO

The controversies and criticisms surrounding RICO are numerous and various. It has been attacked for being vague and too broad, for subjecting defendants to double jeopardy, for violating the Eighth Amendment's protection against cruel and unusual punishment, and for violating due process. The due process criticisms suggest that defendants' Sixth Amendment rights to a speedy trial, right to counsel of their choice, and right to appeal are violated. To date, the statute has withstood each of its constitutional challenges; but a mounting constitutional "void-for-vagueness" challenge is seen to be a real threat.

The statute's author, Professor Blakey, acknowledges that RICO is under attack from a wide range of groups. "Criminally," according to Blakey, "the principal focus of the attack is on large trials and pretrial restraints" (1991:16). The large trial issue refers to the fact that RICO trials are often long and complex, resulting in severe financial burdens and lengthy disruption of defendants' lives. Further, joining together large numbers of defendants (sometimes hundreds) in one "megatrial" poses the risk of defendants being "victims of spill-over prejudice and guilt by association and jurors [being] . . . confused and unable to render proper verdicts" (p. 21). Blakey either dismisses or downplays these arguments. The National Association of Criminal Defense Lawyers and others, however, give these arguments considerable credibility.

Whatever the outcome of the various challenges, if RICO survives, it will undoubtedly continue to be a source of controversy and litigation. The controversies and criticisms remind us that, irrespective of its effectiveness as an instrument of crime control, we must remain mindful of the potential violations of due process posed by RICO. After all, the end of effectively combating organized crime does not justify any means to achieve it.

The Future of RICO

Enacted in 1970, criminal RICO prosecution was not actually used until 1975. Since then, approximately 1,000 RICO indictments have been returned—about 125 per year. Criminal RICO has been used against organized crime groups, political corruption, white-collar crime, and violent groups:

> Roughly 39% have been in the organized crime area (not Mafia alone, but also drugs, gambling, labor racketeering, etc.), while 48% have been in the white-collar crime area (corruption of government, general fraud in the private sector, securities and commodities fraud, etc.). Thirteen percent fall into other categories (violent groups, including terrorists, white-hate, anti-Semitic, etc.). (Blakey, 1991:61)

As previously mentioned, all five New York organized crime families have been the target of RICO indictments and convictions. In *United States v. Luchese Organized Crime Family* (filed June 6, 1989, in the Eastern District of New York), the federal government filed the largest ever civil RICO suit against the Luchese and Gambino organized crime families alleging 486 acts of racketeering by 112 defendants in the private trash carting industry of Long Island.

Twenty-nine states have enacted similar state RICO legislation, the so-called "little RICOs." Future RICO targets for both state and federal investigation include allegations of organized crime money laundering through the million-dollar budgets that movie making now requires. Another target is evasion of millions (possibly billions) of dollars in gasoline and cigarette taxes. Depending on whether and in what form RICO survives its constitutional challenges, numerous targets of opportunity remain.

INVESTIGATIVE GRAND JURIES

There are two types of grand juries in the American system of criminal justice. The typical or standard, accusatory grand jury, made up of 12 to 24 citizens, serves the function of determining whether sufficient evidence exists to prosecute an accused person. If the grand jury decides that there is sufficient evidence—(probable cause), it returns an indictment against the person. The history of grand juries being used for this particular purpose can be traced back to 12th century England. This type of jury is intended to act as a buffer for the individual against the state. Because the grand jury evaluates the state's evidence against the accused, assessing its credibility and weight, and because it does so in secret, it protects individuals from false charges and from being railroaded into being wrongly convicted of crimes on trumped-up charges. In recent years, these accusatory grand juries have been criticized for being nothing more than anachronous tools of the prosecutor, tools that are no longer necessary. It has been charged, for example, that the grand jury is so much under the control of the prosecutor that the prosecutor can get jurors to "indict a ham sandwich." Many jurisdictions have, in part as a result of this, replaced the grand jury with a legal procedure known as the prosecutor's information.

The second type of grand jury, the investigative grand jury, is the focus of our attention here. These special grand juries are generally convened for fixed periods of time (for example, 18 months) to probe into such matters as white-collar crime, political corruption, and organized crime. The extended periods for the jury's impanelment are considered necessary because of the unusually long time required to build organized crime cases. While the accusatory grand jury is reactive—that is, it simply reacts to the presentation of the prosecutor by returning a true bill (an indictment) or a no bill (fails to indict)—the investigative grand jury is proactive. It seeks out evidence and conducts an investigation. In the latter case, individuals may not know that they are the target of a grand jury probe until they have actually been indicted and warrants have been issued for their arrest.

The scope of the investigative grand jury is much broader than that of the conventional grand jury. Its power to investigate complex crimes rests in its ability to subpoena witnesses, books, records, documents, and so on. Issuance of a subpoena compels the appearance of witnesses and the production of records. The 1967 President's Crime Commission Task Force on Organized Crime concluded that a compulsory process was necessary to obtain essential testimony or material. Further concluding that this was most readily accomplished by an investigative grand jury, that commission recommended: "At least one investigative grand jury should be impaneled annually in each jurisdiction that has major organized crime activity" (President's Commission, 1967:16). Twenty years later, the President's Commission on Organized Crime similarly concluded that "the grand jury remains uniquely suited to long-term or large-scale organized crime investigations because of its power to subpoena persons and documents, punish contemnors, and maintain secrecy" (President's Commission, 1987:164). The commission said that it allows for a "more focused and more efficient investigation into sophisticated and geographically diffuse criminal enterprises" (p. 164) and strongly recommended that, similar to the special federal grand juries, state-wide grand juries should have power to subpoena witnesses and documents, grant immunity, and issue indictments or presentments.

Investigative grand juries are usually statewide or multijurisdictional in scope. Title I of the Organized Crime Control Act provides that special grand juries are to be called every 18 months in federal judicial districts of one million or more population. The life of these federal investigative grand juries can extend to 36 months. Because the federal or statewide juries are multijurisdictional, they are removed from potential political pressures often operating at local or county levels. They can better investigate cases that go beyond local or county jurisdictional lines, and they can also help avoid du-plication of effort and resources. The greater insulation from political influence is extremely important in organized crime cases because organized crime employs political corruption as one means of immunizing itself from arrest, prosecution, and conviction. Local prosecutors, who are tied to local politicians, are much more vulnerable to political pressure to quash investi-gations. This does not mean that prosecutors at state and federal levels can-not be corrupted but that it has proven to be more difficult and less likely.

Because organized crime is a continuing criminal conspiracy and be-cause it is covert, investigative grand juries must probe to see who is in-volved to understand any particular organized crime case. "The duty of the grand jury to investigate completely may not be carried out fully without questioning those implicated in order to give them an opportu-nity to explain or implicate others" (Cornell Institute on Organized Crime, 1979:F. 122). To do this, the grand jury relies on the firmly estab-lished duty to testify.

Three types of witnesses may appear before investigative grand juries: (1) targets of the investigation, (2) de jure defendants, and (3) mere witnesses. The first are subjects who the government suspects of wrongdoing and plans to indict. They are potential or virtual defendants. De jure defendants are persons already indicted or against whom formal charges have been filed. Although already indicted, they may be brought before the grand jury as a target where the investigation involves a similar but separate offense. Mere witnesses are persons believed to have relevant information but who are suspected of no crime. It is, of course, the case that just as subjects of the investigation may become de jure defendants so, too, may mere witnesses become targets and then defendants. None of these witnesses may refuse to appear if subpoenaed, but different circumstances apply to each of them in terms of their right to refuse to testify on grounds of the Fifth Amendment privilege against self-incrimination. (The matter of immunity will be discussed in the next section.)

A number of experts are very strong supporters of the use of investigative grand juries against organized crime. Blakey (1967) wrote: "The conclusion seems inescapable: 'As an instrument of discovery against organized crime, the grand jury has no counterpart'" (p. 84). And Robert Rhodes (1984) agreed: "Whether investigating obvious, violent, traditional organized crime, or the subtleties of frauds with respectable cover, the state grand jury's proactive investigative function is critical to combating organized crime" (p. 203).

Certain dangers or risks of abuse of the powers of the investigative grand jury should not be ignored, however. Some prosecutors have used the grand jury to go after and to harass individuals or groups who were considered political undesirables. This happened to a number of political dissidents or antiwar activists in the 1970s. This potential abuse, as real as it is, should not detract from the demonstrated effectiveness of the investigative grand jury in combating organized crime.

GRANTS OF IMMUNITY

The Fifth Amendment to the United States Constitution states that no person shall be "compelled in any criminal case to be a witness against himself." This provision has long been interpreted to mean that not only criminal defendants but also witnesses in both civil and criminal cases have a right not to testify when such testimony would place them at risk of criminal prosecution. This privilege, referred to in the vernacular as "taking the Fifth," is related to the constitutional principles of "presumption of innocence" and "burden of proof." The privilege applies whenever an individual is testifying before an official body authorized to compel testimony under oath, for example, an administrative body such as a state commission of investigation, a congressional committee, or a grand jury. The effect is that any witness, called by subpoena or otherwise to testify before such body, can "plead the privilege" and refuse to answer any question, when the answer might lead to criminal charges against that individual. A witness cannot willy-nilly refuse to answer questions whenever he or she chooses, simply claiming the privilege against self-incrimination. There must be a risk of *criminal* incrimination.

Juxtaposed with this important constitutional protection is much of the character of organized crime. Organized crime is by definition conspiratorial crime in nature: here are hierarchies of organization in which higher-ups are protected and insulated from direct involvement in actually committing crimes; only subordinates can testify to the involvement of these higher-ups; violence is used to intimidate witnesses; and internal bonds and codes bind organization members to secrecy on pain of death. These characteristics make organized crime extremely difficult to infiltrate and to investigate and prosecute.

Witnesses and informants are critical to the success of any investigation and prosecution, but it is difficult to find them. And having found them, it is difficult to overcome their reluctance to talk, especially in the face of threats of retaliation by mobsters who may be their fellow conspirators or in the face of threats of criminal prosecution if they reveal their own criminal involvement. The practice of witness protection to deal with retaliation will be taken up later in this chapter; here we will deal with the issue of avoiding prosecution by offering a grant of immunity.

The prosecutor in the case of a witness who pleads the Fifth Amendment before an investigative grand jury has four options: (1) release the witness and forego the testimony; (2) offer the witness a plea bargain in which certain charges will be brought against the individual but others are downgraded or dropped; (3) prove that the testimony requested could not possibly incriminate the witness and move to invoke a contempt of court citation if the witness still refuses to testify; or (4) offer the witness immunity from prosecution.

The notion of offering immunity has long been upheld by the U.S. Supreme Court. The Court has said that a witness may be compelled to answer incriminating questions if he is granted immunity from prosecution. Two kinds of grants of immunity are important to consider here: transactional immunity and use immunity.

- *Transactional Immunity.* Transactional immunity is a general grant of immunity that "prohibits any prosecution of witnesses for any participation in any criminal acts, whether related to testimony or not, except in circumstances involving perjury or noncompliance with a court order to testify" (Rhodes, 1984:186). This was the only form of granting immunity until 1970.

- *Use Immunity.* Use immunity was adopted in the U.S. Criminal Code in 1970. It guarantees that neither the compelled testimony nor any evidence developed from leads given by the compelled testimony can be used against the witness. The latter is known as derivative use. Use immunity does not, however, bar prosecution of the witness with evidence developed wholly independently from the compelled testimony. Thus, use immunity is only a limited immunity. And in fact, the Supreme Court said in *Kastigar* v. *United States* (406 U.S. 1972, 441) that a witness can be indicted on the basis of evidence gathered "because of," as long as it is "apart from," his testimony.

Use immunity has significant advantages over transactional immunity for the organized crime prosecutor. Under transactional immunity, a witness may give wide-ranging but vague and general testimony, alluding to criminal acts or matters so as to bring them under the immunity grant in such an ambiguous manner that specifics essential to prosecution are not provided. General testimony under a grant of use immunity, on the other hand, will not bar prosecution. There are also greater dangers of granting what is called an "immunity bath" under transactional immunity. "Because the witness could be immunized from prosecution for any crime he referred to while under oath, the witness who had been given transactional immunity could take an 'immunity bath' and escape prosecution simply by mentioning a criminal transaction during testimony" (President's Commission, 1986:155).

Numerous problems can arise in the practice of granting immunity in return for testimony. An inept prosecutor may grant immunity inappropriately to a higher-ranking member of a criminal organization in return for testimony against a lower-ranking criminal. Or an inept or a corrupt prosecutor may (unknowingly in the first case and knowingly in the second) immunize a major crime figure against prosecution in another jurisdiction. Rhodes (1984) cites the argument of some critics that using involuntary immunity to force testimony violates principles of search and seizure. But Rhodes (1984) writes, "the central problem according to critics of use immunity involves using it as an inducement. Since immunized testimony is purchased, it is inherently unreliable" (pp. 192-193). This unreliability is both a real and a perceived problem. It is a real problem when witnesses perjure themselves. It is a perceived problem when jurors are lead to doubt the credibility of immunized witnesses who are painted by defense attorneys as criminals who have "cut a deal" with the prosecutor.

Witnesses who lie under oath after being immunized can be prosecuted for perjury. But in reality, according to the President's Commission on Organized Crime, there are few prosecutions for perjury. There are even fewer cases in which immunized witnesses have been prosecuted, under the stipulations for use immunity, for the crime about which they were forced to testify. A Department of Justice study for the years 1970 to 1977 revealed only one such prosecution in 10,000 grants of immunity (President's Commission, 1986:158).

Witnesses who refuse to testify after having been granted immunity can be held in contempt. The sequence in such cases is that the Court will order the witness to testify, and if the witness still refuses despite the Court's order, the Court can hold the individual in either civil or criminal contempt. This means the court can confine the person in a jail or other corrections facility under one of the following options: (1) until he or she testifies, (2) until the end of the grand jury term if there is continuing refusal, (3) until the end of the terms of any successor grand juries if there is continuing refusal, or (4) to punish the person for violating the Court's order. This last is called criminal contempt.

Numerous experts have supported the critical value of grants of immunity as an important weapon against organized crime. The 1967 Task Force on Organized Crime said: "Since the activities of criminal groups involve such a broad scope of criminal violations, immunity provisions covering this breadth of illicit actions are necessary to secure the testimony of uncooperative or criminally involved witnesses" (President's Commission, 1967:16). They recommended a general immunity statute as being essential in organized crime investigations and prosecutions. Likewise, Rhodes (1984), who has looked at the topic in depth, concludes that the prosecutor's authority to grant immunity is a "vital instrument in the struggle against organized crime" (p. 189). "For low-visibility, conspiratorial crimes," Rhodes says, "there are few alternatives [to use immunity] to obtaining vitally needed testimony" (p. 194). Finally, to the civil libertarian critics of forcing testimony under use immunity, Rhodes responds as follows, and we heartily concur:

> Logic and experience suggest that crimes of conspiracy cannot normally be prosecuted without obtaining testimony from one of the conspirators. If removing use immunity would sharply reduce our ability to investigate and prosecute successfully organized crime and official corruption, that event would be no victory for political freedom. (1984:196)

INFORMANTS

Given the conspiratorial, secretive nature of organized crime, it is very difficult to penetrate it using conventional law enforcement investigative techniques. The use of informants is not particularly unconventional, but they play a significant role in investigations of organized crime (much more so than in other criminal investigations). Who are these informers? Why do they become informers? What is their value to investigators and prosecutors, and what problems attend their use?

An informant, as the name implies, is one who is a source of information. The best informant—the best source of information—is someone particularly "in the know," an insider privy to plans, secrets, and other information. The person most likely to fill this bill is an accomplice—a co-conspirator of the person or persons being investigated. Typically, informants are criminals, and this raises numerous issues and potential problems surrounding their use. There are other, atypical informants, individuals who are not themselves criminals but rather are police buffs who act as pseudo-official investigators. Their information, however, is usually less valuable and is generally not qualitatively different from what police investigators themselves can obtain.

Criminal informants have a number of motives for becoming "stool pigeons," "snitches," or "rats." One principal motive has been characterized as the pleasure–pain principle (M. Brown, 1985); that is, criminals cooperate with investigators in exchange for reduced criminal charges, for lenient sentences, or for immunity from prosecution. A fairly standard investigative technique in going after conspiracies is to catch a "little fish" and squeeze this little fish with threats of severe punishment, using him or her as bait or as the hook to catch a bigger fish. Lower-level criminals are offered a deal in return for their assistance in getting at the higher-ups. This is especially valuable in organized crime investigations where the higher-ups are insulated from direct connections with crimes.

Another motive of informants may be to get into the good graces of law enforcement in case they need a favor some day. Becoming an informant is a sort of insurance policy or an escape hatch. Organized crime operatives live in a cruel world where there are quick ups and downs, and where the "ins" can become "outs" overnight. Thus, they want to have a friend in the right place and inform to curry favor. These kinds of informants may also believe that they are gaining self-esteem and a form of status by associating with the police or the FBI.

A third reason for being an informant is that they get paid. Police departments and other investigative agencies maintain confidential funds to pay for information. This can produce highly valuable and useful information, but the cost may include questionable relationships with various "low-lifes," petty criminals, small-time hoodlums, and assorted street people. This cost can and sometimes does include overlooking or condoning criminal behavior by such persons.

One illustration of the influence of various motives is the case of Tommaso Buscetta, a former member of the Porto Nuova Sicilian Mafia in Palermo, Sicily. Buscetta, who became a Mafia member in 1948, decided to begin cooperating with Italian and American authorities in 1984. He made this decision after being arrested in Brazil in 1983 and extradited to Italy on an Italian warrant for Mafia associations. Buscetta testified before the U.S. Senate in 1988 that he made this decision because he had become disillusioned with the changes in the Mafia. He said that the so-called men of honor in whom you could believe were gone. Gone also were family loyalties and codes of respect. Drugs, he said, had resulted in a changing of the guard—for the worse. But he also testified that in the period 1981 though 1983, there were more than 400 Mafia killings in Palermo. In a mob war with a family known as the Corleones, Buscetta's brother, two sons, three nephews, and son-in-law were gunned down. It would not be surprising if Buscetta's real reason for turning informant (or perhaps his reason in addition to his professed disenchantment) was to bail out and save his own skin.

How valuable was Buscetta as an informant? His 1985 testimony in the important Pizza Connection case in New York City helped convict 35 members of the New York and Sicilian La Cosa Nostra. Likewise, his testimony in 1986 in Palermo, Sicily, helped convict 435 members of the Sicilian Mafia. Informants of the likes of Tommaso Buscetta can be invaluable to the investigation and prosecution of organized crime. They possess information available through no other source. In some cases, it is only through informant testimony that convictions can be obtained. But making a "pact with the devil" can present its own problems.

The potential problems in using informants are numerous and, in some instances, unsettling (Marx, 1982). They may become "loose cannons," setting law enforcement after whatever targets they choose and using the police to settle scores with their enemies for them. Given who they are and what their motives are, they are more likely to lie, to be less accountable for their actions, and to be less constrained in what they say and do than are professional criminal investigators. They may become so intent upon receiving their reward (for example, money or leniency) that they create criminals or use methods to get information that are prohibited to law enforcement.

Marx describes how the desire for "books by crooks" (that is, best sellers by famous criminals) can provide the incentive to come up with dramatic (albeit wholly or partially false) discoveries. The same might be said about drug using informers who are furnished drugs in return for information. Further, given that most informers are criminals, they may continue to commit crimes after becoming informants. Law enforcement is then put in the position of losing their services if they are arrested and convicted or of ignoring and condoning their lawbreaking. This is known as being given a license to commit crime. Informants sometimes sell the same information to several different law enforcement agencies. This is not only unnecessarily expensive but it makes law enforcement into a pawn or stooge. Finally, informants may blackmail the police into granting them a kind of permanent immunity by threatening to reveal police dirty tricks or other government illegality.

The value of informant testimony before a grand jury or trial jury must be balanced against the reliability and credibility problems we have discussed. There is no clear and general rule as to how to proceed in deciding whether or not to offer immunity, just as there is no obvious way to measure the worth of an informant's information against the costs of that information and the risks of unreliability and lack of credibility. This remains an exercise of professional judgment and discretion.

The complex web woven around an informant and his law enforcement handlers is illustrated in this description from *Boss of Bosses*, a book about Paul Castellano, the former head of New York's Gambino crime family:

> There is an ebb and flow in the activities of informants.
>
> It is a common misperception that a source "turns" once and for all, and is thereafter a steady and reliable source of useful news. In the typical case, the dynamic is considerably more subtle. An informant doesn't turn; he flirts, he dances, he plays both sides. Like a man with two girlfriends, he kisses one and screws the other; then, after a while, he reverses them. When he feels secure in the bosom of his criminal organization, he clams up. When he needs a favor from law enforcement, such as keeping him alive, he spills his guts. Mostly, he does some of both—singing enough to establish his worth, holding back the good stuff for when he really needs a place to hide. In certain instances, informants are of less value for what they actually say than for what their willingness to talk reveals of simmering discord. (O'Brien & Kurins, 1991:279–280)

WITNESS PROTECTION

When the so-called Teflon Don, John Gotti, boss of the Gambino crime family, was finally convicted and sentenced to prison in 1992 on murder and racketeering charges, the principal witness against him was his former underboss Salvatore "Sammy Bull" Gravano. Gravano, who had been indicted as a co-defendant with Gotti, agreed to make a deal with the government to testify against Gotti, and along with his wife and two children Gravano entered the federal witness protection program. Without Gravano's critical testimony, which corroborated electronic surveillance information and other evidence, Gotti's conviction would have been much less assured—and, in fact, might not have occurred at all. Gravano's willingness to cooperate with the federal prosecutors is itself testimony to the value of the witness protection program. There is no doubt that his cooperation would not have been secured except under a guarantee that he and his family would be protected from retaliation by Gotti and his followers. As former U.S. Attorney Rudolph Giuliani pointed out, "because of organized crime's demonstrated use of murder and other acts of violence over the years were it not for the Witness Security Program the Government would have few if any witnesses available for its organized crime prosecutions" (Giuliani, 1987:115). One of those who would surely have otherwise been unavailable is Salvatore Gravano.

American citizens generally have a duty to testify in court when summoned to do so. Fear of reprisal or retaliation can, however, deter people from meeting this duty. Individuals may refuse or lie or otherwise avoid putting themselves and their families in jeopardy. When fears of retribution are well founded, such as in cases involving organized crime, avoidance is certainly understandable. Recognizing both the realities of retaliation and the invaluable contribution of personal testimony to convicting mobsters, Congress passed Title V of the Organized Crime Control Act of 1970 which authorized the Attorney General of the United States to protect the lives of witnesses who testify against persons involved in organized crime activity. The witness protection program was subsequently created to meet this mandate.

Participation in the protection program is voluntary. It is also a very major step. Participants have to take on new identities, and they have to start new lives in new locations. They essentially disappear—forever. The three conditions of eligibility for entrance into the program are:

- the person is a qualifying witness in a specific case in process or during and after a grand jury proceeding;
- evidence in possession indicates that the life of the witness or that of a member of his family is in immediate jeopardy; and
- evidence in possession indicates that it would be advantageous to the federal interest for the Department of Justice to protect the witness or family or household member. (Montanino, 1990:124)

The witness protection program is operated by the U.S. Marshals Service. Under the law, the marshals undertake a number of protective measures to safeguard the health, safety, and welfare of witnesses and their family members. These include the following:

> (1) documentation to enable a person to establish a new identity or otherwise achieve protection [this includes new birth certificates, social security cards, drivers' licenses, marriage licenses, and employment, school, medical, and military records]; (2) housing; (3) transportation of household and other personal property to a new residence; (4) a subsidy for living expenses; (5) assistance in obtaining employment; (6) other services necessary to assist the individual in becoming self-sustaining; and (7) a refusal to disclose the person's location or new identity if there is danger that disclosure would endanger the protected individual and work to the detriment of the witness protection program to a greater extent than it would benefit the public and the person requesting disclosure. (George, 1987:19)

Since its inception in 1971, the federal witness protection program has provided protection and relocation services to more than 20,000 persons—of whom, over 5,000 were considered principal witnesses (Safir, 1989). Over the years (but particularly in the beginning), the program has also been much criticized. One major problem is that the program has been so overloaded as to exceed its resources. As opposed to the 30 to 50 people expected in the program per year when it was conceived, the actual numbers have been on the order of 400 to 500 per year. Witnesses themselves have criticized the program for breaking promises to them: documentation was alleged to be slow in coming or nonexistent; jobs did not materialize; and subsistence payments were too low (G. Mitchell, 1981).

A major criticism among public officials and others is that the program is a haven for criminals. Over 95 percent of the people entering the program have extensive criminal records. A sample of protected witnesses studied by the General Accounting Office had 7.2 arrests for 10.3 crimes before entering the program; more than half of these arrests were for violent crimes (U.S. General Accounting Office, 1984). These criminals, nee protected witnesses, have been said to use their new identities as cover for returning to crime. The GAO study found a two-year recidivism rate of 21.4 percent among its sample of protected witnesses. Although that proportion is not unusually large, nor perhaps unexpected given their criminal histories, the victims of these particular crimes are understandably critical of the program. They object to the government moving criminals into their neighborhoods and, in their view, subsidizing and covering up their continuing criminal behavior.

Other criticisms have been leveled by the divorced parent of a child who followed the other parent into the program. These parents claim that their child custody and visitation rights are involuntarily terminated by the government. And then there are the legitimate creditors left holding the bag by the witness's relocation without recourse for collecting debts and obligations (Montanino, 1990).

Congress addressed a number of these problems in the Witness Security Reform Act of 1984. For example, a protected witness's identity, location, criminal records, and fingerprints can now be disclosed (at the discretion of the Attorney General) to state or local law enforcement authorities if the witness is under investigation or charged with a felony or any crime of violence. The Attorney General is also required to assess in writing the risks and benefits of protection in individual cases, including the danger of possible further criminal acts by the protected individual.

Other changes brought about by the 1984 legislation include a requirement that court ordered child support payments be deducted from subsistence payments by the government and paid over, that children not be relocated if a person other than the protected witness has legal custody, and that certain civil actions against protected witnesses be facilitated by the government.

There is a further and continuing concern that the use of the program has changed over time to dilute its intended focus on organized crime. Whereas more than 60 percent of the witnesses entering the program in the early 1970s testified in organized crime prosecutions, ten years later this proportion had fallen to 27 percent (U.S. General Accounting Office, 1984). Despite this and other problems, there is reason to consider the program a success.

Howard Safir, an administrator of the program with the Marshals Service, had this to say about it:

> On balance, the Witness Security Program is a very successful operation. Information provided by protected witnesses helped to convict over 89 percent of the defendants against whom they have testified. The testimony of just one witness helped to convict five underworld bosses, severely crippling organized criminal activity on the west coast and in the mid-west. Not only do witnesses feel safe to speak out against their confederates, but in the majority of cases, they go on to live normal law-abiding lives. (1989:22)

Corroboration of Safir's observations can be found in an independent review of 220 cases involving testimony of protected witnesses: 75 percent of the defendants were found guilty, and of 150 so-called ringleader defendants, 88 percent were convicted and received median prison sentences of 11.2 years (U.S. General Accounting Office, 1984:11). Thus, good evidence of the success of this method of combating organized crime is plentiful.

In addition to Salvatore "Sammy Bull" Gravano, during the more than 20 years of its existence, other big name organized crime figures have entered the program, including Vincent Teresa and Jimmy "the Weasel" Fratianno. One whose name was initially not so big later became better known as the subject of the book *Wiseguy* (Pileggi, 1985), which in turn was the basis for the movie *GoodFellas*. His name is Henry Hill.

Henry Hill exemplifies both the pluses and the minuses of the witness protection program. On the plus side, as Pileggi pointed out, Hill was a very valuable witness: "It is safe to say that the Federal Witness Program got its money's worth out of Henry Hill. He took the stand and testified with such detached authenticity . . . that juries came back with one conviction after another" (1985:244). Just as with every other protected witness, Hill's survival literally depended on his willingness to betray his former criminal associates. Pileggi said of Hill: "He willingly turned on the world he knew and the men with whom he had been raised with the same nonchalance he had used in setting up a bookie joint or slipping a tail. For Henry Hill giving up the life was hard, but giving up his friends was easy" (1985:246). Just how hard was it? Too hard apparently. And this is where Hill is illustrative of a major concern about the program. Hill continued his criminal activities under the cover of his new identity and initially at least with the protection of the government. As a result, Henry Hill was ultimately booted out of the program and sent off on his own.

Witness protection is a valuable tool, but it is not without risks and negatives. In that regard it is like just about every other weapon against organized crime, including our next topic—wiretapping and electronic surveillance.

USING TECHNOLOGY
AGAINST THE MOB

Electronic surveillance incorporates a number of techniques that are governed by different laws and rules and that are more or less invasive of the privacy of the targets of the surveillance. Some techniques are nonconsensual, meaning none of the parties are aware of what is going on. Others use what is called one-party consensual monitoring. An undercover investigator may, for example, use a concealed tape recorder to record conversations, or one party to a telephone conversation may consent to it being recorded without the knowledge of the other party. Not all states permit one-party consensual monitoring.

Wiretapping, which is one of the methods used most extensively against organized crime, is the electronic interception of communications over a telephone line. Investigators tap into the telephone line of the target to listen in on and also to record these conversations. This is usually done without the consent of the parties to the conversation.

Eavesdropping and bugging involve the use of body tape recorders or hidden transmitters (microphones attached to walls, lamps, or internal sprinkler systems) to intercept and record oral communications. In the case of transmitters, this again is usually done without the consent of the participants. Also included in what has been referred to as "electronic snooping" is the use of TV cameras with videotapes and audio surveillance and recording equipment. Beepers can be attached to cars or packages or briefcases, for example, to emit a signal that permits tracking the target.

Electronic surveillance is utilized for many different purposes in investigating and prosecuting organized crime, including: (1) developing strategic intelligence in which the persons and criminal enterprises to be targeted for investigation are identified; (2) setting up specific investigations; (3) developing witnesses by, for example, approaching individuals who have been overheard to become informers; (4) corroborating witness testimony; and (5) as a substitute for witness testimony.

Intercepting oral communications is especially important in investigating organized crime because mobsters and racketeers use a minimum of written communications. Most of their criminal business is conducted over the telephone and in meetings. Thus, it is difficult or impossible to construct a "paper trail" that documents their criminal transactions. Lacking written records and documents that can be used as evidence, investigators must resort to producing their own records and documentation. Recordings and transcripts of wiretapped telephone conversations are one form of such documentation. Law enforcement officials generally view wiretapping as essential to controlling organized crime. Shieber summed up this view:

> Of the methods available to law enforcement personnel for securing information, only electronic surveillance is effective against higher echelon organized crime leaders. Infiltration and physical surveillance do not work: infiltration, because organized crime's methods for recruitment and screening of members and insulation of leaders make it almost impossible for a law enforcement agent to penetrate its upper levels. . . . Physical surveillance is inadequate

because it does not disclose the purpose of meetings or the substance of conversations at meetings or by telephone. If there is no informant, only electronic surveillance can provide this essential information to law enforcement agencies. And, even if an informant will provide information, usually he will not testify. (1982:1344–1345)

Despite its acknowledged value and effectiveness, the use of electronic surveillance in its various forms is a controversial policy because it constitutes a considerable invasion of privacy. Stepping back somewhat from the narrower issue of its use to combat organized crime, we must not lose sight of the fact that the privacy of communication is, in general, something to be preserved and protected. Totalitarian governments provide the best examples of the ugly side of surveillance—of what can happen when privacy is not respected. Under intrusive government, dissent is discouraged and intellectual controversies are smothered. The kind of thought and creativity essential to democracy, which is linked to the privacy of communications, is inhibited by the fear of surveillance. There have been unfortunate instances in our own history of the illegal use of electronic surveillance. At various times the FBI and the CIA illegally monitored political dissidents, antiwar protestors, professors, journalists, Dr. Martin Luther King, Jr., and the Socialist Workers Party. As the technological capabilities and sophistication of surveillance increase, these concerns are heightened. We now have miniaturized equipment, voice-activated equipment, parabolic microphones, lasers, and other highly sensitive devices that vastly increase the capacity for invading people's privacy. These serve to emphasize and reemphasize questions about their legitimate use. We must defend against simply exchanging "Big Brother" for the "Godfather."

In trying to strike a balance between law enforcement benefits and threats to privacy, certain rules have been developed to govern the use of electronic surveillance. Title III of the Omnibus Crime Control and Safe Streets Act of 1968 is one major source of these rules. Wiretaps, for example, require a warrant. Applications for warrants must be approved by the chief prosecutor (the Attorney General at the federal level) before being reviewed by a judge. Generally a rather high level of probable cause is required for such warrants. This means that there are good reasons for suspecting that the individuals to be targeted are engaging in criminal activity. The individuals and the probable crimes must be named. There must also be indication that alternative, traditional investigatory methods have been tried unsuccessfully and are likely to continue to be unsuccessful. When warrants are issued, there is usually a time limit, for example, 30 days (with a possibility of extensions). When the investigator monitoring the telephone tap overhears nonincriminating conversations, they are to be turned off. For example, the child of a surveillance target talking on the phone to a school classmate about homework would be an example of a nonincriminating conversation that is not supposed to be monitored. Upon termination of the wiretap, the recordings are sealed by a judge and all named defendants are notified. Judges also have the discretion to notify nondefendants or unindicted suspects that they have been recorded to protect individual privacy from undue public disclosure. Despite all these precautions, there is still considerable room for abuse and for innocent people to be hurt.

Beyond the operational value of the information produced about organized crime from electronic surveillance, which is our main concern here, this information is also of considerable value for criminologists and researchers who are trying to explain the nature and structure of this unique form of crime. It is extremely difficult to get hard, empirical data about organized crime. Kip Schlegel's work (1987) is a demonstrative example of the value of electronic surveillance information for research. Schlegel analyzed information produced by the FBI in its four-year electronic surveillance (wiretaps and eavesdropping devices) of the De Cavalcante and De Carlo crime families in New Jersey. He used this information to empirically test some of the assumptions about the nature and function of violence in organized crime. This work expands our knowledge and increases our understanding. With that idea in mind, we turn, finally, to a more recent example of information that can be used for both law enforcement purposes (as it was very effectively in this case) and for purposes of understanding and explaining the broader phenomenon that is organized crime.

The Gotti Tapes

In 1989, as part of the federal investigation of John Gotti and his Gambino crime family—and based on the probable cause that criminal activity had occurred and was likely to occur again—the FBI was authorized to bug several of the family's leading hangouts: the Ravenite Social Club in New York City, a hallway outside the club, and a private apartment above the club. Blumenthal (1992) described the results produced in this way: "The harvest of revelation the government would reap from its electronic eavesdropping would yield a bounty beyond expectation. The Gotti tapes would open a vista into a sinister and darkly humorous world riven by greed and paranoia and ego run amok" (p. xxi).

The surreptitiously recorded conversations among Gotti and his criminal associates, of which the following is an example, were transcribed by the

FBI. This sample, from the book, *The Gotti Tapes* (1992), is presented both to give a flavor of the kinds of things discussed by organized crime figures and to suggest the value to law enforcement of such electronic surveillance. This particular recording was made in the apartment above the club on January 24, 1990. Gotti, Salvatore Gravano, and two associates, Frank Locascio and John D'Amato, are discussing the very threat to them of government wiretapping and bugging. Gotti begins by talking about the recorded conversations that were used as evidence against him in previous trials. He also explains how he is much more cautious now.

> GOTTI: And from now on, I'm telling you if a guy just so mentions "La," or if he wants to say, "La, la, la, la." He just says "La," the guy. I'm gonna strangle the cocksucker. You know what I mean? He don't have to say, "Cosa Nostra," just "La," and they go. No, you know why (inaudible). Look, I heard other people's—I heard nine months of tapes of my life. Gambling, I put the guy's head up his mother's cunt, and I'll kill him about this, (inaudible) all that shit. It, er, once in a while you heard "a nice fellow," something like that. It bothered me, but it didn't bother me. This actually is fucking bothering me today. I was actually sick and I don't wanna get sick. Not sick for me—sick for this "thing of ours." Sick for that—how, how naive we were five years ago. This was '85. This is fuckin' April '85, ah, up until, ah, till May of '86. And, I'm, I'm sick that we were so fucking naive. Me number one! (p. 121)

After several brief comments by the others during this same conversation, Gotti expounds on the problem of conversations being recorded by the government and proposes taking people outside where they cannot be overheard when he wants to talk business.

> GOTTI: Yeah, but let me give ya an example. I'm telling Angelo, "Hey, you gotta do me a favor," I tell him. "Don't make nobody come in. Don't make nobody talk. This [is] how we get in trouble—we talk. You don't have to be in this club". . . . But I'm telling you, I'm sort of more guilty than any of you are simply because, I'm telling you, I know better. "Get the fuck out!" I'm supposed to tell them. "I wanna talk to you." Two blocks up I'm talking to you. Six blocks around I'll talk. (p. 122)

Prior to the start of his RICO trial in January 1992, John Gotti's lawyers tried to get the hundreds of hours of tapes suppressed. Such motions to suppress evidence gained through electronic surveillance are a typical defense tactic in organized crime cases. In this case, the motion was denied. The tapes, along with the already mentioned testimony of underboss Salvatore Gravano, were critical in bringing about Gotti's conviction on racketeering and murder charges.

CONCLUSION

Each of the various methods of combating organized crime we have just examined is controversial in its own way. The IRS's giving information to investigators and prosecutors—information it has gained from personal income tax forms—is an invasion of privacy. Sometimes, however, this may be the only effective way to build a criminal case against an organized crime figure. Considering such disclosure presents a clash of values and a policy dilemma prosecutors and judges and sometimes legislators must resolve. The stark choice is between protecting the rights of innocent parties on the one hand and effectively going after organized professional criminals on the other. This choice occurs repeatedly in organized crime cases.

RICO is unquestionably the most effective legislative tool ever devised to combat organized crime in the United States. However, it has been and continues to be misused and abused. The misuse and abuse have occurred especially by characterizing certain groups inappropriately as "racketeering enterprises" and by using civil forfeitures against innocent people who were far removed from the actual criminal activity.

Similarly, investigative grand juries have become "runaway" grand juries: suspects who are innocent under the law have been granted immunity from prosecution but then incarcerated for lengthy periods because of refusal to testify; informants and protected witnesses have practically been given a license to commit crimes; major criminals have been exonerated and turned loose on society in return for their testimony; and eavesdrops and wiretaps have been overused.

Does this mean that we should forgo or eliminate these various tools? No. To do so would, in effect, render us toothless in our struggle against the most pernicious forms of crime. What it does mean is that we must be ever vigilant in safeguarding the use of powerful weapons. The principle of last resort should govern in most cases. Judicial approval and oversight should be required. We, as a society, should ask whether the ends justify the means and be guided by the thought that there are few (if any) ends that justify any and all means.

13

⊷⇒◉⇐⊶

Policy Issues in Dealing with Organized Crime

I n this final chapter, we conclude our discussion of organized crime in America by examining what we consider to be some of the major policy issues for the foreseeable future. We will look at the public's understanding of this phenomenon and how that understanding is influenced by the media and by government agencies and actions. We will look, too, at new tools and weapons government is employing in combating organized crime. Last, we will take up the controversial question of legalizing at least some of the goods and services now being provided—generally for huge profits—by organized crime.

Why is public understanding of organized crime important? Without understanding the true nature and costs to society of the illicit activities of organized crime, there will not be public antipathy and revulsion for such activities. And without strong antipathy, there will not be the necessary public support for policies to control and reduce organized crime.

The American public has a sort of love–hate relationship with organized crime. This ambivalence seems to result from a combination of fascination and even tacit admiration for certain "glamorous" criminals; a desire for the "things" that organized crime provides; feelings of fear and helplessness at what is perceived to be the awesome power of organized crime; and an abhorrence of the corruption and violence that often attend organized crime. Public ambivalence sends mixed signals both to organized crime and to the agencies of law enforcement and criminal justice. Ambivalence and mixed signals are not solid foundations for public policy.

> The existence of . . . constituencies [for illicit goods and services], together with the absence of widespread awareness of the broader implications of organized crime group operations, such as public corruption, derivative crime such as that flowing from the need to service drug and gambling habits, and diversion of resources from productive to consumer channels, makes it most difficult to marshal the public support that is vital to assuring continuous and consistent provision of resources to combat these organized criminal groups. (Edelhertz & Overcast, 1990:4)

Let us begin by understanding where, how, and in what form the public receives its information.

THE MEDIA AND ORGANIZED CRIME

In Chapter 9 we described the role of popular culture in helping to promulgate and maintain the so-called Mafia myth. Here we want to examine and describe, in a broader fashion, the part the media generally play in bringing about a public understanding of organized crime. Public understanding, and the ensuing support or opposition, are essential elements in the development and success of government policies to combat organized crime. Some critics have been particularly harsh on the media for their poor coverage of organized crime. Martens and Cunningham-Niederer (1985) are examples: "Simply stated, the mass media have done little to encourage high quality research of organized crime. Competition is woefully lacking, and as a result, we are treated to very superficial, mediocre, and sensational portrayals of organized crime" (p. 62). We believe that this criticism is overstated and paints with too broad a brush. While it is an accurate assessment of some media coverage, particularly the more sensational entertainment-oriented media, it is certainly not true of all.

By media we mean serious newspaper, television, and radio news media as well as radio and television entertainment programming and also books, movies, and national magazines. The extent to which the media permeate our lives is enormous; and the degree to which they inform, educate, and shape our attitudes and opinions should not be underestimated. Take, for example, just the number of TV channels, given cable, that one can watch 24 hours a day, 7 days a week. All forms of media have played a role in determining what the public understands, doesn't understand, and misunderstands about the mysteries of organized crime.

The nature of the understanding seems to be closely tied to the form of the media sending the message. The message from the news media is rather different from the message of the entertainment media. But to complicate things further, there is overlap within the forms of media themselves. Television, for example, the principal source of information for most Americans, presents both news and entertainment programs dealing with organized crime—and sometimes even mixes up entertainment and news in a form known as the *docudrama*. A host of books fall into the categories of fact-based fiction or fictionalized biographical works. What the consumer understands from all this is, therefore, not simple to sort out. In Chapter 1, we defined organized crime by examining the attributes of its activities and of its actors. The entertainment media take a selective form of the latter focus when presenting information about organized crime. They concentrate on the individual personalities of particular organized crime figures, making "media personalities" of them.

The informing and educating done by the serious news media are complicated and sometimes undermined or countermanded by the entertainment media, which is accused of distorting organized crime and glamorizing organized crime figures. A veteran reporter and editor for the *Chicago Tribune* described the difficulties faced by news reporters covering organized crime: "sometimes getting those stories [of organized crime] into the paper becomes more difficult today. . . . Editors tend to overlook the fact that the impact of organized crime and the lack of public awareness can be almost as devastating to the economy and the lifestyle of a local community as the events in some far off place" (Wiedrich, 1984:15). On the mixed messages (informing versus entertaining) problem, Wiedrich said: "All of us have to strive in some way to keep the image of organized crime alive before the public so that people do not accept the glamorous presentation that television and the movies very often portray" (p. 15).

Newspapers such as the *New York Times*, the *Wall Street Journal*, *Newsday*, and the *Arizona Republic* have done an excellent job covering organized crime. A reporter for the *Arizona Republic*, Don Bolles, was murdered in 1976 while investigating and writing about organized crime activity in Arizona. Excellence in coverage is also true of national magazines such as *Fortune*, *Time*, *The New Yorker*, and *Reader's Digest*. Attesting to the role of the *New York Times* in this area, and notwithstanding the fact that one of us is affiliated with the University of Nebraska, a colleague who is a specialist on the subject remarked that one of the reasons he had to leave Nebraska was because the *New York Times* was not readily available on a timely basis in Nebraska and that it was impossible to work in that specialty under those circumstances.

The Media World of Crime

"Because relatively few people have extensive direct experience with crime, it seems reasonable to assume that the public's mental images of crime—as well as of criminals, victims, and criminal justice—are shaped, to a great extent, by the mass media," concluded James Garofalo (1981:334) after a comprehensive review of the research on crime and the mass media. We believe it is safe to assume that even fewer people have direct personal experience with organized crime than they do with crime in general. Therefore, the role of the vicarious experience in shaping their views is probably even greater. Unfortunately, from the point of view of accuracy, the nature of the media shaping was described by Garofalo as more a process of misinforming than informing, because "the depictions of crime and violence in the media differ from the reality of crime and violence" (1981:339).

Nearly ten years later, a similar conclusion was reached in another study of the media and crime: "We are on the way to a communication-conditioned mass-media society in which fiction, fantasy, and the definition of reality assume a greater role than reality itself" (Schneider, 1990:115). The media, according to Schneider, influence societal stereotypes that then enter human interaction as interpretation. In one ironic form of this interpretation, Schneider says that the "law violator adopts the picture that he thinks society holds of him" (p. 120). O'Brien and Kurins (1991) describe how this phenomenon affects organized criminals: "Mobsters look to the media for a sense of their own history. The Tradition, the Code—it is not too much of an exaggeration to say that these things have now been given over to the keeping of editors and screenwriters, who feed them back to a new generation of thugs with no real sense of the past, no real sense of the Old Country—just a crew of mutts who happen to have Italian surnames and would like to feel that they are part of something slightly less mean and sordid than their own criminal impulses" (p. 227). These thugs, according to the authors, have been given (by the Godfather movies and their genre) "a whole range of ready-made things to say when they wanted to sound tough, sincere, righteous, or even wise" (p. 47).

Kooistra (1989) likewise accused the press of treating crime as entertaining drama and of often misrepresenting tales as informative news. Why do they do this? The answer is not too surprising: "Newspapers found that stories about noted criminals [for example, Bonnie and Clyde, Billy the Kid, John Dillinger] helped to sell papers. Magazines, movies, and books found such criminals to be profitable topics" (Kooistra, 1989:127). Kooistra has developed an interesting theory about criminals as heroes, which we take up in the conclusion of this section on the media.

Organized Crime in the Movies A number of references have been made to the influence of movie portrayals on public understanding of organized crime. Let's take a closer look at this particular form of media, whose importance we ought not to underestimate. About movies, Garofalo (1981) concluded that "it is possible that movies have greater effects on the public than might be expected [because] theater movie viewing is probably a more intense form of media exposure" (p. 341).

The decade of the 1990s was ushered in by a spate of movies dealing with organized crime. We had *GoodFellas, My Blue Heaven, The Godfather Part III, State of Grace, Miller's Crossing,* and *Mobsters,* just to name the most prominent films. The movie reviewer for *Time* magazine analyzed the public's fascination with these movies as follows: "Watching *GoodFellas* is like going to the Bronx Zoo. You stare at the beasts of prey and find a brute charisma in their demeanor. You wonder how you would act if you lived in their world, where aggression is rewarded and decency is crushed. Finally you walk away, tantalized by a view into the darkest part of yourself, glad that that part is still behind bars" (*Time,* September 24, 1990:84). But to carry the analogy a step further, if the knowledge and understanding of organized crime gleaned from *GoodFellas*-type movies is comparable to the knowledge of jungle animals gained from visiting the Bronx Zoo, then the degree of our enlightenment is certainly questionable.

In a similar vein, Peter Maas, writing about *Godfather Part III,* concluded that the Mafia embodies and reflects our deepest anxieties, yearnings, wonderment and imagination. "What better mirrors fierce free enterprise with everyone's . . . life literally on the line. . . . Its heroes are flawed, not superhuman projections of good over evil. Its personas are caught in destinies not of their own making. Never mind that loyalty and honor play no part in the actual Mafia. Perceived reality is what counts here" (the *New York Times,* September 9, 1990:23, 45). Perceived reality and its conscious creation are important elements in understanding the media's handling of the subject of organized crime.

Mobsters, a film about the rise of Lucky Luciano, Meyer Lansky, Bugsy Seigel, and Frank Costello, paints Luciano and Lansky especially as heroes. Young men on the make on the violent streets of the Italian neighborhoods of New York City in the 1930s, they are portrayed as little guys who suffer but ultimately prevail against big "bad" guys. Their world is presented as a glamorous world of excitement, beautiful women, high living, nice clothes, and whatever else goes along with being a mobster. It is exactly this kind of treatment critics such as Robert Wiedrich are attacking. And, it is contrary to Schneider's conclusion that the media portray offenders as psychopaths, monsters, and mentally abnormal people deserving of hate and contempt. "In the 'media world of crime,' the offender is an unfair, disagreeable, reckless, and egotistical character" (Schneider, 1990:121). The Luciano and Lansky of *Mobsters* may be reckless and egotistical, but they are certainly not disagreeable and contemptible. We will have more to say about the notion of criminals as heroes shortly.

Organized Crime in the News Media In Smith's (1975) development of what he called the Mafia mystique, he reviewed the news media coverage of organized crime or more accurately that of the Mafia. Using the *New York Times Index*, Smith found that "in the seven-year period from the Kefauver hearings [in 1950] to the eve of Apalachin [in 1957], there were a total of 19 items in the *Times* . . . in which 'Mafia' was a subject worth citing. . . . In the six-year period from November 1957 to the first public comment on [Joseph] Valachi, there were a total of 35 items of 'Mafia' significance" (pp. 240-241). In the 1950s, *Times* coverage ranged from 5 to 11 pieces. In 1963, the year of Valachi's testimony, there were 67 pieces, and in 1967, there were 148.

By way of contrast, the *New York Times Index* for 1989 had 27 references for Mafia, Unione Siciliano, or Black Hand, but 98 for organized crime, and 175 for racketeering and racketeers. The *Readers' Guide to Periodical Literature* for 1989 had 15 references to Mafia and 17 to RICO; the *Guide* for 1990 had 2 references to organized crime, 22 to Mafia, and 6 to RICO. These latter results indicate a Mafia fascination is still prevalent in these particular media. But there has been a dramatic new emphasis on and coverage of racketeering and particularly of RICO. This reflects the government's increasingly effective use of the RICO statute against racketeering enterprises. This kind of media attention is more relevant to the issue of government policy.

Finally, as a measure of the magnitude of news media coverage of organized crime, the *National Newspaper Index* (which covers the *New York Times*, the *Christian Science Monitor*, the *Wall Street Journal*, the *Los Angeles Times*, and the *Washington Post*) had 423 references to organized crime between January 1988 and July 1991. It is not possible to say whether this is a lot or a little without a comparative study, but information about organized crime is certainly being provided to readers of the nation's leading newspapers.

Similar to the observations already reported from others, Smith criticized the media at that time for providing "little substantive knowledge or analysis" for the "popular reader" (1975:182). What was provided was, he said, for "popular consumption," in other words, entertainment rather than enlightenment.

More recently, Morash and Hale (1987) examined a case example of the news media's handling of organized crime. They too echo the concern of others that "crime news generally presents a selective perception of reality" (p. 130). In their examination, they added another important dimension to the effects of media treatment: "coverage of organized crime is of particular interest because it shapes not only public but also some academic understanding. News accounts of organized crime activity have a significant influence in academia because, probably more than in any other area of criminological research, they have been accepted as data sources. . . . The picture of organized crime and corruption that is established in the news influences the views of college and university students, who often become criminal justice practitioners and policy-makers" (p. 131). Morash and Hale criticized news accounts for inadequate sampling of both illegal acts and actors; for emphasizing discrete events and individual's crimes rather than organizational crime; and for stressing "temporal and spatial interrelationships between people and actions . . . rather than interactions between people that can explain how an illegal activity came to pass" (p. 147). Although certainly legitimate criticisms, some of these may be asking too much of the typical news media. After all, every reporter is not a criminologist or even a social scientist, and every newspaper is not the *New York Times* or the *Washington Post*.

The Heroic Criminal: John Gotti, alias Mob Star

Paul Kooistra (1989) has developed a thesis about criminals being portrayed and seen as heroes. He describes the heroic criminal as follows: "They are driven to a life of crime either as a victim of injustice or for committing an act which the state, but not the community, considers as criminal; they are considered by large portions of the public as moral and honorable men; these . . . are men who violate the law but who represent a 'higher' justice; they rob from the corrupt rich and give to the deserving poor; others are harmed only when 'justice' requires it or in self-defense; the legitimacy of the state is not challenged, only the corrupt practices of the oppressors of the people" (p. 9).

Kooistra admits that the so-called gangster does not readily fit into this "Robin Hood" role, that is, robbing from the rich to give to the poor. But Kooistra offers Al Capone as the prototype big city gangster who comes closest to fitting the definition: "Of all the noted Godfathers of American history, Capone comes closest to being an American Robin Hood" (p. 139). Capone was regularly quoted in the Chicago newspapers, with which he had "a good working relationship." "Stories of his support for soup kitchens to feed the poor, of his providing tickets for boy scouts to attend football games, of his protection of show business personalities and common folk from the predations of street criminals, of his gifts of thousands of turkeys to the poor on holidays, all had a way of appearing in print and keeping the public informed of Capone's philanthropy" (Kooistra, 1989:138). A popular figure and public benefactor who "provided alcoholic beverages to a thirsty populace"(p. 138), Capone had no less than seven biographies about him published between 1929 and 1931. Kooistra points out that Capone and his influential supporters actively attempted to cultivate the hero image. Let's look at a modern-day Al Capone in the context of the criminal as hero thesis. What Al Capone was to the 1920s and 1930s, John Gotti was to the 1980s and early 1990s.

In one biographical work, John Gotti was called a "mob star" and "Al Capone in an $1800 suit" (Mustain & Capeci, 1988). As such, he was said to be the most powerful criminal in America—head of the New York–based $500 million (or $5 billion, depending on whom you believe) Gambino crime empire of drugs, loan-sharking, extortion, hijacking, robbery, and murder. Gotti was also known as the Dapper Don for his expensive style of dress and the Teflon Don for having been indicted three times in the late 1980s but not convicted. Gotti took over the Gambino crime family when its boss, Paul Castellano, was murdered in December 1985. Gotti was ultimately convicted of masterminding Castellano's murder and of racketeering; he was finally sent to prison in 1992.

Another book about Gotti described him as being "as publicly visible as a movie star . . . strolling into the city's finest restaurants." "In the city that worships power, the New York City tabloids chronicled every move and public utterance of the man they called 'the Dapper Don.' He was the subject of cover stories in *Time*, *People*, and *The New York Times Magazine*, a tribute to the phenomenon of national media, whose nerve centers are in Manhattan. . . . Gotti was also chronicled in that ultimate tribute to fame in America, the 'Doonesbury' comic strip" (Cummings & Volkman, 1990:226).

Do John Gotti and the Gotti media phenomenon fit the heroic criminal idea? Again, as in the Capone case, Gotti was neither construed as nor perceived as being some sort of American Robin Hood. But the media are obviously fascinated with Gotti the personality, and so are the public. Gotti had sex appeal. He had that intangible thing called animal magnetism. He exuded a sense of power and invulnerability. He was crude, but tough. He thumbed his nose at the white-collar establishment in a way that is appealing to blue-collar, working-class types in particular. The best example of this was his annual Fourth of July block party in Ozone Park, Queens. This celebration, complete with illegal fireworks, was held in defiance of the law and fire department regulations. Cummings and Volkman described the 1987 version this way: "The [three-thousand-dollar diamond pinky] ring glinted in the light as he waved to the crowd of more than two thousand people gathered along a six-block stretch. . . . They cheered, as though Gotti was some kind of hometown hero. . . . If the people of Ozone Park were cheering his accession to power in the Mafia and his victory in a federal racketeering case a few months before, then there was cause to wonder about the civic education of citizens who thought it worthwhile to cheer a murderer, heroin trafficker, and extortionist" (1990:225).

Gotti and his treatment by the media exemplify the entertainment versus information conflict the media face in creating a public understanding of organized crime. The Task Force on Organized Crime of the National Advisory Committee on Criminal Justice Standards and Goals recognized this complication. Nevertheless, they recommended that "the media have an essential role in the control of organized crime," because they are necessary to inform the public about the meaning of government actions, to identify for the public the true nature, magnitude, and seriousness of organized crime, and "to reveal governmental failures and inadequacies in dealing with problems" (President's Commission, 1976:85). It is in this way that the role of the media is a policy issue in dealing with organized crime.

Moving from the outside to the inside, we turn next to the role of the federal government in bringing about a public understanding of organized crime.

EDUCATING THE PUBLIC ABOUT ORGANIZED CRIME

Our focus here will be on the government's role in enhancing understanding of organized crime and not on its role in enforcement and prosecution. Consequently, we will be looking at several national commissions, at the United States Senate, and the General Accounting Office, and not at such federal agencies as the FBI or the Department of Justice. Further, we will focus on roughly the last decade after briefly reviewing the history of the most significant government efforts that predate the 1980s.

National Studies of Organized Crime, 1950 to 1980

The Kefauver Investigation The U.S. Senate Special Committee to Investigate Organized Crime in Interstate Commerce, under the chairmanship of Senator Estes Kefauver of Tennessee, came into being in 1950. The committee conducted the first nationwide investigation of organized crime by means of 92 days of hearings, in different major cities, lasting nearly a year (Blakey, 1987). The Kefauver committee's part in defining organized crime and in contributing to the Mafia myth have already been described. Notwithstanding the criticisms of the committee, particularly with regard to the myth issue, we think it is appropriate to conclude that "the Kefauver committee was successful in arousing the consciousness of the public and stirring its sensitivity to organized crime" (Blakey, 1987:20). Whether consciousness and sensitivity are the same as understanding, or whether they are nevertheless important in their own right, are debatable questions.

The McClellan Hearings Seven years after Kefauver, in June and July 1958, the Senate Select Committee on Improper Activities in the Labor or Management Field, under the chairmanship of Senator John McClellan, also held hearings on organized crime. In 1963, McClellan's Permanent Subcommittee on Investigations, of the Senate Committee on Government Operations, took the testimony of mobster Joseph Valachi about the existence and workings of La Cosa Nostra. The committee also probed links between the International Brotherhood of Teamsters labor union and organized crime. As with the Kefauver committee, there was certainly heightened public consciousness and increased sensitivity as a result of these investigations. But also again, there is controversy especially regarding the validity of the Valachi disclosures—controversy that bears on the question of public understanding.

The 1967 Task Force on Organized Crime This task force of the President's Commission on Law Enforcement and Administration of Justice made a national report of findings and recommendations relating to the problems of organized crime. The exact extent to which this report enhanced public understanding of these problems is unknown, but it is questionable on several grounds. First, the American public in general is not made up of voracious consumers of government reports on anything (and their avoidance in many instances is quite understandable). Second, the paperback, popular publication of the President's Commission's general report, *The Challenge of Crime in a Free Society* (Avon Books, 1968), contained a fairly critical or dismissive review of the organized crime piece by a criminologist. This could have had the effect of diminishing its credibility. But probably most important, the circulation of the report in particular, but also of the paperback book as well, would have been pretty narrow and selective—mostly to libraries, the criminal justice community, and academics, researchers, and students of organized crime. This is not an unimportant audience, but it is clearly not the general public. Public knowledge of the contents of this report would, for the most part, have come from the news media. And that, of course, would have been subject to the concerns and problems previously described.

The 1976 Task Force on Organized Crime This body, one of the task forces of the National Advisory Committee on Criminal Justice Standards and Goals, issued its report on organized crime in 1976. We suspect that its circulation to the general public and its effect upon general public understanding were even less than that of the 1967 report. This is ironic because the foreword to the report emphasized that "an increased concern by the private citizen is an indispensable prerequisite . . . to the success of an organized crime control program" (National Task Force on Organized Crime, 1976:vii). The reasons for our suspicions are, first, the thrust of the report was toward recommending standards and goals to help state and local criminal justice agencies. That means its principal audience was intended to be police, prosecutors, judges, and lawyers. Second, unlike the 1967 report, this report on organized crime did not even have the benefit of a popularized paperback edition. There was a general volume, but it was issued in 1975, before there was an organized crime report. Thus, we conclude that this task force and its report probably had little if any effect on the public's understanding of organized crime.

President's Commission on Organized Crime, 1983 to 1986

Established by the Reagan administration, this was the first national commission devoted exclusively to investigating and reporting on the problems of organized crime. Among other things, it was directed to conduct public hearings in numerous cities across the country and to make use of a variety of investigative techniques to "alert the public to the scope and pernicious effects of organized crime in American society" (President's Commission, 1983:vi). The commission held seven public hearings in different regions of the country, focusing on the federal law enforcement perspective, money laundering, Asian organized crime, cocaine trafficking, heroin trafficking, labor–management racketeering, and gambling. It also produced five major reports.

Commission Chairman Judge Irving Kaufman seemed to feel that the commission had largely accomplished its goal of alerting the public. Kaufman agreed with the premise that "public awareness of its pernicious effect must be heightened if any concerted campaign against organized crime is to succeed" (President's Commission, 1986:4). Kaufman indicated in the final report that the commission had focused public attention on organized crime and had suggested ways to implement a concerted national strategy against it. The commission's success in this informational aspect of its work, he wrote, "was an important achievement." Similarly, a statement of supplemental views by a subset of commissioners agreed that "the Commission has . . . made a significant contribution to public understanding of some key aspects of the problem of organized crime in America" (President's Commission, 1986:173).

Unfortunately, as far as public understanding is concerned, we again have reservations about how broad and deep was the nature of understanding created or stimulated by this commission. Undoubtedly, people who attended the public hearings learned something about organized crime, but this was an extremely limited subsample of American citizens. Those who availed themselves of the media coverage in cities where hearings were held would have gained some selective information. The vast remainder would have had to depend on their own media or read the commission reports. To add to our earlier comments about the readership for government reports, and just to furnish an impressionistic view of the likelihood of any broad reading audience having materialized, not one of nearly a dozen criminal justice faculty colleagues surveyed at Rutgers was even aware of this commission and its reports, let alone having actually read one.

Finally, one additional problem in this case negatively affected the intent of the publicity given the commission's findings and recommendations. A supplemental report was made by a large group of commissioners. In their report, this group, who represented some of the most knowledgeable and influential of the commissioners, took the President's Commission to task for what they termed a "saga of missed opportunity" (President's Commission, 1986:173). They were referring mainly to the failure to assess the effectiveness of federal and state antiorganized efforts. It was this controversy that received most of the media attention. As a result, even people who did pay attention to the media coverage of the commission and its reports mostly heard or read about the controversy.

Does this mean that commissions like this one and the others mentioned earlier are a waste of time, effort, and money? Or, minimally, are they a waste at least as far as public understanding is concerned? No. But it does mean that expectations need to be limited and realistic. As many efforts as are possible need to be made to reach out to and involve the public. Influential and recognizable citizen members need to be appointed. Video technology needs to be exploited in creative ways to educate the public. Well-advertised public hearings need to be held in diverse locations. And most important, the news media need to be heavily involved, kept fully informed, and even cultivated.

Other Senate Investigations:
Twenty-Five Years after Valachi

In April 1988, the U.S. Senate Permanent Subcommittee on Investigations held five days of public hearings on organized crime. The subcommittee also produced a hearings report of 1255 pages (U.S. Senate, 1990). A number of statements and testimony during these hearings are instructive, both in terms of the role of the hearings themselves in bringing about greater understanding and in the importance attached to such public understanding:

> CHAIRMAN SAM NUNN: That testimony [by Joseph Valachi], coupled with the extensive work done by this Subcommittee under the chairmanship of the late Senator McClellan, profoundly affected not only our understanding of organized crime in America, but also how our Government was to respond to it during the years that followed. . . . public information, public awareness, public dedication . . . are absolutely crucial to the fight that lies before us now in so many realms. (pp. 2, 4)
>
> SENATOR MITCHELL: These hearings will serve their purpose if they revive public intolerance for these and other lawbreakers. (p. 10)
>
> DIRECTOR DAVID WILLIAMS (Office of Special Investigations, General Accounting Office): We must continue to focus public attention on the LCN and its activities. Publicity, like that provided by today's hearing, increases public understanding of how the LCN operates. Publicity also increases the risk of exposure for those participating in the LCN's activities, particularly the political figures and businesspeople who are enticed by the LCN's promises of power and easy profits. (p. 78)
>
> COMMISSIONER JAMES R. ZAZZALI (Chairman, New Jersey State Commission of Investigation): The helpful weapons are hearings such as these, education, sense of commitment, and an expenditure of resources and manpower. (p. 174)

JOSEPH PISTONE (Former undercover agent for the FBI; as "Donnie Brasco," infiltrated the LCN for six years): Law enforcement and society in general have to be aware of this subcultural phenomenon in order to succeed in eliminating it. As long as this subculture exists and to some extent is supported by the rest of society, there will be new subculture members ready and willing to replace those who are convicted or killed by rival gang members. (p. 205)

SENATOR ROTH: How does publicity or public exposure hurt the LCN?

PISTONE: Well, I think it hurts them in that if they are exposed, it takes away our movie image of them, that they are invincible and that they all walk around in $2,000 suits and that they cannot be touched. Also, if they are exposed along these lines, it may help to have legitimate businessmen who at this point would think twice before becoming involved with a Mafia member if he knows that this individual has been in the newspapers or there has been articles about this individual as being associated with the mob. (p. 215)

While subject to many of the limitations already outlined, the Senate and its Permanent Subcommittee on Investigations clearly made a laudatory effort to increase public appreciation of the problem of organized crime. And these were only the latest in a series of similar efforts. In 1980, this subcommittee held hearings and released a report on organized crime and the use of violence; in 1984, they profiled organized crime in the mid-Atlantic region, and they put out a report on waterfront corruption (U.S. Senate, 1980, 1984a, 1984b). Likewise, the Senate Committee on the Judiciary (U.S. Senate, 1983) held hearings and released several reports on organized crime in America. Thus, the United States Senate has been fairly active in this area of public education over the last ten years.

United States General Accounting Office

The General Accounting Office (GAO) is an investigative arm of the United States Congress. They undertake investigations at the request of various congressional committees. They provide the requesting committees with reports and publish investigative reports for the use of the general public. In 1989, the GAO published two such reports following investigations into organized crime. One was an examination of the Department of Justice Organized Crime Strike Force efforts against organized crime groups

(U.S. General Accounting Office, 1989b). The other was an investigation of Colombian, Jamaican, Chinese, and Vietnamese criminal gangs operating in the United States, and street gangs in Los Angeles (U.S. General Accounting Office, 1989a).

These investigations and the resulting reports assisted the Senate in its exposure efforts. They also provided information to law enforcement, researchers, and other students of organized crime. Limitations on reaching the general public are the same as previously described.

Federal Support for Research

Following the assumption that research produces knowledge and that knowledge brings understanding, another avenue or means by which the federal government can enhance understanding of organized crime is by supporting research. Historically, such financial support has been extremely limited and sporadic. "Organized crime is not a field for which there has been a steady supply of grant opportunities" (Reuter, 1987:184). One of the factors that may account for this is the absence of solid theoretical foundations. Federal funding agencies like the National Academy of Sciences and the National Science Foundation place great emphasis upon sound conceptual and theoretical underpinning in the research proposals they support. Organized crime theory is notoriously weak.

The National Institute of Justice (NIJ), the principal research support arm of the Department of Justice, is the primary source of research funding for criminal justice research in the United States. It developed a special research program for white-collar and organized crime in 1988. NIJ's research program plan for 1990 described some of its prior projects and outlined its focus of priorities for 1990 funding. Asserting that the institute "has a long history of sponsoring research directed toward the improvement of law enforcement detection, prevention, and control of organized crime" (National Institute of Justice, 1990:41), that plan referred to specific studies of illegal bookmaking and numbers operations in New York City, of corruption in the waste disposal industry, and of racketeer-dominated or influenced labor unions, as examples of its past support.

The 1990 plan proposed supporting research in such new areas as the impact of civil and criminal RICO legislation on organized criminal groups and their operations; on broadening the focus of enforcement efforts to a wide range of organized criminal groups such as Asian racketeering organizations, Latin American drug cartels, and motorcycle and prison gangs; and on identifying reliable direct and indirect measures to detect the presence, types, and levels of organized crime activity. These certainly are important topics to include on the national organized crime research agenda.

In 1991, however, organized crime disappeared from the NIJ research plan (National Institute of Justice, 1991). Practically lost among the new research priorities of gang violence, drugs, domestic terrorism, multiple murder, occult crime, and community-based policing were just two even bearing on organized crime: money laundering (focused on laundering drug money) and control of organized crime drug trafficking groups. Without going into either the merits or the politics of these priorities, it appeared that strong financial support for organized crime research had been abandoned by NIJ. Fortunately for the producers and consumers of organized crime research, financial support was restored in 1992 and 1993. Since accurate and publicly available information is considered to be so crucial to the fight against organized crime, this research support is essential if there is to be a well-grounded and well-informed policy to guide this fight.

EXPANDING THE POWERS
OF ENFORCEMENT

In Chapter 12, we examined the Racketeer Influenced and Corrupt Organizations Act (RICO) in some detail. Here we want to focus on one specific feature of that statute that has greatly expanded government's ability to combat organized crime—provision for the use of civil remedies. Section 1964 of the RICO statute provides:

(a) The district courts of the United States shall have jurisdiction to prevent and restrain violations of section 1962 of this chapter by issuing appropriate orders, including, but not limited to: ordering any person to divest himself of any interest, direct or indirect, in any enterprise; imposing reasonable restrictions on the future activities or investments of any person, including, but not limited to, prohibiting any person from engaging in the same type of endeavor as the enterprise engaged in, the activities of which affect interstate or foreign commerce; or ordering dissolution or reorganization of any enterprise. . . .

(b) The Attorney General may institute proceedings under this section. Pending final determination thereof, the court may at any time enter such restraining orders or prohibitions, or take such other actions . . . as it shall deem proper.

(c) Any person injured in his business or property by reason of a violation of section 1962 . . . may sue therefor . . . and shall recover threefold the damages he sustains and the cost of the suit, including a reasonable attorney's fee.

What this somewhat formidable legal language means is that the government is given enormous powers to employ civil sanctions against persons and enterprises engaging in a pattern of racketeering activity. A U.S. judge can, for example, require such persons to sell their holdings in a business enterprise (perhaps at a loss) and to pay back any earnings they have gained from the enterprise. The judge can also break up the enterprise or reorganize it. Private individuals, as well as the Attorney General, can institute civil actions against racketeer-influenced enterprises. And, most important, these powers can be exercised independent of any criminal proceedings. A criminal conviction, therefore, is not a prerequisite to seeking any civil remedies.

This provision is the key to the expansion of enforcement powers, because civil actions are much easier than criminal actions because the civil rules of evidence are more relaxed than the criminal rules. Protections against self-incrimination are generally not applicable and standards of proof are lower (preponderance of the evidence versus guilt beyond a reasonable doubt). But, at the same time, heavy fines or other economic penalties can be imposed. Successful civil suits under RICO can result in treble damages, which can amount to multimillion dollar awards for the plaintiff. Thus, the economic infrastructure of organized criminal enterprises can be very effectively attacked, huge economic sanctions and penalties can be levied, and all this can be done under a civil procedure that makes it much easier to accomplish.

Not surprisingly, the advantages of this approach have not been lost on state and local governments although some claim that these same advantages, at least initially, seemingly escaped most federal prosecutors (President's Commission, 1986). In fact, in the period 1970 to 1985, it was at the state and local level that civil RICO saw its greatest use. Twenty-nine states presently have "little RICOs." New York, for example, has the New York Organized Crime Control Act of 1986. Notwithstanding its earlier timidity, there have been some significant examples of the federal government's use of civil RICO since 1986. Approximately 82 civil RICO cases are now being filed each month in federal courts. We will survey a few of these cases and examine one case example in particular detail.

Consent Decrees and Trusteeships

The President's Commission on Organized Crime (1986) strongly recommended that trusteeships be systematically used by the courts to prevent organized crime from continuing to do business as usual. The government seeks court-appointed trusteeships under civil RICO where there is evidence that a business or labor union has been controlled by organized crime. A consent decree means the government and the defendants reach a formal, legal agreement or settlement on how to resolve the dispute. Under a trusteeship, the existing leadership of a target enterprise is removed, and a trustee is appointed to run the operation on behalf of the court. One major effort in this direction was the government's move against the largest labor union in the United States, the International Brotherhood of Teamsters.

The International Brotherhood of Teamsters In June 1987, the United States Department of Justice indicated that it was moving for the first time to use civil racketeering statutes to take over an entire union. That union, the 1.7 million member International Brotherhood of Teamsters, had had a long and sordid history of alleged involvement with mobsters. The President's Commission declared that the International Teamsters had been firmly under the influence of organized crime since the 1950s.

Suit was actually filed in federal court in New York on June 28, 1988. This suit sought to oust the senior leadership of the Teamsters and to have the court appoint a trustee to supervise new union elections, review appointments and expenditures, discipline misconduct, and seek court orders to block any improper actions by the union's executive board.

The legal brief of the Justice Department, outlining the bases for the legal action, said that organized crime's control of the Teamsters was "so pervasive that for decades the IBT's leadership has permitted La Cosa Nostra figures to dominate and corrupt important teamsters' locals, joint councils and benefit funds." "The IBT leadership has made a devil's pact with La Cosa Nostra—La Cosa Nostra figures have insured the elections of the IBT's top officers, including the union's last two presidents" (*New York Times*, June 29, 1988). The Department of Justice charged that organized crime had deprived Teamster members of their rights through a pattern of racketeering—"a campaign of fear" that included 20 murders, dozens of bombings and other violent acts, bribes, extortion, and theft. At a news conference announcing the lawsuit, U.S. Attorney Rudolph W. Giuliani denied that the government was seeking to take over the union. "We are," he said, "using the racketeering statute in a surgical way to take back the union from the Mafia" (*Wall Street Journal*, June 29, 1988).

On March 13, 1989, it was announced that an out-of-court settlement had been reached between the Department of Justice and the IBT with regard to the government's legal action (*New York Times*, March 14, 1989). Under a consent decree, the union's top national officers were to remain in place and the government would stop seeking to replace them. But the court was to appoint officers to monitor corruption and to oversee union operations, such as elections and expenditures of union funds. The court ordered that direct, secret ballot elections be held in 1991; and these were considered to be "the linchpin" in the government's effort to purge the union of the influence of organized crime. The federal judge supervising the consent decree said: "An election under these rules beacons the coming of the light of freedom to this dark union" (*Wall Street Journal*, July 11, 1990).

Local 814—International Brotherhood of Teamsters Also in 1987, a consent agreement was reached between the Department of Justice and Local 814 of the Teamsters Union in New York. This action was likewise intended to rid a union local of mob control. Federal prosecutors charged that the Bonanno organized crime family had a "stranglehold" on the union (*New York Times*, October 10, 1987). Under the terms of the consent decree, union officials named in the civil suit had to resign their positions, and a court appointed trustee was named to run the daily affairs of the union.

Philadelphia Roofers Union Local 30/30b The Philadelphia Roofers Union had a history of violence and corruption and was tied to the Philadelphia-based organized crime family of Nicodemo Scarfo. In 1989, Scarfo was sentenced to prison for life plus 55 years for murder and racketeering. Thirteen union officials and employees were convicted under RICO of extortion, racketeering, and other crimes. The leader of the union was given 15 years in prison. Local 30/30b was declared to be a criminal enterprise, and a trustee was named by the federal court to supervise the union. Under this trustee, who continues to run the union, free elections have been held. The trustee believes, however, that it will take another five years before real freedom for dissent and airing grievances by union members is restored (*Wall Street Journal*, May 29, 1990).

New York's Fulton Fish Market For at least a decade, it had been reported that this 150-year-old, $300 million a year fish market in New York City had been controlled by organized crime (Cook, 1982). In October 1987, U.S. Attorney Giuliani announced a civil racketeering suit that sought court supervision in the form of a trusteeship over the market itself and over a local of the United Seafood Workers Union (*Wall Street Journal*, January 25, 1989). The move to take over the market was the first time the government had sought control of an entire commercial area allegedly dominated by organized crime. The government effort to impose a trusteeship over the union local was denied by a federal judge. The judge said that the government had not proved its claim "that the Genovese family currently controls, and in recent years has controlled, Local 359 and its principal officers." But,

he said, "this is not to say that there is no evidence of the presence of organized crime, particularly Genovese family operatives," in the fish market
(*Wall Street Journal*, January 25, 1989). Again, under the terms of a consent
decree, defendants allegedly associated with the Genovese organized crime
family were barred from further dealings with the market. In addition, the
court ordered appointment of an administrator and an investigative staff to
oversee operations in the market and to make sure that consent decrees bar-
ring mob control were not violated.

Teamster Local 560

For 30 years, the 7,800 member Teamster Local 560 in Union City, New
Jersey, had been dominated by a family with well-established and well-publicized links to organized crime. The boss of the local was Anthony (Tony
Pro) Provenzano, an alleged captain of New York's Genovese organized
crime family. Tony Pro and his brothers used the union to engage in a broad
range of criminal activities: extortion, loan-sharking, kickbacks, hijacking,
and murder. Two union dissidents were murdered, union funds were misused, former convicts were illegally put on the payroll, and employers paid
union officers illegal kickbacks for so-called sweetheart contracts that allowed them to pay below-scale wages (*Wall Street Journal*, May 29, 1990).

The second of two court-appointed trustees of Local 560, Edwin H.
Stier, who had been New Jersey's chief prosecutor of organized crime, described the situation in the union this way: there was a "condition that had
existed in the Teamsters union for approximately 30 years, a condition of
continuous, unabating corruption. Successive prosecutions reflected a pattern of racketeering in that union that was beyond the control of the Government through traditional law enforcement means. It was also either beyond the control of the membership or was a condition that satisfied some
interests of the membership because they didn't seem to do anything about
it" (U.S. Senate, 1990:19). In 1984, Judge Harold Ackerman of the Federal
District Court of New Jersey determined that the conditions surrounding
the local met the criteria for classifying it as a "captive enterprise" under
RICO. In June 1986, after his decision had been affirmed by appeals courts
up to the U.S. Supreme Court, Judge Ackerman replaced the elected officers and the executive board of the union local with a trustee.

Judge Ackerman had decided that Local 560 was "the quintessential organized crime dominated union organization" (Kaboolian, 1990:7).
Kaboolian says that the history of Local 560 led to the conclusion that it fit
the criteria of "susceptibility and desirability" put forth by the President's
Commission on Organized Crime as a basis for assessing vulnerability to

organized crime infiltration and takeover. The local was particularly vulnerable, she says, because its members were poorly skilled, they were dispersed over scattered work sites, they were dependent upon whimsical employers for work, and the work was mainly in two industries heavily influenced by organized crime—transportation and construction.

The court-appointed trustee was charged with eliminating organized crime from Local 560 and with restoring union democracy, which meant having free and fair elections of union leaders who would protect the union and its members from future infiltration by organized crime. Stier indicated that his trusteeship had three goals: (1) to run the day-to-day affairs of the union in the interests of the membership, (2) to investigate other allegations of corruption, and (3) to "democratize" the union and return it to the rank and file. This trusteeship, according to Kaboolian, was "the primary example of a court takeover of the complete range of functions of a union organization" (1990:13).

On December 6, 1988, after 20 months of trusteeship, union elections were held. To the surprise and disappointment of many, a majority of the membership elected a Provenzano-connected slate to once again lead the local. This outcome has been variously interpreted, some give it a more pessimistic slant and others are more optimistic. Kaboolian, for example, suggests that the membership may have been reacting to a feeling that they were being persecuted by the Justice Department. "Instead of accepting the court's determination that the union was victimized by the mob, many members saw the union as victimized by the government. . . . The remedial government intervention to reform Local 560 was the dominant issue in the campaign, inadvertently strengthening the hand of the former leadership and allowing it to prevail in the election" (Kaboolian, 1990:27). Stier, on the other hand, concludes that the RICO trusteeship clearly had a positive effect, as witness the fact that the elections were the first contested elections in 25 years. Elected officers now run Local 560. "Only time will tell," he says, "whether the patterns of behavior that were so deeply ingrained in the union have been altered" (U.S. Senate, 1990:20). Stier continued to retain control of the union's pension and welfare funds after the elections and was later asked by the Local 560 executive board to become the permanent, paid overseer of these funds after the union trusteeship expired.

Civil RICO: Some Conclusions and Recommendations

Not surprisingly, given the degree of controversy about RICO in general and civil RICO in particular, there are somewhat mixed reviews of its effectiveness and its success, and mixed recommendations for its continued use. A report of the Permanent Subcommittee on Investigations, of the U.S.

Senate Committee on Governmental Affairs, recognized the enormous powers granted to government under RICO:

> In theory, a judge has broad latitude in civil RICO suits to create remedies that will not only remove existing corruption and racketeering activity in a given entity, but also prevent it from recurring. In practice, that power has authorized the reorganization and Government monitoring of both labor unions and private commercial entities, something clearly unprecedented in law enforcement efforts in this country. (U.S. Senate, 1990:32)

The subcommittee was evidently concerned that the tools provided in the statute be used with caution and discretion. Its report said, for example, that without clearcut limitations on the use of civil remedies, there is a "valid public concern that the tremendous power which the statute offers may be abused" (U.S. Senate, 1990:33). It recommended less drastic alternatives to removal of elected officials and direct government control when these alternatives would be potentially as effective as the more punitive approaches. Finally, the subcommittee recommended that a permanent liaison or "pathway of communication" be established among the AFL-CIO, the Department of Justice, the Department of Labor, and the FBI to prevent and detect criminal activity in the labor movement.

Kaboolian similarly cautions against overly ambitious use of civil RICO. She says that a court-imposed trusteeship of a union or other commercial enterprise "must be designed around the court's findings about the source of the problem to be solved" (1990:29). Given that the task of the trusteeship is to act on whatever problems are identified, this task "must be one which can in fact be accomplished by a court-imposed remedy." "The government," she says, "is best equipped to remove criminal elements and reform administrative practices" (p. 29). Other actions, such as bringing about broader cultural reforms, are essentially beyond its scope and, therefore, ought to be beyond its mandate.

Former United States Attorney Giuliani, who aggressively used RICO to go after organized crime, is much less reluctant to strongly advocate its extensive use:

> [In RICO], Congress provided an extremely powerful tool for permanently dissolving criminal enterprises and preventing organized crime figures from infiltrating and corrupting legitimate businesses. The use of these remedies has become an important— indeed crucial—part of a strategic approach where particular businesses or industries have historically fallen prey to the influences of organized crime. United States Attorneys should be seeking to

utilize these tools whenever possible, particularly as a follow-up measure to successful criminal prosecutions. . . .

Through RICO's civil remedies, the prosecutors have the power to permanently divest organized crime of its corrupt economic base. With a strong commitment to the use of these civil remedies, entire industries and the citizens that they serve may once again enjoy the benefits of an economy free of the corrosive influence of unrestrained greed. (Giuliani, 1987:112–113)

In view of the fact that labor racketeering—extortion of employers and embezzlement of union and pension funds—is a principal source of revenue for traditional La Cosa Nostra organized crime, civil RICO will seemingly have to be continued to be looked to as a critically important weapon in the government's powers of enforcement. Further, this weapon or tool will, in all probability, have to shift or expand its focus as other organized criminal groups become more sophisticated in development of racketeering enterprises.

LEGALIZING THE ACTIVITIES OF ORGANIZED CRIME

In Chapter 7, we examined the controversial idea of legalizing drugs as a way of taking their supply and distribution (and the profit from such supply and distribution) out of the hands of organized crime. Here we want to look at the companion idea of legalizing other goods and services that have likewise become lucrative sources of power and profit for organized crime at least in part because they are illegal. As with drugs, the idea of legalizing that which heretofore has been criminal (and in the view of some immoral) is similarly controversial. We will not deal with the general merits and demerits of the arguments in this controversy except as they specifically relate to dealing with organized crime.

Legalization of drugs and gambling has been most vigorously discussed and advocated, partly because these activities have the largest consumer markets and are thus the major income producers for organized crime. Drugs and gambling, along with labor racketeering, are organized crime's most lucrative ventures. The President's Commission on Organized Crime (1985) estimated the take from gambling to be $26 to $30 billion annually. This constitutes more than half the estimate of the revenues for organized crime.

Some on and off discussion about legalizing other forms of vice, such as prostitution, has been active over the years. Haller (1990) described the regulation of the red-light districts that took place in the United States around 1900. This regulation of prostitution, he said, represented an attempt to deal with vice activities that despite being illegal were regarded as inevitable. However, unlike drugs and gambling, the money in prostitution is minuscule, and its legal status is of much less importance as an anti–organized crime policy issue.

In the case of other organized crime activities, extortion, loan-sharking, hijacking, and various frauds and scams, there has understandably been little or no issue of legalizing. Given these realities, the discussion here will concern itself largely with the question of legalizing gambling.

We use the term *legalization* because it is the preferred approach of those who advocate legal reforms in this direction. Legalization means making an activity or aspects of an activity legal, while keeping it subject to certain regulations. Under legalization, government would maintain a role as a regulator. The consumption of alcohol is an example of a legal but regulated activity. It is restricted by licensing requirements and age restrictions. Violations of these restrictions can result in loss of license and possible criminal penalties. Regulated legal gambling is currently permitted in a number of states, such as Nevada and New Jersey.

Another, much less popular, approach to changing our posture toward illicit goods and services is *decriminalization*. This means literally removing all criminal sanctions and allowing people to buy goods or services or to engage in an activity pretty much as they wish.

The Arguments For and Against Legalization

The National Advisory Committee Task Force on Organized Crime outlined the pro-legalization and con-legalization arguments as these related to the question of combating organized crime:

Pro

- Laws which prohibit goods and services for which there is a large public demand—a demand which requires capital, expertise, and continuing organization to meet the supply—create a lucrative market for organized crime. Such laws should be changed to deprive organized crime of this market.

- Organized crime's earnings from the so-called victimless crimes are used to finance other illegal activities which are clearly detrimental to the public interest. Loan-sharking, and the strong-arm tactics and violence surrounding loan-sharking, for example, flow from organized crime's involvement in illegal gambling.

- The unenforceability of the current laws against drugs, gambling, prostitution, etc., lead to official corruption.
- Shifting the emphasis from the generally ineffective enforcement attempts against low-level vice operatives to a more concerted attack on the upper echelons of organized crime would be much more effective in the long run

Con

- Legalization (or decriminalization) would simply allow organized crime to continue to engage in victimless crimes, but on a legal basis.
- Because legalization involves licensing and regulation, there would continue to be many opportunities for corruption. Thus legalization is not the answer to public corruption.
- Legal activities to provide the formerly outlawed goods and services will not be able to compete with the services and advantages that organized crime can offer. Their skills, expertise, experience, contacts, and capital will enable them to dominate the market. (National Task Force on Organized Crime, 1976:231–232)

The Advocates

One of the influential supporters of legalized gambling is Jerome Skolnick. Skolnick testified before the President's Commission on Organized Crime during its hearings on gambling in 1985, and argued for legalized casino gambling on the grounds of revenue raising and resort renewal. But his third reason for legalized gambling was, he said, the most important:

> There is a third reason for legalized gambling, and I think it is the most important and the most legitimate that a government has for legalizing gambling, and that is to control those who are the purveyors of gambling. That is, given the frank recognition that the activity is socially acceptable—enough to be widespread and to encourage organized crime—the government should legalize primarily to control. . . . England legalizes casinos not to raise revenue, not to renew resorts, but to keep organized crime out of the casino business. It legalizes bookmaking for the same reason. Sports bookmaking could be legalized in this country—if done properly. (President's Commission, 1985:26)

Skolnick's principal argument is that legalization of gambling is a way to undercut the benefits flowing to organized crime from illegal gambling.

The New Jersey Gambling Study Commission undertook a study before gambling casinos were introduced to Atlantic City and arrived at this position on legalized gambling:

> Regulation within a framework of law is necessary. A prerequisite to such regulation is legalization of the activity to be regulated. State policy should recognize not only the futility of total suppression, but also the . . . social ills and corrupting influence which arise from attempting to maintain a set of suppressive laws which generate hypocrisy in their enforcers and resentment among the general citizenry. (New Jersey State Commission of Investigation, 1991c:3)

Another advocate of legalization is Albanese (1989, 1991). Albanese uses the term *decriminalization*, but since he suggests government regulation of gambling, prostitution, drugs, and even loan-sharking, he seems to really mean legalization. He argues that legalization would accomplish two important purposes that relate directly to organized crime: (1) it would "reduce the opportunity for survival and profit for organized criminal enterprises that provide these goods and services" (1989:180), and (2) it would "force police and policymakers to devote more time to the investigation of more serious organized crimes" (1989:180). Legalization, according to Albanese, would have the positive result that illicit markets would be greatly reduced and the major sources of funds for organized crime would be seriously impaired.

Several assumptions underpinning Albanese's and others' conclusions are at least debatable. First, he says that "it is clear that organized crimes with direct victims . . . are more significant and deserve more attention than do crimes resulting from the provision of illicit goods and services" (1989:176). Clear to whom? If there was consensus on this point, it would not be so controversial. But on the contrary, many believe that drug trafficking and large-scale gambling are significant and do deserve considerable law enforcement attention. Second, he indicates that "if state-sponsored gambling was designed to better compete with illegal games. . . , illicit gambling would be seriously eroded" (1989:177). As will be illustrated shortly, a number of law enforcement and other government officials, as well as people in organized crime, believe that such competition from a position of any kind of parity is a practical impossibility. Third, Albanese argues that "the purpose of the criminal law is not to legislate morality, but rather to maintain social control" (1989:177). This, too, oversimplifies a complex and controversial issue. Putting aside the philosophical questions about legislating morality, criminal law does have more purposes than simply maintaining social control, and it can be argued that at least one of those purposes is symbolizing society's views about permissible and impermissible behavior. It is the lack of any general consensus on just these kinds of issues that makes the question of legalization such a complex one. To illustrate, let us now turn to the antilegalization side.

The Opponents

A number of law enforcement officials have spoken out forcefully against legalizing gambling. Among them is Justin Dintino, a member of the President's Commission on Organized Crime and the superintendent of the New Jersey State Police. In testimony before the U.S. Senate he said: "A number of surveys have been taken and all the surveys have indicated that wherever gambling is legalized, there is an increase to organized crime's money making capacity in the illegal market, because legalized gambling creates a new clientele, it creates a new market, and some of these new clients do turn to the illegal gambling market" (U.S. Senate, 1988:162). At these same hearings, Ronald Goldstock, head of the New York State Organized Crime Task Force, likewise testified that "wherever there is legalized gambling, whether it be off-track betting, whether it be legalized numbers or any experiment that a state does, rather than competing successfully with the illegal gamblers, it in fact creates a better and bigger market for them" (U.S. Senate, 1988:162).

In testimony before the President's Commission on Organized Crime, the then superintendent of the New Jersey State Police, Clinton Pagano, made this statement:

> I would like to dispel the myth, the ever-popular myth, that legalized gambling dries up sources of revenue for organized crime. We in New Jersey law enforcement have found that despite the legalization of state lottery, we continue to make a substantial number of [illegal] lottery arrests. . . . [The] easy availability of credit, the odds which are substantially better in the illegal lottery, and the avoidance of taxes all contribute to the existence of an illegal lottery. . . . If we examine casino gambling we find that illegal casinos—illegal casinos—are [still] being run by organized crime. (President's Commission, 1985:211–212)

Pagano argued that legal gambling begets illegal gambling and that illegal gambling thus benefits from legal gambling.

To be placed in the strange bedfellows category, several organized crime figures and their associates have proffered information supporting the position of the opponents of legalized gambling. Jimmy Fratianno, for example, suggested that the real opportunities for organized crime were not in illegal gambling but in the skim and scam possibilities that existed in legal gambling in places like Las Vegas and Atlantic City (Demaris, 1981). This certainly throws doubt on the idea that legalization would remove a huge profit-making opportunity from organized crime. In a similar vein, the so-called Benguerra organized crime family described by Anderson (1979) was in favor of, indeed enthusiastic about, legalization of casino gambling in areas near their city. They made business investments in nearby areas and saw opportunities for making loans to gamblers that would be collected through a loan-sharking organization. Joseph Fay, who cooperated with organized crime in the distribution of video gaming devices (but who himself was ostensibly not a member or associate of any organized crime family) had this to say in testimony before the New Jersey State Commission of Investigation:

> Q: In your opinion, is it possible that, in the kind of business that you were engaged in, is it possible to exist without the involvement of organized crime?
>
> A: Impossible to exist.
>
> Q: Why is that?
>
> A: Because you can't operate these, anything to do with gambling, wiseguys are there. Anything to do with cash, they're always there and, you know, they can get, they'll take legitimate people and put them up front and threaten them and make them do things that they don't want to do. They will definitely be in back of any gambling that's involved anywhere.
>
> Q: Do you feel legalization might lessen the impact of organized crime?
>
> A: No way. (New Jersey State Commission of Investigation, 1991c:25–26)

So, What to Do?

The final decision on whether and under what conditions to legalize gambling, or any other activities traditionally infested with organized crime, is up to the people and their representatives. It may be that Albanese is right that strict government controls over all forms of legal gambling can "ensure that dishonest operators do not corrupt the integrity of the games" and that "there is no reason that, as a well-regulated industry, legal gambling could [not] do as well [as] any other legitimate entertainment business" (1991:16).

There is no quarreling with the fact that people want to gamble and that there is a lot of money to made from gambling. On the other hand, with specific regard to the organized crime connection, we agree with this conclusion of the New Jersey State Commission of Investigation: "No one should delude himself into thinking that legalizing such games will have any but the slightest impact on organized crime. Such action, however, probably will create more gamblers" (1991c:4).

CONCLUSION

From the foregoing discussion of policy issues and organized crime, several conclusions are fairly clear, but some others are much less so. It is clear that there is a great need for much more public knowledge and understanding of organized crime. This will lead to greater public support for government initiatives against racketeers and racketeering and against various other activities that bring money and power to organized crime at the expense of innocent victims. It is also clear that both the media and the government have major roles to play in bringing about the necessary understanding. With the possible exception of certain civil liberties groups and perhaps some others, it also seems obvious that there is considerable support for expanded use of RICO and other law enforcement tools against organized crime.

In the much less clear category, on the other hand, is the degree to which there will be public support for aggressively going after gambling, in particular. At the same time, it is also not obvious (and in fact it is quite doubtful) that there will be great public support for widespread legalization of either gambling or drugs. Thus, policymakers are left on the horns of a dilemma. Anderson (1979) pinpoints three questions that have to be addressed in resolving this policy dilemma: (1) Should the resources and laws against organized crime be increased and extended, or be decreased? (2) How should available resources be allocated? (3) What specific goals and strategies should be used to combat organized crime in particular cities and in particular illegal markets?

We close by returning to the questions we posed at the outset:

Q: Is organized crime synonymous with the Mafia or La Cosa Nostra?

A: No, it definitely is not.

Q: Is there even such an entity as the Mafia or La Cosa Nostra?

A: Yes, there clearly is such an entity. La Cosa Nostra, although in a state of demise because of the success of law enforcement initiatives, the aging or incarceration of its leadership, intrafamily infighting, and a general breakdown of internal discipline, is still the best organized and most sophisticated national organized crime entity.

Q: Can other criminal groups be considered examples of organized crime?

A: Yes, there are a number of such groups. The Chinese, the Jamaicans, the Japanese Yakuza, and the Russians are the best examples of immigrant, ethnically based, organized criminal groups. Among the homegrown variety are the motorcycle and prison gangs. Some of these groups are seriously challenging the historical preeminence of La Cosa Nostra in a number of areas.

Q: Is there a myth of organized crime, and particularly of the Mafia, that is exploited for political purposes and by the media?

A: Yes, there is unquestionably a mythology surrounding the Mafia, and this mythology has been exploited by various government agencies over the years for various purposes. It has also been profitably exploited by books, magazines, newspapers, movies, and television. But what we have tried to make clear, and what deserves repeating, is that concluding that there is a Mafia myth is not the same as concluding that there is not a Mafia involvement in organized crime.

Q: Does organized crime thrive in the United States because Americans want certain goods and services that are illegal?

A: Yes, this is certainly a major part of the explanation for the existence of organized crime. But, it is not the only explanation. Organized crime is also heavily involved in schemes and scams regarding goods and services that are otherwise perfectly legal. These particular activities often constitute a form of white-collar crime. The bootleg gasoline or motor fuel racket of Russian emigre organized crime is a prime example of this. These kinds of criminal enterprises lend support to theories about illegal markets, spectrums of legal and illegal enterprises, and so on—theories that demand further examination and testing.

Organized crime is not unique to the United States or American society. However, the wealth, the economic, social, and political structures, and the criminal opportunities available in the United States present a unique set of circumstances that enable organized crime to achieve its highest form here. One of the greatest challenges for us all concerning organized crime in the United States may be to look in the mirror. In the words of Pogo, "We meet the enemy; and the enemy is us."

Bibliography

Abadinsky, H. (1981). *Organized crime.* Boston, MA: Allyn & Bacon.

———. (1985). *Organized crime* (2nd ed.). Chicago, IL: Nelson-Hall.

———. (1990). *Organized crime* (3rd ed.). Chicago, IL: Nelson-Hall.

Adams, N. (1992, August). "Menace of the Russian Mafia." *Readers Digest,* pp. 33–40.

Akers, R. (1992). *Drugs, alcohol, and society.* Belmont, CA: Wadsworth.

Albanese, J. (1987). "Predicting the incidence of organized crime: A preliminary model." In T. Bynum (Ed.), *Organized crime in America: Concepts and controversies* (pp. 103–114). Monsey, NY: Willow Tree Press.

———. (1989). *Organized crime in America.* Cincinnati, OH: Anderson Publishing.

———. (1991). "Organized crime and the oldest vice." Paper presented at the meeting of the American Society of Criminology, San Francisco, CA.

Albini, J. (1976) "Syndicated crime: Its structure, function, and modus operandi." In F. Ianni & E. Ruess-Ianni (Eds.), *The crime society: Organized crime and corruption in America* (pp. 24–41). New York: Times-Mirror.

———. (1988). "Donald Cressey's contributions to the study of organized crime: An evaluation." *Crime and Delinquency, 34*(3), 338–354.

Albini, J., & Bajon, B. (1978). "Witches, Mafia, mental illness and social reality: A study in the power of mythical belief." *International Journal of Criminology and Penology, 6*(4), 285–294.

Allsop, K. (1961). *The bootleggers: The story of Chicago's prohibition era.* London, England: Hutchinson & Company.

American Law Institute. (1985). *Model penal code.* Philadelphia: American Law Institute.

Anderson, A. (1979). *The business of organized crime.* Stanford, CA: Hoover Institution.

Asbury, H. (1927). *The gangs of New York: An informal history of the underworld.* New York: Knopf.

————. (1932). *Sucker's progress.* New York: Dodd, Mead.

————. (1940). *Gem of the prairie: An informal history of the Chicago underworld.* Garden City, NY: Garden City Publishing Company.

————. (1950). *The great illusion: An informal history of prohibition.* Garden City, NY: Doubleday.

Barker, W. (1985). "Linkages and co-participation in right-wing groups." Paper presented to the Academy of Criminal Justice Sciences, Las Vegas, NV.

Beck, M. (1993, June 14). "Kicking the prison habit." *Newsweek.*

Bell, D. (1953). "Crime as an American way of life." In Marvin E. Wolfgang, Leonard Savitz, & Norman Johnston (Eds.), *The sociology of crime and delinquency* (pp. 213–225). New York: John Wiley & Sons.

————. (1963, December 23). "The myth of the Cosa Nostra." *The New Leader, 46*(26), 12–15.

Berger, M. (1940, August 4). "Gang patterns: 1940." *New York Times Magazine.*

Berthe & Chaw [no initials given]. (1984). "Motorcycle gangs." *International Criminal Police Review, 40* (390), 170–179.

Blakey, G. (1967). "Aspects of the evidence gathering process in organized crime cases." In President's Commission on Law Enforcement and Administration of Justice, *Task force report: Organized crime* (pp. 80–113). Washington, DC: Government Printing Office.

————. (1987). *Organized crime in the United States: A review of the public record.* Bellevue, WA: Northwest Policy Studies Center.

————. (1990). "Foreword." *Notre Dame Law Review, 65*(5), 873–884.

————. (1991). "Dispelling some myths about RICO." Paper presented to the Rutgers University Criminal Justice Assembly, New Brunswick, NJ.

Block, A. (1978). "History and the study of organized crime." *Urban Life, 6,* 455–474.

————. (1991). *Masters of paradise: Organized crime and the Internal Revenue Service in the Bahamas.* New Brunswick, NJ: Transaction Publishers.

Block, A., & Scarpitti, F. (1984). *Poisoning for profit: The Mafia and toxic waste in America.* New York: William Morrow.

Blocker, J. (1976). *Retreat from reform: The prohibition movement in the United States—1890–1913.* Westport, CT: Greenwood Press.

Blumenthal, R. (1992). Foreword. In *The Gotti Tapes.* London, England: Arrow Books.

Bonanno, J. (1983). *A man of honor: The autobiography of Joseph Bonanno.* New York: Simon & Schuster.

Brace, C. (1967). *The dangerous classes of New York and twenty years' work among them.* Montclair, NJ: Patterson Smith.

Bremner, R. (1956). *From the depths: The discovery of poverty in in the United States.* New York: New York University Press.

Brown, E. (1973). "CORE warns Harlem: Beware of OTB and Howard Samuels." *Amsterdam News* (New York).

Brown, J. (1929). "Modernize the federal judicial system." In W. Durant (Ed.), *Law observance: Shall the people of the United States uphold the Constitution?* (pp. 91–96). New York: Durant Award Office.

Brown, M. (1985). "Criminal informants: Some observations on use, abuse, and control." *Journal of Police Science and Administration, 13*(3), 251–256.

Browning, F., & Gerassi, J. (1980). *The American way of crime.* New York: G.P. Putnam & Sons.

Bruere, M. (1927). *Does prohibition work: A study of the operation of the Eighteenth Amendment made by the National Federation of Settlements, assisted by social workers in different parts of the United States.* New York: Harper & Brothers.

Buckley, W. (1992, July 7). "No one attacks failure of drug prohibition." *Omaha World Herald,* p. C-22.

Bureau of Organized Crime and Criminal Intelligence, California Department of Justice. (1987). *Organized crime in California.* Sacramento: Author.

Burnham, J. (1968). "New perspectives on the prohibition 'experiment' of the 1920s." *Journal of Social History, 2*(Fall), 51–68.

Burnstein, D. (1983, May). "Death of a hustler." *New York,* pp. 25-29.

Callow, A. (1966). *The Tweed ring.* New York: Oxford University Press.

Camp, M., & Camp, C. (1985). *Prison gangs: Their extent, nature and impact on prisons.* Washington, DC: U.S. Department of Justice.

Chaiken, M. (1993). *The rise of crack and ice: Experiences in three locales.* Washington, DC: National Institute of Justice, Research in Brief.

Cherrington, E. (1920). *The evolution of prohibition in the United States of America: A chronological history of the liquor problem and the temperance reform in the United States from the earliest settlements to the consummation of national prohibition.* Westerville, OH: The American Issue Press.

Chin, K. (1986). *Chinese triad societies, tongs, organized crime, and street gangs in Asia and the United States.* Ann Arbor, MI: University Microfilms International.

Cloward, R., & Ohlin, L. (1960). *Delinquency and opportunity.* Glencoe, IL: The Free Press.

Coates, J. (1987). *Armed and dangerous: The rise of the survivalist right.* New York: Hill & Wang.

Cohen, S. (1968). "A quarter century of research with LSD." In J. Ungerleider (Ed.), *The problems and prospects of LSD.* Springfield, IL: Charles C Thomas.

Colvin, D. (1927). *Prohibition in the United States: A history of the prohibition party and of the prohibition movement.* New York: George Doran Company.

Combating organized crime. (1966). Report of the 1965 Oyster Bay Conferences on Combating Organized Crime.

Cook, J. (1982, April 26). "Fish Story." *Forbes,* pp. 61–67.

Cordner, G. (1989). *Police organization and methods to prevent and investigate illicit trafficking in narcotic drugs and other psychotropic substances.* Washington, DC: Police Foundation.

Cornell Institute on Organized Crime. (1979). *Techniques in the investigation and prosecution of organized crime—grand jury examination of the recalcitrant witness: contempt and perjury.* Ithaca, NY: Author.

Cornwell, T. (1992). *Russian Mafia.* Unpublished manuscript.

Cressey, D. (1969). *Theft of the nation: The structure and operations of organized crime.* New York: Harper & Row.

————. (1970, April). "Organized crime and inner city youth." *Crime and Delinquency,* pp. 129–138.

Cummings, J., & Volkman, E. (1990). *Goombata: The improbable rise and fall of John Gotti and his gang.* Boston: Little, Brown.

Curry, G., & Spergel, I. (1988). "Gang homicide, delinquency, and community." *Criminology, 26*(3), 381–405.

Custer, A. (1929). "Offer large rewards." In W. Durant (Ed.), *Law observance: Shall the people of the United States uphold the Constitution?* (pp. 172–174). New York: Durant Award Office.

Daley, R. (1978). *Prince of the city.* Boston, MA: Houghton Mifflin.

Davis, J. (1929). "A police chief's plan." In W. Durant (Ed.), *Law observance: Shall the people of the United States uphold the Constitution?* (pp. 181–185). New York: Durant Award Office.

Defoe, D. (1972). *A general history of the pyrates* (M. Schonhorn, Ed.). Columbia, SC: University of South Carolina Press.

Delfs, R. (1991, November 21). "Feeding on the System." *Far Eastern Economic Review,* pp. 28–35.

Demaris, O. (1981). *The last mafioso: The treacherous world of Jimmy Fratianno.* New York: Times Books.

Dennis, R. (1990, November). "The economics of legalizing drugs." *The Atlantic Monthly,* pp. 126–132.

Dibrell, A. (1929). "Use the navy more." In W. Durant (Ed.), *Law observance: Shall the people of the United States uphold the Constitution?* New York: Durant Award Office.

Dobyns, F. (1940). *The amazing story of repeal: An expose of the power of propaganda.* New York: Willett, Clark & Company.

Dolan, P. (1986). "The rise of crime in the period 1830–1860." *Journal of Criminal Law, 30,* 859–861.

Doyle, T. (1929). "Deprive offenders of citizenship." In W. Durant (Ed.), *Law observance: Shall the people of the United States uphold the Constitution?* (pp. 207–208). New York: Durant Award Office.

Dunham, F. (1929). "Hasten and multiply trials by using U.S. Commissioners." In W. Durant (Ed.), *Law observance: Shall the people of the United States uphold the Constitution?* New York: Durant Award Office.

Dusek, D., & Girdano, D. (1980). *Drugs: A factual account* (3rd ed.). Reading, MA: Addison-Wesley.

Edelhertz, H. (1987). *Major issues in organized crime control: Symposium proceedings.* Washington, DC: National Institute of Justice.

Edelhertz, H., & Overcast, T. (1990). *A study of organized crime business-types activities and their implications for law enforcement.* Washington, DC: Government Printing Office.

Esquemeling, J. (1951). *The buccaneers of America.* London, England: George Allen & Unwin, Ltd.

Ezell, J. (1960). *Fortune's merry wheel: The lottery in America.* Cambridge, MA: Harvard University Press.

Fagan, J. (1988). *The social organization of drug use and drug dealing among urban gangs.* New York: John Jay College.

Fagan, J., Kelly, R., & Chin, Ko-lin (1989a). *Patterns of organized crime activities in Asian businesses in the New York area.* Newark, NJ: Rutgers University School of Criminal Justice.

————. (1989b). *Extortion and victimization of Asian business persons in the New York metropolitan area.* Newark, NJ: Rutgers University School of Criminal Justice.

Fantel, H. (1988, May 8). "Myths of the audio wonderland." *New York Times,* p. H24.

Feldman, H. (1930). *Prohibition: Its economic and industrial aspects.* New York: D. Appleton & Company.

Fino, P. (1955, November). "Let's legalize gambling." *Coronet.*

Fisher, I. (1928). *Prohibition still at its worst.* New York: Alcohol Information Committee.

Fishman, S., Rodenrys, K., & Schink, G. (1986). *The income of organized crime.* Philadelphia, PA: Wharton Econometric Forecasting Associates.

Florez, C., & Boyce, B. (1990). "Colombian organized crime." *Police Studies, 13*(2), 81–88.

Fox, S. (1989). *Blood and power: Organized crime in 20th century America.* New York: William Morrow.

Friedman, M., & Friedman, R.. (1984). *Tyranny of the status quo.* New York: Harcourt Brace Jovanovich.

Friedman, R. (1993, January). "Brighton Beach Goodfellas." *Vanity Fair,* pp. 26–41.

"Frontline" (television show). (1991). "Guns, drugs, and the CIA."

————. (1993). "What Happened to the War on Drugs?"

Fund for the City of New York. (1972). *Legal gambling in New York: Discussion of numbers and sports betting.* New York: Author.

Galeotti, M. (1992). "Organized crime in Moscow and Russian national security." *Low Intensity Conflict and Law Enforcement, 1*(3), 237–252.

Galliher, J., & Cain, J. (1974, May). "Citation support for the Mafia myth in criminology textbooks." *The American Sociologist,* pp. 68–74.

Garofalo, J. (1981). "Crime and the mass media: A selective review of research." *Journal of Research in Crime and Delinquency, 18*(2), 319–350.

George, B. (1987). "New developments in victim and witness protection in the United States." In *Resource Material Series No. 32.* Fuchu, Tokyo, Japan: UNAFEI.

Gerster, P., & Cords, N. (1977). *Myth and the American experience.* Encino, CA: Glencoe Press.

Giancana, A., & Renner, T. (1985). *Mafia princess: Growing up in Sam Giancana's family.* New York: Avon Books.

Giuliani, R. (1987). "Legal remedies for attacking organized crime." In *Major issues in organized crime control* (pp. 103–130). National Institute of Justice (Symposium Proceedings). Washington, DC: Government Printing Office.

———. (1991). "Government's memorandum of law in support of its motion for preliminary relief." In A. Block (Ed.), *The business of crime: A documentary study of organized crime in the American economy* (pp. 245–276). Boulder, CO: Westview Press.

Goldberg, S. (1985). "Putting science in the Constitution: The prohibition experience." In D. Kyvig (Ed.), *Law, alcohol, and order: Perspectives on national prohibition.* Westport, CT: Greenwood.

Goodwin, G. (1929). "Make all violations felonies." In W. Durant (Ed.), *Law observance: Shall the people of the United States uphold the Constitution?* (pp. 260–263). New York: Durant Award Office.

Gosse, P. (1934). *The history of piracy.* New York: Tudor Publishing Company.

Gottfredson, M., & Hirschi, T. (1990). *A general theory of crime.* Stanford, CA: Stanford University Press.

Hagan, F. (1983). "The organized crime continuum: A further specification of a new conceptual model." *Criminal Justice Review, 8,* 52–57.

Haller, M. (1976). *History of organized crime: 1920–1945.* Washington, DC: National Institute of Law Enforcement and Criminal Justice (#75–NI–99–0109), Government Printing Office.

———. (1985). "Bootleggers as businessmen: From city slums to city builders." In D. Kyvig (Ed.), *Law, alcohol, and order: Perspectives on national prohibition* (pp. 139–157). Westport, CT: Greenwood.

———. (1990, May). "Illegal enterprise: A theoretical and historical interpretation." *Criminology, 28*(2), 207–235.

———. (1992). "The changing structure of American gambling in the twentieth century." In E. Monkkonen (Ed.), *Prostitution, drugs, gambling, and organized crime—Part 1* (pp. 294–365). New York: K. G. Saur.

Haller, M., & Alvitti, J. (1992). "Loansharking in American cities: Historical analysis of a marginal enterprise." In E. Monkkonen (Ed.), *Prostitution, drugs, gambling, and organized crime—Part 1* (pp. 366–397). New York: K. G. Saur.

Handelman, S. (1993, January 24). "Inside Russia's gangster economy." *New York Times Magazine,* pp. 12–15, 50.

Hawkins, G. (1969). "God and the Mafia." *The Public Interest, 14,* 24–51.

Healy, P. (1984). "Organized crime: A new dimension." In Thomas M. Frost & Magnus Seng (Eds.), *Organized crime in Chicago* (pp. 18–23). Chicago: Loyola University of Chicago.

Henry, L. (1929). "Punish oath-breaking officials." In W. Durant (Ed.), *Law observance: Shall the people of the United States uphold the Constitution?* (pp. 280–282). New York: Durant Award Office.

Hobson, R. (1929). "An educational organization." In W. Durant (Ed.), *Law observance: Shall the people of the United States uphold the Constitution?* (pp. 290–295). New York: Durant Award Office.

Hoffman, D. (1987). "Tilting at windmills: The Chicago Crime Commission versus organized crime, 1980–1984." In T. Bynum (Ed.), *Organized crime in America: Concepts and controversies* (pp. 83–100). Monsey, NY: Willow Tree Press.

————. (1992). *Scarface Al and the crime crusaders: Chicago's private war against Capone.* Unpublished manuscript, University of Nebraska at Omaha.

Hofstadter, R. (1955). *The age of reform: From Bryan to F.D.R.* New York: Knopf.

Holden, R. (1985). "Historical and international perspectives on right-wing militancy in the United States." Paper presented to the Academy of Criminal Justice Sciences, Las Vegas, NV.

Huff, C. (1989). "Youth gangs and public policy." *Crime and Delinquency, 35*(4), 524–537.

Husak, D. (1992). *Drugs and rights.* New York: Cambridge University Press.

Ianni, F. (1972). *A family business.* New York: Russel Sage.

————. (1974). *Black Mafia: Ethnic succession in organized crime.* New York: Simon & Schuster.

Ianni, F., & Reuss-Ianni, E. (1976). "A family business: Business and social organization in the Lupollo family." In F. Ianni and E. Reuss-Ianni (Eds.), *The crime society: Organized crime and corruption in America* (pp. 239–254). New York: Times-Mirror.

Inciardi, J. (1986). *The war on drugs: Heroin, cocaine, crime, and public policy.* Palo Alto, CA: Mayfield.

————. (1989). *Narcotic drugs, coca products, and other psychoactive substances.* Washington, DC: Police Foundation.

————. (1991). "American drug policy and the legalization debate." In J. Inciardi (Ed.), *The drug legalization debate* (pp. 7–15). Newbury Park, CA: Sage.

Inciardi, J., & McBride, D. (1990). "Legalizing drugs: A gormless, naive idea." *The Criminologist, 15*(5), 1–4.

————. (1991). "The case against legalization." In J. Inciardi (Ed.), *The drug legalization debate.* Newbury Park, CA: Sage.

International Opium Conference, The Hague, December 1, 1911–January 23, 1912. Summary of the minutes. The Hague: National Printing Office.

Iwai, H. (1986). "Organized crime in Japan." In R. Kelly (Ed.), *Organized crime: A global perspective* (pp. 208–233). Totowa, NJ: Rowan & Littlefield.

Jenkins, P., & Potter, G. (1987). "The politics and mythology of organized crime: A Philadelphia case study." *Journal of Criminal Justice, 15*, 473–484.

Johnson, D. (1992). "A sinful business: The origins of gambling syndicates in the United States, 1840–1887." In E. Monkkonen (Ed.), *Prostitution, drugs, gambling, and organized crime—Part 2* (pp. 500–512). New York: K. G. Saur.

Johnson, H. (1967). "Introduction." In D. Lowe, *Ku Klux Klan: The invisible empire* (p. 10). New York: W. W. Norton.

Jones, J. (1973). *Gambling yesterday and today: A complete history.* Devon, England: David & Charles.

Joselit, J. (1983). *Our gang: Jewish crime and the New York Jewish community, 1900–1940.* Bloomington, IN: Indiana University Press.

Kaboolian, L. (1990). *Local 560 IBT: A case study of a court-appointed RICO trusteeship.* Unpublished manuscript.

Kaplan, D., & Dubro, A. (1986). *Yakuza: The explosive account of Japan's criminal underworld.* Reading, MA: Addison-Wesley.

Kaplan, J. (1987). *Crime file: Heroin* (Study Guide). Washington, DC: National Institute of Justice.

Karchmer, C., & Ruch, D. (1992). *State and local money laundering control strategies.* National Institute of Justice (Research in Brief). Washington, DC: National Institute of Justice.

Karraker, C. (1953). *Piracy was a business.* Rindge, NH: Richard R. Smith.

Keene, L. (1989). "Asian organized crime." *FBI Law Enforcement Bulletin, 58*(10), 12–17.

Kefauver, E. (1951). *Crime in America.* Garden City, NY: Doubleday.

Kelly, R. (1986). *Organized crime: A global perspective.* Totowa, NJ: Rowman & Littlefield.

Kelly, R., Chin, K., & Fagan, J. (1993). "Chinese organized crime in New York City." *Crime, Law and Social Change, 19,* 245–269.

Kenney, D., Ginger, J., Sapp, A., & McNamara, R. (1990). *Domestic terrorism: Developing a coordinated response.* Washington, DC: Police Foundation.

King, R. (1969). *Gambling and organized crime.* Washington, DC: Public Affairs Press.

———. (1972). *The drug hang-up: America's fifty-year folly.* Springfield, IL: Charles C Thomas.

Klein, M. (1971). *Street gangs and street workers.* Englewood Cliffs, NJ: Prentice-Hall.

Klein, M. W., & Maxson, C. L. (1987). "Street gang violence." In Marvin E. Wolfgang & Neil Weiner (Eds.), *Violent crime, violent criminals* (pp. 198–234). Newbury Park, CA: Sage.

Kobler, J. (1971). *Capone: The life and world of Al Capone.* New York: G. P. Putnam & Sons.

Kooistra, P. (1989). *Criminals as heroes: Structure, power and identity.* Bowling Green, OH: Popular Press.

Kyvig, D. (1979). *Repealing national prohibition.* Chicago, IL: University of Chicago Press.

———. (1985). "Sober thoughts: Myths and realities of national prohibition after fifty years." In D. Kyvig (Ed.), *Law, alcohol, and order: Perspectives on national prohibition* (pp. 3–20). Westport, CT: Greenwood.

Lasswell, H., & McKenna, J. (1972). *The impact of organized crime on an inner city community.* New York: The Policy Sciences Center.

Lender, M. (1985). "The historian and repeal: A survey of the literature and research opportunities." In D. Kyvig (Ed.), *Law, alcohol, and order: perspectives on national prohibition* (pp. 177–205). Westport, CT: Greenwood.

Levi-Stauss, C. (1963). *Structural anthropology.* New York: Basic Books.

Lewis, L., & Smith, H. (1929). *Chicago: The history of its reputation.* New York: Harcourt, Brace.

Lidz, C., & Walker, A. (1980). *Heroin, deviance and morality.* Beverly Hills, CA: Sage.

Light, I. (1992). "Numbers gambling among blacks: A financial institution." In E. Monkkonen (Ed.), *Prostitution, drugs, gambling, and organized crime—Part 2* (pp. 578–590). New York: K. G. Saur.

Lightner, L. (1929). "Return to wholesale education." In W. Durant (Ed.), *Law observance: Shall the people of the United States uphold the Constitution?* (pp. 232–237). New York: Durant Award Office.

Lintner, B. (1992). "Heroin and highland insurgency in the golden triangle." In A. McCoy and A. Block (Eds.), *War on drugs: Studies in the failure of U.S. narcotics policy* (pp. 281–318). Boulder, CO: Westview Press.

Lodhi, A., & Vaz, E. (1980). "Crime: A form of market transaction." *Canadian Journal of Criminology, 22*(2), 141–150.

London, H., & Weeks, A. (1981). *Myths that rule America.* Washington, DC: University Press of America.

Longstreet, S. (1977). *Win or lose: A social history of gambling in America.* New York: Bobbs-Merrill.

Lupsha, P. (1981). "Individual choice, material culture, and organized crime." *Criminology, 19*(1), 3–24.

———. (1986). "Organized crime in the United States." In R. Kelly (Ed.), *Organized crime: A global perspective.* Totowa, NJ: Rowman & Littlefield.

———. (1987). "La Cosa Nostra in drug trafficking." In T. Bynum (Ed.), *Organized crime in America: Concepts and controversies.* Monsey, NY: Willow Tree Press.

Lyman, M. (1989). *Gangland—Drug trafficking by organized criminals.* Springfield, IL: Charles C Thomas.

Lynch, G. (1990). "A conceptual, practical, and political guide to RICO reform." *Vanderbilt Law Review, 43*(3), 769–803.

Maas, P. (1968). *The Valachi papers.* New York: G. P. Putnam & Sons.

MacDonald, A. (1980). *The Turner diaries* (2nd ed.). Arlington, VA: National Vanguard Books.

Mallewe, M. (1983, May). "From Russia with guns." *Philadelphia,* pp. 104–107, 142–150.

Maltz, M. (1976). "On defining 'organized crime.'" *Crime and Delinquency, 22,* 338–346.

———. (1985). "Towards defining organized crime." In H. Alexander and G. Caiden (Eds.), *The politics and economics of organized crime.* Lexington, MA: D. C. Heath.

———. (1990). *Measuring the effectiveness of organized crime control efforts.* Chicago, IL: Office of International Criminal Justice, University of Illinois.

———. (1992). "Defining organized crime." Unpublished paper.

Marshall, J. (1992). "CIA assets and the rise of the Guadalajara connection." In A. McCoy and A. Block (Eds.), *War on drugs: Studies in the failure of U.S. narcotics policy* (pp. 197–208). Boulder, CO: Westview Press.

Martens, F., & Cunningham-Niederer, M. (1985). "Media magic, Mafia mania." *Federal Probation, 49*(2), 60–68.

Marx, G. (1982). "Who really gets stung? Some issues raised by the new police undercover work." *Crime and Delinquency, 28* (2), 165–193.

McBride, D., & Swartz, J. (1990). "Drugs and violence in the age of crack." In R. Weisheit (Ed.), *Drugs, crime, and the criminal justice system* (pp. 141–170). Cincinnati, OH: Anderson.

McCall, G. (1963). "Symbiosis: The case of hoodoo and the numbers racket." *Social Problems, 10,* 361–367.

McCoy, A. (1972). *The politics of heroin in Southeast Asia.* New York: Harper & Row.

———. (1992). "Heroin as a global commodity: A history of Southeast Asia's opium trade." In A. McCoy and A. Block (Eds.), *War on drugs: Studies in the failure of U.S. narcotics policy* (pp. 237–280). Boulder, CO: Westview Press.

McGuire, P. (1986). "Outlaw motorcycle gangs: Organized crime on wheels." *National Sheriff, 37*(2), 68–75.

Mencken, H. (1926). *Notes on democracy.* New York: Knopf.

Merton, R. (1957). *Social theory and social structure.* Glencoe, IL: The Free Press.

Miller, P., McFarland-Benedict, G., & Salzman, R. (1986). *Organized crime's involvement in the waste hauling industry.* Albany, NY: New York State Environmental Conservation Committee.

Miller, W. B. (1958). "Lower class culture as a generating milieu of gang delinquency." *Journal of Social Issues, 14*(3), 5–19.

Mitchell, A. (1992, April 11). "Russian emigres importing thugs to commit contract crimes in the U.S." *New York Times,* p. 1.

Mitchell, G. (1981, March). "The life and hard times of the protected witness program." *Police Magazine,* pp. 51–57.

———. (1992). *Janus-faced justice: Political criminals in Imperial Japan.* Honolulu, HI: University of Hawaii Press.

Moldea, D. (1978). *The Hoffa wars.* New York: Charter Books.

Montanino, F. (1990). "Protecting organized crime witnesses in the United States." *International Journal of Comparative and Applied Criminal Justice, 14* (1), 123–131.

Moore, W. (1974). *The Kefauver committee and the politics of crime.* Columbia, MO: University of Missouri Press.

Morash, M., & Hale, D. (1987). "Unusual crime or crime as usual? Images of corruption at the Interstate Commerce Commission." In T. Bynum (Ed.), *Organized crime in America: Concepts and controversies* (pp. 129–148). Monsey, NY: Criminal Justice Press.

Morgan, H. (1981). *Drugs in America: A social history, 1800–1980.* Syracuse, NY: Syracuse University Press.

Mullen, K. (1993, July 29). "Magazine: Betting boomed last year." *Omaha World-Herald,* p. 1.

Mullins, W. (1988). *Terrorist organizations in the United States.* Springfield, IL: Charles C Thomas.

Mustain, G., & Capeci, J. (1988). *Mob star: The story of John Gotti.* New York: Franklin Watts.

Musto, D. (1987). *The American disease: Origins of narcotic control* (expanded ed.). New York: Oxford University Press.

————. (1990). "If past is prologue, drug epidemic may weaken." Issue 2 in a Police Foundation Series on Drugs and Violence. Washington, DC: Police Foundation.

Nadelmann, E. (1989, September 1). "Drug prohibition in the United States: Costs, consequences, and alternatives." *Science, 245,* pp. 939–947.

————. (1991). "The case for legalization." In J. Inciardi (Ed.), *The drug legalization debate* (pp. 17–44). Newbury Park, CA: Sage.

Nash, J. (1975). *Bloodletters and bad men.* New York: Warner Books.

National Institute of Justice. (1990). *Fiscal year 1990 program plan.* Washington, DC: U.S. Department of Justice, Office of Justice Programs.

————. (1991). *Fiscal year 1991 program plan.* Washington, DC: U.S. Department of Justice, Office of Justice Programs.

National Task Force on Organized Crime. (1976). *Report of the task force on organized crime.* Washington, DC: Government Printing Office.

Nelli, H. (1976). *The business of crime.* New York: Oxford University Press.

————. (1985). "American syndicate crime: A legacy of prohibition." In D. Kyvig (Ed.), *Law, alcohol, and order: Perspectives on national prohibition.* Westport, CT: Greenwood.

Ness, E. (1987). *The untouchables.* New York: Pocket Books.

New Jersey State Commission of Investigation. (1989). *Twenty-first annual report.* Trenton, NJ: Author.

————. (1991a). *The New Jersey garment industry.* Trenton, NJ: Author.

————. (1991b). *Twenty-third annual report.* Trenton, NJ: Author.

————. (1991c). *Video gambling.* Trenton, NJ: Author.

New York State Commission of Investigation. (1971). *An investigation concerning the awarding of contracts and the purchases of supplies by the city of Yonkers.* Albany, NY: Author.

————. (1991). "An investigation of the loan-shark racket." In A. Block (Ed.), *The business of crime: A documentary study of organized crime in the American economy* (pp. 29–62). Boulder, CO: Westview Press.

Nimmo, D. D., & Combs, J. E. (1980). *Subliminal politics: Myths and myth makers in America.* Englewood Cliffs, NJ: Prentice-Hall.

Notre Dame Law Review (1990). " 'Mother of mercy—Is this the end of RICO?' Justice Scalia invites constitutional void-for-vagueness challenge to RICO 'pattern.' " *Notre Dame Law Review, 65*(5), 1106–1162.

O'Brien, J., & Kurins, A. (1991). *Boss of bosses.* New York: Simon & Schuster.

Odegard, P. (1930). *The American mind.* New York: Columbia University Press.

Osgood, H. (1924). *The American colonies in the eighteenth century—Volume II.* New York: Columbia University Press.

————. (1930). *The American colonies in the seventeenth century—Volume I.* New York: Columbia University Press.

Osofsky, G. (1966). *Harlem; The making of a ghetto; Negro New York, 1890–1930*. New York: Harper & Row.

Pace, D., & Styles, J. (1983). *Organized crime: Concepts and control*. Englewood Cliffs, NJ: Prentice-Hall.

Pennsylvania Crime Commission. (1990). *Organized crime in Pennsylvania: A decade of change (1990 report)*. Conshokocken, PA: Author.

———. (1991). *1991 report*. St. Davids, PA: Author.

Peterson, V. (1952). *Barbarians in our midst: A history of Chicago crime and politics*. Boston, MA: Little, Brown & Company.

———. (1983). *The mob: 200 years of organized crime in New York*. Ottawa, IL: Green Hill.

Pileggi, N. (1985). *Wiseguy: Life in a Mafia family*. New York: Simon & Schuster.

Poland, J. (1988). *Understanding terrorism: Groups, strategies, and responses*. Englewood Cliffs, NJ: Prentice-Hall.

Posner, G. (1988). *Warlords of crime: Chinese secret societies—the new Mafia*. New York: McGraw-Hill.

President's Commission on Law Enforcement and Administration of Justice, Task Force on Organized Crime. (1967). *Task force report: Organized crime*. Washington, DC: Government Printing Office.

President's Commission on Organized Crime. (1985). *Organized crime and gambling. Record of hearing VII, June 24–26, 1985, New York, NY*. Washington, DC: Government Printing Office.

———. (1986). *The impact: Organized crime today*. Washington, DC: Government Printing Office.

Puzo, M. (1969). *The godfather*. New York: G. P. Putnam & Sons.

Rankin, H. (1969). *The golden age of piracy*. New York: Holt, Rinehart & Winston.

Reavis, D. (1992, Febuary 23). "Fighting the battle in the trenches." *San Antonio Light*, p. 1.

Rebovich, D. (1992). *Dangerous ground: The world of hazardous waste crime*. New Brunswick, NJ: Transaction.

Reinarman, C., & Levine, J. (1989). "The crack attack: Politics and media in America's latest drug scare." In J. Best (Ed.), *Images of issues* (pp. 115–134). New York: Aldine.

Report of Interpol General Secretariat. (1984, May 10–11). "Motorcycle gangs." Report presented at St. Cloud, MN, pp. 170–179.

Reuter, P. (1983). *Disorganized crime: Illegal markets and the Mafia*. Cambridge, MA: MIT Press.

———. (1985). *The organization of illegal markets: An economic analysis*. Washington, DC: U.S. Department of Justice.

———. (1987). "Methodological problems of organized crime research." In H. Edelhertz (Ed.), *Major issues in organized crime control: Symposium proceedings*. Washington, DC: National Institute of Justice.

———. (1990). "Can the borders be sealed?" In R. Weisheit (Ed.), *Drugs, crime and the criminal justice system* (pp. 13–26). Cincinnati, OH: Anderson.

Reuter, P., & Rubinstein, J. (1982). *Illegal gambling in New York: A case study in the operation, structure, and regulation of an illegal market.* Washington, DC: Government Printing Office.

Reuter, P., Rubinstein, J., & Wynn, S. (1983). *Racketeering in legitimate industries: Two case studies.* Washington, DC: National Institute of Justice.

Rhodes, R. (1984). *Organized crime.* New York: Random House.

Ritchie, R. (1986). *Captain Kidd and the war against the pirates.* Cambridge, MA: Harvard University Press.

Rosenthal, J. (1990, June 24). "Russia's new export: The mob." *Washington Post*, p. C4.

Rosner, L. (1986). *The Soviet way of crime: Beating the system in the Soviet Union and the U.S.A.* South Hadley, MA: Bergin & Garvey.

Ross, J. (1988). "Attributes of domestic political terrorism in Canada, 1960–1985." *Terrorism, 11*, 213–233.

Safir, H. (1989). "The United States witness protection program." In H. Smith (Ed.), *Transnational crime: Investigative responses.* Chicago, IL: OICJ.

Salerno, R., & Thompson, J. (1969). *The crime confederation: Costa Nostra and allied operations in organized crime.* Garden City, NY: Doubleday.

Salmony, S., & Smoke, R. (1988). "The appeal and behavior of the Ku Klux Klan in object relations perspective." *Terrorism, 11*, 247–262.

Sante, L. (1991, August 12). "These are the good old days." *New York*, pp. 26–36.

Sapp, A. (1987). "Organizational linkages of right-wing extremist groups." Paper presented to the Academy of Criminal Justice Sciences, Saint Louis, MO.

Sasuly, R. (1982). *Bookies and bettors: Two hundred years of gambling.* New York: Holt, Rinehart & Winston.

Scarpitti, R., & Block, A. (1987). "America's toxic waste racket: Dimensions of the environmental crisis." In T. Bynum (Ed.), *Organized crime in America: Concepts and controversies* (pp. 115–128). Monsey, NY: Willow Tree Press.

Schelling, T. (1971). "Organized crime: A symposium." *Journal of Public Law, 20*(1), 33–165.

———. (1976). "What is the business of organized crime?" In F. Ianni and E. Ruess-Ianni (Eds.), *The crime society—organized crime and corruption in America* (pp. 69–82). New York: Times-Mirror.

Schlegel, K. (1987). "Violence in organized crime: A content analysis of the De Cavalcante and De Carlo transcripts." In T. Bynum (Ed.), *Organized crime in America: Concepts and controversies* (pp. 55–70). Monsey, NY: Willow Tree Press.

Schneider, H. (1990). "The media world of crime: A study of social learning theory and symbolic interaction." In W. Laufer and F. Adler (Eds.), *Advances in criminological theory* (vol. 2) (pp. 115–143). New Brunswick, NJ: Transaction.

Schoenberg, R. (1992). *Mr. Capone: The real—and complete—story of Al Capone.* New York: William Morrow & Company.

Schrag, C. (1971). *Crime and justice: American style.* Rockville, MD: National Institute of Mental Health, Center for Study of Crime and Delinquency.

Scott, P. (1992). "Honduras, the Contra support networks, and cocaine: How the U.S. government has augmented America's drug crisis." In A. McCoy and A. Block

(Eds.), *War on drugs: Studies in the failure of U.S. narcotics policy.* Boulder, CO: Westview Press.

Sellin, T. (1938). *Culture conflict and crime.* New York: Social Science Research Council.

Serio, J. (1993). "Organized crime in the former Soviet Union." Unpublished master's thesis, University of Illinois, Chicago.

Shaw, C. R., & McKay, H. D. (1942). *Juvenile delinquency and urban areas.* Chicago: University of Chicago Press.

Sherry, F. (1986). *Raiders and rebels.* New York: Hearst Marine Books.

Shieber, B. (1982). "Electronic surveillance, the Mafia, and individual freedom." *Louisiana Law Review, 42*(4), 1323–1372.

Short, M. (1984). *Crime inc.: The story of organized crime.* London, England: Thames Methuen.

Silberman, C. (1978). *Criminal violence, criminal justice.* New York: Random House.

Simis, K. (1982). *USSR: The corrupt society.* New York: Simon & Schuster.

Smith, D. (1975). *The Mafia mystique.* New York: Basic Books.

————. (1980). "Paragons, pariahs, and pirates: A spectrum-based theory of enterprise." *Crime and Delinquency, 26*(3), 358–386.

Solomon, R. (1985). "Regulating the regulators: Prohibition enforcement in the seventh circuit." In D. Kyvig (Ed.), *Law, alcohol, and order: Perspectives on national prohibition* (pp. 81–96). Westport, CT: Greenwood.

Strong, G. (1952). *The diary of George Templeton Strong.* A. Nevins and M. Thomas (Eds.). New York: Macmillan.

Sutherland, E., & Cressey, D. (1960). *Principles of criminology* (6th ed.). New York: Lippincott.

Sykes, G., & Matza, D. (1957). "Techniques of neutralization: A theory of delinquency." *American Sociological Review, 22,* 664–670.

Talese, G. (1971). *Honor thy father.* New York: World Publishing.

Terry, C., & Pellins, M. (1928). *The opium problem.* New York: The Committee on Drug Addictions.

Thompson, C., & Raymond, A. (1940). *Gang rule in New York.* New York: Dial Press.

Thornton, M. (1991). *The economics of prohibition.* Salt Lake City, UT: University of Utah Press.

Thoroughbred Racing Communications, Inc. (1993). *Wire to wire: Enjoying a day at the races.* New York: Author.

Thrasher, F. (1927). *The gang.* Chicago, IL: University of Chicago Press.

Timasheff, N. (1957). *Sociological theory: Its nature and growth.* New York: Random House.

Timofeyev, L. (1992). *Russia's secret rulers: How government and criminal Mafia exercise their power.* New York: Knopf.

Trebach, A. (1982). *The heroin solution.* New York: McGraw-Hill.

————. (1987). *The great drug war: Radical proposals that could make America safe again.* New York: Macmillan.

Turkus, B., & Feder, S. (1951). *Murder, inc.: The story of the syndicate.* New York: Farrar, Straus, & Young.

Tyler, G. (Ed.). (1966). *Combatting organized crime.* Philadelphia, PA: American Society of Political and Social Science.

United States Congress, Office of Technology Assessment. (1987). *The border war on drugs.* Washington, DC: Government Printing Office.

United States Department of Justice. (1989). *Drug trafficking: A report to the president of the United States.* Washington, DC: Government Printing Office.

————. Office of the Attorney General. (1990). *Attacking organized crime—program report.* Washington, DC: Government Printing Office.

————. (1991). *Attacking organized crime—national strategy.* Washington, DC: Government Printing Office.

United States General Accounting Office. (1984). *Witness security program: Prosecutive results and participant arrest data.* Washington, DC: Government Printing Office.

————. (1989a). *Nontraditional organized crime—law enforcement officials' perspectives on five criminal groups.* Washington, DC: Government Printing Office.

————.(1989b). *Organized crime: Issues concerning strike forces.* Washington, DC: Government Printing Office.

United States Senate. (1951). *Special committee to investigate organized crime in interstate commerce.* New York: Didier.

————. Permanent Subcommittee on Investigations. (1963). *Organized crime and illicit traffic in narcotics: Hearings (Part I).* Washington, DC: Government Printing Office.

————. (1980). *Organized crime and use of violence: Hearings, April 28–May 5, 1980.* Washington, DC: Government Printing Office.

————. (1983). *Hearings before the committee on the judiciary (holding hearings on organized crime).* Washington, DC: Government Printing Office.

————. (1983). *Organized crime in America. Hearings, Committee on the Judiciary, January 27, February 16, March 2–3, 1983.* (Part I, Serial No. J-98-2). Washington, D.C.: Government Printing Office.

————.(1984a) *Profile on organized crime: Great Lakes region: Hearings on January 25, 26, 31 and February 4, 1984.* Washington, DC: Government Printing Office.

————.(1984b). *Profile on organized crime: Great Lakes region: Report, together with additional views.* Washington, DC: Government Printing Office.

————. (1990). *Organized crime: 25 years after Valachi.* Washington, DC: Government Printing Office.

————. Permanent Subcommittee on Investigations of the Committee on Governmental Affairs. (1991). "Oversight inquiry of the Department of Labor's investigation of the Teamsters central states pension fund." In A. Block (Ed.), *The business of crime: A documentary study of organized crime in the American economy.* Boulder, CO: Westview Press.

Walker, W. (1991). *Opium and foreign policy: The Anglo-American search for order in Asia, 1912–1954.* Chapel Hill, NC: University of North Carolina Press.

Walsh, M. (1983). *An overview of organized crime.* Washington, DC: National Institute of Justice.

Ward, R., & Smith, H. (1987). *International terrorism: The domestic response.* Chicago, IL: Office of International Criminal Justice, University of Illinois at Chicago.

Warner, W., & Junker, B. (1941). *Color and human nature.* Washington, DC: American Council on Education.

Weisheit, R. (1990a). "Challenging the criminalizers." *The Criminologist, 15*(4), 1–5.

————. (1990b). "Declaring a 'civil' war on drugs." In R. Weisheit (Ed.), *Drugs, crime and the criminal justice system* (pp. 1–16). Cincinnati, OH: Anderson.

Wiedrich, R. (1984). "Organized crime and public apathy." In Thomas M. Frost & Magnus Seng (Eds.), *Organized crime in Chicago* (pp. 13–16). Chicago: Loyola University of Chicago.

Wiley, H. (1912, August 12). "An opium bonfire." *Good Housekeeping.*

Will, G. (1988, March 28). "A west coast story." *Newsweek*, p. 76.

Wilson, J. (1974). *Thinking about crime.* New York: Basic Books.

————. (1989). "The drug war: Victory will come slowly; fight must be on all fronts." Issue 1 in a Police Foundation Series on Drugs and Violence. Washington, DC: Police Foundation.

————. (1990). "Against the legalization of drugs." *Commentary, 89*(2), 21–28.

Wilson, J., & Herrnstein, R. (1985). *Crime and human nature.* New York: Simon & Schuster.

Wisotsky, S. (1991). "Beyond the war on drugs." In J. Inciardi (Ed.), *The drug legalization debate.* Newbury Park, CA: Sage.

Woodiwiss, M. (1987). "Capone to Kefauver: Organized crime in America." *History Today, 37*, 8–15.

Yablonsky, L., & Haskell, R. (1988). *Juvenile delinquency* (4th ed.). New York: Harper & Row.

Zinn, H. (1980). *A people's history of the United States.* New York: Harper Colophon Books.

Author Index

Subject Index